Justifying Ballistic
Missile Defence

Technology is championed as the solution to modern security problems, but also blamed as their cause. This book assesses the way in which these two views collide in the debate over ballistic missile defence: a complex, costly and controversial system intended to defend the United States from nuclear missile attacks. Columba Peoples shows how, in the face of strong scientific and strategic critique, advocates of missile defence seek to justify its development by reference to broader culturally embedded perceptions of the promises and perils of technological development. Unpacking the assumptions behind the justification of missile defence initiatives, both past and present, this book illustrates how common-sense understandings of technology are combined and used to legitimate this controversial and costly defence programme. In doing so it engages fundamental debates over understandings of technological development, human agency and the relationship between technology and security.

COLUMBA PEOPLES is a lecturer in International Relations in the Department of Politics at the University of Bristol. His research focuses on the question of technology and its impact on international relations and global security. He received the British International Studies Association Thesis Prize for International Studies in 2007, and has published widely in the fields of International Relations and Security Studies.

D1557346

Cambridge Studies in International Relations: 112

Justifying Ballistic Missile Defence

Cambridge Studies in International Relations is a joint initiative of Cambridge University Press and the British International Studies Association (BISA). The series will include a wide range of material, from undergraduate textbooks and surveys to research-based monographs and collaborative volumes. The aim of the series is to publish the best new scholarship in International Studies from Europe, North America and the rest of the world.

Cambridge Studies in International Relations

Series list continued after index

Justifying Ballistic Missile Defence

Technology, Security and Culture

COLUMBA PEOPLES

CAMBRIDGE UNIVERSITY PRESS

CAMBRIDGE UNIVERSITY PRESS
Cambridge, New York, Melbourne, Madrid, Cape Town, Singapore, São Paulo, Delhi

Cambridge University Press
The Edinburgh Building, Cambridge CB2 8RU, UK

Published in the United States of America by Cambridge University Press, New York

www.cambridge.org
Information on this title: www.cambridge.org/9780521130417

First published 2010

Printed in the United Kingdom at the University Press, Cambridge

A catalogue record for this publication is available from the British Library

ISBN 978-0-521-11329-8 Hardback
ISBN 978-0-521-13041-7 Paperback

Contents

Acknowledgements

The process of writing this text has followed an intellectual and personal trajectory that has criss-crossed the west of Wales, west coast of the United States, south coast of Wales and south-west of England. Along the way I've been fortunate to benefit from the guidance and friendship of a number of people who helped make that journey possible. The original project on which this text builds began at the Department of International Politics in Aberystwyth, where it developed under the supervision of Richard Wyn Jones, Doug Stokes and Michael C. Williams. Without their comments, suggestions and encouragement I doubt that this project would have even got off the ground, and the influence of Richard Wyn Jones in particular, whose critical thinking has constantly spurred my own efforts, has been a crucial factor in the development of this research. I owe a debt of gratitude to all three, and the same to Pauline Ewan, Peter Jackson and Stuart Croft for their comments on the first stage of this project, and for encouraging me to pursue it further post-Aberystwyth.

Likewise I would like to thank the Department of International Politics in Aberystwyth for providing the means to conduct this research in the form of an E. H. Carr scholarship. Whilst studying there I was also fortunate to be part of an incredibly vibrant and close-knit intellectual community, and Cian O' Driscoll, Nick Vaughan Williams, Alexej Behnisch, Darren Brunk and Rens van Munster were amongst many friends who lent their support and comments on the project as it evolved. Part of the research was conducted as a visiting scholar in the School of International Relations at the University of Southern California, and I was grateful for the help and friendship of Steve Lamy and Hayward Alker in particular during that period.

The latter stages of writing this book were completed whilst at the Department of Politics and International Relations, Swansea

University. There Roland Axtmann and Mike Sheehan gave thoughtful guidance on the direction of the project, and Alan Finlayson, Sam Chambers, Alan Collins, Helen Brocklehurst and Rebecca Brown provided both intellectual engagement and great camaraderie. The same goes for Judith Squires and Terrell Carver at the Department of Politics, University of Bristol, and Jutta Weldes who has supported and encouraged this project from an early stage right up until its present form.

The recognition accorded by the British International Studies Association through the award of the International Studies Thesis Prize for 2007 was also a great source of encouragement. With regard to transferring that research into book form thanks are due to those at Cambridge University Press, especially John Haslam, Carrie Parkinson and Carol Fellingham Webb, who helped in putting the final version together in book form, Nicholas Wheeler and Chris Reus-Smit, editors of Cambridge Studies in International Relations, and two anonymous reviewers for their detailed and encouraging comments. Some of the research presented in chapters 2 and 4 of this book appeared in an earlier version as '*Sputnik* and "Skill Thinking" Revisited: Technological Determinism in American responses to the Soviet Missile Threat', *Cold War History*, 8:1 (2008) pp. 55–75, and I am grateful to the reviewers for their comments on that article which helped strengthen the arguments presented in those chapters. Otherwise the material here is previously unpublished.

Most of all my thanks go to Tony, Pat and Julie Peoples for their love and support and it is to them that I dedicate this book.

Abbreviations

ABM	anti-ballistic missile
ARPA	Advanced Research Projects Agency
BMD	ballistic missile defence
BMDO	Ballistic Missile Defense Organization
BMEWS	Ballistic Missile Early Warning System
CIA	Central Intelligence Agency
CND	Campaign for Nuclear Disarmament
CPB	charged particle beam
CPD	Committee on the Present Danger
CSP	Center for Security Policy
CSS	Critical Security Studies
DEW	directed energy weapon
DoD	Department of Defense
DR&E	Defense Research and Engineering
GMD	Ground-Based Midcourse Defense
HOE	Homing Overlay Experiment
ICBM	intercontinental ballistic missile
JNIC	Joint National Integration Center
MAD	mutual assured destruction
MDA	Missile Defense Agency
MDAA	Missile Defense Advocacy Alliance
MIC	military-industrial complex
MIRV	multiple independently targetable re-entry vehicle
MIT	Massachusetts Institute of Technology
MTCR	Missile Technology Control Regime
NFIRE	Near Field Infrared Experiment
NIE	National Intelligence Estimate
NIPP	National Institute for Public Policy
NMD	National Missile Defense
NORAD	North American Aerospace Defense Command
NPR	Nuclear Posture Review
NRA	National Rifle Association
NSC	National Security Council

NSPD	National Security Presidential Directive
PAC	Patriot Advanced Capability
QDR	Quadrennial Defense Review
R&D	research and development
RMA	revolution in military affairs
SAM	surface-to-air missile
SBL	space-based laser
SDI	Strategic Defense Initiative
SDIO	Strategic Defense Initiative Organization
SLV	space-launch vehicle
SORT	Strategic Offensive Reduction Treaty
SRI	Stanford Research Institute
TMD	Theater Missile Defense
UCS	Union of Concerned Scientists
WMD	weapons of mass destruction

Introduction

The contemporary global security agenda is dominated by issues where technology is seen as central: the so-called 'Revolution in military affairs', the future of nuclear weapons, the proliferation of conventional and nuclear weapons globally, their prospective use in terror attacks, 'cyber-terrorism' and so the list goes on. One such case where consideration of technology comes to the fore in relation to security is ballistic missile defence in the United States. Ballistic missile defence (or BMD) is a weapons system intended to protect America from nuclear missile attack by shooting down incoming intercontinental ballistic missiles (ICBMs). This current concept has had previous incarnations as the anti-ballistic missile programmes of the 1960s, the Strategic Defense or ('Star Wars') Initiative of the 1980s and National Missile Defense in the 1990s.

Under the leadership of President George W. Bush, missile defence underwent a resurgence in its fortunes in the United States. The fledgling elements of a system were put in place with several interceptor missiles deployed in silos at two separate locations – Fort Greely, Alaska and Vandenberg airbase in California – since late 2004. Missile defence attracted consistent support from the Bush administration, ostensibly justified by concerns over ballistic missile and nuclear weapons proliferation particularly in relation to 'rogue states' such as North Korea and Iran. Of concern to many outside the USA, however, is the fact that BMD is predicated upon a particular variant of strategic thought that assumes the efficacy of defensive technology for the post-Cold War era, as distinct from traditional theories of deterrence which generally tended to downplay the role of defences. This has engendered a considerable amount of debate over the intentions behind this system, its potential impact on the nuclear arsenals of other states such as Russia and China, and its consequent implications for global security.[1] More recently the potential extension of BMD to Eastern Europe has sparked fears of a 'New Cold War' between the USA and Russia.

This latest phase of debate over missile defence represents only the most recent chapter in a catalogue of contentious efforts to provide America with a shield against nuclear missiles. Throughout its history, missile defence has remained highly controversial owing to the nature of its aims and the technical challenges it faces, challenges that persist up to the present day. ICBMs, the proposed targets of the current BMD system, travel at a speed of 7km per second and are routinely designed to deploy a range of countermeasures capable of overcoming defences. The contentious nature of the system is further assured by the fact that missile defence is extremely costly: BMD has consistently remained the single biggest defence technology pro-gramme in budgetary terms, around $7–8 billion per annum since 2001, rising to just over $10 billion in 2006, no mean feat given that the 'War on Terror' became the more prominent priority of the Bush administration.[2] Yet even with this significant outlay no one is sure that missile defence will work, and a significant proportion of the American scientific community believe that it won't. The poor test and evaluation record of missile defence to date ensures that doubts persist over the ability of proposed technologies to deal both with countermeasures deployed during the 'mid-course' of an ICBM's flight (the proposed format for the currently deployed interceptors),[3] and with the initial velocity and trajectory of nuclear missiles during their 'boost-phase'.[4] The head of the Pentagon's Missile Defense

[1] See Keir A. Lieber and Daryl G. Press, 'The End of MAD? The Nuclear Dimension of US Primacy', *International Security*, 30:4 (2006) pp. 7–44.
[2] Congressional Budget Office, *The Long-Term Implications of Current Defense Plans and Alternatives: Detailed Update for Fiscal Year 2006* (2006), www.cbo.gov/showdoc.cfm?index=7004&sequence=0&from=7 [last accessed 7 March 2007].
[3] See 'Countermeasures': Excerpts from a Report by the Union of Concerned Scientists and the Massachusetts Institute of Technology Security Studies Program, www.armscontrol.org/subject/md/?print [last accessed 7 March 2007]; see also Lisbeth Gronlund, David Wright and Stephen Young, 'An Assessment of the Intercept Test Program of the Ground-based Midcourse National Missile Defense System', *Defense and Security Analysis*, 18:3 (2002) pp. 239–60.
[4] David K. Barton, Roger Falcone, Daniel Kleppner *et al.*, 'Report of the American Physical Society Group on Boost-Phase Intercept Systems for National Missile Defense: Scientific and Technical Issues', pp. xxi–xxii, www.aps.org/

Agency (MDA), General Henry 'Trey' Obering, admitted in 2006 that the recently deployed ground-based system only has a 'better-than-zero-chance' of stopping an incoming missile warhead;[5] even today, few would confidently rate the prospects for missile defence any higher than this.

In this sense BMD is a perfect example of investment in technology in pursuit of security. The very nature of technological development – and its limits – in terms of achieving security is in question in this defence programme. As a recent commentary notes, 'Missile defence is a fait accompli. Yet it remains technically immature, poorly evaluated, largely untried and extremely controversial.'[6] The way technology is represented and articulated in its promotion is therefore of critical importance. Missile defence not only represents the ongoing struggle to come to terms with the more deadly applications of nuclear physics, it also deals – quite literally – in the finer points of 'rocket science'. The aim of this book, therefore, is to help account for American persistence with this highly contentious initiative. It does so by concentrating on the narratives of technological development and understandings of technology employed in the advocacy of ballistic missile defence since the concept was first proposed in the post-World War II era. By drawing on previous work in the field of Critical Security Studies, and by combining the Critical Theory of the Frankfurt School (on the issue of technology) and Antonio Gramsci (on the strategic use of language), the book aims to show how proponents of missile defence have consistently articulated and reiterated two pervasive 'common sense' understandings of technology that parallel and invoke broader sociocultural narratives of technological development. The first assumes technological innovation as a particularly American trait that can be used to overcome even the monumental technical challenges

public_affairs/popa/reports/nmd03.cfm [last accessed 7 March 2007]; also published in special issue of *Review of Modern Physics*, 76, S1 (2004).

[5] A spokesman for the MDA later sought to clarify that the statement was made on the more positive basis that 'we [previously] had nothing, i.e. zero chance, and now we have the means to defend ourselves'. Quotes from Wade Boese, 'Missile Defense Aims to Hit Target in '06', *Arms Control Today*, September 2004, www.armscontrol.org/act/2005_09/MissileDefenseAims.asp?print [last accessed 20 January 2009]. Obering's comment was picked up by Ann Scott Tyson, 'US Missile Defense being Expanded, General Says', *Washington Post*, 22 July 2005, p. A10.

[6] Aaron Karp and Regina Karp, 'Preface: From Strategy to Domestic Debate', *Contemporary Security Policy*, 26:3 (2005) pp. v–vi, p. v.

presented by missile defence – what some have termed the search for a 'technological fix'. The second understanding of technology in missile defence advocacy presents technology (specifically contemporary proliferation of nuclear and ballistic missile technology) as a largely autonomous source of insecurity to the United States, one that is beyond control, invalidates Cold War theories of deterrence and thereby necessitates that missile defence form a priority of the American defence infrastructure.

These understandings, as explored in chapter 1, have analogous counterparts identified (and expounded) in critical theories of technology and, moreover, it is argued in chapter 2 that these understandings are homologous with a particularly 'American' experience of technology that runs from the establishment of the US state to the present day. Focusing on these two countervailing understandings of technology as an organising frame, Parts Two, Three and Four examine the occurrence of these two conceptions historically in the three 'great debates' over American missile defence: the anti-ballistic missile (ABM) controversy in the late 1960s; the Strategic Defense Initiative (SDI) of the 1980s; and contemporary BMD. The advantage of this structure is that it allows for comparison and evaluation of the concrete manifestations of these understandings over time, and the manner in which they have been combined at various points in the promotion of missile defence. Hence chapter 3 examines the extent to which an optimistic conception of technological development pervaded early arguments for ABM systems, whilst chapter 4 evidences a sub-current of fear that future US security policy would be determined by a technologically superior Soviet Union. This countervailing narrative, it is argued, is represented most prominently in the rhetoric of bomber, missile and ABM 'gaps', Robert McNamara's 'action–reaction' thesis and, most prominently, American reactions to the launch of *Sputnik*.

Similarly, Part Three traces a similar pattern in relation to the Strategic Defense Initiative of the 1980s. On the one hand, the promotion of strategic defence in the speeches of the Reagan administration and the writings of SDI proponents more broadly invoked and rearticulated America's technological heritage to defend the viability of missile defence, and elevated the notion of a 'technological fix'; on the other, SDI proponents also exploited fears of technological constraints as evidenced in the arguments of groups such as the 'Committee on the Present Danger' and 'Team-B', as well as in the

Reagan administration's co-optation of the language of technological fears as employed by the anti-nuclear movement.

Part Four undertakes a complementary reading in relation to contemporary BMD. Analysing recent arguments for BMD, chapter 7 indicates how technology is, in one sense, understood simply as an instrument we use to 'make life better', and missile defence should be no exception to this logic. Yet, as chapter 8 illustrates, BMD is simultaneously justified on the basis of an alternative understanding of technology, most evident in BMD proponents' discussion of nuclear proliferation, which connotes helplessness in the face of inevitable technological advance and is founded on the notion that technological development is increasingly moving beyond human control.

The overall aim of the book is to point to the fundamental operation of understandings of technology as a form of 'common sense' (understood in the Gramscian sense) used in the legitimation of missile defence. In Gramsci's definition, common sense refers to a conception that is fragmentary, incoherent and thus, potentially, contradictory.[7] The approach taken here is thus to piece together the fragments of both instrumental and substantive understandings of technology in missile defence advocacy and then, ultimately, to illustrate how they work together to form a contradictory whole. The central contention of this volume, then, is this: common sense understandings of technology (as both a uniquely American solution to security problems *and* a source of global insecurity in terms of the spread of weapons technology) have been consistently employed by missile defence advocates to insulate a problematic system from criticism. These discursive articulations serve to legitimate and naturalise a range of other practices – spending patterns, the assignment and distribution of defence contracts, research and institutional arrangements, testing and technical development procedures. Ultimately they help legitimate BMD itself, a programme which, it can be argued, makes little real contribution to enhancing American or global security in the twenty-first century but which favours sectional political and industrial interests in the short term and helps to sustain America's immense defence infrastructure in the post-Cold War era. Moreover, in the process, this articulation of

---

[7] Antonio Gramsci, *Selections from the Prison Notebooks*, ed. and trans. by Quintin Hoare and Geoffrey Nowell Smith (London: Lawrence and Wishart, 1973) p. 419.

American technological common sense also constitutes ideas about identity, threats, technology and security in very specific ways.

This book thus claims an important contribution to the study of security in its theoretical approach, methodological rigour and empirical analysis. In a general sense it adds to work utilising social theory to enhance our understanding of the political practice of nuclear security,[8] contributing an original and theoretically informed approach to a case that has been relatively under-theorised in security studies.[9] More specifically, the argument is made that Critical Security Studies,[10] by drawing on its philosophical groundings in Frankfurt School and Gramscian theory, still has much to contribute to the study of 'real world', 'traditional' security issues such as nuclear security. As Bradley Klein noted some time ago, 'Having paid too much attention to weapons for decades, there is now a danger of not paying enough attention.'[11] As the nuclear arsenals of the Cold War continue to atrophy, and 'new' initiatives are put forward in their stead, we would do well to ensure that embedded dynamics of strategy and militarisation do not continue to dominate our thinking. As is illustrated here, the philosophical-theoretical resources that underpin Critical Security Studies can contribute substantially in 'helping to nail the half-truths and distortions by which governments perpetuate the national security state' and 'help ensure the continuation of human society after the nuclear revolution'.[12] They can do so, though, by deepening our understanding of how these 'half-truths and distortions' continue to hold sway, particularly in humanity's continuing effort to come to terms

---

[8] See Simon Dalby, *Creating the Second Cold War: the Discourse of Politics* (London: Pinter, 1990); Bradley S. Klein, *Strategic Studies and World Order* (Cambridge: Cambridge University Press, 1994).

[9] Exceptions include: Ernest J. Yanarella, *The Missile Defense Controversy: Technology in Search of a Mission* (Lexington, KY: University Press of Kentucky, 2002), on ABM, although this is mainly historical in focus; Edward Reiss, *The Strategic Defense Initiative* (Cambridge: Cambridge University Press, 1992), on SDI; and Natalie Bormann, *National Missile Defense and the Politics of US Identity* (Manchester: Manchester University Press, 2008) on missile defence under Bill Clinton and George W. Bush as theorised from a poststructuralist perspective.

[10] Referring specifically here to the variant espoused by Richard Wyn Jones in his *Security, Strategy and Critical Theory* (London: Lynne Rienner, 1999).

[11] Klein, *Strategic Studies and World Order*, p. 5.

[12] Richard Wyn Jones, 'The Nuclear Revolution' in Alex Danchev (ed.) *Fin de Siècle: the Meaning of the Twentieth Century* (London: I. B. Taurus, 1995) p. 106.

with the nuclear revolution itself as is manifested in projects such as missile defence. The insight proffered here into the construction of the case for American missile defence thus constitutes a new, critical understanding of missile defence advocacy. In this sense the argument remains true to the spirit of immanent critique in Max Horkheimer's sense that immanent confronts 'the existent, in its historical context, with the claim of its conceptual principles, in order to criticize the relation between the two and thus transcend them'.[13]

---

[13] Max Horkheimer, *Eclipse of Reason* (New York: Seabury Press, 1974) pp. 182–3.

PART ONE

Technology, security and culture

1 | *Critical theory, security and technology*

The impact of technology on warfare has been a constant consideration of strategists running from Sun Tzu through to Clausewitz, increasing to such a degree by the twentieth century that the British strategist J. F. C Fuller declared that 'Tools, or weapons, if only the right ones can be discovered, form 99% of victory.'[1] The advent of the 'nuclear revolution' only served to heighten the salience of this question of technology for the makers of modern nuclear strategy such as Bernard Brodie and Thomas Schelling, and the unprecedented destructive power of nuclear weapons spurred the emergence of the cognate discipline of security studies.[2] In short, the question of technology's role and impact has traditionally been seen as central within both strategic thought and security studies.

The orientation of the argument made here is somewhat counter-intuitive in this light. It begins from the premise that though strategic and security studies have devoted significant space to the consideration of (weapons) technology, they have actually been remarkably unreflective on the relationship between technology and security in spite of the amount of research devoted to this issue. This assertion is based on the fact that even accounts which place technology and technological change at their heart reduce the role these factors play to a series of familiar dichotomies: capabilities versus intentions; 'push' versus 'pull' factors in military technological development; manpower versus matériel; and,

---

[1] J. F. C. Fuller, *Armament and History: a Study of the Influence of Armament on History from the Dawn of Classical Warfare to the Second World War* (London: Eyre and Spottiswoode, 1946) p. vi. On the general theme see Martin Van Creveld, *Technology and War: From 2000 BC to the Present* (New York: The Free Press, 1989); Peter Paret (ed.) *Makers of Modern Strategy: From Machiavelli to the Nuclear Age* (Oxford: Clarendon Press, 1986).

[2] See John Baylis and John Garnett (eds.) *Makers of Nuclear Strategy* (London: Pinter, 1991) on Brodie's and Schelling's roles as 'makers' of modern nuclear strategy in terms both of their influence on policy and as founding fathers of strategic studies.

most fundamentally, whether technology determines the nature of international security or vice versa.[3] Technology itself constitutes a relatively discrete, well-defined and unproblematic variable within such debates,[4] perpetuating the acceptance of technology as a 'natural' part of strategic discourse.[5] There has, however, been little reflection on this acceptance *itself* as a phenomenon. As Judith Reppy points out:

> It is ironic that political theorists, apparently ignorant of the extensive litera-
> ture in the fields of economics and the sociology of science on technological
> change, have been willing to accept a 'black box' explanation of these pro-
> cesses, processes that are in reality deeply dependent on social institutions and
> government policy.[6]

Such black-boxing is not the sole preserve of political theory. Security studies has likewise been charged with an understanding of technology that 'has been confused, crude and unreflective' as a result of the fact that 'strategists have paid almost no heed to work in the fields of the history of science and technology'.[7] Traditional security studies, in short, stands accused of maintaining a particularly emaciated conception of technology even though it ostensibly prioritises the relationship between technology and security.

If this is indeed the case, it begs the question of how the ways in which technology and technological development have traditionally been conceptualised impact upon the theory and practice of security. In this spirit, the argument undertaken here attempts to illustrate how understandings of technology inform a particular policy and vision of American nuclear security, namely ballistic missile defence (BMD). The approach it takes originates in a more general concern (alluded to above) with the relationship between security, technology and culture

---

[3] See, for example, Barry Buzan and Eric Herring, *The Arms Dynamic in World Politics* (London: Lynne Rienner, 1998).

[4] As argued by Bradley S. Klein, *Strategic Studies and World Order* (Cambridge: Cambridge University Press, 1994) p. 21.

[5] Indeed Barry Buzan has argued that strategic studies should be thought of as the study of the military-technological variable in International Relations – see Barry Buzan, *An Introduction to Strategic Studies: Military Technology and International Relations* (Basingstoke: Macmillan, 1987).

[6] Judith Reppy, 'The Technological Imperative in Strategic Thought', *Journal of Peace Research*, 27:1 (1990) pp. 101–6, p. 105.

[7] Richard Wyn Jones, *Security, Strategy and Critical Theory* (London: Lynne Rienner, 1999) p. 133.

that has recently emerged in the field known as Critical Security Studies (CSS). The CSS project has been described variously by its key progenitors as 'an ambitious attempt to combine the insights of previous alternative work in the field with a particular set of metatheoretical principles and precepts to develop a new, emancipation-oriented paradigm for the theory and practice of security'[8] and as 'an issue-area study, developed within the academic discipline of international politics, concerned with the pursuit of critical knowledge about security in world politics' where 'Security is conceived comprehensively, embracing theories and practices at multiple levels of society, from the individual to the whole human species.'[9] Critical approaches to security, broadly conceived, set out to assess the taken-for-granted realms and objects of enquiry within strategic and security studies.[10] Hence, an important constituent of this effort is a conceptualisation that 'recognizes the mutual implication of technology and culture – a conceptualization that recognizes their dialectical interdependence rather than collapses one into the other or draws strict dividing lines between them' by encouraging 'long overdue cross-pollination between the study of military technology with the more general literature on the relationship between technology and society'.[11]

Towards a critical approach to security and technology

The stated commitment to emancipation and the linkage to the Marxian tradition from which this emanates, particularly Frankfurt School and Gramscian theory,[12] has generally been seen to distinguish CSS from other 'critical' approaches to security associated with the 'postpositivist'

---

[8] Ibid., p. ix.
[9] Ken Booth, 'Critical Explorations' in Ken Booth (ed.) *Critical Security Studies and World Politics* (Boulder, CO: Lynne Rienner, 2005) pp. 15–16.
[10] See Wyn Jones, *Security, Strategy and Critical Theory*; in a more broadly defined sense, Keith Krause and Michael C. Williams (eds.) *Critical Security Studies: Concepts and Cases* (London: UCL Press, 1997); Jutta Weldes, Mark Laffey, Hugh Gusterson and Raymond Duvall (eds.) *Cultures of Insecurity: States, Communities, and the Production of Danger* (Minneapolis, MN: University of Minnesota Press, 1999).
[11] Wyn Jones, *Security, Strategy and Critical Theory*, p. 142.
[12] On the links and origins of Critical Security Studies see in particular Wyn Jones, *Security, Strategy and Critical Theory*, and Ken Booth, 'Critical Explorations' and 'Beyond Critical Security Studies' in *Critical Security Studies and World Politics*, pp. 1–18, 259–78.

turn in international relations theory.[13] Wyn Jones distinguishes the two variants as 'CSS-as-project' (referring to the specifically Frankfurt School inspired or 'emancipation-oriented' variant) and 'CSS-as-label' (the wider spectrum of 'critical' or postpositivist approaches to security) respectively in consequence.[14] Certainly the approach taken in this volume owes more to the former conception of Critical Security Studies than to the latter (and it is to this that the acronym CSS refers throughout this text). Where the two variants have frequently been united, though, is in the critique of 'traditional' approaches to security.[15] The use of the term 'traditional' refers primarily to mainstream strategic and security studies (most prominently Realist approaches to security) which, Booth argues, have been characterised by three elements. The traditional approach to security has 'emphasised military threats and the need for strong counters; it has been status quo oriented; and it has centred on states.'[16] It has been marked, as Booth eloquently puts it, by 'statism, strategizing and stability'.[17]

Whereas traditional approaches to strategy and security have tended to take the security of the state as the primary goal, Critical approaches to security question this assumption for a variety of reasons. Within CSS in its Frankfurt School inspired variant, the challenge to this 'state-centrism' has generally been based on the identification of a relationship between security and 'emancipation', which opens the definition of security up to a much wider range of issues than in the traditional

---

[13] Compare, for example, Krause and Williams, *Critical Security Studies*; on the postpositivist turn generally see Steve Smith, Ken Booth and Marysia Zalewski (eds.) *International Theory: Positivism and Beyond* (Cambridge: Cambridge University Press, 1996), specifically Andrew Linklater, 'The Achievements of Critical Theory', pp. 279–300, in the same volume.

[14] See Richard Wyn Jones, 'On Emancipation: Necessity, Capacity, and Concrete Utopias' in Booth, *Critical Security Studies and World Politics*, pp. 215–35. Wyn Jones argues that the citation of commitment to emancipation as a distinguishing factor has been overplayed, especially in relation to poststucturalist accounts of security which, he argues, frequently incorporate an implicit commitment to emancipatory change or at least something closely resembling it.

[15] As the various contributions to Krause and Williams's *Critical Security Studies* attest.

[16] Ken Booth, 'Security and Emancipation', *Review of International Studies*, 17:4 (1991) pp. 313–26, p. 318. See also Wyn Jones, *Security, Strategy and Critical Theory*, pp. 94–102.

[17] Booth, 'Critical Explorations', p. 7.

military focus.[18] In his seminal statement on this issue, Booth argues that:

'Security' means the absence of threats. Emancipation is the freeing of people (as individuals and groups) from those physical and human constraints which stop them carrying out what they would freely choose to do. War and the threat of war is one of those constraints, together with poverty, poor education, political oppression and so on. Security and emancipation are two sides of the same coin. Emancipation, not power or order, produces true security. Emancipation, theoretically, is security.[19]

This definition, indeed the very invocation of the concept of emancipation, has been the source of much debate, and this has been covered at much length elsewhere.[20] For the moment we might simply note that the potential role of technology in relieving these constraints on emancipation in accordance with Booth's definition has not been taken for granted. Indeed Booth has frequently taken state-sponsored 'technological momentum' as an inherent cause of insecurity in the international realm.[21] For him the entirety of nuclear strategy, including presumably strategic arguments for missile defences, 'is an illustration of the danger of instrumental reason. Its evolution shows how a belief in the absolute priority of national defence, and the subsequent immersion in its processes and goals, perverts intuitions and ideas about humanity, society, and nature and so opens up the possibility of war crimes, environmental disaster, genetic damage and untold human catastrophe.' The idea of using technological instruments to achieve a sense of security entails a simultaneous acceptance of the prospect of large-scale conflict as a fact and thus is not only misguided but, Booth borrows the phrase from Robert Lifton and Eric Markusen, 'encourages "the genocidal mentality".'[22]

---

[18] Booth, 'Security and Emancipation'; Wyn Jones, *Security, Strategy and Critical Theory*; in relation to International Relations theory more generally see the various contributions to Richard Wyn Jones (ed.) *Critical Theory and World Politics* (Boulder, CO: Lynne Rienner, 2001).
[19] Booth, 'Security and emancipation', p. 319.
[20] For overviews of such debates see Booth, 'Critical Explorations', Wyn Jones, 'On Emancipation' and Hayward Alker, 'Emancipation in the Critical Security Studies Project' in Booth, *Critical Security Studies and World Politics*, pp. 189–213.
[21] Booth, 'Critical Explorations', p. 1.
[22] Booth, 'Beyond Critical Security Studies', pp. 267–8. See Robert Jay Lifton and Eric Markusen, *The Genocidal Mentality: the Nazi Holocaust and Nuclear Threat* (London: Macmillan, 1991).

Technology then, like state-centrism, would appear to be potentially part of the problem when it comes to achieving security even, and perhaps especially, when it is proffered as a solution (as in the case of proposals for missile defence, for example). Within CSS this issue, or rather the issue of technology and this 'problem-solving' perspective of it, has been given more sustained consideration by Richard Wyn Jones. To some extent Wyn Jones shares Booth's concern with technological momentum, acknowledging that 'During the twentieth century technology has developed at a bewilderingly rapid pace', and nowhere has this been epitomised more so than in the 'nuclear revolution' with which so much of strategic studies has largely concerned itself in recent decades. 'However,' he adds, 'neither the direction of these developments nor their implications are predetermined.'[23] In fact Wyn Jones explicitly ties the question of technology to the question of emancipation and in turn, following Booth's definition, to security. 'Critical Theorists and concerned citizens', he exhorts, 'must seek to intervene in this process [Booth's 'technological momentum'] in order to try to ensure that new technologies are not developed and imposed in ways which simply re-create and reinforce present patterns of domination and injustice. More positively, they must try to ensure that the liberating potential of technology is fulfilled.'[24]

Wyn Jones argues that such intervention is necessitated not just by the practical commitments, or practice-oriented commitment of CSS, but also by its theoretical foundations in Frankfurt School Theory which was deeply concerned with the relationship between technology and society, and the bearing this relationship might have on the prospects for emancipation.[25] What these foundations are and how they apply are closely examined later. Suffice to note for the moment that Wyn Jones makes the argument that in tandem with its fetishisation of the state, the traditional approach to security studies has also shown an alarming tendency to fetishise technology, specifically military hardware.[26] This latter fetishisation, he argues, has led to a consequent lack of sustained reflection: 'the strategists' conception of technology remains curiously underdeveloped. Though strategy texts discuss the relationship between

---

[23] Richard Wyn Jones, 'The Nuclear Revolution' in Alex Danchev (ed.) *Fin de Siècle: the Meaning of the Twentieth Century* (London: I. B. Tauris, 1995) p. 106.
[24] Ibid.
[25] See ibid. and Wyn Jones, *Security, Strategy and Critical Theory*, pp. 84–8, 125–44.
[26] Wyn Jones, *Security, Strategy and Critical Theory*, p. 5.

strategy and technology, these discussions tend not to move beyond rather superficial speculation about the pace of technological change.' As a result, 'The deeper issues concerning the nature of the relationship between technology and society are hardly ever addressed.'[27]

Nowhere is this tendency more apparent than in the study of nuclear weapons technology. Specifically, Wyn Jones, drawing on terms and ideas developed in Andrew Feenberg's *Critical Theory of Technology*,[28] sees the greater part of such studies dividing into one of two camps, neither of which addresses the relationship between technology and society beyond a superficial level. In one camp are those who adopt an 'instrumental approach'. The instrumental approach to technology 'argues that technology does not affect the social, political and cultural fundamentals in either domestic or international politics'.[29] It is, as Wyn Jones characterises it, the extension of the National Rifle Association's argument that 'it's not the gun, it's the person holding the gun' to the level of international security. Politics and strategy dictate the use of weapons, no matter how powerful or 'revolutionary' those weapons might be. This is epitomised, Wyn Jones argues, in an unlikely coalition of disparate, politically opposed strategic thinkers that ranges across Colin S. Gray, John Mueller and Mao Zedong. The view is encapsulated by Gray, famed for his espousal of nuclear war fighting, in both the title and content of his treatise *Weapons Don't Make War*; by Mueller in his argument for the 'essential irrelevance' of nuclear weapons in East–West relations during the Cold War; and by Mao in his view that 'the outcome of a war is decided by the people, not by one or two new types of weapon'.[30]

The other camp Wyn Jones describes as adopting a 'substantive' approach. This approach suggests that 'technology has an autonomous logic of its own which determines a particular form of social organization'.[31] In other words, far from being simply a range of neutral tools we

[27] Wyn Jones, 'The Nuclear Revolution', p. 93.
[28] Andrew Feenberg, *Critical Theory of Technology* (Oxford: Oxford University Press, 1991).
[29] Wyn Jones, 'The Nuclear Revolution', p. 100.
[30] Colin S. Gray, *Weapons Don't Make War: Policy, Strategy and Military Technology* (Lawrence, KS: University Press of Kansas, 1993); John Mueller, 'The Essential Irrelevance of Nuclear Weapons: Stability in the Postwar World', *International Security*, 13:2 (1998) pp. 55–79; Mao Tse-Tung, 'The Chinese People Cannot Be Cowed by the Atom Bomb', *Selected Works of Mao Tse-Tung*, Vol. V (Beijing: Foreign Languages Press, 1977) pp. 152–3.
[31] Wyn Jones, 'The Nuclear Revolution', p. 102.

use to achieve certain ends, technology itself has a tangible, substantive impact in shaping social relations. Again, this categorisation throws up an odd coalition of thinkers: Kenneth Waltz, who argued that 'more nuclear weapons may be better' on the basis that the graduated proliferation of such technology would determine greater international stability by itself; McGeorge Bundy, exponent of 'existential deterrence'; and Edward P. Thompson who, in his nuclear activism, created the concept of 'exterminism' to describe the way in which the human race was seemingly hell-bent on creating its own destruction during the Cold War, enslaved to fascination with creating ever more sophisticated and deadly weapons.[32]

Most contributions to the literature on nuclear weapons, Wyn Jones contends, fall into one or other of these two camps, but neither completely captures the relationship between technology and society. A more critical approach, he argues, must be based in an awareness that 'Technology *does* have a logic in that it simultaneously creates and constrains the choices available to society, yet technology *does not* predetermine which one of those particular choices is made. That decision is a social one, and as such reflects a whole series of social, cultural and power relations. The fact that these relations are contestable leads to the argument that technology is a scene of struggle.'[33] In place of the traditional approach, Wyn Jones argues for 'an alternative conceptualization of strategy that embraces ends, regarding normative issues as intrinsic to the study and is based on a dialectical understanding of technology'.[34]

Technology, strategy and contradiction?

A primary move made in this text is to reassess the way in which this typology is formulated, applied and evaluated as a means of developing

[32] Kenneth Waltz, *The Spread of Nuclear Weapons: More May be Better*, Adelphi Paper No. 171 (London: International Institute of Strategic Studies, 1981); McGeorge Bundy, 'Existential Deterrence and Its Consequences' in Douglas McClean (ed.) *The Security Gamble: Deterrence Dilemmas in the Nuclear Age* (Totowa, NJ: Rowman and Allenheld, 1984) pp. 3–13; Edward P. Thompson, 'Notes on Exterminism, the Last Stage in Civilization' in Edward P. Thompson (ed.) *Exterminism and Cold War* (London: Verso, 1982) pp. 1–34.
[33] Wyn Jones, 'The Nuclear Revolution', p. 99, emphasis in original.
[34] Wyn Jones, *Security, Strategy and Critical Theory*, p. 5.

its potential application to the study of security issues, in this case the issue of missile defence. A good starting point in this regard is an assessment of the possible limitations of the instrumental/substantive characterisations of strategic thinking outlined above. Colin S. Gray, for example, is cited by Wyn Jones as an archetypal instrumental strategist, as noted previously. Wyn Jones is on extremely firm ground in identifying Gray's *Weapons Don't Make War* as an instrumentalist text. Yet a few years later, in his *The Second Nuclear Age*, Gray implicitly draws upon a substantially different understanding of (nuclear) technology.[35] Here Gray argues that we are currently living in 'a second nuclear age'. Immediate post-Cold War optimism notwithstanding, there is 'a nuclear quality to world politics beyond the erstwhile great East–West Cold War. The prospectively even less good news is that a third nuclear age probably lurks in the wings and could see the return of a single dominant political axis of nuclear armed hostility.'[36] Thus, not only are we left with a 'nuclear problem', we are suffering from a 'nuclear condition': 'nuclear weapons provide a particular character of condition as well as constituting a problem'.[37] Political change seems entirely incidental in this regard: 'It just so happens that the dominant differences between the first and second nuclear ages were wholly political.'[38] Such assertions seem to be diametrically opposed to Gray's earlier 'weapons don't make war' argument. Instead of policy dictating technology, as consistent with instrumentalism, nuclear weapons are argued to be constitutive of (world) politics rather than the other way around. Indeed they become epochal, era-defining technologies.

This seems to move Gray much closer to Kenneth Waltz's substantivist approach to nuclear weapons as identified by Wyn Jones. In fact, Gray explicitly tips his hat to Waltz's 'more may be better argument', with minor qualifications. Waltz, Gray argues, 'has performed a most valuable service with his powerfully argued deflation of some of the most overexpanded balloons of nuclear menace that have been floated in recent years'. Gray largely agrees, though looks to add a sense of pessimism that is again predicated on the character of nuclear weaponry in itself, not on policy or policy-makers: 'one should not discount nuclear threats. Indeed, it is the unique potency of nuclear threats

---

[35] Colin S. Gray, *The Second Nuclear Age* (Boulder, CO: Lynne Rienner, 1999).
[36] Ibid., p. 1.   [37] Ibid., p. 5.   [38] Ibid., pp. 7–8.

upon which Waltz's thesis leans most essentially.'[39] Gray thus prioritises (literally explosive) change over Waltz's focus on nuclear technology as a potential source of stability, and is elsewhere less favourable to Waltz's assertion that managed proliferation encourages states to act rationally: 'The rigorous semi-nonsense of Waltz's neorealism would have us treat the actors in world security politics [*sic*] largely as if they were black boxes.'[40] Gray expects nuclear catastrophe to be an ever-increasing likelihood resulting from the inevitable spread of nuclear weapons.

Once again, this results in some unlikely alignments. Despite his frequent self-identification as a 'realist', Gray cannot be listed among what Richard K. Betts has termed 'Utopian Realists', such as Kenneth Waltz and John Mearsheimer, who have held out hope in the past for 'managed proliferation'.[41] Gray is, paradoxically, probably better classed with the 'Liberal Pessimists' of the arms control school who 'view the spread of nuclear weapons with alarm ... assuming that increased numbers of nuclear-armed states means an increased likelihood that nuclear weapons eventually will be used.'[42] Gray, however, places little faith in the power of international law to control the spread of technology. In good technological determinist fashion he argues that new technologies will emerge to modify, though not replace, the determinative quality of nuclear weapons. 'In principle, and one day for near certain, nuclear weapons might be superseded by functionally superior substitutes; indeed for some purposes and for some countries – one in particular, the United States – such substitution is already far advanced. Nonetheless, the nuclear era endures.'[43] Here Gray hints both at his disdain for the notion of a 'revolution' in military affairs and at his positive endorsement of technologies capable of defending against nuclear weapons. His role as a major proponent of the latter is explored in more detail in later chapters.

---

[39] Ibid., p. 10 in reference to Waltz, *The Spread of Nuclear Weapons*, and Scott D. Sagan and Kenneth N. Waltz, *The Spread of Nuclear Weapons: a Debate* (New York: W. W. Norton, 1995).

[40] Gray, *The Second Nuclear Age*, p. 61.

[41] See Waltz, *Spread of Nuclear Weapons*; John Mearsheimer, 'Why We Will Soon Miss the Cold War', *The Atlantic Monthly*, 266:2 (1990) pp. 35–50.

[42] Richard K. Betts, 'Universal Deterrence or Conceptual Collapse? Liberal Pessimism and Utopian Realism' in Victor A. Utgoff (ed.) *The Coming Crisis: Nuclear Proliferation, US Interests, and World Order* (Cambridge, MA: MIT Press, 2000) p. 8.

[43] Gray, *The Second Nuclear Age*, p. 2.

What this account is intended to illustrate for the moment, though, is that (consciously or not) strategic thinkers can draw upon and hold instrumentalist and substantivist conceptions at different times, and seeming paradoxes and juxtapositions emerge as a result. Gray is but one example. Likewise Kenneth Waltz, Wyn Jones's archetype of a substantivist approach to nuclear weapons, has at times expressed highly instrumentalist views. For example, just two years prior to his espousal of the 'more may be better argument', Waltz seems to argue in his seminal work *Theory of International Politics* that the impact of nuclear technology in international politics is relatively minimal and superseded by the condition of international anarchy:

> Nuclear weapons did not cause the condition of bipolarity; other states by acquiring them cannot change the condition ... Nuclear capabilities reinforce *a condition that would exist in their absence*: Even without nuclear technology the United States and the Soviet Union would have developed weapons of immense destructive power. They are set apart from the other [states] not by particular weapons systems but by their ability to exploit military technology on a large scale and at the scientific frontiers. Had the atom never been split, each would far surpass others in military strength, and each would remain the greatest threat and source of potential damage to the other.[44]

In this light, the idea of a 'nuclear condition' has a much diminished status. States use whatever military instruments are available to them to achieve their political ends under the condition of anarchy. This, for Waltz, is a timeless truth that exists independently of technological change. As Waltz asserts, 'Gunpowder did not blur the distinction between great powers and the others ... nor have nuclear weapons done so.'[45] Thus with very little distance in a temporal sense Waltz – seemingly unconsciously – maintains an inversion of his later view of nuclear technology's impact on world politics.

Interrogating the instrumental/substantive taxonomy

Wyn Jones's application of the instrumental/substantive taxonomy does not seem to give much consideration to what oscillation between

---

[44] Kenneth N. Waltz, *Theory of International Politics* (New York: MGraw Hill, 1979) pp. 180–1, emphasis added. Waltz's *The Spread of Nuclear Weapons* was published in 1981.
[45] Ibid., p. 180.

these seemingly juxtaposed understandings of technology might mean or even how it might be possible. Of course, we should not dismiss this application on this basis alone. As an initial attempt to explicate and critique dominant conceptions of military technology within strategic studies, the adaptation of Feenberg's approach succeeds in substantially realigning thought on this subject, thus potentially opening up the discipline as a whole to critique in this regard. This is of particular benefit given the reluctance to theorise or engage substantively with the social, political and ethical implications of modern military technology in a subject area that, paradoxically, ostensibly elevates weaponry as its object of analysis. In this regard, the deployment of Feenberg's typology does indeed add 'welcome broadness and sophistication to a field where these qualities have been absent'.[46]

As the above argument attests, though, there are limits – and possibly ultimately limited benefits – to the delineation of ideal types along instrumental and substantive lines within strategic thought. These ideal types can overlap and intersect in ways that make it difficult to speak of purely instrumental or purely substantivist understandings of technology in the analysis of nuclear strategy as a whole, or particular issues within it such as defensive technology. Revision of the application of this taxonomy, and of the reasons we apply it, might therefore be a necessary and fruitful move.

A key starting point of this volume is that instrumental and substantive understandings of technology are at their most interesting, and potentially most powerful, precisely when they overlap, intersect and even contradict each other. The instrumental/substantive distinction is therefore maintained throughout, but is maintained with specific qualifications and on a substantially revised basis. In order to understand this basis more fully, we need to trace both the delineation of the instrumental/substantivist taxonomy and its intellectual lineage in more detail. As noted previously, Wyn Jones adopts the terms 'instrumental' and 'substantive' from the work of the critical theorist Andrew Feenberg, in particular his *Critical Theory of Technology*.[47] Feenberg defines the 'instrumental' approach to technology as the 'common sense

---

[46] Wyn Jones, *Security, Strategy and Critical Theory*, p. 133.

[47] Feenberg, *Critical Theory of Technology*, more recently revised and updated, in less expansive form, as *Questioning Technology* (London: Routledge, 2001) and *Transforming Technology: a Critical Theory Revisited* (New York: Oxford University Press, 2002).

idea that technologies are "tools" standing ready to serve the purposes of their users'.[48] Technology in this sense is 'neutral' in and of itself and indifferent to the variety of ends it can be employed to achieve. This instrumental conception is, Feenberg argues, typical of modern government in so far as it treats technology as subservient to values and goals established in other spheres such as politics and economics.[49]

Intuitive and commonsensical as it may seem, Feenberg argues that even this instrumental or 'technicist' view of technology rests on deep-seated philosophical assumptions. These assumptions often go unspoken in the modern association of technological 'progress' with a fitter, happier, more productive society, but the broad acceptance of these assumptions does not diminish the fact that this unquestioning view of technology still represents a position. Feenberg identifies the most obvious and well-developed philosophical exposition of this position in the work of Jürgen Habermas.[50] Habermas's thinking on technology represents his contribution to a long-standing debate within Western Marxism on the place and effects of technology in modern industrialised societies, and specifically on the transferability of technological means in any transition to a genuinely socialist society. The possibility that technology was itself an implicit cause of relations of domination in modern capitalist society was considered to varying degrees by the earlier Frankfurt School thinkers from whom Habermas followed on. They had become increasingly pessimistic about any progressive or emancipatory qualities technology might have.

Habermas, by contrast, seeks to uphold the neutrality of technology as one aspect of a potentially 'rational society'. He argues that the reason his Frankfurt School predecessors had considered technology as a negative determinant of social relations was that they failed to distinguish between purposive-rational (technical) and communicative spheres of action. As Thomas McCarthy puts it, Habermas's view is that 'while the specific historical forms of science and technology

---

[48] Feenberg, *Critical Theory of Technology*, p. 5.
[49] This view generally accords with the emergence of 'technology' as specialisation in the mechanical arts that emerged in the mid-eighteenth to mid-nineteenth century – see Raymond Williams, *Keywords: a Vocabulary of Culture and Society* (London: Fontana, 1983) pp. 315–16.
[50] See in particular Jürgen Habermas, 'Technology and Science as "Ideology"' in his *Toward a Rational Society: Student Protest, Science and Politics*, trans. J. J. Shapiro (London: Heineman, 1971) pp. 81–122.

depend on institutional arrangements that are variable, their basic
logical structures are grounded in the very nature of purposive-rational
action'.[51] In other words we should separate social relations from
technology which is part of the structure of purposive-rational action
and, therefore, is a 'project of the human species *as a whole*'.[52]
Consequently, 'the achievements of technology' are 'indispensable as
such' even allowing for the destructive potential of modern technology.[53] Habermas continues that 'Realizing this, it is impossible to
envisage how, as long as the organization of human nature does not
change and as long therefore as we have to achieve self-preservation
through social labor and with the aid of means that substitute for work,
we could renounce technology, more particularly *our* technology, in
favour of a qualitatively different one.'[54] As a result, Habermas places
tremendous weight on the ability of human beings, at the 'species level',
to negotiate the rational ends to which technology should be put, and
his views on technology arguably effect an illusory separation between
society and technology that has been rejected by most of the recent work
in the sociology of technology.[55] In regard to the implications of his
views in regard to weapons technology Habermas has even been
accused of filtering out the 'politics of mass destruction'.[56]

The second and seemingly opposed conception of technology
argues that human subordination to technology is an inherent and
inescapable concomitant of modern technology itself. This is what
Feenberg classifies as the 'substantive' theory or understanding of

---

[51] Thomas McCarthy, *The Critical Theory of Jürgen Habermas* (Cambridge, MA: MIT Press, 1981) p. 21.

[52] Habermas states it thus: 'technology, if based at all on a project, can only be traced back to a "project" of the human species *as a whole*, and not to one that could be historically surpassed'. Habermas, 'Technology and Science as "Ideology"', p. 87, emphasis in original.

[53] Ibid.; see also his 'Technical Progress and the Social Life-World' also in *Toward a Rational Society*.

[54] Habermas, 'Technology and Science as "Ideology"', p. 87, emphasis in original.

[55] See, for example, Wiebe E. Bjiker, Thomas P. Hughes and Trevor J. Pinch, *The Social Construction of Technological Systems: New Directions in the Sociology and History of Technology* (Cambridge, MA: MIT Press, 1989). Habermas's position on the relation between humans and technology has, more recently, been pessimistically revised in relation to biotechnology – see his *The Future of Human Nature* (Cambridge: Polity Press, 2003).

[56] John B. Thompson, 'Rationality and Social Rationalization: An Assessment of Habermas' Theory of Communicative Action', *Sociology*, 17:2 (1983) pp. 278–294, p. 293.

technology.[57] This approach claims that the very existence of technologies, and the possibilities which by design (so to speak) they
allow, have a determinative or substantive impact on the way we
live. Technology creates a finite amount of (technological) choices
and therefore has a determining, almost autonomous quality that
outlives and supersedes human input and involvement. Moreover,
what the very employment of technology does in conditioning humanity and nature is of more consequence than the ostensible goals it is
used towards.[58]

In philosophy this view is most prominently represented by Martin
Heidegger. It is impossible entirely to do justice to the scope of his
argument here, but at base Heidegger argues that the 'essence' of
modern technology is to turn man and nature into quantifiable
resources or 'standing reserves', a process that Heidegger terms
'enframing'. This process, in his view, compromises the true revealing
of our own human 'essence': 'The threat to man does not come in the
first instance from the potentially lethal machines and apparatus of
technology. The actual threat has already affected man in his essence.
The rule of Enframing threatens man with the possibility that it could be
denied to him to enter into a more original revealing and hence to
experience the call of a more primal truth.'[59] Thus, if we are thinking
in terms of military technology from the Heideggerian perspective, its
destructive potential is only the most obvious and ephemeral manifestation of a more fundamental form of subjugation that resides in modern
technology itself.

These two understandings, Feenberg implies in passing, extend
beyond the worlds of philosophical speculation. In a strict philosophical
sense, there is no value judgement associated with either instrumentalism or substantivism: they do not say whether technological advance is
a 'good' or a 'bad' thing, they simply try to understand where technology fits in social life. Beyond the philosophical realm, though, the two
understandings have tended to be manifested as normative evaluations

---

[57] See his *Critical Theory of Technology*, and also *Questioning Technology*, pp. 14–20.
[58] See Feenberg, *Critical Theory of Technology*, pp. 7–8.
[59] Martin Heidegger, *The Question Concerning Technology, and Other Essays*,
trans. W. Lovitt (London: Harper and Row, 1977) p. 28. Feenberg also associates
substantivism closely with the work of Jacques Ellul – see Ellul's *The
Technological Society*, trans. J. Wilkinson (New York: Vintage, 1964).

of technological development.[60] As Feenberg suggests, technology has a 'cultural character' and a 'connotative dimension' that arises from the cultural significance attributed to a particular technology or technologies.[61] So too, in consequence, as becomes clear from examining the understandings of technology outlined by Feenberg, do these understandings have a connotative dimension. The view of technology as simply an instrument has often been conflated with the view of *technology as an instrument of progress*. The understanding of technology as a neutral instrument, Feenberg argues, leads in turn to an assumption that it can be univerally applied across different settings to achieve greater productivity, efficiency and modernisation.[62] Yet, instrumentalism is by consequence clearly imbued with a value content even as it stipulates the neutrality of technology: productivity, efficiency and modernity all require judgements as to how such standards are measured and achieved. In this sense, instrumentalism is not simply limited to philosophical treatises, but is in fact more prevalent in political and practical discourse.[63] Instrumentalism not only underpins the progressivist impulses of both liberalism and orthodox Marxism in terms of political theory, but is also manifested in popular thought extending from utopian science fiction to advertising rhetoric and even, as noted previously, in specific variants of strategic thought. In the process it takes on a range of connotations – of progress, improvement and modernity in particular – and has tended to be imbued with a sense of optimism and faith in technology as an instrument of human progress and achievement.

Likewise substantivism is not simply bound or exhausted in philosophical debate, and it similarly possesses a range of value connotations. Heideggerian resignation to a technologically determined future has often been equated with a sense of pessimism and the view that *technology corrodes humanity's ability to control its own destiny*.[64] As Feenberg argues, Heidegger's vision is an 'apocalyptic' one, and its claims are 'all too believable' in light of unintended cultural consequences of technology.[65] A characterisitic example he cites in this vein

---

[60] William Leiss, *Under Technology's Thumb* (Montreal: McGill-Queen's University Press, 1990) pp. 23–35, offers a parallel analysis to that given here, examining the often opposed visions associated with technological 'imperatives'.
[61] Feenberg, *Critical Theory of Technology*, pp. 7, 109.
[62] Ibid., p. 6.   [63] Ibid., p. 7.
[64] Ibid., p. 8. See also Leiss, *Under Technology's Thumb*, p. 26.
[65] Feenberg, *Critical Theory of Technology*, p. 7.

is drawn from Norbert Wiener, the early pioneer of cybernetics, who cautioned against the dangers of increasing over-reliance on computerisation. Reliance on computers without the capacity to learn, Wiener warned, would be unwise owing to the risk of system failure or inadequacy; but reliance on computers with the capacity to learn raised the prospect that decision-making would be taken out of human hands and might be completely automated on certain occasions. 'For the man who is aware of this', Wiener concluded, 'to throw the problem of his responsibility on the machine, whether it can learn or not, is to cast his responsibility to the winds, and to find it coming back seated on the whirlwind.'[66] Clearly, then, substantivism has its own value content and connotations that are 'apocalyptic', pessimistic and cautionary. It warns of diminishing human capacity to control human affairs in the face of technological development, and in this regard aligns closely with forms of technological determinism. And since its ominous portents are 'all too believable', it is unsurprising that as a literary trope substantivism is well represented in dystopian literature and science fiction and has its own counterparts in political and strategic thought.[67]

It is possible, therefore, to align a variety of character-dichotomies between these two understandings – hope and fear, human agency versus determinism, optimism versus pessimism (as regards the impact of technology on social life) and so on – and some have gone so far as to argue that analyses of the social consequences of technological change have tended to become 'trapped' in such polarisations.[68] Feenberg alludes to these connotations of instrumentalism with progressive and utopian thought and substantivism with an opposed tendency towards dystopian thinking. However, he is less concerned with the development of these connotations within particular cultural contexts than he is with charting a path between these two apparently juxtaposed understandings towards a genuinely critical theory of technology. The rationale for doing so lies, he argues, in the fact that, for all their ostensible differences, instrumentalism and substantivism essentially amount to the same thing: technological determinism. The apparent dichotomy between instrumentalism and substantivism belies a shared 'take it or leave it' attitude to technology:

---

[66] As cited in Feenberg, *Critical Theory of Technology*, p. 111.
[67] See Langdon Winner, *Autonomous Technology: Technics-out-of-Control as a Theme in Political Thought* (Cambridge, MA: MIT Press, 1978).
[68] See Leiss, *Under Technology's Thumb*, p. 28.

On the one hand, if technology is a mere instrumentality, indifferent to values, then its design and structure is not at issue in political debate, only the range and efficiency of its application. On the other hand, if technology is the vehicle for a culture of domination, then we are condemned to pursue its advance toward dystopia or to regress to a more primitive way of life. In neither case can we change it: in both theories, *technology is destiny*.[69]

Feenberg, as Wyn Jones would later argue with regard to nuclear technology, wants to establish a dialectical conception of technology that allows a certain amount of autonomy to technology without era-dicating or obfuscating the role of human agency entirely. Thus he argues on the one hand that 'What human beings are and will become is decided in the shape of our tools no less than in the action of statesmen and political movements. The design of technology is thus an ontologi-cal decision fraught with political consequences.'[70] At the same time he argues that we should not conflate these consequences with predeter-mined societal ends: 'the lower we descend toward the [technological] foundations of rational institutions, the more ambiguous are the ele-ments from which they are constructed, and the more these are compa-tible with a variety of different hegemonic orders'.[71] On this view, 'technology is not a destiny but a scene of struggle. It is a social battle-field, or perhaps a better metaphor would be a *parliament of things* on which civilizational alternatives are debated and decided.'[72] This is what Feenberg terms the 'ambivalence' of technology. Technology may not be produced or used entirely under conditions of our choosing at present, but the fundamental ambivalence of technology allows for the possibility that it can be informed by and used towards more emancipatory ends.

A short genealogy of critical theory on technology

As indicated previously, the analysis undertaken later maintains Feenberg's taxonomy as a heuristic device, but does so in a qualified and differentiated manner compared with the way it has been used both by Feenberg himself and by Wyn Jones within CSS. Rather than seeking to create a new critical theory of technology in reference to missile

---

[69] Feenberg, *Questioning Technology*, p. 8, emphasis in original.
[70] Ibid., p. 3.   [71] Feenberg, *Critical Theory of Technology*, p. 83.
[72] Ibid., p. 14.

defence, or explicitly to look for evidence of elements of a critical understanding of technology latent within the discourse of missile defence advocacy, the following chapters attempt to show how this discourse is saturated with understandings of technology that are homologous to the instrumental/substantive conceptions. Hence the analysis undertaken here is better identified as a *critical approach to* understandings of technology as opposed to a critical theory of technology per se, even if this is a related issue.

The underlying argument of the later chapters is that the simultaneous presence of instrumental and substantive understandings – which are frequently referenced and used in combination within a particular form of security discourse associated with justifications of missile defence – does not necessarily lead to the development of a critical understanding of technology. In fact it may well inhibit any such development. Missile defence stands as an archetypal 'problem-solving' or 'traditional' approach to both technology and security, to put it in the terms used by Robert Cox or in the prior and broadly analogous terms used by Max Horkheimer.[73] Based on the evidence to date, there is very little 'critical' thinking either within missile defence advocacy or, indeed, in commentaries within the academic literature on missile defence as a programme.[74] With regard to the justifications and arguments for American missile defence, one of the key aims of the analysis is to show how the discourse of missile defence advocacy seeks to represent the ambivalent potentiality of technological development – which Feenberg sees as a critical source of opportunity – via common sense derivatives of the previously described philosophical understandings of technology. In short, the analysis here is motivated by a concern that CSS must tie its development of a critical understanding of (military) technology to a critique of extant understandings of technology present in contemporary forms of security discourse, in keeping with the mode of 'immanent critique' – the criticism of an extant theory or philosophy

---

[73] Robert W. Cox, 'Social Forces, States and World Orders: Beyond International Relations Theory', *Millennium: Journal of International Studies*, 10:2 (1982) pp. 126–55; Max Horkheimer, 'Traditional and Critical Theory' [originally published in 1937] in *Critical Theory: Selected Essays*, trans. Matthew J. O'Connell and others (New York: Seabury Press, 1972).

[74] On the latter aspect see Columba Peoples, 'Technology and Politics in the Missile Defence Debate: Traditional, Radical and Critical Approaches', *Global Change, Peace and Security*, 19:3 (2007) pp. 265–80.

that 'measures the present on the basis of a conception of actually existing but not yet actualized' critical understanding of technology.[75]

The allusion to immanent critique makes the orientation of this argument closer to the (admittedly problematic) critique of technology advanced by the early Frankfurt School critical theorists. Prominent figures associated with the Frankfurt School – most notably Max Horkheimer, Theodor Adorno, Herbert Marcuse and to some extent Walter Benjamin – were all concerned with the 'question of technology' and the role it played in modern society.[76] This concern can be seen as emanating from the genus of Marxist thought itself. Marxian social theory must, of necessity, concern itself on some level with technology, specifically as a component part of the means of production. But Marx's own views on technology are somewhat ambiguous, and several different readings have been taken in this regard. The first is what Monika Reinfelder and others identify as the 'technicist' form of Marxism: a belief in the pure instrumentality of technology such that under the command of the proletariat, technology could, without major modification, be used towards the creation of a socialist society.[77] Several challenges to this view emerged in revisionist Marxian thought, however, as confidence in the technicism found in the arguments of Engels and Karl Kautsky dissipated by the 1920s. Aspects of this critique are implied in the work of Rosa Luxemburg, Karl Korsch and Antonio Gramsci,[78] but were pursued in much more depth by Georg Lukács initially and later by the Frankfurt School. Lukács rejects the technological determinism implicit in technicism, arguing that 'this attempt to find the underlying determinants of society and its development in a principle other than that of the social relations between men in the process of production ... leads to fetishism'.[79] Against the technicists

---

[75] Wyn Jones, 'On Emancipation', p. 228.

[76] For overviews see Feenberg, *Critical Theory and Technology* and Wyn Jones, *Security, Strategy and Critical Theory*.

[77] Monica Reinfelder, 'Breaking the Spell of Technicism' in Phil Slater (ed.) *Outlines of a Critique of Technology* (London: Ink Links, 1980) pp. 12–19.

[78] See Reinfelder, 'Breaking the Spell'.

[79] What Marx terms the 'fetishism of commodities', which is in turn attributed an illusory explanatory power, the market. 'Competition is used to explain everything,' Marx declares in *The Economic and Philosophical Manuscripts of 1844* (London: Lawrence and Wishart, 1977) p. 62. Hence, the common sense idea that market dynamics drive technological change is at one and the same time plausible and a logical fallacy. See Leiss, *Under Technology's Thumb*, p. 57.

Lukács went so far as to say, 'it is altogether incorrect and unmarxist to separate technique from the other ideological forms and to propose for it a self-sufficiency from the economic structure of society'.[80]

The potential problem of viewing technology in this manner is what Feenberg terms the 'paradox of reform from above': how could socialism hope to revolutionise technological development if it was accepted that 'technology is not neutral but fundamentally biased toward a particular hegemony', and hence 'all action undertaken within its framework tends to reproduce that hegemony'?[81] To Lukács this paradox could be overcome through the attainment of class consciousness, presupposing the ability of social subjects to extricate themselves from social relations far enough to be able to recognise the role that technology plays in reproducing these relations, and to act accordingly. The idea that such consciousness was immanent in society was taken up by the Frankfurt School, though, as we shall see, they became increasingly pessimistic as to its actual existence.

The work of the Frankfurt School not only added to the debate about the possible role of technology in any transition to socialism but also sought to assess the role technology might play in allowing exacerbated forms of domination and exploitation – in Nazi Germany, the USSR and latterly in the post-war United States – as a broader aspect of social relations. Initially at least, the theorists now commonly associated with the Frankfurt School rubric were sanguine about a potentially emancipatory role for technology. Max Horkheimer's essay 'Traditional and Critical Theory', for example, can be argued to represent such a benign attitude to technology.[82] Here Horkheimer's proposes a vision of an emancipated society in which humans are free from the vicissitudes of nature (or 'outer nature') to the greatest possible extent allowed by the rational utilisation of the forces of production. This is, according to Wyn Jones, 'predicated on a benign view of technology' in which technological developments 'are seen as creating ever greater possibilities for the domination of nature and, hence, emancipation'.[83]

---

[80] Georg Lukács, 'Technology and Social Relations', *New Left Review*, 39 (1966) pp. 27–34, p. 29.

[81] Feenberg, *Critical Theory of Technology*, p. 65.

[82] Horkheimer, 'Traditional and Critical Theory'.

[83] Wyn Jones, *Security, Strategy and Critical Theory*, p. 27. In a similar vein, Walter Benjamin initially welcomed the 'Age of Mechanical Reproduction'

Hence there does seem to have been some stake placed in an instrumental, technicist understanding of technology in early Frankfurt School thought. In the main, however, there is a palpable shift to a negatively construed subtantivist understanding of technology across the later writings of the School, undoubtedly influenced by the School's increased engagement with the ideas of Max Weber.[84] At the risk of oversimplification, the School fused Weber's 'iron cage' of bureaucratic rationality with the instrumental rationality they perceived as inherent in modern technology.[85] This strand became particularly prominent in the School's post-war writings, but was already present by the 1930s. Walter Benjamin, for example, lamented in 1936 that:

The destructiveness of war furnishes proof that society has not been mature enough to incorporate technology as its organ, that technology has not been sufficiently developed to cope with the elemental forces of society ... Instead of draining rivers, society directs a human stream into a bed of trenches; instead of dropping seeds from airplanes, it drops incendiary bombs over cities; and through gas warfare the aura is abolished in a new way.[86]

Against this background the Frankfurt School developed the concept of 'technological rationality' which, like Marx's market rationality, is seen as constitutive of elite control of society but in which 'control is not simply an economic purpose served by neutral systems and machines but is internal to their very structure'.[87] For Herbert Marcuse in particular this technological rationality is the leitmotif of 'One-Dimensional' modern society – a world devoid of critical consciousness.[88] To him, 'Not only the application of technology but technology itself is domination (of nature and men) – methodical, scientific, calculated, calculating

on the basis that 'for the first time in world history, mechanical reproduction emancipates the work of art from its parasitical dependence in ritual' – see 'The Work of Art in the Age of Mechanical Reproduction' in his *Illuminations* (New York: Shocken Books, 1969) p. 224.

[84] Andrew Feenberg, 'From Essentialism to Constructivism: Philosophy of Technology at the Crossroads', undated paper available from www-rohan. sdsu.edu/faculty/feenberg/talk4.html [last accessed 20 January 2009]. See, for example, 'Industrialism and Capitalism in the Work of Max Weber' in Herbert Marcuse's *Negations: Essays in Critical Theory* (London: Allen Lane, 1968).

[85] Terry Maley, 'Max Weber and the Iron Cage of Technology', *Bulletin of Science, Technology and Society*, 24:1 (2004) pp. 69–86.

[86] 'The Work of Art in the Age of Mechanical Reproduction', p. 242.

[87] Feenberg, *Critical Theory of Technology*, p. 69.

[88] Herbert Marcuse, *One-Dimensional Man*, 2nd edition (London: Routledge, 1991).

control. Specific purposes and interests of domination are not foisted upon technology "subsequently" and from outside; they enter the very construction of the technical apparatus.'[89]

A difficulty quickly arises with this position though, which is that if technological rationality is so dominant in itself, and perpetuates relations of domination, how can we account for any forms of change or resistance? As early as 1941 Marcuse's fellow-traveller Max Horkheimer had stated that 'The new order contradicts reason so fundamentally that reason does not dare to doubt it. Even the consciousness of oppression fades. The more incommensurate become the concentration of power and the helplessness of the individual, the more difficult for him to penetrate the human origin of his misery. The tattered veil of money has been replaced by the veil of technology.'[90] Elements of Marcuse's work, and certainly works such as Adorno and Horkheimer's *Dialectic of Enlightenment*, tend to accept the impenetrability of this veil and the inability of human beings to do anything about it.[91] In effect this drew later Frankfurt School thinking towards substantive theory by identifying the values embodied in current technology with the essence of technology as such. This would be exemplified in Adorno's later claim that 'No universal history leads from savagery to humanitarianism, but there is one leading from the slingshot to the megaton bomb.'[92] The technological ensemble the Frankfurt theorists analysed may have been the product of contingent historical social relations, but through its reproduction of domination and instrumental reason had now, apparently, reached a catastrophic endpoint.

[89] Marcuse, *Negations*, p. 223. See also Herbert Marcuse, 'Some Social Implications of Modern Technology' in Andrew Arato and Eike Gebhardt (eds.) *The Essential Frankfurt School Reader* (Oxford: Blackwell, 1978) pp. 138–62 and 'From Ontology to Technology: Fundamental Tendencies of Industrial Society' in Stephen Eric Bronner and Douglas MacKay Kellner (eds.) *Critical Theory and Society: a Reader* (New York: Routledge, 1989) pp. 119–27, in which the influence of Marcuse's former tutor, Heidegger, as well as his own reading of Lewis Mumford, on Marcuse's thinking on technology is apparent.

[90] Max Horkheimer, 'The End of Reason' in Bronner and Kellner, *Critical Theory and Society*, p. 44.

[91] Theodor Adorno and Max Horkheimer, *Dialectic of Enlightenment*, trans. J. Cumming (London: Allen Lane, 1973).

[92] Theodor Adorno, *Negative Dialectics* (London: Routledge and Kegan Paul, 1973) p. 320. The strength of Adorno's feeling on this is embellished by his contradictory claim in the same paragraph that 'Universal history must be construed and denied.'

Technology and dialectics

Elements of a more positive view of technology do remain in, for example, the writings of Marcuse, who would later (in the 1960s) attempt to identify elements of resistance to a totally administered society. However, the portrayal of a society dominated by technological rationality itself seems to preclude such forms of protest. Marcuse seems to foster this contradiction without ever coming to a sustainable account of its existence or how it might be overcome. In the preface to *One-Dimensional Man*, for example, he states that: '*One-Dimensional Man* will vacillate throughout between two contradictory hypotheses: (1) that advanced industrial society is capable of containing qualitative change for the foreseeable future (2) that the forces and tendencies exist which may explode the society.'[93] The word 'containing' here is important, as it suggests the ability of the existing system of social relations to both absorb and co-opt countervailing tendencies and its ability to *contain* these tendencies. Feenberg criticises Marcuse on this point:

The mutually cancelling formulae do actually add up to a theory, but it is buried in the interplay of the inadequate concepts used to present it. In any case, Marcuse's rhetorical strategy is clear enough: from a variant of the Marxist position, he extracts results that one would expect from the substantivist position. He has his conceptual cake and eats it, making the strongest possible critique of technology without paying the 'Luddist' price. The ambiguous results reveal the limitations of Marcuse's approach.[94]

A key aim of Feenberg's 'Critical Theory of Technology' is to get away from such potential contradictions and limitations and form a truly dialectical understanding of technology that is not reducible simply to either Habermasian-style instrumentalism or Heideggerian substantivism.

We should, however, pause before dismissing the Frankfurt School entirely on the basis of its seeming contradictions, disparity and occasional fatalism on the subject of technology. In seeking to solve or resolve the apparent inadequacies of Frankfurt School thinking on technology, Feenberg potentially obscures one of the fundamental concerns of Critical Theory: contradiction. This latter aspect is one which David Held elevates as a *key* characteristic that can be observed as common among

---

[93] Marcuse, *One-Dimensional Man*, p. xlvii.
[94] Feenberg, *Critical Theory of Technology*, p. 76.

those thinkers conventionally associated with the rubric of the Critical Theory of the Frankfurt School. Held argues that: 'Critical theory ... seeks to explicate human reality as a self-structured, self-unfolding and contradictory whole. If it is to pursue its task successfully it must proceed ... through the analysis of the creation, maintenance, and change of people's inter-subjective, historical *concepts*' and '*by refusing to ignore and smooth over contradictions and contradictory claims at the phenomenal level*'.[95]

This precept is one which, following Held's assessment of Critical Theory, is common to the early Frankfurt School, particularly Horkheimer, Adorno and Marcuse, or at least homologous between them in the sense of being a common characteristic employed in different critical exercises. More specifically, it is common to the form of dialectical method employed by all three. What distinguishes dialectical method at a general level is

its recognition of the insufficiencies and imperfections of 'finished' systems of thought. The dialectical method is a critical method for it reveals incompleteness where completeness is claimed. It embraces that which is in terms of that which is not, and that which is real in terms of potentialities not yet realized. Through continuous criticism and reconstruction, however, the partiality of perspectives can be progressively overcome.[96]

Horkheimer, Marcuse and Adorno all adapted the Hegelian–Marxist form of dialectical method into the broader project of immanent critique: the attempt to identify the closed-off possibilities immanent in the extant socio-political order that have not yet become realised or realisable. A major revision they add in this sense is captured by Horkheimer's notion of the 'unconcluded' dialectic (*unabgeschlossene Dialektik*) where 'progress is not guaranteed in history; it depends on the productive and reproductive practices of historically acting subjects'.[97] Horkheimer sees the role of the critical theorist in this sense as attempting to 'salvage relative truths from the wreckage of false ultimates', and in this sense it is the contradiction in dialectics that is more important than its expected 'product'.[98] Similarly, though in a more pessimistic vein, Adorno's *Negative Dialectics* 'sets out to free dialectics from affirmative traits which are entailed in Hegel's notion of the

[95] David Held, *Introduction to Critical Theory: Horkheimer to Habermas* (London: Hutchison, 1980) p. 173, second emphasis added.
[96] Held, *Introduction to Critical Theory*, p. 177. [97] Ibid., p. 178.
[98] Max Horkheimer, *Eclipse of Reason* (New York: Seabury Press, 1974) pp. 182–3.

negation of the negation'.[99] Contradiction is pivotal to Adorno's theory
of negative dialectics where 'To proceed dialectically means to think in
contradictions, for the sake of the contradiction once experienced in the
thing, and against that contradiction.'[100]

This emphasis on contradiction within words, concepts and understandings is suggestive of a subtly different approach to understandings
of technology. That is, it suggests that at least as important as the type of
understanding of technology employed (which has been well captured
by Feenberg's typology) is the way these understandings overlap, intersect and contradict each other. Moreover, it suggests that where such
contradictions exist they do not necessarily lead either to the collapse
of an argument (as would be expected by logical analytical thought) or
to an improved, synthetic argument.[101] In the spirit of this approach
then, what becomes important is to see how such contradiction between
'false ultimates' endures, and with what effects. With respect to understandings of technology, one major effect, specifically, might be to produce a sense of linear motion through technological determinism. That
is, if instrumentalism and substantivism really are 'false ultimates' in
Adorno's sense – and Feenberg seems to acknowledge as much in his
association of both with technological determinism[102] – then the presence
and combination of both within arguments may have the effect of portraying a seemingly predetermined line of technological development.

With respect to the proceeding analysis of the discourse surrounding
missile defence this has several implications. The first is that it throws
the use of ostensibly contradictory understandings of technology within
this discourse into a different light. Secondly, and by consequence, the
characteristics of instrumentalism and substantivism might be seen to be
more fluid and less exclusive as a result. This suggests that one need not
be a *bona fide* instrumentalist or substantivist to borrow tropes, metaphors and references from one another. Hence we might still see, for
example, Colin Gray as espousing (on some occasions at least) an
instrumentalist view of technology that is forever optimistic about
progress in defensive technology even though Gray is a thoroughgoing
pessimist of human progress based on his 'realist' view of human

---

[99] Held, *Introduction to Critical Theory*, p. 203.
[100] Adorno, *Negative Dialectics*, pp. 144–5.
[101] For a relevant application in security studies see Michael C. Williams,
      'Rethinking the "Logic" of Deterrence', *Alternatives*, 17 (1992) pp. 67–93.
[102] As does Leiss in *Under Technology's Thumb*, p. 24.

nature.[103] Finally, when combined within the discourse of missile defence advocacy, a specific and unavoidable line of defensive development – a sense of 'technological momentum' – may be precisely what is being effected by the use and combination of instrumental and substantive understandings of technology, where missile defence is portrayed, to borrow Feenberg's phrase, as destiny by those promoting it.

Limitations of the Frankfurt School approach to technology

Taken in this light, Horkheimer, Adorno, Marcuse and their fellow-travellers might be somewhat exonerated from their apparent internal contradictions over the issue of technology. The early Frankfurt School thinkers as a whole can be said to oscillate, in good Marcusian fashion, between Heidegger and Habermas on the question of technology. Indeed it might be said that a prime value of the development of the Frankfurt School thinking on technology lies in its allegorical illustration of the shifts that can occur between instrumental and substantive conceptions and representations of technology. There are, however, significant criticisms of the Frankfurt School that need to be borne in mind for any project, such as this one, that seeks to continue this spirit in application to a concrete case. The first is that, as Held notes, 'the level at which some of the critical theorists work often makes the relevance of their ideas to social and political events hard to grasp'.[104] This criticism arguably applies not only to the frequently esoteric nature of, for example, Adorno's later writings, but also to Feenberg who tends to work at the level of a grand, overarching philosophical project.

Secondly, as Tom Bottomore argues, the early Frankfurters had a tendency to draw overly broad conclusions from their immediate context. In his view the School 'tended to be excessively influenced in its social analysis by immediate and sometimes ephemeral phenomena' – such as National Socialism, the virulent anti-Semitism of 1930s Germany and the 'culture industry' of the 1950s – 'which were not systematically

---

[103] See Colin S. Gray, *Another Bloody Century: Future Warfare* (London: Weidenfield Military, 2005). By the same token, Waltz's 'more may be better' argument may be based on an implicit substantivist logic, but offers a generally optimistic assessment of the spread of nuclear weapons under certain conditions.
[104] Held, *Introduction to Critical Theory*, p. 364.

integrated from a historical and comparative perspective'.[105] Bottomore contends that this tendency to focus on immediate context led to an 'unhistorical approach' and that, for example, the School also 'largely ignored economic analysis'.[106] David Held concurs to some extent on the School's capacity for overstatement. The experience of Fascist rule led, in Held's view, to 'an exaggerated notion of the cohesion of capitalism' and 'an unsatisfactory notion of domination' based on a general overestimation of state-administrative power.[107] Held also cites this as a potential cause of the School's 'overestimation of the significance of instrumental reason, technique and technology in the shaping of political attitudes and demands'.[108]

Bottomore is less than forgiving in his final assessment of the early Frankfurt School for these reasons. In its original form, he asserts, 'The Frankfurt School ... is dead',[109] and one suspects he does not think this an entirely bad thing. He is particularly critical of the School's elision of class as an object of analysis, describing it ultimately as 'Marxism without the proletariat'.[110] This echoes the more general point, made by Lukács among others, that the Frankfurt School generally distanced themselves from popular political struggles (Marcuse in the 1960s being a possible exception, but even then only obliquely in his somewhat unintended elevation as the figurehead of '60s counter-culture). Although, as Wyn Jones points out, this has the benefit of distancing the School from political parties or agendas and the rigid focus on class associated with orthodox Marxism, it has a negative effect in concurrently exacerbating the distance of philosophy from 'real life' politics and practices.[111] This leads to a situation in which, somewhat paradoxically, 'despite [their] orientation towards practice, there have been no particularly convincing answers by the members of the Frankfurt tradition of critical theory to the question of how theorizing can become a force for change in contemporary society'.[112] Implicit in this judgement is the feeling that the Frankfurt tradition has also not performed especially well in accounting for how and why particular institutions and situations develop over time and 'get the way they are'.

---

[105] Tom Bottomore, *The Frankfurt School* (London: Tavistock, 1984) p. 72.
[106] Ibid., pp. 71–3.   [107] Held, *Introduction to Critical Theory*, p. 366.
[108] Ibid., p. 367.   [109] Bottomore, *The Frankfurt School*, p. 76.
[110] Ibid., p. 74   [111] Wyn Jones, *Security, Strategy and Critical Theory*, p. 71.
[112] Ibid., p. 145.

Technology, common sense and critical theory

The aim of this section is to point briefly to possible ways to address some of the inherent limitations of the Frankfurt School approach. Specifically, it is argued here that the thought of Antonio Gramsci (and the further work he has inspired) provides a logical supplement to the Frankfurt School's more philosophically developed work on understanding technology and points to ways in which we might develop this into a framework of analysis.

The potential overlaps, homologies and compatibility between Frankfurt School and Gramscian thought have been partially broached by a variety of authors.[113] This subject has been of particular interest to those working within the CSS project, where Gramsci is frequently seen to offer the resources for analysing how theory informs political practice that Frankfurt School theory lacks.[114] As Wyn Jones argues, this move is partially justifiable on the basis that both the 'Italian' and 'German' schools of Critical Theory have shared roots in the Hegelian–Marxist tradition. They are in this sense species-form of the 'same broad intellectual project'.[115] Indeed the rationale for linking the two traditions becomes clear precisely when we acknowledge that the Frankfurt School is itself more a loose coalition of associated thinkers than a specific school of thought. As Wyn Jones notes:

Once we view the Frankfurt School ... not as a unified whole but as a series of different and indeed contradictory strands, it is then possible to clarify its relationship(s) with Gramscian critical theory ... both approaches are rooted in the same Marxian productivist paradigm, and both seek to develop a social theory oriented toward social transformation. They are recognizably variations on a theme rather than different in any fundamental way.[116]

If we look to the subject of technology, however, Gramsci would initially appear to add little to the general thinking of the Frankfurt School. Gramsci rarely addresses technology as a separate issue. When

[113] Most notably Renate Holub, *Antonio Gramsci: Beyond Marxism and Postmodernism* (London: Routledge, 1992) and Peter Ives, *Gramsci's Politics of Language: Engaging the Bakhtin Circle and the Frankfurt School* (Toronto: University of Toronto Press, 2003).
[114] See Wyn Jones, *Security, Strategy and Critical Theory*, pp. 151–60.
[115] Richard Wyn Jones, 'Introduction: Locating Critical International Relations Theory in Social Theory' in Wyn Jones, *Critical Theory and World Politics*, p. 10.
[116] Ibid., p. 8.

he does, he seems to replicate the broader 'Problem of Marxism' (in his own phrase) on the question of technology, as is exemplified in the following passage:

In reality the philosophy of praxis does not study a machine in order to know about and to establish the atomic structure of its materials or the physical, chemical and mechanical properties of its natural components (which is the business of exact science) but only in so far as it is a moment of the material forces of production, is an object of property of particular social forces, and expresses a social relation which in turn corresponds to a particular historical period.[117]

The reference here to the 'moment' of the material forces of production seems to reduce the study of technology simply to a question of the ends to which it is put; but the simultaneous reference to the way in which a machine 'expresses a social relation' seems to hint at something deeper than a simple instrumentalist or technicist view. Gramsci, it could be argued, is broadly analogous to the Frankfurt School in this sense but adds little to the framework outlined previously.

Gramscian theory, nevertheless, is still a useful resource for addressing the question of technology's use in missile defence advocacy. Indeed, Gramsi's notion of 'common sense' forms one of the central concepts of the argument made here. An initial point of support in this regard is the fact that Gramsci himself viewed determinism in all its manifestations as something that should be critically interrogated. 'It is essential at all times', he argues 'to demonstrate the futility of mechanical determinism: for, although it is explicable as a naïve philosophy of the mass and as such, but only as such, can be an intrinsic element of strength, nevertheless when it is adopted as a thought-out and coherent philosophy on the part of intellectuals, it becomes a cause of passivity, of idiotic self-sufficiency.'[118] Secondly, as Stuart Hall argues, utilising Gramsci does not require a 'claim that in any simple way ... Gramsci "has the answers" to our present troubles'. But, as Hall continues, 'I do believe that we must "think" our problems in a Gramscian way – which is different.'[119] We

---

[117] Antonio Gramsci, *Selections from the Prison Notebooks*, ed. and trans. by Quintin Hoare and Geoffrey Nowell Smith (London: Lawrence and Wishart, 1973) p. 465.

[118] Ibid., p. 337.

[119] Stuart Hall, *The Hard Road to Renewal: Thatcherism and the Crisis of the Left* (London: Verso, 1988) p. 161.

can acknowledge the limited nature of Gramsci's attention to the question of technology in comparison with the Frankfurt School tradition whilst simultaneously recognising the superiority of the Gramscian constellation of concepts for interrogating the way that theory informs practice, and the role understandings of technology play in the process. The closing sections of chapter 2 deal with the broader spectrum of Gramsci's vocabulary and its methodological implications. For the moment the relevance of Gramscian thought is shown here initially by reference to one of his most fundamental concepts: common sense.

Gramsci's notion of 'common sense' denotes, as Mark Rupert puts it, 'an amalgam of historically effective ideologies, scientific doctrines and social mythologies'.[120] The concept is used to signify instances where a largely uncritical and unconscious way of perceiving the world has 'become "common" in any given epoch'.[121] It occurs, according to Gramsci, when 'one's conception of the world is not critical and coherent but disjointed and episodic' and contains both 'Stone Age elements and principles of a more advanced science, prejudices from all past phases of history at the local level and intuitions of future philosophy'.[122] Hence common sense is viewed by Gramsci as a dynamic but relatively permanent 'terrain of struggle' in which the development of 'future philosophy' is always immanent but not guaranteed.

In this light common sense is not univocal or reducible to 'false consciousness', even if it is frequently pressed into the service of particular political ideologies.[123] Common sense is understood by Gramsci to be 'a syncretic historical residue, fragmentary and contradictory, open to multiple interpretations and potentially supportive of very different kinds of social visions and political projects'.[124] In his thoughts on culture and politics, Gramsci is himself constantly 'grappling with

---

[120] Mark Rupert, 'Globalising Common Sense: a Marxian–Gramscian (re-)Vision of the Politics of Governance/Resistance', *Review of International Studies*, 29 (2003) pp. 181–98, p. 185.

[121] Gramsci, *Prison Notebooks*, editors' note, pp. 321–2.

[122] Gramsci, *Prison Notebooks*, p. 324.

[123] See, for example, Stuart Hall's work on Thatcherism in *The Hard Road to Renewal* and 'The Toad in the Garden: Thatcherism among the Theorists' in Cary Nelson and Lawrence Grossberg (eds.) *Marxism and the Interpretation of Culture* (Urbana: University of Illinois Press, 1988) pp. 58–74 for a broader discussion. In security studies see Simon Dalby, *Creating the Second Cold War: the Discourse of Politics* (London: Pinter, 1990).

[124] Rupert, 'Globalising Common Sense', p. 185.

common sense and folklore, as structures that are as much determined as determining'.[125] Common sense is thus seen to have a structural quality to it (in the sense that it is impossible to extricate oneself entirely from it), but is not wholly determining. Indeed, Gramsci indicates, though 'multiple elements of "conscious leadership" ' may invoke common sense arguments, 'no one of them is predominant or transcends the level of a given social stratum's "popular science" – its "common sense" or traditional conception of the world'.[126]

The concept of common sense, Marcia Landy claims, 'is the linchpin in [Gramsci's] analysis of existing and future hegemonic formations, which brings together his discussions of politics, economics and culture'.[127] Furthermore, the reason that Gramsci's notion of common sense is prioritised herein is that it explicitly seeks to make and interrogate the linkages between philosophy and more 'everyday' forms of discourse. As Gramsci defines the concept:

Common sense is not a single unique conception, identical in time and space. It is the 'folklore' of philosophy, and, like folklore, it takes countless different forms. Its most fundamental characteristic is a conception which, even in the brain of one individual, is fragmentary, incoherent and inconsequential, in conformity with the social and cultural position of those masses of whose philosophy it is.[128]

This follows from Gramsci's assumption that every human being is possessed of a critical faculty and hence 'all men are philosophers' and their philosophy manifests itself in three main ways: 'This philosophy is contained in: 1. language itself, which is a totality of determined notions and concepts and not just of words grammatically devoid of content; 2. "common sense" and "good sense"; 3. popular religion and, therefore, also in the entire system of beliefs, superstitions, opinions, ways of seeing things and acting, which surface collectively under the name of "folklore".'[129]

---

[125] Marcia Landy, *Film, Politics and Gramsci* (Minneapolis, MN: University of Minnesota Press, 1994) p. 75.
[126] Gramsci, *Prison Notebooks*, pp. 196–7.
[127] Landy, *Film, Politics and Gramsci*, p. 78.
[128] Gramsci, *Prison Notebooks*, p. 419.
[129] Ibid., p. 323. As Hoare and Smith note in a footnote to this extract, 'Broadly speaking, "common sense" means the incoherent set of generally held assumptions and beliefs common to any given society, while "good sense" means practical empirical common sense in the English sense of the term' – ibid., p. 323, fn.1.

More than this, though, the concept of common sense helps to connect the 'high' level philosophical understandings of technology expanded upon in the previous chapter to more everyday forms of discourse and to explain the possible connections between these two realms of discourse. As Hoare and Smith note, 'The critique of "common sense" and that of the "philosophy of the philosophers"' are seen by Gramsci as complementary aspects of a single ideological struggle.[130] In a key passage Gramsci asserts that:

> Every social stratum has its own 'common sense' and its own 'good sense', which are basically the most widespread conception of life and of man. Every philosophical current leaves behind a sedimentation of 'common sense': this is the document of its historical effectiveness. *Common sense is not something rigid and immobile, but is continually transforming itself, enriching itself with scientific ideas and with philosophical opinions which have entered ordinary life.* 'Common sense' is the folklore of philosophy, and is always half-way between folklore properly speaking and the philosophy, science, and economics of the specialists. Common sense creates the folklore of the future, that is as a relatively rigid phase of popular knowledge at a given place and time.[131]

How then might philosophical and commonsensical understandings of technology overlap? There is little evidence to show that, in the discourse of missile defence advocacy for example, anyone reads Habermas, Heidegger or the Frankfurt School! This, however, is taking the connection between philosophy and common sense too literally. Landy argues that Gramsci's conception of common sense is based on the notion of 'borrowing' – the assimilation by intellectuals and groups (in this case those seeking to justify and advocate missile defence) of attitudes and dispositions from both philosophical and popular thinking. Hence critical analysis of common sense 'needs to be traced in terms of these borrowings, to locate their sources and their particular deployment, particularly to identify and expose how they produce and maintain consent'.[132] A further consideration is that 'The philosophy of common sense is not represented in folklore, popular culture and mass media as simply false consciousness but as a means of negotiating lived, if distorted and counterproductive, conditions endemic to one's

---

[130] Ibid., editors' note, pp. 321–2.
[131] Gramsci, *Prison Notebooks*, p. 326, fn. 5, emphasis added.
[132] Landy, *Gramsci, Film and Politics*, p. 80.

social group.'[133] Hence, in keeping with Gramsci's materialist and quasi-phenomenological bent, lived experience and contemporary conditions play a part in generating philosophical understandings, and this must necessarily apply to both *bona fide* and everyday philosophers: 'One's conception of the world is a response to certain specific problems raised by reality, which are quite specific and "original" in their immediate relevance,' as Gramsci notes.[134]

As Landy argues, Gramsci's prioritisation of common sense and focus on popular culture distinguished him from earlier Marxist critics and, she argues, moves him closer to the Frankfurt School.[135] Indeed a linkage between the two schools of thought can clearly be seen in the manner in which both place strong emphasis on what might be termed the power of contradiction. For Gramsci it is precisely the inchoate and contradictory nature of common sense that makes it so powerful and gives it mass appeal. Again the shared roots in Hegelianism are important in this regard. Gramsci speaks of history as a *'concordia discors'* (discordant concord) 'which does not start from unity, but contains in itself the reasons for a possible unity'.[136] Building on Marx, with simultaneous echoes of Marcuse, Gramsci states in regard to dialectics that: 'One must keep permanently in mind the two points between which this process oscillates: that no society poses for itself problems the necessary and sufficient conditions for whose solution do not already exist or are coming into being; and that no society comes to an end before it has expressed all its potential content.'[137]

Conclusion

One qualifier to this constellation of critical thought is that Gramsci ostensibly seems more optimistic about the prospects of such oscillation leading to a 'new common sense', and that even within common sense there remains a kernel of 'good sense' – relative truths to be salvaged. The Frankfurt School, even in their more pessimistic moments, maintained the power of critique in overcoming partial perspectives. By the same token, Gramsci does not naively assume that critically informed 'good sense' will simply emerge over time: 'the movement toward good

---

[133] Ibid., p. 79.   [134] Gramsci, *Prison Notebooks*, p. 324.
[135] Landy, *Film, Politics and Gramsci*, p. 77.
[136] Gramsci, *Prison Notebooks*, p. 356.   [137] Ibid., p. 367.

sense is provisional and not absolute'.[138] Gramsci declares a critical approach to common sense that necessitates critical investigation 'does not mean that there are no truths in common sense. It means rather that common sense is an ambiguous, contradictory and multiform concept, and that to refer to common sense as a confirmation of truth is nonsense.'[139] What this suggests, then, is that we think about understandings of technology as informed by Frankfurt School critique, but in a Gramscian way: in short that we should seek to unite the philosophical orientation of the Frankfurt School with Gramsci's focus on the relations between culture and politics. As Gramsci puts it, 'an introduction to the study of philosophy must expound in synthetic form the problems that have grown up in the process of the development of culture as a whole and which are only partially reflected in the history of philosophy'.[140] The next move therefore, before moving on to the specific case of missile defence advocacy, is to observe the historical development of common sense attitudes towards technology with reference to the particular cultural context of the American experience of technology.

[138] Landy, *Film, Politics and Gramsci*, p. 82.
[139] Gramsci, *Prison Notebooks*, p. 423.   [140] Ibid., p. 331.

2 | *Technology and common sense in America*

Introduction

Building on the previous analysis, the purpose of this chapter is to help develop the possible application and investigation of the instrumental-substantive taxonomy by adding a further level of cultural-historical awareness to it. Its aim is to 'fill in' elements of the content of American common sense on technology by illustrating its manifestations, and to indicate how – in methodological terms – we might identify this form of common sense in the discourse of missile defence advocacy. As Gramsci puts it,

> From our point of view, studying the history and logic of the various philosophers' philosophies is not enough. At least as a methodological guide-line, attention should be drawn to the other parts of the history of philosophy; to the conceptions of the world held by the great masses, to those of the most restricted ruling (or intellectual) groups, and finally to the links between these various cultural complexes and the philosophy of the philosophers.[1]

This chapter takes several related steps in this light. The first is to establish, at a broad level, what American attitudes to technology are in a *longue durée* sense and how they have developed over time.[2] Here it is argued that the historical development of these attitudes has generally been understood and articulated in terms that are frequently comparable to the instrumental and substantive categories. These broad cultural-historical archetypes, the chapter argues, have also been incorporated into analyses of American strategic and political culture, two relevant examples being the notions of 'American strategic man' and the

---

[1] Antonio Gramsci, *Selections from the Prison Notebooks*, ed. and trans. by Quintin Hoare and Geoffrey Nowell Smith (London: Lawrence and Wishart, 1973) pp. 344–5.
[2] Fernand Braudel, *On History*, trans. Sarah Matthews (London: Weidenfeld and Nicolson, 1980).

'military-industrial complex'. Adherence to these archetypes in these two instances has, however, tended to encourage cultural and economic reductionism respectively. Building a critique of such reductionism based on Gramsci's ideas, the final section of the chapter outlines an approach that not only maintains historical and cultural awareness, but adds reflexive attentiveness to the role language and discourse play in the articulation of common sense understandings of technology. This approach in turn forms the basis of the analysis of that more 'restricted' intellectual group, missile defence advocates, undertaken in subsequent chapters.

Technology, everyday life and the 'American ideology'

Common sense from a Gramscian perspective is, to put it simply, the apparently taken-for-granted view of what the world is and how it works. In this light the relationship between technology and everyday life becomes potentially important. As James Moore writes: 'Part of everyday life are people's ideas about the world, including their ideas or beliefs about science and technology.' These ways of thinking, according to Moore, 'belong to the wider cultural context of technological change and subsist in a reciprocal relationship to it', hence 'it makes sense to talk both about the impact of technology on everyday ideas about the world and about the influence of everyday ideas on technological change, although any real separation of the two would be artificial'.[3] This, Moore argues, gives rise to 'ideology' in everyday life by changing the horizon of the taken-for-granted:

technology gives rise to ideology in everyday life; ideology in everyday life serves to justify or 'legitimate' technology. The success with which scientists and engineers control the physical world changes the quality of people's lives and thereby alters their perceptions of space and time, health and disease, life and death – in short the natural order of things. This is the *ideological impact* of technology.[4]

Indeed, he continues, 'At the same time . . . and in so far as everyday life is transformed, people's perceptions of technology also change. They

---

[3] James R. Moore, 'Ideology' in Colin Chant (ed.) *Science, Technology and Everyday Life 1870–1950* (London: The Open University, 1990) pp. 29–30.
[4] Ibid., p. 30, emphasis in original.

may come to believe, for example, that technology *per se* is a good thing, that more and more problems will be found to have technological solutions – in short, the more technology the better.[5] This is what the author terms the 'ideological legitimation' of technology, and Moore characterises the form this takes in industrialised societies as 'the American ideology'.[6] Although there are, as we shall see, reasons for denoting this understanding as specifically 'American' in character, Moore argues that it represents the dominant view of technology in all industrialised societies. In its most explicit formulation it prescribes that

All problems, whether of nature, human nature, or culture, are seen as 'technical' problems capable of rational solution through the accumulation of objective knowledge, in the form of neutral or value-free observations and correlations and the application of that knowledge in procedures arrived at by trial and error, the value of which is to be judged by how well they fulfil their appointed ends ...[7]

Hence, 'the American Ideology, becomes "instrumental rationality" incarnate' and is, in this respect, clearly consistent with the instrumental conception of technology as discussed in previous chapters. What makes the American Ideology 'ideological' is precisely this 'separation it creates between technology and values – between purely instrumental techniques on the one hand, and the human ends they are supposed to serve on the other'.[8] This, Howard P. Segal concurs, develops an apparent 'belief in the inevitability of progress and in progress precisely as technological progress'.[9]

Enrico Augelli and Craig Murphy draw similar conclusions from an explicitly Gramscian perspective. A key element of American common sense, they argue, is 'Scientism': 'the faith that the systematic methods of the natural sciences can be applied with advantage to all fields, an idea that has been part of the common sense of American managers, both public and private, since the end of the

---

[5] Ibid.
[6] Ibid. The term was used originally by H. T. Wilson in his *The American Ideology: Science, Technology, and Organization as Modes of Rationality in Advanced Industrial Societies* (London: Routledge and Kegan Paul, 1977).
[7] Moore, 'Ideology', p. 31.   [8] Ibid.
[9] Howard P. Segal, *Technological Utopianism in American Culture* (Chicago: University of Chicago Press, 1985) p. 1.

nineteenth century'.[10] Scientism combines elements of Enlightenment faith in progress and engineering philosophy, and Augelli and Murphy note that the term 'Scientism' is somewhat misleading given that 'it was engineering, applied science, rather than theoretical science that was the source of American faith in science and technology'.[11] This in part helps accounts for the 'quiet' (that is, unquestioned) nature of the 'American ideology': 'The distrust of theory explains why many Americans, especially American managers or those who aspire to be like them, insist that they have accepted no ideology, no system, but are only guided by practical considerations.'[12] Here Augelli and Murphy deliberately echo Gramsci's notes on Fordism, where Gramsci suggested that 'Americanism' should be understood in relation to 'Gentile's little formula about "philosophy which is not expressed in verbal formulations, but is affirmed in action" ... if the formula has any value at all, it is precisely in Americanism that it finds its justification.' Americanism, Gramsci speculated, is 'creating a future which is intrinsic to its objective activity and which it prefers to keep quiet about'.[13]

The instrumental/'American' conception of technology

The appellations 'American ideology' and 'Americanism' suggest a broad acceptance that the understanding of technology described above applies especially to the American context. For most historians of technology this is itself a commonsensical assumption. Carroll Pursell boldly declared in the late 1960s that:

Technology holds a special place in both the hearts and history of Americans. Although tools have always played an important role in the history of man, it is commonly admitted that they have played a special and magnified role in the New World. Whether we [Americans] are envied for our refrigerators,

[10] Enrico Augelli and Craig Murphy, *America's Quest for Supremacy and the Third World* (London: Pinter, 1988) p. 36.

[11] Ibid., p. 50. Decades earlier Hans J. Morgenthau had identified Scientism as 'the belief in the power of science, to solve all problems, more particularly, all political problems which confront man in the modern age' and the concurrent belief that modern technology 'could not fail to be beneficial to the social world as a whole' – *Scientific Man versus Power Politics* (London: Latimer House, 1947) p. v, p. 77.

[12] Augelli and Murphy, *America's Quest*, p. 50.

[13] Gramsci, *Prison Notebooks*, p. 307, emphasis added.

despised for our transistor radios, or feared for our nuclear weapons, the American way of life is viewed throughout the world as one in which gadgets, tools, and machines play a dominant part.[14]

Pursell's statement makes the case that this view of technology not only persists but has its lineage in the process of carving modern America out of the New World. The other implication of Pursell's statement is that technology, as understood and applied in this way, has also irreversibly affected America's position in the world. Walter LaFeber recounts the entirety of American history in microcosm through this theme:

> Columbus depended on ... calculations that indicated the world was round, not flat. He proved those calculations correct by using the latest compasses, astrolabe, and elaborate tables that measured longitude. From these first voyages of discovery through the Yankee clipper ship that conquered world trade, the Colt .44 revolver that conquered the West, the airplane that conquered distance, the atomic bomb, and the multistage rocket that conquered space, American foreign policy cannot be understood apart from the technology that transformed the world and made diplomacy ever more complex ...[15]

Likewise, Segal, historian of 'technological utopianism' – the view that technological progress would eventually realise an American utopia – argues that the prevalence and popularity of this strand of thought in literature between the publication of John Macnies's *The Diothas; Or a Far Look Ahead* in 1883 and Harold Loeb's *Life in a Technocracy: What it Might Be Like* in 1933 points to 'the persistence of a firm, even rigid set of beliefs about contemporary American society' during this period and implies 'the pre-existence of a coherent view of reality, which may properly be called ideology'.[16]

This instrumental view of technology can be dated even further back. In fact, several authors argue, it precedes even the introduction of the very concept of 'technology' as an agent of change in 1829, and is integrally tied up in the foundation and establishment of the US republic

[14] Carroll W. Pursell Jr., *Readings in Technology and American Life* (New York: Oxford University Press, 1969) p. 3.

[15] Walter LaFeber, *The American Age: United States Foreign Policy at Home and Abroad, 1750 to the Present* (New York: Norton 1994) p. 8. LaFeber continues by adding that technology made American diplomacy 'more complex – and dangerous. Those technological conquests also help us to understand why Americans have too often believed that crisis in foreign affairs might well be solved through new scientific breakthroughs.'

[16] Segal, *Technological Utopianism*, p. 4.

itself.[17] Of course, as Segal notes, 'It is impossible to date precisely the initial consciousness among Americans of the concept of technology, much less their initial consciousness of the transformations that were increasingly incorporating technology into daily life.'[18] While this is the case Leo Marx argues that there is a 'special affinity' between 'the machine', as metaphor of technological progress, and the emergence of the new American republic in the late eighteenth and early nineteenth century, basing this assertion on the views of prevalent themes in art and literature of the time. Marx sees this affinity as exemplified in Thomas Jefferson's passion for utilitarian improvement, gadgetry and the potential of labour-saving devices for American production. 'From Jefferson's perspective', Marx argues, 'the machine is a token of that liberation of the human spirit to be realized by the young American Republic.'[19]

Indeed, architects of the US constitution such as Jefferson and Benjamin Franklin and contemporary inventors such as Robert Fulton increasingly came to share in the belief that technology could act as the instrument to advance the survival and success of the nascent republic, the view that 'the shining city on the hill will be created by experiment, efficient planning and the application of technology'.[20] By incorporating this new emphasis on technology's importance into existing pastoral-puritan ideas there was an increasing consensus that manufacturing technology was both essential to and compatible with the success of the new republic. According to Marx the 'Report on the Subject of Manufactures' (1791) prepared by the early industrial entrepreneur Tench Coxe and influential member of the constitutional convention Alexander Hamilton (who presented it to the convention) 'reflects the considerable shift in attitudes towards manufacturing that coincided with the formation of the new government'. This shift was clearly indicated in Hamilton's assertion that 'The expediency of encouraging manufactures in the United States which was not long since deemed very questionable appears at this time to be pretty generally admitted.'[21]

In fact by the time Harvard Professor Jacob Bigelow introduced the very term 'technology' to the American context in his *Elements of*

---

[17] Most prominently Leo Marx, *The Machine in the Garden: Technology and the Pastoral Ideal in America* (New York: Oxford University Press, 1964) p. 149.
[18] Segal, *Technological Utopianism*, p. 92.
[19] Marx, *The Machine in the Garden*, p. 150.
[20] Augelli and Murphy, *America's Quest*, p. 50.
[21] Quoted in Marx, *The Machine in the Garden*, p. 167.

Technology (1829), Marx argues, Coxe's notion that the advancement of republican values was bound up with the power of machine production had evolved into the 'official American ideology of industrialism' – a 'loosely composed scheme of meaning and value so widely accepted that it seldom required precise formulation'.[22] In keeping with the formulation of the American ideology as an unreflective, unquestioned worldview – 'philosophy affirmed in action', as Gramsci puts it – Marx and Segal argue that its wide diffusion is attested to by the fact that technological progress, apparently unquestioned, occurs so frequently as the leitmotif of nineteenth-century American art and literature. The benefits of technological progress existed as a self-evident truth. It is for this reason, Marx notes, that 'no summary in paraphrase will convey the subtle influence of industrialization upon mass consciousness. Not that this familiar and all-too-simple body of ideas requires further elucidation. Anyone can understand it, and, of course, that is just the point: it is the obviousness and simplicity of the machine as a symbol of progress that accounts for its astonishing power.'[23]

It is tempting to close the book on conventional understandings of technology in the American context at this point. Developments such as electrification, advances in transport and communication, medicine and science and numerous other stories of technical success could all be cited as contributory factors in the formulation and maintenance of the American ideology. This conception is also often assumed to be characteristic of post-war American culture. Meier argues as much when he states that although 'The assimilation of the technological concept was a gradual process, uneven in degree and haphazardly directed by the self-interest and the enthusiasm of inventors, engineers, mechanicians, interested politicians, publishers and writers', it was 'a very real thing ... and the admittedly "technological frame of reference" of the present day American is in large degree the result'.[24]

It is also tempting to argue that the 'technological frame of reference' identified with this American ideology, the view that technology potentially promises the solution to any sort of social or political problem, would be the key frame of reference in relation to American missile

---

[22] Ibid., p. 181.   [23] Ibid., p. 192.

[24] Hugo A. Meier, 'The Technological Concept in American Social History: 1750–1860', PhD dissertation, University of Wisconsin, 1956, p. 546.

defence advocacy.[25] In this regard a relevant historical illustration might be provided by an example cited by H. Bruce Franklin.[26] In 1807, with the onset of a British–American war increasingly likely, Robert Fulton proposed to his frequent correspondent and backer President Jefferson novel methods of deploying 'torpedoes' (essentially comparable to modern floating mines) to neutralise the offensive capability of the British fleet. Fulton's rhetoric in promoting the use of a defensive floating shield of torpedoes to repel the British fleet is, as Franklin notes, remarkably similar to the language of the Strategic Defense Initiative. Fulton argued that since science had equipped the British ships, making them the ultimate offensive weapon of the time, then 'may not science, in her progress, point out a means by which the application of the violent explosive force of gunpowder shall destroy ships of war, and give to the seas the liberty which shall secure perpetual peace between nations?'[27] Franklin notes, with some justification, that Fulton's language 'would need only minor stylistic revisions to be incorporated into a speech advocating star wars'.[28] The theme seems to chime clearly with the American ideology: a constant search for a technological solution to the problem of military security.[29]

The rise of substantivist understandings of technology in America

While the instrumental conception represented by the American ideology of technology is pervasive and, as will be shown in later chapters, one that is recurrent within missile defence advocacy, it would be

[25] See Gerald M. Steinberg, 'The Limits of Faith' in Gerald M. Steinberg (ed.) *Lost in Space: the Domestic Politics of the Strategic Defense Initiative* (Lexington, MA: Lexington Books, 1988) pp. 145–58.

[26] H. Bruce Franklin, *War Stars: the Superweapon and the American Imagination* (New York: Oxford University Press, 1988).

[27] Quoted in ibid., p. 15.

[28] Ibid., p. 15; compare President Reagan's 1983 speech announcing the birth of strategic defense – 'I call upon the scientific community in our country, those who gave us nuclear weapons, to turn their great talents now to the cause of mankind and world peace, to give us the means of rendering these nuclear weapons impotent and obsolete' Full text available from www.atomicarchive.com/Docs/Missile/Starwars.shtml [last accessed 20 January 2009].

[29] Franklin, *War Stars*; see also Russell F. Weigley, *The American Way of War: a History of the United States Military Strategy and Policy* (New York: Macmillan, 1973).

inaccurate to portray this as the sole, definitive or monolithic understanding of technology in the American context. Complementary to the
account given above, most historians of technology and culture in
America recognise that the impact of technology on everyday life has
given rise to more than just the conception of technology encapsulated
in the term 'American ideology'. As Segal notes, 'What can be stated
with assurance is that American attitudes towards technology have
shifted over time and have occasionally been quite critical.'[30]
Certainly by the early nineteenth century less positive understandings
of technology – largely developed outside the USA – attracted widespread attention among American intellectuals.[31] Among the more
significant of these impacting upon the American intelligentsia of the
time were the ideas of the German writer Friedrich Schiller, one of the
first to use the machine metaphor to denote a 'mechanistic' social
system, and the influential English commentator Thomas Carlyle,
who argued that the increasing role of technology in society had fostered an excessive emphasis on means as against ends.[32] Carlyle's views
challenged the dominant American understanding of technology in the
mid-nineteenth century, introducing as it did the metaphor of 'runaway'
technology (as against the association of the 'machine' with progress):
'we have argued away all force from ourselves', Carlyle declared, 'and
stand lashed together, uniform in dress and movement, like the rowers
of some boundless galley'.[33]

   This view of the negative, substantive impact of technology (in the
sense that technology was seen to determine human ends, not vice versa)
on society developed into something of an undercurrent – Marx, Segal
and others argue – of the dominant instrumental approach to technology
and its subsidiary association of technology with progress in nineteenth-
century America. Its provocative nature resulted in one of the few sustained attempts to expand upon this instrumental understanding of
technology, Timothy Walker's (1831) 'Defence of Mechanical

[30] Segal, *Technological Utopianism*, p. 78.
[31] See especially Christopher Lasch, *The True and Only Heaven: Progress and its Critics* (New York: W. W. Norton, 1991) pp. 168–295.
[32] Marx, *The Machine in the Garden*, pp. 170–3.
[33] Carlyle from his 1829 essay 'Signs of the Times', quoted in ibid. William Leiss identifies a similar theme in the works of Thoreau, Emerson, Melville and Henry Adams – *Under Technology's Thumb* (Montreal: McGill-Queen's University Press, 1990) p. 38.

Philosophy'. Written in response to Carlyle's pessimistic account, Walker's essay fitted better with the general feeling of nineteenth-century America that rapid industrialisation was integral to national success. Walker defended the instrumental view of technology, citing technology as 'the instrument appointed to fulfil the egalitarian aims of the American people'.[34] His defence, Marx argues, 'expounds the doctrine of unlimited economic development as if the American people had always been committed to it'. In one sense, Walker's defence was an explicitly political appeal to sustaining and increasing American productive power and, implicit in this, the class relations associated with it; however, since machine technology was commonly assumed to benefit all Americans, there was no contradiction in regarding technology as apolitical and neutral in this view. Moreover, Marx contends, it is precisely the fact that Walker's 'Defence' is so unoriginal in propounding this view that makes it 'a fine exhibit of pervasive attitudes toward the new machine power' of the nineteenth century.[35]

This is not to say that the substantive understanding of technology and its impact disappeared completely as a result. First of all, it should be noted that the contours of the exchange between Carlyle and Walker indicated an already accepted 'mechanical social order', as Segal puts it. Carlyle's and especially Walker's positions are important not so much in themselves but because they suggest the pervasive acceptance by most Americans of technology as a fact of life by the mid-nineteenth century. Beyond this broad characterisation though, most historians of technology posit a complex relationship between actual technological developments, attitudes towards these developments, and overall conceptions of technology. As Thomas P. Hughes notes, 'There has never been a single American attitude toward technology.'[36] 'American' attitudes to technology, as with attitudes to technology in general, alter and fluctuate over time at least in part in response to actual, material technological developments and their effects. As Hughes puts it, 'Depression, wars and vistas of unexploited land and resources have stimulated reactions or attitudes towards the uses or potential of technology. But what influences these attitudes at any one time is a complex

---

[34] Quoted in Marx, *The Machine in the Garden*, p. 187.   [35] Ibid., p. 182.
[36] Thomas P. Hughes, 'Introduction' in Thomas P. Hughes (ed.) *Changing Attitudes Toward American Technology* (New York: Harper and Row, 1975) p. 1.

combination of events, trends and ideas; a war or depression may be only the most obvious immediate cause of the crystallization of attitudes.'[37] Thus, for example, the social problems that came to be associated with industrialisation (mass unemployment, periodic depression, resultant social unrest, etc.) gave greater credence to the negative conception of technology proposed by Carlyle and, according to Segal, 'there is evidence that to at least some Americans in the early and mid-nineteenth century, as to more Americans later in the century, technology appeared to be as much a problem as a solution to problems'.[38]

Historians have again attempted to chronicle the development of this counter-conception in some detail. Suffice to say here that by the early twentieth century, when the 'electrification' of America was being lauded, the 'runaway engine' could be employed negatively as the metaphor for the unstoppable march of technology just as convincingly as the locomotive could be as the driver of progress; and while the Fordist factory system may have run 'like clockwork', by 1936 viewers of *Modern Times* could also relate to scenes of its star Charlie Chaplin literally caught between the cogs of a great machine, or earlier still to workers deep underground attending the identical machines powering Fritz Lang's *Metropolis* (1926). The general conception of technology was no longer as overwhelmingly positive as it had been in the earlier period of industrialisation.

According to Hughes, though, the instrumental understanding of technology remained dominant well into the twentieth century. He asserts that for the most part from the late nineteenth century until the end of World War II, 'Americans commonly considered invention, industrial research and systems of production the source of goods for the good life and', paraphrasing President Roosevelt, 'an arsenal of weapons for the great democracy'.[39] Post-World War II, though, Hughes argues, 'the temper of the times began to change markedly'. Engineers, managers, financiers, workers, the military and others dependent on modern, large-scale production technology for livelihood and status 'continued to take a positive attitude toward technological change, and even spoke of progress in ways reminiscent of the

---

[37] Ibid., pp. 7–8.   [38] Segal, *Technological Utopianism*, p. 92.
[39] Thomas P. Hughes, *American Genesis: a Century of Invention and Technological Enthusiasm, 1870–1970* (Chicago: University of Chicago Press, 2004) p. 443.

nineteenth century'.[40] Thus the view of technology as an instrument of progress continued to have a presence. However, 'countless others' began to reflect on the potential consequences and dangers of seemingly unremitting technological advance. By the mid-1970s David Dickson felt safe in asserting that 'contemporary [American] society is characterized by a growing distrust of technology',[41] and Segal argues that contemporary Americans, generally speaking, display, if not distrust of, then at least a 'healthy scepticism about unadulterated technological advance'.[42] He contends that major factors contributing to this sceptical attitude towards technology derive from technology-related environmental crises, repeated disappointments over nuclear power and other alleged technical panaceas, and distrust of both public officials and technical experts arising from the Vietnam experience and the Watergate scandal.[43] Here the *Challenger* disaster and Chernobyl, though less close to home, are usually also cited as pivotal moments.[44]

Undoubtedly, the post-war questioning of the association between technology and progress was in no small measure due to 'the increasing awareness of the destructiveness of atom bombs and the threat that their proliferation posed for the future of civilization' which 'greatly stimulated among the public a counterreaction to technology'.[45] The development of this technological capacity for mass destruction also arguably stimulated sustained development of the substantivist 'technics-out-of-control' conception of technology, most obviously in the work of Jacques Ellul, Herbert Marcuse and Lewis Mumford.[46] Mumford, in particular,

---

[40] Ibid.

[41] David Dickson, *Alternative Technology and the Politics of Technical Change* (Glasgow: Fontana, 1974) p. 9.

[42] Howard P. Segal in interview with G. Ganiel, 'Umaine Today', March/April 2003 – www.umaine.edu/issues/u312/technology.html [last accessed 10 January 2005]. See also Segal's *Future Imperfect: the Mixed Blessings of Technology in America* (Amherst: University of Massachusetts Press, 1994).

[43] Ibid.

[44] See John Manley, 'Simple and Complex Technologies' (1987) reprinted in Richard Rhodes (ed.) *Visions of Technology: a Century of Vital Debate about Machines, Systems and the Human World* (New York: Simon and Schuster, 1999) pp. 348–50.

[45] Hughes, *American Genesis*, p. 444.

[46] Jacques Ellul, *The Technological Society*, trans. J.Wilkinson (New York: Vintage, 1964; Herbert Marcuse, *One-Dimensional Man*, 2nd edition (London: Routledge, 1991); Lewis Mumford, *The Pentagon of Power: the Myth of the Machine, Volume II* (New York: Harvest, 1970).

argued that nuclear weapons, which could potentially dictate the future of civilisation, were themselves products of modern, bureaucratically administered military-industrial projects – epitomised by the Manhattan Project – where authority centred not in any particular hands but in the system itself.[47] This sentiment was captured at its most hyperbolic in Marshall McLuhan's claim that human beings had become 'the sex organs of the machine world'.[48]

In contemporary American culture, this substantivist trope now recurs most commonly (as it does elsewhere in industrialised nations) in fears surrounding the spread and consequences of bio-technology (think of 'Frankenstein' foods), and advances in reproductive and cloning technology. The increasing role of computers in everyday life has also given rise to substantivesque interpretations. Jaron Lanier, the computer scientist who coined the term 'virtual reality', speculates that 'as we hurtle toward more and more powerful computers, eventually there'll be some sort of very dramatic Omega point at which everything changes – not just in terms of our technology but in terms of our basic nature'.[49] This theme of a technologically determined future remains a staple of popular culture, as the success of movies such as the *Terminator* series and *The Matrix* attests to.[50] Some have even argued that the events of 11 September 2001 have reinforced such apprehensions about technological progress: 'The attacks fed a growing undercurrent of fear that new technologies were fostering new dangers, dangers that were hard to understand, much less resolve.'[51]

William Leiss goes so far as to argue that the idea 'That established ways of life are challenged by unremitting technological novelty is something of a cliché for us by now.'[52] Yet its very status as a cliché in itself implies

[47] Mumford, *Pentagon of Power*, p. 264.
[48] Marshall McLuhan, *Understanding Media: the Extensions of Man* (London: Sphere, 1967) p. 46.
[49] Jaron Lanier, 'Omega Point' (1997) reprinted in Rhodes, *Visions of Technology*, p. 367. See also Mark Brosnan, *Technophobia: the Psychological Impact of Information Technology* (London: Routledge, 1998).
[50] For a more detailed reading of the original (1984) movie *The Terminator* along these lines see Paul N. Edwards, *The Closed World: Computers and the Politics of Discourse in Cold War America* (Cambridge, MA: MIT Press, 1996) pp. 22–5.
[51] Loren B. Thompson, 'Emerging Technologies and Security' in Michael E. Brown (ed.) *Grave New World: Security Challenges in the 21st Century* (Washington, DC: Georgetown University Press, 2003) p. 115.
[52] Leiss, *Under Technology's Thumb*, p. 40.

widespread resonance. Likewise, the theme of 'technology-making-life-better' continues implicitly to saturate American advertising discourse, and defenders of technological progress in the mould of Timothy Walker remain, for example, the artificial intelligence proponent Marvin Minsky:

> The world was *terrible* before people came along and changed it. So we don't have much to lose by technology. The future of technology is about shifting to what people like to do, and that's entertainment. Eventually, robots will make everything.[53]

Where Walker once lauded technological progress as represented by American manufacturing, Minsky now predicts the latter's eventual transcendence as the next logical step in America's technological development.

Instrumentalism, substantivism and American strategic culture

As the previous section shows the 'common sense' of technology, as understood historically in the American context, is precisely the sort of fluid and contradictory composite of ideas that Gramsci identified with the term. The broad acceptance of technology as a taken-for-granted aspect of everyday life seems relatively unchallengeable. Beyond this, though, the way technology has been understood has divided into two broad conceptions: the first a positive, instrumental understanding of technology as a potential panacea to any kind of problem; the second a subsidiary but recurring pessimistic conception of technology as the source of problems often more intractable than those it is supposed to solve, most notably the problem of apparently increasing human subservience to unremitting technological advance. Thus the history (or perhaps more accurately interpretations of the history) of technology in America evidences two understandings of technology that seem broadly to accord with the instrumental/substantive categorisation identified in chapter 1. While both may exist in the more developed philosophical forms examined in the previous chapter, the historical analyses examined here suggest that they have also (co-)existed as widely diffused, often fragmentary and disparate, conceptions of the role of technology in American life, and this virtually throughout the duration of the history of America from independence onwards. What might be termed

---

[53] Marvin Minsky, 'R.U.R Revisited' (1997) reprinted in Rhodes, *Visions of Technology*, p. 369, emphasis in original.

the 'American common sense of technology' is, on this reading, precisely the kind of 'syncretic historical residue' that is 'fragmentary and contradictory' in nature, as Mark Rupert identifies the Gramscian conception of common sense. It is also, by consequence, 'open to multiple interpretations and potentially supportive of very different kinds of social visions and political projects'.[54]

The permeation of this residue is equally clear in accounts of American strategic and political culture. Once again, instrumentalism is the more obvious of the two understandings in this regard. Nicholas Wheeler and Ken Booth, for example, criticised the instrumentalist orientation of what they termed the 'engineering approach' of American strategic planning in the late 1980s:

Since we have grown up in a world in which technology shapes so much of what we do, as individuals and groups, we almost intuitively come to invest it with a significance in international security that is not justified by the historical record. US strategists in particular have been prone to this. They have tended to believe that since technological change throws up the problems, it can also provide the solutions. Out of the fact of technological innovation has been born a faith in the technological fix.[55]

This they link to a broader current – 'that "can do" attitude which runs so strongly through US life'.[56]

Booth and Wheeler draw heavily here on ideas first developed by Stanley Hoffman with respect to the conduct of American foreign policy in the 1960s. Hoffman not only coined the term 'engineering approach', he also pre-empts the analogous concept of 'scientism' as used by Enrico Augelli and Craig Murphy.[57] Indeed, there are even echoes of Gramsci's

---

[54] Mark Rupert, 'Globalising Common Sense: a Marxian–Gramscian (re-)Vision of the Politics of Governance/Resistance', *Review of International Studies*, 29 (2003) pp. 181–98, p. 185.

[55] Nicholas J. Wheeler and Ken Booth, 'Beyond the Security Dilemma: Technology, Strategy and International Security' in Carl G. Jacobsen (ed.) *The Uncertain Course: New Weapons, Strategies and Mind-Sets* (Oxford: Oxford University Press, 1987) p. 314.

[56] Ibid. See also Colin S. Gray, *Nuclear Strategy and National Style* (London: Hamilton Press, 1986).

[57] Stanley Hoffman, *Gulliver's Troubles, Or the Setting of American Foreign Policy* (New York: McGraw Hill, 1968) p. 146. There are strong parallels here with Morgenthau's critique of (what he saw as) the liberal fallacy of generalising technological progress in the domestic realm to international affairs. See Morgenthau, *Scientific Man versus Power Politics*.

'philosophy affirmed in action' in Hoffman's assertion that 'What I have in mind is a pragmatism that is a way of acting, not a mode of thought – a *praxis*, not a philosophy, unless one describes it as an *implicit* philosophy, a pattern of behaviour resting on submerged assumptions all of which correspond, once more, to the American experience writ large and projected upon the outside world.'[58] This experience, Hoffman claims, 'from the Puritans to the space age, has been primarily one of mastering nature'.[59]

In foreign policy, this is manifested as what he terms 'skill thinking' – the 'substitution of instruments for policies' – and it is a label that he associates in particular with Robert McNamara's tenure as Secretary of Defense. 'The engineering or instrumental outlook has always been characteristic of *homo oeconomicus* and *homo militaris*,' hence the 'military-industrial complex' is less important in the formulation of American defence policy than is the 'commitment to a certain way of thinking'.[60] Suggestive of the expected prevalence of this mode of thinking in arguments for missile defence is Wheeler and Booth's contention that 'Hoffman's words were written over 20 years before President Reagan's Star Wars speech, but they could have been written the day after.'[61] In terms of the broader relevance of such thinking, Matthew Evangelista concedes that this emphasis on technology 'contributes some understanding of how new weapons are promoted to a broader public', citing General Omar Bradley's reference to 'the permanent American desire to substitute machines for men and magic weapons for conventional armaments'.[62] Others see this view as having come to dominate the risk-averse 'Western way of war' that not only includes but now also extends beyond the USA.[63]

There are, however, necessary subtleties to be added to this somewhat stereotypical portrayal of American strategic culture. Prior to his

---

[58] Hoffman, *Gulliver's Troubles*, p. 144, emphasis in original.
[59] Ibid., p. 147. [60] Ibid., pp. 148–9.
[61] Wheeler and Booth, 'Beyond the Security Dilemma', p. 314.
[62] Matthew Evangelista, *Innovation and the Arms Race: How the United States and the Soviet Union Develop New Military Technologies* (Ithaca: Cornell University Press, 1988) p. 222.
[63] See Christopher Coker, *Waging War without Warriors? The Changing Culture of Military Conflict* (London: Lynne Rienner, 2002); Martin Shaw, *The New Western Way of War: Risk-Transfer War and its Crisis in Iraq* (Cambridge: Polity Press, 2005).

collaboration with Wheeler, Booth had on other occasions been much more critical of such a characterisation: 'In war, as in other aspects of life, it has always been tempting ... to relegate Americans to the fashionably inferior category of "doers" rather than "thinkers". The evidence from strategic history is much more mixed than this cliché about the great "Can Do" society might suggest.'[64] Booth goes on to state that 'the argument that Americans "seek refuge" in technology away from the hard problems of strategy is scarcely supportable in the light of the extensive debating of strategic issues in the last twenty years. The image of *American Strategic Man* as being nine-tenths technology and one-tenth brain never has been valid, and is certainly not valid in the contemporary period.'[65] Though Booth does not pursue this line himself, one can identify opposed (that is, substantivist) elements to American strategic thought as epitomised in, for example, theories of arms racing during the Cold War.[66] In contrast to Hoffman's appraisal chapter 4 attempts to show, for example, how substantivist tropes featured in the thinking of Secretary of Defense McNamara, and chapter 6 adds a missing dimension to Wheeler and Booth's assessment of SDI by illustrating the ways in which the 'engineering approach' predicated on the idea of technological fix was both parasitic of and complementary to a contemporaneous discourse of technological fears.

A further relevant manifestation of substantivist thinking in the study of the strategic-political culture of the USA is the ubiquitous notion of the 'military-industrial complex' (MIC). The term is, of course, most closely associated with Dwight D. Eisenhower's 1961 farewell address, which arguably remains the most recognisable formulation of the idea. Referring to the massive rise in US defence expenditure post-World War II and the increasing institutional ties between the US state, industry and military, Eisenhower proclaimed that:

---

[64] Ken Booth, 'American Strategy: The Myths Revisited' in Ken Booth and Moorhead Wright (eds.) *American Thinking about Peace and War* (Sussex: Harvester Press, 1978) p. 22.

[65] Ibid., p. 22, emphasis in original.

[66] For a contemporaneous analysis of arms races see, for example, Michael Sheehan, *The Arms Race* (Oxford: Martin Robertson, 1983).

This conjunction of an immense military establishment and a large arms industry is new in the American experience. The total influence – economic, political, even spiritual – is felt in every city, every State House, every office of the Federal Government. We recognize the imperative need for this development. Yet we must not fail to comprehend its grave implications. Our toil, resources and livelihood are all involved; so is the very structure of our society ... In the councils of government, we must guard against the acquisition of unwarranted influence, whether sought or unsought, by the military-industrial complex.[67]

The issue of the military-industrial complex has spawned a massive literature that debates its existence, specific form, content and consequences.[68] Its concern is with the relationship between state, industry and society as an aspect of the structuring of economic relations within (American) society.[69] This is an issue that has been broached already by several authors in relation to missile defence, where radical critics commonly claim that the persistence of missile defence as a project is best explained by the presence of industrial interests.[70]

Why should we particularly identify theories of the MIC with substantivist understandings of technology? The argument can be made that accounts of the MIC are frequently underpinned by an implied correlation between the power of technological development and the development of the 'complex' itself. Eisenhower continued his assessment above by claiming that 'Akin to, and largely responsible for the sweeping changes in our industrial military posture, has been the

---

[67] Eisenhower's Farewell Address (1961) reprinted in Pursell, *Readings in Technology and American Life*, p. 461.

[68] MIC-lit mushroomed in the late 1960s and early '70s. For overviews see (amongst others) Sam C. Sarkesian (ed.) *The Military-Industrial Complex: a Reassessment* (Beverley Hills, CA: Sage, 1972). A more contemporaary example is Ken Silverstein, *Private Warriors* (New York: Verso, 2000).

[69] Various assessments of this intertwining are to be found in C. Wright Mills, *The Power Elite* (London: Oxford University Press, 1956); J. K. Galbraith, *The New Industrial State* (Harmondsworth: Penguin, 1974); David F. Noble, *Forces of Production* (Oxford: Oxford University Press, 1986).

[70] See, for example, William D. Hartung with Frida Berrigan, Michelle Ciarrocca and Jonathan Wingo, 'Tangled Web 2005: a Profile of the Missile Defense and Space Weapons Lobbies', report by the World Policy Institute, www.worldpolicy.org/projects/arms/reports/tangledweb.html [last accessed 20 January 2009]; Silverstein, *Private Warriors*, see pp. 242–58; Helen Caldicott, *The New Nuclear Danger: George W. Bush's Military-Industrial Complex* (New York: The New Press, 2004).

technological revolution during recent decades.'[71] In one and the same
breath he attributes an autonomous and deterministic quality not simply to the military-industrial complex but to technology itself; both take
on a momentum of their own. At its most developed, this substantivist
understanding has manifested itself in conceptions of the 'pentagon of
power' operating at the heart of the 'megamachine' that is modern
life,[72] of the 'iron triangle' of defence economics,[73] and now even,
apparently, a technologically mediated network of military, media
and industry.[74]

It should be acknowledged that the figurative conceptions of
Mumford or Der Derian are far outnumbered by more prosaic efforts
to 'unmask' the workings of the military-industrial complex. Even here,
though, the mechanical metaphor looms large. Although there is a
frequent focus on the self-serving actions of individuals within the
complex, these individuals are simultaneously seen as cogs in a larger
mechanism of corporate and governmental structures that is ultimately
beyond their control. This results in a (potentially misguided) attribution of mechanical causality to the 'complex' itself and, as Jerome Slater
and Terry Nardin argue, risks the danger of missing 'various possibilities for explanation which refer to social wholes of various kinds (such
as beliefs, rules, practices and institutions) and in general overlook a
wide range of factors which must be considered in any reasonably
complete explanation of social and political events'.[75] There is always
a danger that framing the argument in terms of military-industrial
complex risks treating the issues of technological development and the
tightening of military–industrial relations as complicit and inevitable
without ever really questioning the (possible) relationship between the
two. As Chant notes 'it is one thing to *establish*, for example, the
growing interdependence in our period of the technical community,
government and administration, and the "military-industrial complex";
it is quite another to open up the possibility of intervention in these

---

[71] Eisenhower's Farewell Address.   [72] Mumford, *Pentagon of Power*.
[73] Gordon Adams, *The Politics of Defense Contracting: the Iron Triangle* (New
Brunswick, NJ: Transaction Books, 1982).
[74] James Der Derian, *Virtuous War: Mapping the Military-Industrial-Media-
Entertainment Network* (Boulder, CO: Westview Press, 2001).
[75] Jerome Slater and Terry Nardin, 'The Concept of a Military-Industrial Complex'
in Steven Rosen (ed.) *Testing the Theory of the Military-Industrial Complex*
(Lexington, MA: Lexington Books, 1973) p. 34.

relationships, and in consequence to exorcise the spectre of "technics-out-of-control"'.[76]

Beyond the oversimplification of the MIC: common sense, culture and historic blocs

Returning to the Gramsican perspective, we can tie this reflexive awareness of the 'mechanistic' connotations of the MIC, and its cultural resonance, to a broader critique of its attendant tendency towards economic reductionism. Here we might note Gramsci's criticism of proponents of Marxist economism, or what he termed 'economistic superstition': 'they form the habit of considering politics, and hence history, as a continuous *marché des dupes*, a competition in conjuring and sleight of hand. 'Critical' activity is reduced to the exposure of swindles, to creating scandals, and to prying into the pockets of public figures.'[77]

This critique could as easily be applied to those accounts that simply explain away the pursuit of missile defence by reference to the presence of a military-industrial complex, where to be 'critical' is defined precisely in the ability to expose swindles involving defence contractors and to pry into the pockets of those within the Bush administration and congress.[78] No doubt there is value in these accounts in their evidencing of the money trails that criss-cross American defence politics and industry, and in drawing attention to the influential role that economic factors play in defence projects like ballistic missile defence. Beyond this, however, there is very little sense within these accounts as to the

---

[76] Colin Chant, 'Science and Technology: Problems of Interpretation' in Chant, *Science, Technology and Everyday Life*, p. 57, emphasis in original. See, as an example, Ted Greenwood, 'Why Military Technology is Difficult to Restrain', *Science, Technology and Human Values*, 15:4 (1990) pp. 412–29.

[77] Gramsci, *Prison Notebooks*, p. 164.

[78] With regard to the Bush administration's increase in funding of missile defence, Hartung *et al.* 'Tangled Web 2005', point, for example, to the '32 former executives, board members, or major shareholders from arms companies [who were appointed] to key policymaking positions' and the Cheney family's connections to Lockheed Martin; Caldicott, *The New Nuclear Danger*, p. xxx, refers to what she terms 'The Lockheed Martin Presidency and the Star Wars Administration'. For a more extensive overview see Columba Peoples, 'Technology and Politics in the Missile Defence Debate: Traditional, Radical and Critical Approaches', *Global Change, Peace and Security*, 19:3 (2007) pp. 265–80.

extent to which conditions of possibility within the 'social formation' (as Gramsci might have put it) run deeper and might be of more importance than piecemeal 'sleights of hand'.

Of course it is worth noting that although Gramsci seeks to go beyond economic reductionism, he retains an economic dimension to his analysis, particularly in his concept of hegemony: 'though hegemony is ethical-political, it must also be economic, must necessarily be based on the decisive function exercised by the leading group in the decisive nucleus of economic activity'.[79] This suggests that we should not entirely ignore accounts of the post-war American economic-industrial base and the role played by the defence industry in it, either with regard to missile defence or more broadly. But political–economic relations – such as those prioritised by conventional readings of the military-industrial complex – are embedded in and intertwined with broader cultural forms. Particularly important here is Gramsci's fundamental reformulation of the 'base/superstructure' distinction conventionally associated with Marxism. Crucial to this is his notion of 'historic bloc': 'Structures and superstructures form an "historical bloc". That is to say the complex, contradictory and discordant *ensemble* of the superstructures is the reflection of the *ensemble* of the social relations of production.'[80] Once again common sense, as a cultural-ideational sedimentation, has potential centrality here.[81] Gramsci goes on to speak of the 'solidity of popular beliefs':

Another proposition of Marx is that a popular conviction often has the same energy as a material force or something of the kind, which is extremely significant. The analysis of these propositions tends, I think, to reinforce the conception of *historical bloc* in which precisely material forces are the content and ideologies are the form, though this distinction made between form and content has purely didactic value, since the material forces would be

---

[79] Gramsci, *Prison Notebooks*, p. 161.
[80] Ibid., p. 366, emphasis in original. See also p. 137: 'how is the concept of a circle joining the levels of the superstructure to be understood? Concept of "historical bloc", i.e. unity between nature and spirit (structure and superstructure), unity of opposites and of distincts.'
[81] Stephen Gill, 'Epistemology, Ontology and the "Italian School" ' in Stephen Gill (ed.) *Gramsci, Historical Materialism and International Relations* (Cambridge: Cambridge University Press, 1993) p. 26.

inconceivable historically without the form and the ideologies would be individual fancies without the material forces.[82]

As Stephen Gill has noted, 'The social organisation of production, as an aspect of the social world, is thus necessarily constituted partly by inter-subjective meanings, which can be identified and understood, however imperfectly … which suggests how apparently normative forces may have the social power normally associated with "material forces" (such as technology, the forces of production).'[83] This reinforces the need to examine both cultural-ideational as well as economic factors:

Gramsci is concerned with the process of integration and disintegration of historical blocs, and this, of course, is far more than a merely humanist theory of history, for it must not only understand humanity as it is expressed in folklore, culture, art, etc., but also in the general structures that condition human activity. Thus, Gramsci's analysis presupposes and supplements the results of the analysis of political economy; it does not replace them.[84]

Taken in this light, the concept of historic bloc can, potentially, add a level of sophistication and cultural awareness lacking from theories of the military-industrial complex given that 'it encompasses political, cultural, and economic aspects of a particular social formation, uniting these in historically specific ways to form a complex, politically contestable and dynamic ensemble of social relations'.[85]

Investigation of such culturally embedded formations must always countenance the fact that 'culture' is of course itself a necessarily slippery concept.[86] Awareness of this can in turn help to guard against the danger of essentialising strategic culture(s) a priori,[87] or prematurely delimiting it from 'culture' more broadly understood (that is, culture 'writ large' or popular, political and diplomatic culture).[88] Indeed,

---

[82] Gramsci, *Prison Notebooks*, p. 377.

[83] Gill, 'Epistemology, Ontology and the "Italian School"', p. 26.

[84] Esteve Morera, *Gramsci's Historicism: a Realist Interpretation* (London: Routledge, 1990) p. 58.

[85] Mark Rupert, *Producing Hegemony: the Politics of Mass Production and American Global Power* (Cambridge: Cambridge University Press, 1995) p. 30.

[86] Raymond Williams, *Keywords: a Vocabulary of Culture and Society* (London: Fontana, 1983) pp. 87–93.

[87] See Ken Booth, *Strategy and Ethnocentrism* (New York: Homes and Meier, 1979).

[88] Keith Krause, 'Cross-Cultural Dimensions of Multilateral Non-Proliferation and Arms Control Dialogues: an Overview' in Keith Krause (ed.) *Culture and*

much of the following analysis points precisely to the frequently 'inter-textual' nature of political and strategic discourse: the manner in which justifications of missile defence draw upon, incorporate and recontex-tualise ideas and illustrations from a broader cultural heritage.[89] Within the discourse of missile defence, for instance, there is a constant attempt to articulate and rearticulate the cultural legacy of the United States (in terms of a particularly American experience of technology historically) and with it realignments of US defence spending in relation to this project. Of course, there can be no guarantee that such articula-tions will always be successful, find resonance or always further the cause of missile defence. What is of interest, though, is that these articulations *are* framed in common sense terms that are aimed at the American nation as a whole and in which there is an expectancy that the 'average' American should recognise their supposed heritage and hopes and fears for technological advance as their own.[90] They pre-sume, to borrow a phrase from Pierre Bourdieu, 'anticipated conditions of felicity' on the part of those making the argument or, as Krause and Latham put it, that such articulations will 'fit' within existing cultural structures.[91]

Language, discourse and the analysis of common sense

Those who seek to convince others of the efficacy of missile defence therefore, whatever their personal, political or economic motivation might be for doing so, generally seek to espouse its benefits in universal terms rather than in terms of their own particular interests. One of the aims of later chapters is to show that this espousal has occurred, and

   Security: Multilateralism, Arms Control and Security Building (London: Frank Cass, 1999) pp. 13–18. See also Peter J. Katzenstein (ed.) *The Culture of National Security: Norms and Identity in World Politics* (New York: Columbia University Press, 1996).

[89] On intertextuality see Norman Fairclough, *Analyzing Discourse: Textual Analysis for Social Research* (London: Routledge, 2003) p. 17.

[90] As is assumed, for example, in Colin S. Gray's portrayal of American attitudes to BMD in 'European Perspectives on US Ballistic Missile Defense', *Comparative Strategy*, 21 (2002) pp. 279–310.

[91] Bourdieu, 'Price Formation and the Anticipation of Profits' in Pierre Bourdieu, *Language and Symbolic Power*, ed. and introduced by John B. Thompson (Cambridge: Polity Press, 2005) pp. 74–5; Keith Krause and Andrew Latham, 'Constructing Non-Proliferation and Arms Control: the Norms of Western Practice' in Krause, *Culture and Security*, p. 24.

continues to occur, on the basis of relatively consistent principles that are in turn predicated upon particular understandings of technology. Gramsci's association of civil society (broadly defined) as the general locus of efforts at creating consent, and the centrality of 'intellectuals' in this process, suggests the net be cast widely in the empirical sections in terms of seeking out how and where common sense understandings of technological development have been employed in efforts to create a consensus on the efficacy of missile defence. In this spirit, Parts Two and Three take an extended historical scope in order to ground the analysis of contemporary missile defence advocacy, which is assessed in detail in Part Four. It is not the aim of these sections to act as a history or economic analysis of missile defence (for which further references are provided throughout) or as a full-blown history of ideas in this case. The key aim, by combining elements of all three, is to establish patterns of argument that have developed over time in relation to missile defence and technology, and to identify or 'place' key actors and groups associated with the promotion of missile defence.[92] Crucial to the furtherance of this effort is a greater understanding of the role of language and discourse.

The emphasis placed on establishing a historically-informed textual and discourse analysis in Parts Two, Three and Four follows logically from the centrality the analysis gives to the concept of common sense. Gramsci's thought has been critiqued variously for its slippery definitions of state/civil society,[93] and its perceived emphasis on class and 'History' as the motor of social change.[94] While these criticisms are well taken, much recent work has sought to recognise the linguistic foundations of Gramscian concepts and to extricate their potential salience for analysing political discourse. Reviewing theorists as disparate as Michel Foucault, Jacques Derrida, Judith Butler and Jürgen Habermas, Beatrice Hanssen argues that 'what emerges from a survey of the language conceptions that circulate in our critical field is the conclusion that all are in need of a more diversified reflection on how power is deployed concretely in various registers of language politics', and she

---

[92] Richard E. Neustadt and Ernest R. May, *Thinking in Time: the Uses of History for Decision Makers* (New York: The Free Press, 1988) pp. 208–9.

[93] Perry Anderson, 'The Antinomies of Antonio Gramsci', *New Left Review*, 100 (November 1976–January 1977) pp. 5–78.

[94] Ernesto Laclau and Chantal Mouffe, *Hegemony and Socialist Strategy: Towards a Radical Democratic Politics*, 2nd edition (London: Verso, 2001).

references the Sardinian favourably in this regard.[95] This aspect is what Milliken terms the 'productivity' of discourse – 'how [discourse] renders logical and proper certain policies by authorities' – and here she attributes a crucial role to common sense.[96]

In Gramsci's discussion of common sense and culture, it is precisely the role of language in constructing and sustaining intellectual hegemony that emerges:

[P]hilosophy is a conception of the world and ... philosophical activity is not to be conceived solely as the 'individual' elaboration of systematically coherent concepts, but also and above all as a cultural battle to transform the popular 'mentality' and to diffuse the philosophical innovations that will demonstrate themselves to be 'historically true' to the extent that they become concretely – i.e. historically and socially – universal. Given all this, the question of languages in the technical sense must be put in the forefront of our investigation.[97]

Elsewhere, speaking of the relationship between philosophy, politics and economics, Gramsci argues that there is always 'a reciprocal translation into the specific language proper to each constituent element. Any one is implicit in the others, and the three together form a homogenous circle.'[98]

As Trevor Purvis and Alan Hunt argue, even though Gramsci was keenly aware of the connection between language, common sense and hegemony he never fleshed out the details of this to any great extent. But this connection is crucial given his emphasis on the importance of common sense, which is necessarily transmitted in discursive form. Purvis and Hunt equate common sense with popular discourse more broadly speaking and contend that 'Common sense (or popular discourse) is both the medium of social action and constitutive of the social relations they reproduce,' hence it is naturally implicated in the formation and maintenance of a historic bloc.[99] As the quote from Gramsci

[95] Beatrice Hanssen, *Critique of Violence: Between Poststructuralism and Critical Theory* (London: Routledge, 2000) p. 177.
[96] Jennifer Milliken, 'The Study of Discourse in International Relations: a Critique of Research and Methods', *European Journal of International Relations*, 5:2 (1999) pp. 225–54, p. 236.
[97] Gramsci, *Prison Notebooks*, p. 348.   [98] Ibid., p. 403.
[99] Trevor Purvis and Alan Hunt, 'Discourse, Ideology, Discourse, Ideology, Discourse, Ideology ...', *British Journal of Sociology*, 44:3 (1999) pp. 473–99, p. 495.

above indicates, attempts to elaborate coherent concepts are part of a 'cultural battle' to mould and fix the popular 'mentality'.

To ground this conception of common sense more explicitly within the philosophy of language, several authors have noted the parallels between Mikhail Bakhtin's concept of the 'heteroglossia' of words and discourses – broadly definable as the existence of conflicting discourses within any field of linguistic activity.[100] Bakhtin views this struggle as occurring both at the macro-level of languages per se and at the micro-level of the everyday usage of language, where the act of dialogue seeks to overcome this heteroglossic aspect and create a form of 'unitary language', an instantiation of language or discourse that seeks to max-imise mutual understanding by 'crystallizing into a real, although still relative, unity'.[101] He uses the term 'relative' here to denote the way in which the 'unitary language' is always beholden to both 'centripetal' and 'centrifugal' forces: the unificatory intention exercised by the author or speaker has to contend with the further fragmentary force of heteroglossia, that is, the sedimented multiplicity of meanings that develop over time from social and historical context. In this light, the presence of two contradictory understandings of technology, detailed previously, within a specific form of discourse is less surprising. Indeed, Bakhtin argues that 'It is possible to give a concrete and detailed analysis of any utterance, once having exposed it as a contradiction-ridden, tension-filled unity of two embattled tendencies in the life of language.'[102]

This grounds Gramsci's notion of common sense in a compatible and more extensive theory of language, an overlap that has been identified and pursued elsewhere.[103] Compare, for example, Gramsci's stipulation

---

[100] Mikhail Bakhtin, *The Dialogic Imagination: Four Essays*, trans. C. Emerson and M. Holquist (ed.) (Austin, TX: University of Texas Press, 1981). On the complementarity of Bakhtin and Grasmci see: Peter Ives, *Gramsci's Politics of Language: Engaging the Bakhtin Circle and the Frankfurt School* (Toronto: University of Toronto Press, 2003); Craig Brandist, 'Gramsci, Bakhtin and the Semiotics of Hegemony', *New Left Review*, 216 (March–April 1996) pp. 94–109; Craig Brandist, 'The Official and the Popular in Gramsci and Bakhtin', *Theory, Culture and Society*, 13:2 (1996) pp. 59–74.

[101] Pam Morris (ed.) *The Bakhtin Reader: Selected Writings of Bakhtin, Medvedev and Voloshinov* (London: Edward Arnold, 1994) p. 74.

[102] Ibid.

[103] Ives, *Gramsci's Politics of Language*; also Renate Holub, *Antonio Gramsci: Beyond Marxism and Postmodernism* (London: Routledge, 1992) p. 18 and

of the fragmentary nature of common sense with Bakhtin's eloquent assertion that:

> any concrete discourse (utterance) finds the object at which it was directed already as it were overlain with qualifications, open to dispute, charged with value, already enveloped in an obscuring mist ... it is entangled, shot through with shared thoughts, points of view, alien value judgements and accents. The word, directed toward its object, enters a dialogically agitated and tension-filled environment of alien words, value judgements and accents, weaves in and out of complex interrelationships, merges with some, recoils from others, intersects with yet a third group: and all this may crucially shape discourse, may leave a trace in all its semantic layers, may complicate its expression and influence its entire stylistic profile.[104]

A word – in this case 'technology' – is already 'shot through' with meanings sedimented from theoretical reflection, practical usage, cultural specificity and historical experience that simultaneously allow for juxtaposed understandings to co-exist even as it refers to the same object (or range of objects as in the case of technology).[105]

Conclusion

Gramsci's emphasis on common sense and its discursive character, understood within particular and cultural contexts, offers a clear means of comprehending the connections, parallels and homologies between philosophically elaborated ideas and their more localised and popular instantiations. The concept of common sense allows us to identify the 'everyday' articulations of more theoretically developed understandings of technology – instrumentalism and substantivism. As Stuart Hall notes in his own use of the Gramscian conception of common sense, 'One has to investigate quite precisely how more elaborated theoretical ideologies fit, *often very contradictorily*, into people's actual local and immediate experience.'[106] To the extent that this succeeds, as Hall sought to illustrate in his examination of Thatcherism,

---

Marcia Landy, *Film, Politics and Gramsci* (Minneapolis, MN: University of Minnesota Press, 1994) pp. 90–2.
[104] Morris, *The Bakhtin Reader*, p. 78.
[105] Cf., once again, 'Technology' as defined in Williams, *Keywords*, pp. 315–16.
[106] Stuart Hall, 'The Toad in the Garden: Thatcherism among the Theorists' in Cary Nelson and Lawrence Grossberg (eds.) *Marxism and the Interpretation of Culture* (Urbana: University of Illinois Press, 1988) p. 59, emphasis added.

'It's because some of those philosophically elaborated concepts have connected with a deeper groundwork of emotional loyalties and moral sentiments and bits of knowledge and so on. Symbolic identification – that is the real popular field on which those things are sorted out.'[107] As we have seen, instrumental and substantive understandings of technology map on to the American experience of technology in a historical sense, both in terms of contemporaneous experiences of technology in the US context and in retrospective historical representations of that experience. Despite their very different connotations – of agency, control and progress (instrumentalism) on the one hand, and determinism, fatalism and pessimism (substantivism) on the other – it has been shown that both of these understandings exist in the American context. The task of the following chapters is to establish how this pattern also holds true, and with what implications, within justifications of US missile defence.

[107] Ibid.

PART TWO

Post-war missile defence

3 | *Defence in the missile age?*

Introduction

Part One introduced the concept of an 'instrumentalist' understanding of technology: the idea that technologies are neutral, value-free instruments ready to serve the purposes of their users. The argument developed in chapter 2 was that instrumentalism does indeed form a major part of the 'common sense' approach to technology in America, but has in the process come to be synonymous with social improvement. In the American context, historically, technology was primarily seen as an instrument of 'progress'. Though taken as neutral in itself, technology came to be viewed as an invaluable means for furthering social and political ends such as establishing the early US state by effecting improvements in agriculture, industry, transport and weaponry. Despite the fact that this association between technology and progress has come into question at various points, the view of technological improvement as a shortcut to increased political power still persists to some degree. Indeed several authors argue that ballistic missile defence constitutes at least one area where this persistence is particularly evident. One such commentator, for example, argues that the historical attempts at creating an effective missile defence 'can be best characterized as a program concept engaged in a continual quest for the "magic bullet" '.[1] Missile defence, on this view, constitutes a classic case of the search for a technological solution to a political problem, that of American nuclear security.

This chapter examines the debates surrounding missile defence in the immediate post-war period and during the anti-ballistic missile (ABM) debate, and assesses the extent to which pro-ABM arguments were informed by, and articulated, an instrumentalist understanding of

---

[1] Roger Handberg, *Ballistic Missile Defense and the Future of American Security: Agendas, Perceptions, Technology and Policy* (Westport, CT: Praeger, 2002) p. 31.

technology. Here it is shown that debate on ABM systems became a microcosm for a wider debate on the relationship between technology and defence, particularly in the realm of nuclear security, which not only brought scientists directly into the policy process, but also delineated particular schools of thought precisely on the basis of assumptions about technological development. Much of this debate was based on the issue of whether or not technological development could be utilised to enhance security policy in the realm of nuclear weapons, and the extent to which (defensive) technology specifically could provide a 'fix' for the policy problems of the Cold War. The key point argued is that ABM supporters of different backgrounds sought to espouse a broadly instrumentalist viewpoint based on a shared assumption that ABM technology could be an instrument to achieve the positive ends of nuclear security. Through an analysis of sample arguments for ABM, the chapter illustrates how this view was supplemented by references to America's technological heritage and by postulating assumptions and presuppositions about the nature of technological development.

Early arguments for post-war missile defence initiatives

The idea of an American defence against nuclear weapons emerged almost immediately after the world's introduction to the atomic bomb. On 23 October 1945, just weeks after the bombings of Hiroshima and Nagasaki, President Truman assured Congress that 'Every new weapon will eventually bring some counter defence to it.'[2] Public confidence in the potential to develop a defence against nuclear weapons also remained high immediately after World War II.[3] A 1947 Social Science Research Council poll indicated widespread public optimism that the United States would eventually find a way to build defensive systems against nuclear attack based, primarily, on the fact that American scientists had themselves already taken the lead in the development of atomic weapons. The author of the poll found that most respondents thought that 'since the scientists were able to invent the bomb, they can invent a

---

[2] Quoted in Lawrence Freedman, *The Evolution of Nuclear Strategy*, 3rd edition (Basingstoke: Palgrave, 2003) p. 29. For a further discussion of the consequences of the atomic bomb on this view, see pp. 28–31.
[3] Edward T. Linenthal, *Symbolic Defense: the Cultural Significance of the Strategic Defense Initiative* (Urbana: University of Illinois Press, 1989) p. 2.

defence ... The United States "always keeps ahead" ' and she concluded that people expressed 'immense faith in American science, American ingenuity, and American resources'.[4] The presupposition was that a technological solution to the problem of nuclear war was a natural, desirable and characteristically American approach.

Likewise, as the prospects for control of atomic energy began to recede with the Soviet development of the atom bomb and the full onset of the Cold War, several of America's 'scientific celebrities' increasingly began to consider the potential for defence against nuclear attack. In 1953 J. Robert Oppenheimer, 'father' of the A-bomb, conceded that future defences might contribute to 'some measure of an increased freedom of action'.[5] The majority of scientists continued to emphasise the awesome destructive potential of atomic weapons during the 1950s and Oppenheimer himself held out hope for an international accord to restrict US–Soviet competition in nuclear weapons.[6] But a significant portion of the American scientific community dreamed that science might also hold the key to defending against nuclear attack, thus preserving the full political (and, potentially, military) utility of the bomb, especially in an age of intercontinental reach. 'It would be wonderful if we could shoot down approaching missiles before they could destroy a target in the United States,' Edward Teller, credited with a major role in designing the H-bomb, wrote in 1962's *The Legacy of Hiroshima*; 'if we find that we can build an adequate anti-missile defence, we certainly should'.[7]

A clear strain of instrumentalism runs through Teller's and Oppenheimer's lines of thought here: effective missile defences, if achievable, could be used to free up the political value of offensive nuclear missiles for the USA once again. Of course, this implied that

[4] Ibid., p. 2; Sylvia Eberhart, 'How American People Feel about the Atomic Bomb', *Bulletin of the Atomic Scientists*, 3:4–5 (April–May 1947): 146–9, 168; J. Robert Oppenheimer, 'Atomic Weapons and American Policy', *Bulletin of the Atomic Scientists*, 9:6 (July 1953) pp. 202–5; see also Paul S. Boyer, *By the Bomb's Early Light: American Thought and Culture at the Dawn of the Atomic Age* (New York: Pantheon, 1986) p. 2.
[5] Oppenheimer, 'Atomic Weapons and American Policy' quoted in Linenthal, *Symbolic Defense*, p. 4.
[6] Robert Gilpin, *American Scientists and Nuclear Weapons Policy* (Princeton, NJ: Princeton University Press) p. 98.
[7] Edward Teller, *The Legacy of Hiroshima* (Garden City, NY: Doubleday, 1962) pp. 128–9.

the constraints imposed by (offensive) nuclear weapons technology were already something of a problem, an aspect discussed in more detail in the next chapter. But there was a certain attraction to the idea that technology could be *used* (hence instrumentalism) to overcome this problem. Rather than constraining US policy options vis-à-vis the Soviets, nuclear weapons technology would in turn be restored to its supposedly rightful place – as an instrument of policy.

Instrumentalism and defence planning

Supplementing this view, for some, was the belief that American ingenuity was already well on the way to achieving this goal, and here technological optimism fused with the belief that defences could provide US security. Although the fledgling anti-missile systems of the 1950s remained in only an early development stage, Air Force Chief of Staff General Curtis E. LeMay confidently predicted in 1962 that scientists would soon develop 'directed energy weapons' that would 'strike [missiles] with the speed of light'.[8] The profusion of missile defence research projects in development by the military services in the 1950s and '60s (among them the various 'Nike' interceptor systems developed by the US Army, which included a nuclear-tipped variant, later developed into 'Sprint' and 'Spartan'; the US Air Force's 'Wizard' project; and the service-wide 'Sentinel' and 'Safeguard') indicates that hopes for missile defence had not been entirely ruled out despite the offence-oriented nature of US defence planning at the time.[9] Arguably this owes much to the overall orientation of US defence policy in the post-war period which emphasised the utility of technological superiority, providing the scope and funding for such projects. In other words, a general stress on the need for technological superiority in all areas as a means to preserve US preponderance – itself an instrumentalist outlook – helped to initiate and sustain research into anti-missile systems. Handberg associates this with a general trend in which 'advanced technological capabilities, especially since the post-World War II period, becomes the mechanism by which an effective American military presence is maintained.

---

[8] LeMay quoted in William J. Broad, ' "Star Wars" Traced to Eisenhower Era', *New York Times*, 28 October 1986, pp. C1 C3.

[9] See Ernest J. Yanarella, *The Missile Defense Controversy: Technology in Search of a Mission* (Lexington, KY: University Press of Kentucky, 2002) for a more detailed overview.

Substitution of technology for scarce personnel is the hallmark of the American military ... US military formations during World War II were already more technology intensive than their counterparts in other nations and were also larger in numbers.'[10]

More specifically, as argued by Armacost and Yanarella, the doctrinal shift represented by Eisenhower's 'New Look' had a major effect not only on defence decision-making but also on the pace and direction of research and development (R&D) efforts by the military services, including in the realm of missile defences. Key aspects of the New Look (identified by Michael Armacost) in this respect were: 'the emphasis upon strategic retaliation, the faith in novel technology, the "long haul" perspective, the reliance upon nuclear weapons, the depreciation of manpower and conventional capabilities'. Armacost asserts that this resulted in defence programmes 'induced by haste, boldness in technology'.[11] The orientation of US defence planning therefore seemed to be infused by the 'American ideology' discussed in the previous chapter: technological enthusiasm, the use of technology to supplement or even replace human effort, and an unquestioning assumption of the efficacy of technological improvement. New research projects were in this regard intended, Armacost argues, to 'keep the future open', rather than ruling out the possibility of technological innovation even when such innovations were not deemed key to overall strategic doctrine. Technological innovation was viewed as a good thing, so long as a utility value could be shown. Extrapolating from this analysis, Yanarella argues that the overall direction of the New Look 'prompted the services to fund R&D projects relating to air and missile systems and to develop rationales claiming that their programs added something distinctively new and important to the overall goal underlying strategic bombing'.[12]

Technology and weapons development (i): the 'finite containment school'

Given this centralisation and valorisation of weapons innovation and development in the late 1950s, it became incumbent upon defence

---

[10] Handberg, *Ballistic Missile Defense*, p. 15.
[11] Michael H. Armacost, *The Politics of Weapons Innovation: the Thor–Jupiter Controversy* (New York: Columbia University Press, 1969) p. 267.
[12] Yanarella, *The Missile Defense Controversy*, p. 16.

policy-makers of the time to make fundamental judgements as to the character and quality of weapons development, judgements regarding both domestic capabilities and those of the Soviet Union. With the establishment of bodies such as the DR&E (Defense Research and Engineering) and ARPA (the Advanced Research Projects Agency), scientific opinion was increasingly formally incorporated into these judgements. However, the elevated policy-input that American scientists enjoyed in the post-war American defence infrastructure generated conflicting analyses in this regard.[13] During and immediately after World War II, leading American scientists had largely suppressed their own political differences to take part in the Manhattan Project and in the search for a viable plan to freeze military technology at the subnuclear level. With the deepening of the Cold War, 'The scientific community divided over conflicting sets of temporally stable assumptions about the *origin of the arms race, the essence of security and its relation to technology, the nature of the enemy, and the prospects for negotiation*.'[14] A general emphasis on technological innovation that can be seen to accord with a characteristic American emphasis on technology was indeed assumed. But the question of where this emphasis should be placed initiated a divisive debate over the exact relation between security and technology.

The prospects for defences – including missile defence – would come to be at the heart of this debate. By the early 1960s inter-service research into anti-missile systems had been diverted into one effort, the Nike programme. Although Secretary of Defense Robert McNamara publicly expressed some optimism about the programme's progress, most commentators agree that, by the mid-1960s, he held a growing conviction that a more effective way to deter the Soviets was through possession of overwhelming offensive nuclear force. Not only was McNamara backed in this view by nascent theories of deterrence emerging at the same time,[15] but his own scepticism towards the prospects for effective missile defences were also backed by significant voices within the scientific community: Herbert York (ARPA's former chief scientist); Harold Brown (director of the Lawrence Livermore National Laboratory);

[13] See Gilpin, *American Scientists and Nuclear Weapons Policy*.
[14] Ibid., p. 107, emphasis added.
[15] Cf. Bernard Brodie, *Strategy in the Missile Age* (Princeton, NJ: Princeton University Press, 1965).

Hans Bethe (professor of physics at Cornell, Nobel laureate, influential in the development of both the A-bomb and the H-bomb); and Jerome Wiesner (professor of engineering at MIT and science adviser to President Kennedy). Bethe firmly supported the Partial Test Ban Treaty of 1963 and described attempts at missile defence as 'virtually hopeless'.[16] York and Wiesner argued that missile defences would only exacerbate the arms race, locking the USA and USSR into a 'dilemma of steadily increasing military power and steadily decreasing national security'.[17] These arguments were influential on McNamara, whose thinking was already turning towards a strategy of 'assured destruction' and the prosecution of the Vietnam War.[18]

In the terms of the analysis proposed in chapter 2, this conglomeration of missile defence sceptics thus exerted a form of intellectual hegemony. The views of York, Brown, Bethe and Wiesner, which carried the weight of scientific expertise, are instructive as to the view of technological development informing this position. All belonged to what Robert Gilpin has classified as the 'finite containment school':

According to this position it is both technically feasible and politically desirable to limit the nuclear arms race by international agreement at some *finite* point prior to the settlement of political differences between the United States and the Soviet Union, while at the same time it is also necessary to *contain* Soviet aggression.[19]

This school of thought had emerged from the spilt in the scientific community post-1947, had existed in the lower echelons of bureaucracy in the 1950s and attained much greater influence in White House circles late in the Eisenhower administration's incumbency with the appointment of James Killian, president of MIT, as Presidential Special Assistant for Science and Technology in November 1957.[20]

---

[16] Quoted in Donald R. Baucom, *The Origins of SDI, 1944–1983* (Lawrence, KS: University Press of Kansas, 1992) p. 21. See also Hans A. Bethe, 'Countermeasures to ABM Systems: What is the Likelihood of an Enemy's Overcoming an ABM by Using Various Penetration Aids and Strategies?' in Abram Chayes and Jerome B. Wiesner (eds.) *ABM: an Evaluation of the Decision to Deploy an Anti-Ballistic Missile System* (London: MacDonald, 1970) pp. 130–43.

[17] Baucom, *Origins of SDI*, p. 21.   [18] Ibid.

[19] Gilpin, *American Scientists and Nuclear Weapons Policy*, p. 98, emphases in original.

[20] Ibid., p. 176. Killian's influence is discussed in more detail in chapter 4.

The rise to prominence of this school of thought entailed acceptance of key assumptions about the relationship between security and technology, assumptions which, Yanarella argues, subsequently came to define the approach to nuclear weapons and ABM systems during the McNamara era. Here the overlap between the finite containment school and the emerging theories of nuclear deterrence becomes apparent. These assumptions included: (1) that 'The development of nuclear weapons had basically altered the character of general war as a political option'; (2) 'The United States is challenged by a determined adversary with a dynamic technology in military weaponry'; and (3) that 'Historically, the offense has always gotten through.'[21] The policy inferences that followed from these assumptions were that: (a) 'National security should be defined above all by the strategy of nuclear deterrence, i.e., deterrence, not war-winning, is the strategic objective'; (b) 'The offense must always get through'; given the prospect that the Soviets would probably also be investing research into defences, it was incumbent upon the Department of Defense to provide the capacity for overwhelming offensive force; and hence (c) 'Technological momentum in offensive military capabilities must continue unimpeded.'[22] Although the finite containment philosophy started out with the objective of negotiated reductions in nuclear arsenals, McNamara concluded from the same assumptions that the only practical way to bring the Soviets to the negotiating table was qualitatively to improve America's offensive nuclear capabilities. In the meantime, the quality and number of US nuclear missiles was to be considered as essential to containing the Soviets.[23]

Technology and weapons development (ii): 'the infinite containment school'

All this left missile defences as a low priority, and disparaged the idea that ABM could provide a simple technological fix.[24] Though research

[21] Yanarella, *The Missile Defense Controversy*, p. 77.   [22] Ibid.
[23] In this, Colin S. Gray argues, ruefully, that US military officers and civilian analysts during the McNamara era were 'trained on the ideas' of Charles Hitch and Roland McKean's *The Economics of Defense in the Nuclear Age* (New York: Atheneum, 1960) and Thomas Schelling's *The Strategy of Conflict* (Cambridge, MA; Harvard University Press, 1960) – see Colin S. Gray, *Nuclear Strategy and National Style* (London: Hamilton Press, 1986) pp. 169–90.
[24] Indeed, this disparagement of the technological fix approach was frequently based on substantivist precepts, as is detailed in chapter 4.

into missile defences was permitted to continue on the pragmatic basis that it was impossible entirely to rule out a breakthrough in defensive technologies, given the assumption that a nuclear offensive would 'always get through' ballistic missile defences were 'saddled with an impossible task', namely 'the building of a technically perfect system'.[25] But while the finite containment school of thought ended up maligning the prospects for missile defence, another school of thought had emerged from the split consensus of American scientific thought which held much higher hopes for ballistic missile defence. Gilpin traces the origins of this opposing 'infinite containment school' to the debate over whether and when to develop the hydrogen bomb and disagreement over the prospects for control of atomic energy. Specifically, this group of scientists argued that the United States should consciously seek the upper hand in the arms race by developing the H-bomb as quickly as possible, and pursuing other innovations in weaponry across the board.[26]

Physicist Edward Teller was to become the key figure in this school of thought, largely by virtue of his forthright promotion of the H-bomb. Rejecting the prospect of a negotiated settlement to the arms race on the basis that negotiation would never go far enough, Teller's argument was that 'modern science and technology creates novelties which cannot be anticipated, and there is no guarantee that a control system developed on the basis of an existing body of knowledge will be able to detect covert developments made possible by new knowledge'.[27] Since modern science was so closely integrated with functions of government and new developments in weapons technology especially were jealously guarded by different powers, only a radical alteration of the constitution of the state-system (into a single world government) could ensure full transparency in technological development. Hence, as Yanarella summarises this position, 'any effort to control technological advances while the cloak of secrecy veils part of the world would be technically impossible and militarily foolhardy'.[28]

The infinite containment position entailed two further presuppositions that differentiated it from the finite containment school. The first was that whereas the finite containment school tended to emphasise

[25] Yanarella, *The Missile Defense Controversey*, pp. 77–8.
[26] Gilpin, *American Scientists and Nuclear Weapons Policy*, p. 102.
[27] Ibid., p. 103.   [28] Yanarella, *The Missile Defense Controversy*, p. 108.

fairly regular incremental advances in offensive forces which could, potentially, be restricted through negotiation, the infinite containment school stressed that the character of modern technological developments was unpredictable and its pace uncontrollable. Under these conditions, 'technology had largely replaced geography as the prime component of national power. Hence, he who sets the pace of technological development controls the world.'[29] Secondly, negotiated restrictions to arms development were innately liable to contravention since 'a decisive military advantage automatically accrues to the country which is first to construct such weapons'; hence, 'under any system to arrest technological progress, there would always exist a temptation to abrogate the system and achieve a technological coup which would shift the balance decidedly to one's advantage'.[30] This view posited that there exists, in the words of Teller's fellow émigré John von Neumann, a 'competitive premium on infringement' in any arms control agreement, a point that would become a mainstay in later justifications of missile defence.[31] The logical conclusion of this line of thought was that 'the safest course for an open democracy like the United States was to foreswear any effort to shackle technological development in the military realm by bilateral or international agreement until the political system of the USSR was radically transformed into an open and democratic society'.[32]

From this perspective, there was *no* finite point at which technological development could be limited, and the imperative to develop new weapons was in Teller's eyes as much ethical as technological. In this view Teller rearticulated the old association of technology with social progress. As Gilpin notes:

Teller's view that scientists must do that which can be done does have its own inherent ethic. Implicit in this position is the belief that the advance of science is a great force for human progress and world peace. Despite the many

---

[29] Ibid. This view was later paralleled in strategic thought in Colin S. Gray's *The Geopolitics of the Nuclear Era: Heartland, Rimlands and the Technological Revolution* (New York: Crane, Russak, 1977).

[30] Yanarella, *The Missile Defense Controversy*, p. 108.

[31] 'Can We Survive Technology?', from the June 1955 issue of *Fortune*: quoted in Gilpin, *American Scientists and Nuclear Weapons Policy*, p. 105. Von Neumann, seen as the pioneer of modern digital computers, was also key to the development of the H-bomb.

[32] Yanarella, *The Missile Defense Controversy*, p. 108.

dangers it presents, technological advance, including that in weaponry, provides mankind with the wherewithal to maintain peace by threat of retaliation and to eliminate the underlying social-economic causes of war.[33]

Accepting Gilpin's portrayal there are clear consistencies in the outlook of the infinite containment school with the progressivist narrative of American technological development discussed in chapter 2. This portrayal also foregrounds the belief that human ends determine the employment of technology and not vice versa, in keeping with the instrumentalist understanding of technology. However, it is also worth noting at this point that the proponents of infinite containment shared in common with their opponents the assumption that technological development has an autonomous logic or dynamic of its own. Where they differed was in their view that this dynamic was something that could be profitably put to use by the USA.

ABM and the pursuit of infinite containment

The infinite containment worldview positively advocated ceaseless and unrestrained technological development in *both* offensive and defensive weaponry as a desirable and necessary measure.[34] Faith in arms control was presented as sheer foolishness in this light. A 'technological imperative' must apply to technology as a whole and, therefore, to defences as much as offences. If an ABM system could be built, it would be built; ergo failure to match Soviet progress in defensive measures would be detrimental to US national interest because it would place artificial limits on American technological development and consequently limit US policy options – especially if the Soviets stole a march on the USA by deploying a territorial missile defence first.

Seeds of contradiction are, arguably, already present within this viewpoint. For example, the 'Gaither report' to the National Security Council in 1957 (in which Teller had a heavy input) predicted improvements not only in the quality and quantity of long-range ballistic missiles, but also in 'means for detecting and defending against missile attacks', concluding that 'missiles in turn will be made more

---

[33] Gilpin, *American Scientists and Nuclear Weapons*, pp. 106–7.

[34] As evidenced in Teller's testimony to Congress on ABM in *Strategic and Foreign Policy Implications of ABM Systems* (1969), as cited in Yanarella, *The Missile Defense Controversy*, p. 168.

sophisticated to avoid destruction; and there will be a continuing race between the offence and the defence. Neither side can afford to lag or fail to match the other's efforts. There will be no end to the technical moves or countermoves.'[35] Logically defences would therefore be as much part of the problem as a solution – the stance generally adopted by the anti-ABM constituency – and the technological determinism under-pinning this view seemed to point to a very bleak future that fitted uneasily with the optimistic presumptions regarding defensive technol-ogy. The logic that constraints on weapons development would equal constraints on US capacity to use those weapons towards political ends is a broadly instrumentalist one; but the prior assumption of a weapons development *dynamic* is in some ways antithetical to the view of tech-nology as simply an instrument to be used. There is a nascent contra-diction here, explored further in the next chapter, that begins to hint at the combination of opposing understandings of technology into a com-posite 'common sense' form.

For the moment we might simply note how the infinite containment view of technology translated from the context of scientific debate into a broader argument for ABM. Key tenets of this view were in fact adopted by the pro-ABM lobby in the late 1960s as the battle on whether to deploy an ABM system deepened.[36] One of the most important groups supporting ABM deployment was the 'Committee to Maintain a Prudent Defense Policy', organised under the auspices of Paul Nitze and Dean Acheson. Nitze envisaged the committee as an intellectually informed vanguard against the scientific opposition to ABM which he viewed as expounding fuzzy, populist and ultimately erroneous views about nuclear weapons. The majority of the work undertaken by the committee was conducted by four young up-and-coming analysts, Peter Wilson, Paul Wolfowitz, Richard Perle and Edward Luttwak, who, Nitze bragged, 'ran circles' around their 'big name expert opponents on a budget of only fifteen thousand dollars'.[37]

---

[35] Quoted in Freedman, *Evolution of Nuclear Strategy*, p. 152.

[36] For contemporaneous positions on the ABM debate see: Hubert H. Humphrey and William O. Douglas, *Anti-Ballistic Missile: Yes or No?* (New York: Hill and Wang, 1968); Johan J. Holst and William Schneider, *Why ABM? Policy Issues in the Missile Defense Controversy* (New York: Pergamon, 1969); Chayes and Wiesner, *ABM: an Evaluation of the Decision to Deploy an Anti-Ballistic Missile System*.

[37] Quote from Strobe Talbott, *Master of the Game: Paul Nitze and the Nuclear Peace* (New York: Knopf, 1988) p. 112.

To these supporters of Sentinel and Safeguard, the initiatives in question between 1968 and 1972, missile defences may not have been perfected (yet) but were conceptually viable based on improvements in radar and ballistic technologies, tests carried out by the various military services and positive technical assessments from consultancy bodies such as RAND.[38] The requirement of 'perfectibility' was argued to place an undue strain on testing procedures and to put the USA at a comparative disadvantage to its rival, and it was estimated that the Soviet Union had already accepted the feasibility of missile defences with the 'Galosh' system (a ring of missile defences around Moscow). While the USA insisted on high performance and effective operational capabilities before deploying a system, the Soviets tended to develop and deploy systems rapidly, knowing that there would be operational problems with the systems deployed but expecting to use the knowledge gained from operating an imperfect system to develop a better follow-on system.[39]

In short, ABM supporters in the USA argued that by refusing to limit themselves in the search for both offensive and defensive systems, the Soviets were more likely to take advantage of the novel and unpredictable nature of technology and to field an operational ABM system before the USA. What was more, even though they were eventually happy to negotiate away the option of a territorial missile defence in the SALT (Strategic Arms Limitation Treaty) negotiations, 1969–72, the Soviets had expressed committed faith in such developments. In a 1965 *Bulletin of the Atomic Scientists* article, General Nikolai Talensky argued that:

every decisive new means of attack inevitably leads to the development of a new means of defense. The sword produced the shield; the improvement of naval artillery caused battleships to be clad in plate armor; torpedo-carrying submarines produced a specific system of anti-submarine defense ...

---

[38] Edward Reiss, *The Strategic Defense Initiative* (Cambridge: Cambridge University Press, 1992) pp. 26–32.

[39] David S. Yost, *Soviet Ballistic Missile Defense and the Western Alliance* (Cambridge, MA: Harvard University Press, 1988) pp. 25–6; see also Jennifer Mathers, *The Russian Nuclear Shield from Stalin to Yeltsin* (Basingstoke: MacMillan, 2000). Ironically this process is arguably comparable to 'spiral development' as pursued by the Bush administration in contemporary BMD system.

There are no limits to creative human thinking, and the possibilities offered by modern science and technology are tremendous. I think it is theoretically and technically quite possible to counterbalance the absolute weapons of attack with equally absolute weapons of defense, thereby objectively eliminating war regardless of the desires of resisting governments. In our day, the human genius can do anything.[40]

The 'committee', though, was not alone in its support of missile defence to counter this Soviet enthusiasm. Despite Nitze's claim of modest budgetary means, the broader campaign for ABM was backed by significant industrial interests – defence corporations such as Boeing, Lockheed and Raytheon – that stood to gain financially from ABM deployment in the form of Safeguard.[41] In addition, following reports in the press at the height of the ABM debate in Congress, the army admitted that it had undertaken a large-scale public relations campaign to win support for the ABM programme. In February 1969, the Department of Defense released details of the plans for the campaign. Its objectives were 'gaining public understanding of the necessity' for ABM and establishing 'a favourable public attitude'. The campaign was planned by the Secretary of the Army and included Congressional lobbying, co-ordination with defence contractors and efforts to influence editors and reporters. It would encourage articles 'supporting the technical feasibility and operational effectiveness of ABM. Public relations tactics included tours for the media, Congressmen and scientific and civic groups.'[42]

Again, themes stressed by the infinite containment school appeared as basic assumptions within such pro-ABM arguments. The view of ex-USAF General Leon W. Johnson, responding to criticism of the Sentinel programme in 1968, exemplifies several of these positions:

If our scientists can build weapons to penetrate enemy defenses, they can build weapons to stop enemy weapons from penetrating our defenses. Too much is at stake to do less.

---

[40] General Nikolai Talensky, 'Missile Defense: a Response to Aggression' reprinted in Zbigniew Brzezinski (ed.) *Promise or Peril: the Strategic Defense Initiative* (Washington, DC: Ethics and Public Policy Centre, 1986) from *Bulletin of the Atomic Scientists*, February 1965, pp. 211–13.

[41] Reiss, *The Strategic Defense Initiative*, p. 31.

[42] Ibid., p. 29; cf. 'Major Lobby Effort Surrounds Sentinel ABM System', *Congressional Quarterly* (21 March 1969) p. 409.

Do you want the actions of our government colored primarily by Soviet actions rather than actions based upon a reasoned analysis of what is in the best interests of our country and the best interests of our trusting allies?

What is notable about the structure of Johnson's arguments is its contending moves. The first is its personalisation of ABM ('our scientists', 'our defences', 'the actions of our government') which represents (defensive) technology as an instrument of control. The second is the way in which Johnson, in a manner imitative of the above citation from the Soviet General Talensky, goes on to ground ABM efforts on the basis of a natural, depersonalised progression in weapons technology:

Each major weapons change and each spectacular technological advance leads to changes in the basic strategic principles of war. However, the pendulum swings, although sometimes slowly, and the old laws of force and counterforce, of action and reaction hold: When the offense outstrips the defense, intensive defensive efforts are applied, and defense is soon back in the picture.[43]

This, Johnson argued, constituted a 'never-ending contest' which made any talk of an 'ultimate weapon' premature and uninformed. Thus, while the justification for ABM is based on the benefits of human control over technology, the evidence for its feasibility is based on a generalised nominalisation[44] of 'technological advance' – a seemingly autonomous dynamic, but one that could be put to beneficial use.

Strategy, technology and defence

An important source of intellectual succour for ABM supporters also came in the form of a variety of strategic theories on nuclear weapons, and similar discursive techniques can be detected here. Just as several of the assumptions of the finite containment school overlapped with the 'national style' of nuclear weapons policy that had downplayed the role of defence – as seen initially in the assessments of Bernard Brodie and latterly in Thomas Schelling's approach to

---

[43] Quoted in Humphrey and Douglas, *Anti-Ballistic Missile: Yes or No?*, pp. 36–7.
[44] Nominalisation is used here in the sense of transforming a clause into a nominal or noun-like entity – see Norman Fairclough, *Analysing Discourse: Textual Analysis for Social Research* (London: Routledge, 2003), p. 13.

deterrence[45] – the pro-ABM camp drew on an intellectual stream that had much in common with the infinite containment philosophy.

The common ground between the infinite containment school, ABM supporters and this intellectual stream rested upon a shared scepticism towards the concept of mutual assured destruction (MAD). Most significantly, several prominent strategic thinkers at the influential RAND Corporation shared and endorsed the view of assured destruction as an erroneous and distorted basis for nuclear strategy. Although Colin Gray laments the influence of 'glorified accountants' – 'RAND-schooled economists appearing to be strategists' – on the policies of consecutive administrations in the period prior to the SALT talks, Pratt contends, 'Most of the people at RAND saw the ABM Treaty as "nuts" … Rand analysts generally viewed active defences as a good thing and discredited the idea that MAD was inherently stabilizing.'[46] The foremost articulation of this attack on MAD came from Fred Ikle, a long-time analyst for RAND, in his 1971 book *Every War Must End* and an article published in the January 1973 issue of *Foreign Affairs* entitled 'Can Nuclear Deterrence Last Out the Century?',[47] and from Herman Kahn who gave his support to the deployment of a 'thin' ABM system as a means to increase deterrence against attack and, in many situations, decrease casualties in the event of an attack.[48] Such views trickled down into popular debate. Pratt argues that 'Several hawkish senators were influenced by Ikle's writings' including Democratic Senator Henry 'Scoop' Jackson, de facto representative of the pro-ABM constituency in Congress.[49] David Goldfischer notes that in the popular press Kahn

---

[45] As Paul Williams notes, Schelling argued that nuclear weapons enhanced 'the importance of … coercion and deterrence, not of conquest and defence'.
'Thomas Schelling' in John Baylis and John Garnett (eds.) *Makers of Nuclear Strategy* (London: Pinter, 1991) pp. 120–35. See Schelling's *Arms and Influence* (New Haven: Yale University Press, 1966).

[46] Gray, *Nuclear Strategy and National Style*, p. 169; Erik K. Pratt, *Selling Strategic Defense: Interests, Ideologies and the Arms Race* (Boulder, CO: Lynne Rienner, 1990) p. 44.

[47] Fred C. Ikle, *Every War Must End* (New York: Columbia University Press, 1971).

[48] Herman Kahn, 'The Case for a Thin System' in Holst and Schneider, *Why ABM?*, pp. 63–90 and Herman Kahn, *On Escalation: Metaphors and Scenarios* (New York: Frederick A. Praeger, 1965) pp. 157–9.

[49] Pratt, *Selling Strategic Defense*, p. 44. Ikle would later go on to become Undersecretary of Defense for Policy under the Reagan administration. Jackson has been termed 'the Senator from Boeing' – Ken Silverstein, *Private Warriors* (New York: Verso, 2000) p. 231.

and Teller 'were speaking and writing with breezy optimism about how civil defense could make nuclear war tolerable', and missile defense fitted well with this 'optimism'.[50]

The most prominent supporter of missile defence associated with the RAND Corporation was Albert Wohlstetter, although Wohlstetter was actually dismissed from RAND in the early 1960s.[51] While at RAND Wohlstetter had been a key author of reports that heavily criticised the army's Nike–Zeus ABM programme (in favour of the air force's 'Wizard' system), and was also highly influential in the writing of the Gaither report which, as noted earlier, emphasised the necessity for ongoing research into defensive measures. His continued insistence that damage limitation remained a worthy effort placed him firmly in the pro-ABM camp.[52] In the mid-1960s, Wohlstetter 'became intrigued with ABMs' – based on the presumption that 'hardened' nuclear shelters for offensive weapons were no longer viable owing to upgrades in Soviet missiles – and became heavily involved in the Stanford Research Institute, or SRI.[53] The SRI functioned as an army think-tank, the main business of which was 'helping the Army come up with new justifications for a large-scale ABM system', and it formed the hub of the army's ABM public relations campaign noted above.[54] While at the SRI, Wohlstetter espoused the capacity of the Safeguard ABM system 'to defend the offense and, given this, at a small extra cost to provide a light area defense of population'.[55] He cautioned against failure to meet

---

[50] David Goldfischer, *The Best Defense: Policy Alternatives for US Nuclear Security from the 1950s to the 1990s* (Ithaca: Cornell University Press, 1993) p. 204.

[51] Fred Kaplan, *The Wizards of Armageddon* (Stanford, CA: Stanford University Press, 1983) p. 348.

[52] Kaplan (ibid.) cites Wohlstetter as a co-founder of the aforementioned 'Committee to Maintain a Prudent Defense Policy', as well as a telling influence on Paul Wolfowitz and Richard Perle – pp. 387–8. For more on these connections and their influence on recent US defense policy see Ivo H. Daalder and James M. Lindsay, *America Unbound: the Bush Revolution in Foreign Policy* (Washington, DC: Brookings Institution Press, 2003) pp. 24–30, and Andrew Bacevich, *The New American Militarism: How Americans are Seduced by War* (New York: Oxford University Press, 2005) pp. 147–74.

[53] Richard Rosencrance, 'Albert Wohlstetter' in Baylis and Garnett, *Makers of Nuclear Strategy*, pp. 57–69.

[54] Ibid.

[55] Albert Wohlstetter, 'The Case for Strategic Force Defense' in Holst and Schneider, *Why ABM?*, p. 121. For the classic statement of Wohlstetter's views on deterrence, damage limitation and survivability of nuclear forces see his 'The Delicate Balance of Terror', *Foreign Affairs*, 37:2 (1959) pp. 211–34.

innovation in offences, such as MIRVs, with corresponding developments in defences: 'In the 1970s unless we continue to make appropriate
decisions to meet technological change, once again the viability of a
large part of our second-strike force will be put in question.'[56]

The potential for novelty and unexpected advances in technological
development was thus stressed by Wohlstetter as a rationale for pursuing an ABM system, as it was by Johnson, and, in a form of argumentation that will recur in later chapters, construed through a
narrative reconstruction of technological development. 'At earlier
dates', he noted, military men and scientists alike 'were surprised by
the rapid Soviet achievement of the A-bomb, the H-bomb, advanced
jet engines, long-range turbo-prop bombers, airborne intercept radars,
and large-scale fissile-material production'. By the same logic, the
possibility of effective defensive technologies for the USA should not
be ruled out, even by such well-qualified critics of the ABM as Bethe,
Killian, Wiesner and York. Indeed, referring directly to these critics
Wohlstetter noted that:

> We have not been very good at predicting our own or adversary's technolo-
> gies. These matters are intrinsically uncertain. Eminent scientists at the end of
> the 1940s predicted that fusion weapons would be infeasible, and, if feasible,
> undeliverable, and, if delivered, could be used only against cities. Some of
> those who then thought the threat of fusion bombs against cities neither moral
> nor important strategically now take it to be both.[57]

Here Wohlstetter attempts to embed a general principle (technological
development is unpredictable – ergo ABM advances cannot be ruled
out) through direct and indirect intertextual references: directly with the
history of Soviet advances in weaponry; indirectly though historicising
his argument with cautionary tales of prior claims of infeasibility.

Missile defence promotion in the ABM Treaty era

Once the ABM Treaty had been enacted, advocates maintained their
argument that the USA had unnecessarily deprived itself of the opportunity to take advantage of its technological ingenuity in the realm of
defences. In 1977, then Secretary of Defense Donald Rumsfeld asserted

---

[56] Wohlstetter, 'The Case for Strategic Force Defense', p. 123.
[57] Ibid., p. 125, fn. 5.

that while mutual deterrence was perceived as being accepted by both parties in the ABM Treaty, 'It has become equally plausible to believe that the Soviets have never really agreed to this [MAD], and that they entered the ABM Treaty either because of severe resource constraints or because they feared that, without an agreement, US technology over the near term would give us a continuing and even growing advantage in this form of defense.'[58] While the ABM Treaty was supposedly 'in force', some doubted that it was having any effect whatsoever on Soviet efforts at missile defence: 'When we build, they build, when we stop building, they nevertheless continue to build,' Harold Brown, President Carter's Defense Secretary quipped in 1979.[59]

Still, as the 1980s approached, no consensus existed that pursuit of missile defences would leave the USA in a better position than would a strategy of deterrence. As Erik Pratt notes, 'Some saw exotic BMD as a technological saviour, others as a chimera – and still others believed the technologies were simply too premature to be tied to one potential application over another.'[60] With the prospects of 'exotic' BMD uncertain, key individuals and groups took it upon themselves to persuade political leaders in the USA that the time was right for missile defences, although 'Whether one sees these individuals as Don Quixotes or Galileos is largely a matter of faith,' Pratt adds.[61]

Within the literature referring to the immediate pre-SDI period, these groups are generally grouped into three, although with overlapping memberships and all sharing a broad commitment to the idea that missile defences could 'solve' the problem of the Cold War stand-off in favour of the USA. Two, commonly referred to as the 'laser lobby' (led by Republican Senator Malcolm Wallop and his aide Angelo Codevilla) and High Frontier (based around the Heritage Foundation think-tank and fronted by General Daniel Graham), emphasised that their ABM systems represented near-term options. Both sought to stress

[58] Secretary of Defense Donald Rumsfeld, Report to Congress on the FY 1978 Budget, FY 1979 Authorization Request and FY 1978–1982 Defense Programs, 14 January 1977, p. 67, http://www.dod.mil/pubs/foi/reading_room/246.pdf [last accessed 20 January 2009].
[59] Quoted in Keith B. Payne, 'Action–Reaction Metaphysics and Negligence', *The Washington Quarterly*, 24:4 (Autumn 2001) pp. 109–21, p. 115. *While Others Build: the Commonsense Approach to the Strategic Defense Initiative* (New York: Macmillan, 1988) was the title of a pro-SDI treatise by Angelo Codevilla.
[60] Pratt, *Selling Strategic Defense*, p. 72.   [61] Ibid.

that the criteria for a functioning ABM system could already be met, that 'all that was required to build their systems was an engineering effort – no new scientific breakthroughs were necessary'.[62] Wallop and Codevilla drew on presentations made to them by Maxwell Hunter, a senior aerospace engineer at the Lockheed Corporation with a long involvement with ballistic missile defences. By 1977, Hunter was convinced that laser technology could, in the near term, produce a revolution in warfare by ending the dominance of offensive strategic weapons: 'high energy lasers are proliferating, and space transportation is about to become sufficiently economical that, if used to place such lasers in space, an effective defence against even massive ballistic missile exchanges ... is possible'. Hunter, who made it his mission to try and enlighten policy-makers as to the benefits of laser technologies then in development, lamented the fact that the United States had seemingly concluded that its technology could no longer solve the problem posed by ICBMs and had instead 'turned to psychology rather than physics, diplomacy rather than engineering to protect the greatest power on the planet'.[63]

Graham and the High Frontier group also stressed the potential advances in ballistic missile defences allowed by the use of space-based technology, but advocated a non-nuclear option, that is, using interceptor missiles launched from space-based platforms to intercept incoming ICBMs. Graham argued that such interceptors were more feasible than lasers in the near term, and was convinced that adoption of the High Frontier proposal would, in effect, accomplish a 'technological end-run' around the Soviets, re-establishing US strategic superiority.[64] Essentially Graham rearticulated by now familiar themes in missile defence advocacy: the technology to achieve missile defences was already imminent, and the USA should be the first to avail of it in order to free its hands from the bonds of deterrence. The actual fine details of the High Frontier project were less apparent. Although it stressed the interconnection between industrial exploration of space and military command of this 'new high ground', Pratt argues that the High Frontier team 'appears to have had a program that was less a policy blueprint and more an articulation of a popular ideal'[65] – a

[62] Ibid., pp. 91–2.   [63] Hunter, quoted in Baucom, *The Origins of SDI*, pp. 121–2.
[64] Pratt, *Selling Strategic Defense*, p. 96.   [65] Ibid.

popular ideal that assumed the common sense utility of technology in achieving nuclear security.

Teller, speaking as the head of the Lawrence Livermore National Laboratory, shared the enthusiasm of the other two groups and their view on the benefits to be accrued from missile defences, but saw space-based lasers as a longer-term option, one which 'called for a push like that of the Manhattan Project' to accelerate what in his view were potentially revolutionary technologies.[66] Teller also believed it was critical to develop these technologies first, calling for research into directed energy weapons (DEWs) programmes to be paced by technology rather than funding given the importance of the task; in other words, that this research should be pursued regardless of cost. The 1970s had seen a mushrooming of such research projects focused on the development of DEWs, programmes which seemed to be making the fantastical a possibility. Even Donald Baucom, official historian of the Strategic Defense Initiative, gets swept away by the prospects for laser technology in his history of the roots of SDI:

The roots of these exotic weapons are found in science fiction and the realization before World War Two that nature produces radiations that can kill human beings . . . In the third century BC, the Greek scientist Archimedes reportedly used sunlight to destroy the ships of a Roman fleet that had laid siege to the port of Syracuse. Using concave mirrors that he had constructed, Archimedes supposedly set the Roman vessels ablaze by focusing the sun's rays on their sails . . . More recently, a description of a directed energy weapon was presented in H. G. Wells's famous science fiction novel, *The War of the Worlds* [where] he described how the Martians used a heat ray to kill people.[67]

Although the use of such references opened the way for comparisons with science fiction, Teller was convinced that DEWs were feasible, and, in common with the laser lobby and High Frontier, 'expressed a powerful faith in technology and the productive potential of the US capitalist economy to outrace the Soviets'.[68] In addition, missile defence

---

[66] See Teller, *The Legacy of Hiroshima* and *Freedom in an Age of Technology: an Address* (New York: International and Academic Technical Publications, 1972) for the roots of Teller's views. See also William J. Broad, *Teller's War: the Top-Secret Story Behind the Star Wars Deception* (New York: Simon and Shuster, 1992).

[67] Baucom, *The Origins of SDI*, p. 105.   [68] Ibid., p. 79.

enthusiasts were offering an alternative vision of the strategic balance, one which they sought to make more plausible and concrete through stressing the potential applications of new technologies – complete with diagrams and artists' impressions – in the pages of *Aviation Week and Space Technology* and their own publications. Effectively, as Yanarella argues, these three groups 'offered support [to the case for missile defence] by generating a strategic framework and technical vocabulary to justify the right's bipolar views of the world and to lend credence to its technological optimism regarding even the most exotic proposals for weapons development'.[69] In short, through both linguistic and visual texts, post-ABM Treaty proponents of missile defence sought to re-articulate the existing order of the contemporary political and strategic discourse in a manner that rendered missile defence a realistic, desirable and necessary option for the USA.

Conclusion

The development of a pro-ABM constituency as part of this first debate over missile defence is worth noting for a number of reasons. First of all it sought to articulate and promote missile defence as a concept at both intellectual and popular levels. With regard to the latter, the historical record shows the arguments made by this constituency were ultimately trumped by the NIMBY ('Not in my back yard') phenomenon in the debate over ABM, and failed to escape its popular association with (even) more dubious forms of civil defence.[70] However, the effort to promote ABM fostered a strong political and intellectual grounding as well as institutional overlaps and it is during this period that many future proponents of missile defence formed their views on the issue. As we shall see, many of these early views and the methods by which they were articulated have remained central to arguments for missile defence in its later incarnations: the instrumental value of missile defence, the broad assumption of technological improvement, and technological development as a dynamic that should not be constrained. Yet, as we shall see in the following chapter, the pro-ABM constituency was always vulnerable to the counter-claim that an autonomous dynamic of technological development was itself something to be feared.

[69] Yanarella, *The Missile Defense Controversy*, p. 190.
[70] Goldfischer, *The Best Defense*, p. 213.

4 | *Post-war missile defence and the language of technological fears*

Introduction

As discussed at length in Part One, the common sense appeal of instrumental theory is rarely unaccompanied by its substantivist opposite: the view that technology is not just something to be used, but has a determinative impact on social life. This opposition is frequently interpreted as an inversion of the progressive connotations of instrumentalism. 'What makes substantivism so very gloomy', Feenberg asserts, is that whereas instrumentalism started out as 'a cheerful doctrine of progress', substantivism implies that 'technology is inherently biased toward domination. Far from correcting its flaws, further advance can only make things worse'[1] – witness the sense of futility that permeates the philosophy of substantivism as discussed in chapters 1 and 2. The frequent corollary of the substantivist view, then, is that technology, far from being an instrument of human control, is out of control; it now controls us.

To begin to show how this has developed historically, this chapter illustrates the occurrence of this substantivist strain in early debates on missile defence in the United States. It does so by highlighting substantivist understandings and accounts of key issues in relation to missile defence in the period leading up to the ABM treaty of 1972 – the launch of *Sputnik* and reactions to it, Secretary of Defense Robert McNamara's attitude towards missile defence, and broader attitudes towards the nuclear arms race. The chapter shows how these more substantivist interpretations relate to the early case for missile defence, and by way of conclusion it attempts to outline how and why instrumentalist and substantivist elements, though contradictory, began to be combined in discourse promoting missile defence during this period.

---

[1] Andrew Feenberg, *Questioning Technology* (London: Routledge, 2001) p. 3.

Sputnik and substantivism

Initially at least, as noted previously, the United States' status as the world's first nuclear-armed power seemed both to reinforce and increase American faith in technology and further embed the notion of technology as a key instrument of US power. During the post-war decades, however, Soviet advances in the same technology gave cause to rethink the assumption that technology could and would render the USA impervious to attack. In August 1949 came the news that the Soviets too now possessed atomic weapons, and developments in the 1950s further caused a crisis of confidence in the strength of American technology. Chief among these was, of course, the Soviet launch of *Sputnik I*, the world's first artificial earth satellite, on 4 October 1957. 'No event focused popular attention on America's vulnerabilities to attack more,' Lawrence Freedman claims.[2] The Soviet Union's demonstration of its potential reach, as well as its perceived display of technological superiority, struck at the heart of the hopes invested in technology as the guarantor of US security, as well as denting the commonly held American self-perception as the world's leading technological power. The promise of progress associated with instrumentalism seemed to have been revoked. As Freedman notes: 'The US had embarked on a nuclear strategy to ensure an upper hand over the Soviet Union; now the position might be fundamentally reversed.'[3] Hence, he continues, in so far as 'Sputnik demonstrated that the Soviet Union could operate as a modern industrial power in its ability to mobilize and exploit scientific and engineering talent' it served as 'a watershed in American attitudes on technology and the strategic balance'.[4]

Evidence of this 'watershed' in attitudes can be found both in the declarations of the time and in subsequent recollections of the *Sputnik* launch. President Eisenhower's bleak interpretation months later in his 'Introductory Note' to NSC 5814/1 'US Policy on Outer Space' of 20 June 1958 was that:

Perhaps the starkest facts which confront the United States in the immediate and foreseeable future are (1) the USSR has surpassed the United States and

[2] Lawrence Freedman, *The Evolution of Nuclear Strategy*, 3rd edition (Basingstoke: Palgrave, 2003) p. 131.
[3] Ibid.   [4] Ibid.

the free world in scientific and technological accomplishments in outer space, which have captured the imagination and admiration of the world; (2) the USSR, if it maintains its present superiority in the exploration of outer space, will be able to use that superiority as a means of undermining the prestige and leadership of the United States; and (3) the USSR, if it should be the first to achieve a significantly superior military capability in outer space, could create an imbalance of power in favour of the Sino-Soviet Bloc and pose a direct military threat to US security.[5]

Although Eisenhower followed this by immediately adding that 'The Security of the United States requires that we meet the challenges with resourcefulness and vigor', there is in this passage not simply a clear indication of the unexpected, surprise nature of the Soviet launch and its blow to American confidence, but also a real sense that the USA could become subject to the demands, even if only temporarily, of Soviet technological superiority. Here, to some extent at least, the heroic vision of technology as America's strong-suit is replaced by the fear that new technology could become the very means by which American power would be constricted, ironically, as a result of a chain of technological development initiated by the United States with the development of the atomic bomb.

As Paul B. Stares points out, this fear manifested itself both in concern over the capacity for attack allowed by missiles of intercontinental reach and in the less tangible fear that the USA would become 'blackmailed' or 'dominated' from space.[6] Nowhere are these fears more concisely expressed than in the recollections of James Killian, Eisenhower's chief science adviser:

As it beeped in the sky, *Sputnik I* created a crisis of confidence that swept the country like a windblown forest fire. Overnight there developed a widespread fear that the country lay at the mercy of the Russian military machine and that our own government and its military arm had abruptly lost the power to defend the mainland itself, much less to maintain US prestige and leadership in the international arena. Confidence in American science, technology, and education suddenly evaporated.[7]

---

[5] President Dwight D. Eisenhower, as quoted in Paul B. Stares, *Space Weapons and US Strategy: Origins and Development* (London: Croom Helm, 1985) p. 38.

[6] Stares, *Space Weapons and US Strategy*, p. 19. Stares quotes Tom Wolfe's interpretation that 'Nothing less than *control of the heavens* was at stake' – *The Right Stuff* (New York: Bantam, 1980) p. 57.

[7] James R. Killian, *Sputnik, Scientists and Eisenhower* (Cambridge, MA: MIT Press, 1977) p. 7.

Killian's interpretation exemplifies the use of substantivist tropes as a means to comprehend *Sputnik* and its significance. Gone are the hallmarks of instrumentalist optimism: hope, a heroic sense of invention and faith in an increased capacity to act through technology leading ultimately to greater control over national destiny. In its place are fear, foreboding and a sense of crisis that American capacity for action could well be beyond its control. In short, American confidence in its technology and the infrastructure entrusted to produce it is replaced by a vision of enslavement to a foreign power itself almost machine-like in quality: a perfectly substantivist interpretation.

Several historians attest that *Sputnik* had a similar, if not more profound, effect on the American public.[8] Against the heady American technological optimism of the 1950s embodied by 'futuristic' everyday technologies such as the fins of the Cadillac, the sleek modern lines of the Fender Stratocaster guitar, labour-saving devices within the home, and in utopian science fiction of the time,[9] *Sputnik* registered as a major shock to the US popular consciousness. Rip Bulkeley and Graham Spinardi note the widespread public fascination with the possibility of futuristic space weapons in the early 1950s fostered, for example, by the dissemination of plans and blueprints for nuclear-armed space-stations by Wernher Von Braun in *Collier's* magazine; a 'direct result', they argue, was that Americans 'now viewed the Russian achievement with growing apprehension'. *Sputnik* had 'brought the nuclear threat directly and inescapably to every Main Street for the very first time'.[10] Stares notes this widespread sense of panic in the popular press, and Peter J. Roman concurs that Soviet boasts of intercontinental ballistic missile (ICBM) tests months prior 'now took on a grave new light',[11] as does Freedman:

---

[8] As opposed to Eisenhower himself, who was simultaneously relatively sanguine about US ability to respond to the *Sputnik* launch, based on covert intelligence gleaned from U2 reconnaissance, and yet hamstrung in his ability to convey this confidence – see Robert A. Divine, *The Sputnik Challenge* (Oxford: Oxford University Press, 1993) and Saki Dockrill, *Eisenhower's New-Look National Security Policy, 1953–61* (Basingstoke: Macmillan, 1996).

[9] Colin Chant (ed.) *Science, Technology and Everyday Life, 1870–1950* (London: Routledge, 1989); Thomas M. Disch, *The New Improved Sun: an Anthology of Utopian Science Fiction* (New York: Harper, 1976).

[10] Rip Bulkeley and Graham Spinardi, *Space Weapons: Deterrence or Delusion?* (Oxford: Polity Press, 1986) p. 16.

[11] Stares, *Space Weapons and US Strategy*; Peter J. Roman, *Eisenhower and the Missile Gap* (Ithaca, NY: Cornell University Press, 1995) p. 31.

'*Sputnik* pushed these dark thoughts to the fore. This achievement in space captured the popular imagination in a way that sparse and subdued reports of monitored ICBM tests could not.'[12] As Andreas Wenger concludes, 'the shock of *Sputnik* was profound: the United States had been challenged in the one field – science and technology – in which almost everybody had taken American preeminence for granted. *Sputnik* led to a wave of near-hysteria.'[13]

Substantivism and the missile defence debate

This near hysteria forced the Eisenhower administration into a range of actions that would have significant implications for missile defence. Post-*Sputnik* the 'missile gap' seemed to constitute a reality in the public perception. *Sputnik* transformed US efforts on space 'overnight into a national obsession to wrest the lead from the Soviet Union', one which would not end until the moon landing and which, in the intervening period, created pressures for a vastly expanded space effort.[14] This expansion included increased funding and research into a range of space weapons proposals. In practical terms, as Stares notes, construing *Sputnik* as a challenge to be met ensured that 'The services and aerospace companies both sensed that "rich pickings" would be available in the post-Sputnik budgets.'[15] As well as inspiring schemes such as the Argus Project, an ill-fated scheme intended to create an atmospheric shield against ICBMs through exploding nuclear warheads in space, the perceived need to monitor and track Soviet efforts in space led to the formation of the Ballistic Missile Early-Warning System (BMEWS) – a new system of tracking radars deployed in Greenland (Thule), Alaska (Clear) and Britain (Fylingdales) – which would become central components in subsequent missile defence initiatives.

The sense of crisis, Bulkeley and Spinardi contend, led to the consolidation of tentative missile defence initiatives, previously the subject of heated inter-service rivalries, exclusively within the US Army in January 1958. Early missile defence advocates, such as House majority leader John McCormack, were keen to promote the army's Nike–Zeus

---

[12] Freedman, *The Evolution of Nuclear Strategy*, p. 131.
[13] Andreas Wenger, *Living with Peril: Eisenhower, Kennedy and Nuclear Weapons* (Oxford: Rowan and Littlefield, 1997) p. 154.
[14] Stares, *Space Weapons and US Strategy*, p. 39.   [15] Ibid., p. 48.

project – and American industry in general – as up to the challenge posed by the Soviets. McCormack admonished the administration to 'close the gap in our missile posture, muzzle the mad-dog missile threat of the Soviet Union, loose the Zeus through America's magnificent production line'.[16]

At this point, however, no consensus existed that missile defences were feasible, as was discussed in chapter 3 as a characteristic of the split between 'infinite' and 'finite' containment schools within America's scientific-political elite. Nowhere was this spilt better represented than in the respective readings of the two schools on the future development of nuclear weapons technology epitomised in two key reports of the 1950s, the Killian report (1955) and the Gaither report (1957).[17] The Killian panel, centred around the aforementioned James Killian, was representative of the finite containment school discussed in chapter 3. Its report foresaw decades of mutual US–Soviet expansion of nuclear forces which, if left to continue uncontrolled, would proceed to a perilous stalemate. Consistent with this view, the Killian panel saw little future for anti-missile technology.

The Gaither panel incorporated the views of Edward Teller and Albert Wohlstetter, and hence might be said to be representative of the infinite containment school. Compiled during the months immediately before and after the launch of *Sputnik*, the report depicted a 'period of extremely unstable equilibrium' caused by the expansion of offensive arsenals, where a 'temporary technical advance' (such as represented by *Sputnik* or, pertinently, in ABM technology) 'could give either nation the ability to come near to annihilating the other'.[18]

What is interesting here is that though these two reports were diametrically opposed on the issue of missile defence, both relied in common on the overt technological determinism associated with substantivist thought in so far as they both envisaged a reciprocal technological arms race that would determine the future international system.[19] Both the Killian and Gaither reports can in this sense be said to indicate the gradual adoption of substantivist (or at least quasi-substantivist)

---

[16] Quoted in Bulkeley and Spinardi, *Space Weapons*, p. 33.
[17] On the importance of the Killian and Gaither reports in shaping the American strategic debate of the 1950s see Freedman, *Evolution of Nuclear Strategy*, pp. 150–5.
[18] As quoted in Wenger, *Living With Peril*, p. 8.
[19] Freedman, *Evolution of Nuclear Strategy*, pp. 146–62.

thinking into the lexicon of American policy-making, and both constitute influential instances of the formal incorporation of the sense of
'alarm and urgency' and the feared loss of control common in popular
and media reactions to *Sputnik* into the policy debate.[20] In both cases,
though, the picture as painted in the substantivist philosophy of
Heidegger and Ellul, as discussed in chapter 1, is necessarily left incom-
plete. In Heidegger's formulation the only escape from a technologically
determined future is through a return to a 'purer' form of techné found
in classical Greek civilisation, a prospect that he held out little hope
for.[21] The characteristic fallacy of instrumentalism, in Heidegger's
view, was to assume that further technological innovation could provide a way out of the binds that modern technology had itself created.

By contrast the Gaither committee was highly optimistic that missile
defence provided an entirely feasible means to offset Soviet advances in
missile technology. Even the Killian panel qualified its prediction of a
strategic stalemate with the recommendation of an emphasis on technological innovation. Its report predicted that the 1960s would be 'So
fraught with danger to the US' that little option remained except that
'we should push all promising technological developments'.[22] The
report was highly pessimistic in its expectations for decisive technological breakthroughs: 'We see no certainty', it declared, 'that the condition of stalemate can be changed through science and technology.'
Immediately after this apparent rejection of a 'technological fix', however, the Killian report allows a chink of hope: 'This does not mean that
some new unimagined weapon or development, far afield from any
present weapon system, might not provide an advantage to one side
or the other.'[23] Escape from the arms race was therefore expected to be
unlikely, but not impossible.

The Killian report thus represents a hedged form of substantivism
that would come to be the bane of both ABM activists and critics of the
nuclear arms race alike. It seemed to disparage the prospect of a

---

[20] For further expansion on this see Robert H. Johnson, *Improbable Dangers:
US Conceptions of Threat in the Cold War and After* (New York: St Martin's
Press, 1994) p. 42.
[21] Martin Heidegger, 'The Question Concerning Technology' in M. Heidegger,
The Question Concerning Technology, and Other Essays, trans. W. Lovitt
(New York: Harper and Row, 1977). See also chapter 2.
[22] Quoted in Wenger, *Living With Peril*, p. 148.
[23] Quoted in Freedman, *Evolution of Nuclear Strategy*, p. 150.

breakthrough in defensive technology, if not breakthroughs per se, whilst simultaneously endorsing the expansion of offensive forces. The main focal point of this ire in the 1960s was Secretary of Defense Robert McNamara. Initially part of Kennedy's team that came to power on the back of campaigning on the issue of the 'missile gap', McNamara's defence policy arguably represents the political instantiation of the hedged, truncated form of substantivism found in the Killian report. To some extent this might come as a surprise. Superficially, McNamara represents the arch-instrumentalist. In symbolic terms, McNamara could be said to be a true representative of America's technological legacy, the literal inheritor (and saviour) of Fordism during his tenure as president of the same motor company in the post-war years. Simultaneously, the adoption of the same managerial techniques employed at Ford into the Pentagon is a principal reason why Stanley Hoffman famously identified the McNamara era as the prime form of 'skill thinking' in American foreign policy – the 'engineering or instrumental outlook' that every political problem could have a rational, technical solution.[24]

Contrasting with this are McNamara's own reflections on the nature of the arms race and his frequent reference to and use of substantivist metaphors and motifs. As noted above and in the previous chapter, McNamara accepted key precepts espoused by the infinite containment scientists and epitomised in the Killian report: that advances in offensive nuclear weapons technology would always outpace innovation in defensive technology, reinforced in his view once the MIRVing of nuclear missiles became possible. McNamara frequently took this vision of the development of an (offensive) arms race and embellished it with descriptions remarkably resonant with the technology-out-of-control theme of substantivist philosophy and literature. In his reluctant approval of plans for a 'thin' anti-ballistic missile system in September 1967, McNamara warned that 'There is a kind of mad momentum intrinsic to the development of all new nuclear weaponry. If a weapons system works – and works well – there is a strong pressure from many directions to procure and deploy the weapon out of all proportion to the prudent level required.'[25]

---

[24] Stanley Hoffman, *Gulliver's Troubles, Or the Setting of American Foreign Policy* (New York: McGraw Hill, 1968).

[25] From McNamara's speech to the Editors of United Press International in San Francisco, 18 September 1967, reprinted in Hubert H. Humphrey and William O. Douglas, *Anti-Ballistic Missile: Yes or No?* (New York: Hill and Wang, 1968).

Even more explicit in this sense is McNamara's *Essence of Security: Reflections in Office*.[26] Pre-empting the pessimistic tone of Theodor Adorno, for example, he argues that 'The road leading from the Stone Age to the ICBM, though it may have been more than a million years in the building, seems to have run in a single direction.'[27] McNamara shows a keen awareness of the fear that 'somehow society, all society – East and West – had fallen victim to a bureaucratic tyranny of technology that is gradually depersonalizing and alienating modern man himself'.[28] This he argued, in line with the general tenets of substantivism, is a concomitant after-effect of technological progress.[29] Indeed, in keeping with the account put forward in chapter 2, McNamara even reckoned this to be a specifically American fate: 'It has been the American practice from the beginning to take the work loads off the backs of men and put them on the backs of machines.'[30] Here too he references the innately 'Jeffersonian' nature of the American desire to use technology as a means to assert and protect American independence.[31] However, in the process, in McNamara's view, 'it is also true that we are becoming tools'.[32]

In his reflections McNamara advises us not to succumb either to the attractive simplicity of instrumentalism or, equally, to the entire rejection of modern technology:

> It is too simple an answer to reply that technology itself is morally neutral and that man must simply take care to retain his human control. The more profound question is whether or not complex technology narrows or widens the alternatives available for human control. It is clear enough that man conditions his technology; what is less clear is the extent to which technology conditions man. The degree and moral quality of that conditioning is a dilemma we must face, but we must face it and solve it and not merely fall into an escapist and emotional romanticism.[33]

---

[26] Robert McNamara, *The Essence of Security: Reflections in Office* (London: Hodder and Stoughton, 1968).

[27] Ibid., p. 31. Adorno: 'No universal history leads from savagery to humanitarianism but there is one leading from the slingshot to the megaton bomb' – see chapter 2.

[28] McNamara, *Essence of Security*, p. 114.

[29] Ibid. [30] Ibid., p. 115. [31] Ibid., p. 117. See chapter 3.

[32] Ibid., p. 116. [33] Ibid., p. 116.

Elsewhere, however, he notes that 'it is unlikely that today Jefferson would fret much about being folded, bent or mutilated by the computer. It is somewhat more likely that he would invent a better one.'[34]

Hence McNamara seems to reject unconditional instrumental optimism, but at the same time he refuses to endorse completely the substantivist outlook perceived in the 'escapist and emotional romanticism' he associated with anti-nuclear sentiment. As Bulkeley and Spinardi put it, 'McNamara himself embodied the *contradiction between*, firstly, a public acceptance of mutual vulnerability and mutual deterrence, and secondly, a constant striving to discover the "technological fix" that might get deterrence back to its bygone one-way form.'[35] In practical terms, the first of these impulses came to prominence in the widespread dissemination of the 'action–reaction' thesis – an almost mechanical process of spiralling weapons production seemingly in accordance with the substantivist vision of a technologically determined iron cage – as a 'virtual law of strategic relations'.[36] In seeming contradiction, the second impulse saw an increase in efforts at attaining US nuclear superiority through increase and innovation in offensive missile technology, a requirement of the policy of assured destruction.

The popular appeal of substantivism

As the passages above indicate, although McNamara may have couched his policy appeals in the language and images of substantivism he failed to take the logic of this view to its conclusion. The foreboding consequences of nuclear technology-out-of-control could be ameliorated by assuring US nuclear superiority, and latterly, as this prospect seemingly receded into a condition of mutually assured destruction, through the negotiation of arms control agreements.

Others were prepared to carry the substantivist image to its conclusion. As Allan M. Winkler notes, fiction and film provide a window on contemporary perspectives of the nuclear arms race, and here we find several additions to the substantivist canon. Eugene Burdick and Harvey Wheeler's highly popular 1962 novel *Fail-Safe* imagined a scenario in which technical malfunction launched a US nuclear attack. Though fictional, the authors stipulated a 'problem that is already upon

[34] Ibid., p. 117.   [35] Bulkeley and Spinardi, *Space Weapons*, p. 57, emphasis added.
[36] Freedman, *Evolution of Nuclear Strategy*, p. 241.

us ... the erosion of human accountability ... It's as if human beings had evaporated and their places were taken by computers.'[37] A similar premise appeared in Stanley Kubrick's even more familiar and acclaimed *Dr Strangelove or: How I Learned to Stop Worrying and Love the Bomb* (1964) which portrays, as Winkler puts it, 'a more vivid and absurd, even if more pessimistic tale of a mad world become prisoner to its monstrous machines' and 'carried the logic of the nuclear age to its ludicrous extreme'.[38] The prevalence of this theme in *Fail-Safe*, *Dr Strangelove* and subsequent films such as *2001: A Space Odyssey* (1968) and *Colossus: The Forbin Project* (1970) has also been analysed in detail by Paul N. Edwards in his *The Closed World: Computers and the Politics of Discourse in Cold War America*.[39] Edwards argues that anxieties about the increasing automation and computerisation of nuclear and defence systems in 1960s America were manifested in such films via the recurrent theme of 'closed' technological worlds where human control over technology is either radically diminished or even entirely absent.[40] The theme was picked up in social critique too. J.K. Galbraith spoke of a 'technological imperative' emanating from the structure of a new 'industrial system', and Hebert Marcuse's declaration that 'Auschwitz continues to haunt, not the memory but the accomplishments of man – the space flights; the rockets and missiles; the electronic plants', neatly captured the feeling that the technological 'progress' of the post-war years held a darker side.[41]

Such thinking was not merely restricted to Kubrick's parody, nor to the New Left of the 1960s. At what cost, George Kennan likewise wondered, had the USA started down the path of the revolution in weapons technology?

[37] Quoted in Allan M. Winkler, *Life under a Cloud: American Anxiety about the Bomb* (Chicago: University of Illinois Press, 1999) p. 177. *Fail-Safe* was subsequently adapted into a film version released in 1964.
[38] Ibid., pp. 177–8.
[39] Paul N. Edwards, *The Closed World: Computers and the Politics of Discourse in Cold War America* (Cambridge MA: MIT Press, 1996) pp. 316–27.
[40] In *2001: A Space Odyssey*, for example, Edwards argues that HAL, the artificially intelligent computer that controls the spaceship *Discovery* in the film, 'represents computers as self-directed technological juggernauts. HAL controls a closed world, human-made but no longer human-centered' – *The Closed World*, p. 323.
[41] J.K. Galbraith, *The New Industrial State* (London: Penguin, 1974); Herbert Marcuse, *One-Dimensional Man: Studies in the Ideology of Advanced Industrial Society*, 2nd edition (London: Routledge, 1991) p. 247.

The technological realities of this competition are constantly changing from month to month and from year to year. Are we to flee like haunted creatures from one defensive device to another, each more costly and humiliating than the one before, cowering underground one day, breaking up our cities the next, attempting to surround ourselves with elaborate shields on the third, concerned only to prolong the length of our lives while sacrificing all the values for which it might be worth while to live at all.[42]

Even scientists involved in government policy on nuclear weapons seemed to accept the technology-out-of-control motif. Herbert York, physicist on the Manhattan Project, asserted that the 'technological side of the arms race has a life of its own, almost independent of policy and politics', echoing the pessimistic view of human agency characteristic of substantivism.[43] As Yanarella notes, York and other key figures in the infinite containment school became increasingly pessimistic about the possibilities of harnessing military technology as the Pentagon further institutionalised the seemingly relentless pursuit of an improved nuclear arsenal.[44]

Ralph Lapp, another physicist who had worked on both the A-bomb and the H-bomb, provides an even more thoroughgoing and pessimistic account centred on the technology-out-of-control analogue of a 'runaway arms race'. 'Somewhere along this road to destruction', he lamented, 'man has lost his way and let his steps be guided by the compass of technology. Whenever a new weapons possibility beckoned, society meekly moved in this direction, without questioning the consequences. The natural sciences, for so long supreme in the grandeur of their isolation, became the dictators of weapons events.'[45] President John F. Kennedy's declared intention in his inaugural address of 21 January 1961 to close the 'missile gap' ('We dare not tempt them with weakness. For only when our arms are sufficient beyond doubt can we be certain they will never be employed'[46]) may have been an elegant rhetorical

[42] George Kennan, *Russia, the Atom and the West* (New York: Harper, 1958) p. 54. Quoted in Freedman, *Evolution of Nuclear Strategy*, p. 153.

[43] Herbert F. York, *Race to Oblivion: a Participant's View of the Arms Race* (New York: Simon and Schuster, 1970) p. 180.

[44] Ernest J. Yanarella, *The Missile Defense Controversy: Technology in Search of a Mission* (Lexington, KY: University Press of Kentucky, 2002) p. 165.

[45] Ralph E. Lapp, *Arms Beyond Doubt: the Tyranny of Weapons Technology* (New York: Cowles, 1970) p. 3.

[46] Quoted in ibid., p. 8.

move, but, in Lapp's view, the implications of this stance had locked the USA into an unwinnable race.[47] In doing so technology had taken on a life of its own, an apocalyptic but irresistible force that had rendered America a subservient garrison state in the process:

The control of a dictatorial weapons technology has become the nation's most urgent problem. Already it encompasses our lives. Its hidden fruit lies deeply buried in a thousand prairie sites. It would ring our decaying cities with a chain of killer-missiles to fend off an attack that would usher in 'mankind's final war.' It would seduce to its temple the minds of our society. America would in the process become a fortress with ramparts stretched from shore to shore, bracketing a garrison state.[48]

In these visions the nuclear juggernaut seemed unstoppable, and attempts to shield against it were merely prisoner to the same way of thinking.

The technological imperative?

All this is not to say that substantivism enjoyed universal acceptance in the post-war or even post-*Sputnik* years. Proponents of the view often argued that the nuclear arms race was in large part a result of the existence and institutionalisation of a 'technological imperative', the sort of 'mad momentum' identified by McNamara. This concept can be traced to Oppenheimer's well-known reflection in the wake of the atomic bomb that: 'When you see something that is technically sweet, you go ahead and do it and you argue about what to do about it only after you have had your technical success'; and as the US–Soviet arms race seemed to be spiralling out of control in the 1960s, Lapp described the technological imperative as the view that 'if a weapons system *could* be made, then it *would* be made'.[49]

Not all practitioners shared Lapp's characterisation. Jack Ruina, a former director of ARPA (the Pentagon's 'Advanced Research Projects Agency') in the 1960s, directly cautioned against overstating the prevalence of any 'technological imperative' in weapons development:

---

[47] Robert F. Kennedy expressed the general fear of losing control over events in this regard during the Cuban missile crisis in *Thirteen Days: a Memoir of the Cuban Missile Crisis* (New York: W. W. Norton, 1971).
[48] Lapp, *Arms Beyond Doubt*, p. 191.   [49] Ibid., p. 31, emphasis in original.

Some writers refer to a 'technological imperative' at work – that is, if a weapon can be made it will be made. There is no doubt some truth to this, but the concept is overly simplistic. There are restraints to the temptation to develop and deploy, without discrimination, the technologically possible ... we did restrain ourselves from developing shipborne nuclear ballistic missiles, bombs in orbit, 100-megaton bombs, and many other technically feasible systems.[50]

Yanarella and Goldfischer also argue that the seeming self-evidence of a technological imperative has more prosaic political-bureaucratic origins.[51] Weapons R&D had become institutionalised within the Defense Department in the late 1950s; added to this was McNamara's penchant for long-range technological planning (usually five years) which he himself admitted forced speculation as to decisions on deployments 'which our opponents, themselves, may not have made'.[52] As a result, Yanarella argues, 'technological developments in the areas of offensive and defensive weaponry more and more took on the image of rational systems evolving in complete detachment from human control and intervention – even, and especially, to the defence planners whose assumptions, decisions, and actions fueled and perpetuated the pace and course of technological change'.[53]

Less sympathetic critics of the McNamara era argue that very often the Secretary of Defense and Pentagon officials simply used arguments based on the existence of a 'technological imperative', construed in a particular way, in order to justify policy decisions. For Stein, 'McNamara spoke of "technological exuberance" as the driving force in the arms race, a theme that predates McNamara in both the scholarly and the popular literature and one that has been echoed since time and again', but adds that 'It is a theme, however, that is overdrawn.'[54] To John Erickson, reference to a technologically driven arms race was also simply a scapegoat policy-makers employed to avoid responsibility for

---

[50] Jack P. Ruina, 'Aborted Military Systems' in B. T. Feld, G. W. Greenwood, G. W. Rathjens and S. Weinberg (eds.) *The Impact of New Technologies on the Arms Race* (Cambridge, MA: MIT Press, 1971) p. 320.

[51] Yanarella, *The Missile Defense Controversy*, p. 16; David Goldfischer, *The Best Defense: Policy Alternatives for US Nuclear Security from the 1950s to the 1990s* (Ithaca, NY: Cornell University Press, 1993) pp. 116–46.

[52] McNamara, quoted in Yanarella, *The Missile Defense Controversy*, p. 101.

[53] Yanarella, *The Missile Defense Controversy*, p. 100.

[54] Jonathan B. Stein, *From H-Bomb to Star Wars: the Politics of Strategic Decision Making* (Lexington, MA: Lexington Books, 1986) p. 3.

an arms spiral: 'The villain of the piece in more than one case has been made weapons technology along with *Homo technicus*: the creation of the nuclear mystique, which is rubbing off so disastrously throughout the tiers of the international power structure, was a political act, which technology in its various forms was called to undo or unmask. The political determinants remain of primary importance.'[55]

Early missile defence advocacy as pure instrumentalism?

Some of the strongest criticisms of the technology-out-of-control argument came from those positively predisposed towards missile defence. On the face of it at least, the early ABM proponents appear to be wilful instrumentalists in their confident assurance that American missile defence technology would ensure Cold War superiority. The idea of a technological imperative construed as a conditioning arms race by McNamara and, more strongly, as a determinative force by York and Lapp – three ABM opponents – is seemingly anathema to the instrumentalist notion that politics (and hence people) determine the use of technology and not vice versa. Albert Wohlstetter, among those positively disposed towards the idea of strategic defence, described what he saw as the 'narrowly technological component' of such decisions as the development of the atomic bomb and hydrogen bomb, implicitly rejecting the weight attributed by some to the technological imperative in strategic policy. 'Technology', he asserted, 'is an important part, but very far from the whole of strategy.'[56]

Likewise, the notion that the arms race proceeded on the basis of reciprocal technological innovations leading ultimately to stalemate (the 'action–reaction' dynamic), and that this dynamic could therefore be slowed only by mutual agreement, was also rejected by the majority of missile defence advocates. '[A]s to the question of parity', Edward Teller declared in 1963, 'in a very rapidly developing field, where a lot of ingenuity can be involved, I don't see any reason to expect that parity will be accomplished. I think that the harder worker will win out, and so

[55] John Erickson, *The Military Technical Revolution: Its Impact on Strategy and Foreign Policy* (New York: F. A. Praeger, 1966) p. 18.

[56] Albert Wohlstetter, 'Strategy and the Natural Scientists' in Robert Gilpin and Christopher Wright (eds.) *Scientists and National Policy-Making* (New York: Columbia University Press, 1964) p. 178.

far the Russians have worked much harder.'[57] In this vein missile defence advocates continued to see technology as a rapidly developing, unpredictable source of strategic advantage that could and should be harnessed by the USA, just as Americans had in the past through 'working harder'. In doing so they seemed to be reiterating the instrumentalist notion of a technical solution to a political problem.

However, just as McNamara embodied certain contradictions in his espoused views of technological development, there are already anomalies and seeds of contradiction within the early pro-missile defence position. The first is that this position rejected not the existence of a technological imperative per se, but merely the way it had been interpreted by McNamara and others. In fact, a key tenet of the pro-ABM argument was that a technological imperative for missile defence already existed, or would come to exist in the future as the next logical step in weapons technology (as discussed in the previous chapter). ABM opponents, they argued, were for political reasons wilfully blind to this fact and misconstrued the technological imperative to their own ends.

Co-existing with this technological optimism, though, early rationales for missile defence arguably rested at least as heavily on the pessimistic view of technology associated with substantivism as did arguments against ABM. Indeed, if anything proponents of expanded research and investment into ABM technology tended to go further in their assessments of the possible negative consequences of future technological developments. Teller, for instance, claimed that the significance of *Sputnik* was 'more important and greater than Pearl Harbor'.[58] Wohlstetter ominously foresaw further technological innovation, particularly in missile accuracy and defences, as a key factor in upsetting the 'delicate balance of terror'.[59] Their views were directly incorporated in the findings of the previously noted Gaither report that predicted a race in technology in which 'There will be no end to the technical moves and countermoves,' and in which 'Neither side can afford to lag or fail to match the other's efforts.' Consequently the report urged 'the importance of providing active defence of cities or other critical areas demands the development and installation of the

---

[57] Quoted in Bulkeley and Spinardi, *Space Weapons*, p. 58.
[58] Quoted in Fred M. Kaplan, *The Wizards of Armageddon* (Stanford, CA: Stanford University Press, 1983) p. 135.
[59] Albert Wohlstetter, 'The Delicate Balance of Terror', *Foreign Affairs*, 37:2 (1959) pp. 211–34.

basic elements of a [missile defence] system at an early date'.[60] Similarly a December 1957 report of the SAB (Scientific Advisory Board), chaired by Teller, evinces a similar mix of panic and faith at the prospect of future technological development. '*Sputnik* and the Russian ICBM capability' had, the SAB noted, 'created a national emergency'. It recommended as a consequent national priority that the air force 'pursue an active research program on anti-ICBM problems', noting, somewhat prophetically, that 'the critical elements are decoy discrimination and radar tracking. When these problems are solved, a strong anti-ICBM missile system should be started.'[61]

In this respect, several aspects of early ballistic missile defence advocacy are consistent with the 'periods of peril' argument proposed by Robert Johnson.[62] A period of peril, Johnson argues, is characterised by (1) a perceived adverse shift in the strategic nuclear balance that creates uncertainty about (2) an opponent's character and the likely shape of the nuclear danger.[63] Johnson's concept is particularly relevant in that it indicates a sense of concern which effectively 'melds' these two uncertainties. The launch of *Sputnik*, or rather the reaction to it, is a classic case in point. As we saw previously, this perceived technological advance was widely taken to portend ominous consequences for the USA. Not only this, but the nature of the development was itself taken as confirmation of the 'aggressive and adventuresome' nature of Soviet intentions.

Nowhere was this practice more prevalent than in the arguments of missile defence proponents such as Teller and Wohlstetter. By assuming a technologically determined future that would be much worse without missile defence, proponents of missile defence were in keeping with a general tendency to 'explain Soviet behavior on the basis of a combination of broad principles – such as a Soviet goal of world domination or the Soviet view of the correlation of forces – and Soviet advances in military technology, *with the effective emphasis upon the latter*'.[64] Johnson even argues that 'Such thinking involves an assumption of technological determinism, in the sense that it postulates that the

[60] The Gaither Report, quoted in Freedman, *Evolution of Nuclear Strategy*, p. 152.
[61] Thomas A. Stern, *The USAF Scientific Advisory Board: Its First Twenty Years, 1944–1964* (Washington, DC: Government Printing Office, 1986) pp. 82–3.
[62] Robert H. Johnson, 'Periods of Peril: the Window of Vulnerability and Other Myths', *Foreign Affairs*, 61:4 (1983) pp. 950–71.
[63] Ibid., p. 950.   [64] Ibid., p. 955, emphasis added.

broad aggressive purposes of the Soviets are made operative and given specific content and direction by the Soviet acquisition of new military technologies. *Means, in effect, determines goals.*'[65]

Accepting Johnson's characterisation as a fair portrayal of missile defence arguments, we arrive at something of a paradox. Though in one sense missile defence advocates postulated technology as simply an instrument, neutral in content with its ends determined by its user, and tended to reject the argument that technology determined either American goals or the arms race in general, they simultaneously embedded this argument in the view that Soviet character was determined by technology and therefore expansive and determinative in nature. So how, in a view which espouses the 'narrowly technological component' of strategy, do we arrive at a point in which the central tenet of substantivism – means determining both goals and character – applies?

Building on Johnson again, one possible explanation is that the type of thinking embodied in early missile defence advocacy tended to 'project upon the Russians a way of thinking that is characteristic of American foreign policy'.[66] Here Johnson cites Stanley Hoffman's notion (examined in chapter 2 and earlier) that the American 'national style' is characterised by an 'engineering approach' to problems that emphasises technique and technology – *the* common sense instrumental approach.[67] A key factor in the period of peril idea is the transposition of this self-characterisation on to the Soviet character, or 'mirror-imaging', particularly in relation to nuclear and space technologies.[68] Recall that a basic assumption of the pro-ABM constituency was that US policy-makers should pursue missile defence as a self-evident instrument to enhance US defences, restore its technological lead and thereby secure American preponderance. Irrespective of the outcome of the ABM debate, they further assumed, Soviet policy-makers would deploy

---

[65] Ibid., pp. 950–1, emphasis added.   [66] Ibid.
[67] Ibid., p. 951. See Hoffman, *Gulliver's Troubles*.
[68] Johnson, 'Periods of Peril'; Bulkeley and Spinardi, *Space Weapons*, p. 20. There are also parallels here with 'spiral theory', as outlined by Robert Jervis, where it is argued that once an image of the other is developed 'ambiguous and even discrepant information can be assimilated to that image' – see *Perception and Misperception in International Politics* (Princeton, NJ: Princeton University Press, 1976) p. 68. From this perspective, the transposition described above is less surprising given that 'people perceive what they expect to be present' (see ibid.), in this case the same engineering approach that persisted in American foreign policy.

missile defences on *the very same instrumentalist reasoning*. Soviet action on defence, on this reasoning, would occur irrespective of American inaction.

It was further assumed by ABM proponents that the totalitarian nature of the Soviet state and a lack of comparative budgetary constraints would facilitate a much quicker rate of technological development in the case of missile defence. Although the capacities touted for the Soviet Galosh system of the time are now generally regarded as having been vastly exaggerated,[69] Soviet rhetoric in the 1960s fed into this view. Marshal Malinowsky declared to the 22nd party congress that '[T]he problem of destroying enemy missiles in flight has been successfully resolved.' Khrushchev famously boasted in 1962 that Soviet forces could now 'hit a fly in space'. General Nikolai Talensky dreamed of the freedom of action that missile defence would provide the Soviet Union: 'The creation of an effective anti-missile system enables the state to make its defences dependent chiefly on its own possibilities, and not only on mutual deterrence, that is, on the good-will of the other side.'[70]

All this is perfectly in keeping with the picture of technological development envisaged by the infinite containment school as summarised in chapter 3. Arms control could never be any match to the lure of technological advancement, and this was something that US policy-makers failed to realise in relation to ABM – quite literally – at their peril. There are, though, several ironies present in these early missile defence arguments if we examine them closely. The most obvious is that instrumentalism, assumed to be the bedrock of American power, becomes that which the USA should fear most. In perfectly Heideggerian style, a world populated by instrumentalist thinkers, irrespective of their ideological leanings, is destined to become subject to its own inventions, endlessly seeking a reassertion of human control, paradoxically, through further technological advance. Likewise the view that successive generations of weapons technology would determine the nature of the Cold War seems to diminish the

[69] John Prados, *The Soviet Estimate: US Intelligence Analysis and Soviet Strategic Forces* (Princeton, NJ: Princeton University Press, 1986) pp. 151–71.
[70] Malinowsky (*Pravda*, 25 October 1961); Khrushchev (*New York Times*, 17 July 1962); Talensky, 1964, quoted in Bulkeley and Spinardi, *Space Weapons*, p. 28. See Jennifer Mathers, *The Russian Nuclear Shield from Stalin to Yeltsin* (Basingstoke: Macmillan, 2000) for more detail.

freedom of choice that it is assumed technological advance – through the deployment of missile defence – would bring. 'Choice', in this view, is always technologically predetermined. Indeed, the very argument made by the ABM constituency was that missile defence constituted a strategic *necessity* caused by the conditions of the arms race. Hence their argument that policy dictates the direction of technology seems to turn in on itself.

These latent contradictions in the pro-ABM arguments, however, did not necessarily impinge on its aspirations to become the common sense strategic outlook of policy-makers and the general public alike. Common sense, Gramsci notes, is itself constituted by a number of often contradictory 'conceptions of the world'.[71] In practice, those making the case for strategic defence readily combined substantivist elements into their overall instrumentalist outlook. Advocates frequently couched their technological optimism, and the concurrent stress on agential state-capacity this would create, against the backdrop of a grim future should the USA choose to constrain itself in the field of ABM technologies. The first implication of this view was that US policy-makers had a choice in the matter, not – *pace* McNamara, York and Lapp – that technology determined political choices. The second implication, however, was that failure to choose ABM deployment would effectively render the technology-out-of-control image a self-fulfilling prophecy. The USA would effectively become a 'second-class power', existing at the behest of a technologically superior rival. This alternative, more substantivist vision gleefully haunts the account of weapons development espoused by early missile defence proponents and was already present, usually explicitly, in many of their arguments. As a means of gaining public support, ABM proponents invoked popular concern about strategic vulnerability to strengthen their case for defence:

My plea is that we do not accept, as a permanent thing, a distorted version of this strategy ['assured destruction'] that will lead to more and bolder confrontations, directly or by proxy, with the Soviets as they match or exceed our nuclear offensive capability. Such a strategy could lead to the subjugation or destruction of our nation if the Soviets should develop an effective strategic

---

[71] Antonio Gramsci, *Selections from the Prison Notebooks of Antonio Gramsci*, ed. and trans. by Quintin Hoare and Geoffrey Nowell Smith (London: Lawrence and Wishart, 1973) pp. 323–5.

defensive force while, at the same time, we were led to believe that a nuclear balance still existed.[72]

The pattern is also found in General Curtis LeMay's confidence, cited in the previous chapter, in American directed-energy weapons, which likewise extended to the grim consequences of Soviet advantage in the same technology:

beam-directed energy weapons would be able to transmit energy across space with the speed of light and bring about the technological disarmament of nuclear weapons ... Whatever we do, the Soviets already have recognized the importance of these new developments and they are moving at full speed for a decisive capability in space. If they are successful, they can deny space to us.[73]

LeMay's prediction might seem far-fetched in hindsight. But as Erik K. Pratt points out, 'Inflated projections of an opponent's forces', exemplified by the 'bomber gap', the 'missile gap', and the 'ABM gap' serve to illustrate 'how threat analysis may be used in politically useful ways ... claims of gaps between US and Soviet force structures have been a recurring tactic in US defence politics and are used to incite public support for specific weapons systems and increased defence spending in general'.[74] Johnson likewise argues that part of the appeal of what he terms these 'periods of peril' is to further political ends, such as the successful use of the now long-discredited 'missile gap' in Kennedy's election campaign.[75] In short, early arguments for missile defence such as those cited above frequently tended to juxtapose these pessimistic readings of technological development with grand claims for the promise shown by missile defence initiatives. A frequent employer of the tactic, hawkish physicist Dr John S. Foster Jr once declared that there are typically two forces driving weapons R&D: 'Either we see from the field of science and technology some new possibilities, which we think

---

[72] Leon W. Johnson, quoted in Humphrey and Douglas, *Anti-Ballistic Missile: Yes or No?*, pp. 36–7. For Johnson's confidence in defensive possibilities, elicited in the very same passage, see chapter 3.

[73] Quoted in the *New York Times*, March 1962 and then in William J. Broad, ' "Star Wars" Traced to Eisenhower Era', *New York Times*, October 28 1986, p. C3. See chapter 3.

[74] Erik K. Pratt, *Selling Strategic Defense: Interests, Ideologies and the Arms Race* (Boulder, CO: Lynne Rienner, 1990) pp. 3, 45.

[75] Johnson, 'Periods of Peril', p. 965. Johnson also details the use of a similar framework in grounding the instrumental orientation of the 'New Look policy' (see chapter 3) and argues it is common to both the Killian and Gaither reports.

we ought to exploit, or we see threats on the horizon, possible threats, usually not something the enemy has done but something we have thought ourselves that he might do, we must therefore be prepared for.'[76] Early missile defence advocacy certainly seemed to combine elements of both to build its case, and in this we can begin to see more clearly the emergence of a 'common sense' form of argumentation in early justifications for ballistic missile defence in the form of ABM systems.

Conclusion: a period of peril postponed

Of course, as Pratt notes, and as was the case in the ABM debate, inflated threat projections and a sense of pessimism are not always a guarantee of political success.[77] The unprecedented combination of local opposition and scientific scepticism, uncertainty in Congress, and an increasing consensus within the Johnson and then Nixon administrations that ABM was expendable in return for mutual limitation in offensive nuclear weapons were all factors that combined against the appeals of the ABM constituency.[78] The important point to note, however, is that though ABM proponents' use of pessimistic projections ultimately failed to create a popular and political consensus behind missile defence, in doing so they effectively sought to embellish their instrumentalist, optimistic arguments examined in chapter 3 with a range of arguments seemingly at odds with this approach. Why?

Robert Johnson goes so far as to argue that such a move is more than either a simple rationalisation of perceived vulnerabilities or an exploitation of such perceptions for the benefit of parochial interests. This may or may not occur as a consequence, but he suggests:

In a curious way, pessimistic predictions . . . may be almost as reassuring – and possibly even more reassuring – than optimistic predictions. By suggesting the need for action, they respond to the culturally rooted American compulsions toward activism and toward believing that all problems have solutions. It is reassuring to think that by 'doing something' we can eliminate the threats to our survival posed by the existence of nuclear weapons.[79]

---

[76] Quoted in Pratt, *Selling Strategic Defense*, p. 3.   [77] Ibid., pp. 3, 45.
[78] For an expanded account see Yanarella, *The Missile Defense Controversy*, pp. 120–86.
[79] Johnson, 'Periods of Peril', p. 967.

Certainly, ballistic missile defence advocacy seems to be part of the increasing prevalence of 'periods of peril'-style argumentation identified by Johnson in American strategic debates of the 1950s and '60s, the perfect foil for an appeal to America's activist, instrumentalist heritage. More than this, the pattern of argumentation and forms of justification examined here and in chapter 3 *come together* to form a common sense whole in this manner, even if the individual understandings of technology examined in each are opposed. Within early justifications for missile defence (and indeed, within early opposition to it as exemplified in the views expounded by Robert McNamara), two contending visions of the role and meaning of technology – the progressivist view of technology as an instrument of US security, and the pessimistic view of technology as ever more autonomous – were increasingly amalgamated.

This has two important implications for expanding our understanding of where 'technology' figures in the discourse of missile defence advocacy. The first is that even if this style of argumentation was used for purely functional purposes by missile defence advocates, its assumptions still indicate a particular view of the relationship between strategy and technology by which ABM proponents sought to 'justify their sense of alarm and make it intelligible and tangible to others'.[80] A second possible implication, building on Johnson's reading, is that where such espoused fears of a technologically determined future 'seems sometimes to have emerged, in part, out of efforts to rationalize the undertakings of particular defense programmes desired for other reasons', such as personal or political gain, bureaucratic or economic interests, 'like other myths that have their origins in some more concrete human need, the period of peril myth, once articulated, has taken on a life of its own with an independent influence on thinking and behaviour'.[81] In the Gramscian perspective, myth, folklore and common sense all serve to embed political and economic relations. As we shall see later in Part Three, the strategic discourse promoting SDI exhibits even more heavily an integration of substantivist thinking and the period of peril myth into the common sense case for missile defence along with its instrumentalist counterpart, helping to embed further the political economy of strategic defence.

---

[80] Ibid., p. 969.   [81] Ibid.

The Strategic Defense Initiative

5 | *The Strategic Defense Initiative and America's technological heritage*

Introduction

Ronald Reagan's speech on 23 March 1983 announcing the Strategic Defense Initiative (SDI) stands, arguably, as the archetypal manifestation of instrumental thinking in a political address. Reagan followed his commentary on the moral and political inadequacy of reliance on nuclear weapons – 'Wouldn't it be better to save lives than avenge them?' – with an exhortation to 'turn to the very strengths in technology that spawned our great industrial base and that have given us the quality of life we enjoy today'. American scientists had been the first to produce the means of mass destruction; why shouldn't they be able to produce protection against these means? 'I call upon the scientific community in our country, those who gave us nuclear weapons, to turn their great talents now to the cause of mankind and world peace, to give us the means of rendering these nuclear weapons impotent and obsolete.' Moreover, Reagan argued, the American industrial base was already producing technology that had 'attained a level of sophistication where it's reasonable for us to begin this effort'. The promise of a technological solution was deemed to be worth 'every investment necessary to free the world from the threat of nuclear war'.[1]

The reason why Reagan's appeal can be viewed as particularly instrumentalist is its emphasis on the (re)assertion of popular control over technology, and, hence, the notion of technology as instrument of politics. For Kenneth Zagacki and Andrew King, SDI 'works within the idiom of the people, therefore preserving public sentiment and creating a sense – not necessarily a false sense – of participation in public

---

[1] Ronald Reagan, 'Address to the Nation on Defense and National Security', 23 March 1983. The President spoke at 8:02pm from the Oval Office at the White House. The address was broadcast live on nationwide radio and television. Full text available from www.atomicarchive.com/Docs/Missile/Starwars.shtml [last accessed 20 January 2009].

debate'.[2] Reagan's 1983 appeal, they argue, reasserted the primacy of politics and popular will over technology. '[T]he legacy of Star Wars', they therefore speculated in a 1989 article, 'may be that Reagan's rhetoric pointed to the potential for continued democratic control over technology, by advocating a nascent argumentative framework accessible to the public.'[3] Gordon Mitchell takes a more sceptical view of the populist rhetoric used to advocate SDI on the basis that, to the contrary, 'evidence has mounted that the cold war military apparatus (including SDIO) used frustration of democratic control over technology as a political modus operandi to trigger cycles of defense-spending jackpots'.[4]

Mitchell makes a convincing argument based on extensive archival research.[5] Yet the fact that such an array of 'defense-spending jackpots' (Mitchell estimates the cost of SDI at \$70.7 billion since 1983[6]) could be enacted can in some ways be taken as an indication of Reagan's initial success in portraying his SDI appeal as what Norman Fairclough terms a 'nuclear conversation' – 'a series of shifting articulations between the technical/strategic, political and moral public domains'.[7] Fairclough adjudges this 'conversation' (specifically referring to the nuclear discourse of the Reagan administration) as being, in actuality, 'a struggle to produce configurations of these domains capable of dominating the discursive field'.[8] What we need to pay particular attention to, therefore, is 'how the strategic moves within this struggle are textually enacted', and here he highlights the role that intertextual analysis can play.[9]

Focusing in particular on the inter-articulation of technical and strategic discourses, this chapter traces the ways in which the instrumentalist underpinning of Reagan's appeal for strategic defence was textually

[2] Kenneth Zagacki and Andrew King, 'Reagan, Romance and Technology: a Critique of "Star Wars"', *Communication Studies*, 40 (1989) pp. 1–12.
[3] Ibid., p. 10.
[4] Gordon R. Mitchell, *Strategic Deception: Rhetoric, Science and Politics in Missile Defense Advocacy* (East Lansing: Michigan State University Press, 2000) p. 78.
[5] Ibid., pp. 47–120.   [6] Ibid., p. 87.
[7] Norman Fairclough, 'Linguistic and Intertextual Analysis within Discourse Analysis' in Adam Jaworski and Nikolas Coupland (eds.) *The Discourse Reader* (London: Routledge, 2004) p. 198.
[8] Ibid. Fairclough makes his assessment in relation to Hugh Mehan, Charles E. Nathanson and James M. Skelly, 'Nuclear Discourse in the 1980s: the Unravelling Conventions of the Cold War', *Discourse and Society*, 1:2 (1990) pp. 134–65.
[9] Fairclough, 'Linguistic and Intertextual Analysis', p. 198.

embedded and enacted in the broader promotion of SDI. Examining the literature on the origins of SDI, it argues that subsequent accounts have been retrospectively cast in terms of technological optimism and progressivism as associated with the instrumentalist view as outlined in chapters 1 and 2. In combination with direct references to America's technological heritage, such moves became a fundamental part of the promotion of SDI and played an important role in the debate over strategic defence by offsetting scientific criticisms and legitimating investment in the programme, as well as drawing attention away from political and economic challenges to the Reagan administration more generally.

The Reagan era: instrumentalism resurgent

The rise of the ideological right within the Reagan administration brought with it the overall emphasis on technological innovation as the key to strategic superiority that had characterised the thinking of Teller, Wohlstetter *et al.* in the 1960s and '70's. The notion that technology had replaced geographical control as the mark of military superiority was now in the ascendancy: Reagan, Secretary of Defense Caspar Weinberger and many of the political appointees in the DoD, among them Richard Perle, all held the view that 'Western technological sophistication would offset Soviet quantitative and geographic advantages. Since the Soviet Union lacked resources in this area, new hi-tech weaponry could also provide the United States with "strategic leverage" or, if the Soviet Union tried to keep pace, could bankrupt the Soviet economy and lead to civil unrest and instability.'[10] As the Strategic Defense Initiative entered the height of its prominence, Weinberger would declare that: 'We are entering into a period of rapid technological change that can work to our advantage. We have superior skills in the development of military systems embodying some of the leading technologies and superior manufacturing techniques and skills.'[11]

[10] G. Allen Greb, 'Short-Circuiting the System: Science Advice to the President in the SDI' in Gerald M. Steinberg (ed.) *Lost in Space: the Domestic Politics of the Strategic Defense Initiative* (Lexington, MA: Lexington Books, 1988) p. 26. See also Robert W. Tucker, *The Nuclear Debate: Deterrence and the Lapse of Faith* (New York: Holmes and Meier, 1985) pp. 96–102.

[11] Caspar W. Weinberger, 'US Defense Strategy', *Foreign Affairs*, 64 (1986) pp. 695–6.

The instrumentalist view that defences held the key to restoring the political utility of the US nuclear arsenal also came to be expressed by Weinberger among others in this context: 'If we can get a system which is effective and which we know can render their weapons impotent, we could be back in a situation we were in, for example, when we were the only nation with a nuclear weapon.'[12] New technology could be the instrument to solve the Cold War dilemma. In this Weinberger could count on the backing of at least a portion of the strategic studies community, with Colin S. Gray declaring that 'In the event that the United States succeeded in deploying a population defense that was technically robust, a considerable measure of US freedom of political action should be restored as a logical consequence.'[13] A new generation of strategists including Gray, Keith B. Payne and William Van Cleave (several of whom had direct influence on Reagan's defence policy) would take up the case for strategic defence much as Ikle and Wohlstetter had done previously.[14] Indeed, Gray, while critical of the systems analysis approach developed out of RAND, echoed many of Wohlstetter's arguments. He asserted that a defence for cities against ICBMs was not necessarily required to be '100% effective', recommending that 'A measure of "hardening" for urban-industrial America through civil defense should be the principal policy response to the "leakage" problem.'[15] Thus it can be argued that the advent of the Reagan era brought with it a renewed emphasis on the instrumentalist principle that new technologies, including defensive technologies,

[12] Statement to the Senate Armed Services Committee, 1984, quoted in Edward P. Thompson (ed.) *Star Wars* (Harmondsworth: Penguin, 1985) p. 138.
[13] From *The Progressive*, July 1985, p. 26, quoted in Thompson, *Star Wars*, p. 138.
[14] See, for example, Colin S. Gray, *The Geopolitics of the Nuclear Era: Heartland, Rimlands, and the Technological Revolution* (New York: Crane, Russak, 1977); Keith B. Payne, *Strategic Defense: 'Star Wars' in Perspective* (London: Hamilton Press, 1986); William Van Cleave, *Fortress USSR: the Soviet Strategic Defense Initiative and the US Strategic Defense Response* (Stanford, CA: Hoover Institution Press, 1986). Ikle's political influence increased as Deputy Director of Defense for Policy from 1981 to 1988; see his 'Nuclear Strategy: Can There be a Happy Ending?', *Foreign Affairs*, 63:4 (1985) pp. 810–26. Gray served as an adviser on the General Advisory Committee on Arms Control and Disarmament and Van Cleave headed Reagan's Defense Department transition team.
[15] Colin S. Gray (1981) 'The Missile Defense Debate in the Early 1970s' reprinted in Z. Brzezinski (ed.) *Promise or Peril: the Strategic Defense Initiative* (Washington, DC: Ethics and Public Policy Centre, 1986) p. 37.

stood ready to advance America's interests should the political will be found to do so.[16]

Hence, the Reagan administration shared many of the views of the 'missile defence missionaries' who argued that the dream of an anti-ballistic missile system could become a reality.[17] However, the announcement of the Strategic Defense Initiative came as a shock even to some within the administration. The day after it was announced, Paul Thayer, Deputy Secretary of Defense, began a meeting at the Pentagon by asking 'What are we going to do with this mess?'[18] The lack of a firm blueprint and fluctuation in stated strategic rationales (from replacing deterrence to enhancing deterrence) indicate the lack of any well-planned, long thought-out agenda. How much did the technological optimism and proposals of missile defence advocates such as Wallop, Graham and Teller influence this 'surprise' decision?

Reagan's vision: origins and influences

Probing the depths of the origins of SDI is not a clear-cut enterprise. As Erik Pratt notes, 'Analyzing the gestation of Reagan's decision to initiate his Star Wars plan has become something of a minor literary enterprise … not even Reagan could likely reconstruct all the factors behind the decision and assign them their proper weight.'[19] What is particularly interesting, though, is the manner in which this gestation has subsequently come to be recounted in terms of a quasi-mythical realisation on the part of Reagan as to the potential of defensive technology.[20]

[16] Cf. Steve Smith, 'SDI and the New Cold War' in Richard Crockatt and Steve Smith (eds.) *The Cold War Past and Present* (London: Allen and Unwin, 1987) pp. 149–70.

[17] Erik K. Pratt, *Selling Strategic Defense: Interests, Ideologies and the Arms Race* (Boulder, CO: Lynne Rienner, 1990) p. 112.

[18] Quoted in Gerald M. Steinberg, 'A Presidential Initiative' in Steinberg, *Lost in Space*, p. 2.

[19] Pratt, *Selling Strategic Defense*, p. 101.

[20] Pratt, *Selling Strategic Defense*, Steinberg, *Lost in Space*, Donald R. Baucom, *The Origins of SDI, 1944–1983* (Lawrence, KS: University Press of Kansas, 1992), Edward T. Linenthal, *Symbolic Defense: the Cultural Significance of the Strategic Defense Initiative* (Urbana: University of Illinois Press, 1989) and H. Bruce Franklin, *War Stars: the Superweapon and the American Imagination* (New York: Oxford University Press, 1988) all subscribe to this account to some extent, as do several political memoirs and reflections such as Martin Anderson's *Revolution: the Reagan Legacy* (New York: Harcourt Brace Jovanovich, 1988).

This 'myth of origins' variously combines elements of popular culture, strategic thinking and technological optimism into the kind of folkloric *mélange* Gramsci associates with common sense. Several accounts contextualise Reagan's decision against the background of his career before going into politics. A possible influence usually cited is Reagan's appearance as the male lead in the 1940 film *Murder in the Air*, in which he starred as secret agent 'Brass Bancroft'. The film portrays Bancroft, the hero of the hour, foiling communist spies who are attempting to steal a secret weapon, the 'inertia projector'. With its ability to down any incoming aircraft by disrupting their electrical currents, the inertia projector promises a flawless air defence for the United States, and effectively renders it invulnerable to attack. Pratt is not alone in noting 'some uncanny similarities between elements in the film and Reagan's Star Wars vision'.[21] Reagan's aides would also refer to uncanny parallels between the President's vision and another motion picture, this time Alfred Hitchcock's *Torn Curtain*, a 1966 film centring on an attempt to develop an anti-missile system. Playing the role of an American agent, Paul Newman declares that 'We will produce a defensive weapon that will make all nuclear weapons obsolete, and thereby abolish the terror of nuclear warfare.'[22]

Reagan the politician, we are told, could also have been influenced by formative contacts with the issue of defences against nuclear attacks, or rather the lack of such defences. In 1967, as governor of California, Reagan visited the Lawrence Livermore National Laboratory where, according to Pratt, Edward Teller 'shared with the future president his dream of constructing a strategic defence system'.[23] Later, in 1979, Reagan paid a visit to NORAD (North American Aerospace Defense Command) in Colorado and was reportedly 'deeply concerned by the realization that a nation which had spent hundreds of billions of dollars for national security and had the best, most technologically sophisticated equipment in the world was "powerless to protect our country

[21] Pratt, *Selling Strategic Defense*, p. 102. See also Franklin, *War Stars*, p. 202.
[22] Strobe Talbott, *Master of the Game: Paul Nitze and the Nuclear Peace* (New York: Knopf, 1988) p. 188. See also Frances Fitzgerald, *Way Out There in the Blue: Reagan, Star Wars and the End of the Cold War* (New York: Simon and Schuster, 2000) p. 23.
[23] Pratt, *Selling Strategic Defense*, p. 102.

and its people"'.[24] Indeed, Reagan recalled his own astonishment that for all America's technological achievements – exemplified by the computer displays, satellite tracking and communications technology at NORAD – the USA still remained entirely defenceless:

> I think the thing that struck me was the irony that here, with this great technology of ours, we can do all this yet we cannot stop any of the weapons that are coming at us. I don't think there's been a time in history when there wasn't a defense against some kind of thrust, even back in the old-fashioned days when we had coast artillery that would stop invading ships if they came.[25]

A few days after the trip to Colorado, Martin Anderson, Reagan's security adviser, put together a memo on defence and foreign policy including a section proposing the development of a 'protective missile system'. Anderson argued that 'the idea is probably fundamentally far more appealing to the American people than the questionable satisfaction of knowing that those who initiated an attack against us were also blown away', and that 'there have apparently been striking advances in missile technology during the past decade or so that would make such a system technically possible'.[26] Assuming the innate appeal of this technological utopianism, Anderson claims he set out to write a defence policy based on what he 'thought the American people would like if they could have their wishes come true'[27], and came up with SDI.

A myth of origins

More recent assessments of the history of SDI (particularly those of Frances Fitzgerald and Gordon R. Mitchell) have expressed deep scepticism about these standard accounts of the origins of the programme.[28] Regarding the commonly referred to instances of revelation – Reagan's first encounter with Teller at Livermore and the NORAD visit as retold by Martin Anderson – Fitzgerald points out

[24] Martin Anderson, *An Insurance Missile Defense* (Stanford, CA: The Hoover Institution, 1986) pp. 1–2.
[25] Quoted in Robert Scheer, *With Enough Shovels: Reagan, Bush, and Nuclear War* (New York: Random House, 1982) p. 233.
[26] Quoted in Fitzgerald, *Way Out There in the Blue*, p. 21.
[27] Anderson, *Revolution*, p. 83.
[28] Fitzgerald, *Way Out There in the Blue*; Mitchell, *Strategic Deception*.

that there is 'a high narrative gloss to the story': 'Because it first appeared in public long after Reagan's 1983 speech, it has always been understood in the light of that speech, and as a reflection upon his exhortation to the scientific community to make "nuclear weapons impotent and obsolete".'[29] Essentially, Fitzgerald makes the argument that these supposedly formative events in Reagan's pre-presidential career have been retrospectively reconstructed in order to contextualise his 'epiphany' regarding ballistic missiles. The standard narrative as recounted tallies well with the content of the 1983 announcement: 'to read it [Anderson's narrative] without irony, as most SDI historians have, is to see that it has a very rich symbolic content. But then the same is certainly true of the speech.' Although mutual assured destruction (MAD) is not mentioned in Reagan's recollection of his NORAD visit, an alternative to it is postulated through the recounting of his personal experience and his reading of American history.

For Fitzgerald, the narrative of this 'story' is trite, bordering on implausible: did it really take a visit to NORAD for a presidential candidate finally to appreciate the common-knowledge vulnerability of the USA to nuclear attack?[30] The cinematic allusions cited by most also form part of this 'myth of origins' for Fitzgerald.[31] They add further symbolic, but superficial, evidence to the notion that defence against nuclear weapons had been incubating in the President's mind for some time, that the idea had not just appeared 'out of the blue'. Fitzgerald is similarly sceptical about the direct influence often attributed to missile defence advocates.[32] Reagan and his advisers were, to varying extents, aware of the schemes of Teller, Graham and Wallop, each of whom had some degree of access, either directly or through political and military connections. By July 1981, for example, the High Frontier panel, which counted both Daniel Graham and Edward Teller among its membership, was being sponsored by the White House. But there is mixed evidence as to the extent to which administration officials were actually convinced by their technological optimism. A letter of 24 November

[29] Fitzgerald, *Way Out There in the Blue*, p. 21; Anderson's account in *Revolution* was only published in 1988.
[30] For a slightly more forgiving reading see Lawrence Freedman, *The Evolution of Nuclear Strategy*, 3rd edition (Basingstoke: Palgrave, 2003) p. 395. See also Richard N. Lebow, *Nuclear Crisis Management: a Dangerous Illusion* (Ithaca: Cornell University Press, 1983) p. 121.
[31] Fitzgerald, *Way Out There in the Blue*, p. 23.   [32] Ibid., p. 194.

1982 from Weinberger to Graham stated that: 'Although we appreciate your optimism that technicians will find the way [to defend against ICBMs] and quickly, we are unwilling to commit this nation to a course which calls for growing into a capability that does not currently exist.'[33] This seems further to support Fitzgerald's assertion that Reagan's key advisers 'were not in the grip of any technological enthusiasm'.[34]

This, however, only makes all the more salient the apparent switch made by the administration to the language of technological optimism as associated with instrumentalism. By 1982 the Reagan administration was in a severe logjam with regard to its strategic policy. Members of the Joint Chiefs of Staff were known to be concerned about the status of the administration's MX missile programme. Congress had refused to appropriate further funds for the MX until the basing-mode issue had been successfully dealt with, and the House was due to vote on a nuclear-freeze resolution again in the spring. Public support for strategic modernisation was also haemorrhaging. While the anti-nuclear movement continued to grow, popular backing for increased military spending had fallen from 80 per cent to 20 per cent in just two years. Concerns about the wisdom of a military build-up, combined with the onset of economic recession, caused Reagan's approval rating to drop sharply.[35]

In this light, it might be argued, the technological optimism of missile defence advocates, honed over the previous decades and compatible with the administration's emphasis on developing the US defence infrastructure, provided a ready-made vocabulary to secure and renew Reagan's defence agenda. At a meeting with the Joint Chiefs of Staff in early 1983, the military's top brass expressed concern about the direction of strategic policy, especially in light of growing opposition from the nuclear-freeze movement and the Catholic bishops. The Chief of Naval Operations, James D. Watkins, reportedly impressed by Teller's enthusiastic proposals which he had heard some months earlier, suggested:

[33] Quoted in ibid., p. 143.   [34] Ibid., p. 145.
[35] Rebecca S. Bjork, *The Strategic Defense Initiative* (Albany, NY: State University of New York Press, 1992) pp. 16–17; see also Paul N. Edwards, *The Closed World: Computers and the Politics of Discourse in Cold War America* (Cambridge, MA: MIT Press, 1996) p. 284.

Why don't we use our applied technological genius to achieve our deterrent instead of sticking with an offensive land-based rocket exchange which [the Soviets] will win every time?

[Foreign policy adviser Robert McFarlane] I believe that Jim is suggesting that new technologies may offer the possibility of enabling us to deal with a Soviet missile attack by defensive means.

[Reagan] I understand; that's what I've been hoping.[36]

Watkins embellished his appeal to American 'technological genius' by espousing the moral superiority of defences ('Wouldn't it be better to save lives than to avenge them?'). McFarlane contends that he then seconded the idea of strategic defence as a means of 'leveraging Soviet behaviour' but claims that such arguments were lost on Reagan for whom 'the idea of anti-missile defences had an appeal in itself'.[37]

Again, Fitzgerald finds this narrative slightly implausible: 'Only the President seems to be in character – or at least in the character ascribed to him by Martin Anderson: Ronald Reagan the dreamer, the nuclear abolitionist, the naïve.' The positions of the other players in this dialogue – McFarlane and Watkins – are tinged with a technological optimism which, for Fitzgerald, is out of character, a retrospective embellishment crafted to fit with the 'myth of origins', and masks the role of other pressing political concerns. No doubt exists, though, that SDI captured the imagination of the American public and in so doing relieved at least some of the political pressures on the Reagan administration. As Eisendrath *et al.* note: 'SDI ... looked to defense rather than offense, as in the case of the MX missile, and ... could be seen as turning the public image of the president from a warmonger to a man of peace. The Democrats, who backed mutual deterrence, could in this calculus be depicted as the military aggressors.'[38]

Fitzgerald makes a convincing case that missile defence advocates had less influence on the administration than commonly thought. Despite advisers initially attributing the inspiration for the 1983 speech to High Frontier and the infectious enthusiasm for lasers and 'third generation' technologies, 'Years later ... the very same officials told historians that

---

[36] Fitzgerald, *Way Out There in the Blue*, p. 197; events as recounted in Lou Cannon, *President Reagan: the Role of a Lifetime* (New York: Simon and Schuster, 1991) and Baucom, *Origins of SDI*.

[37] Quoted in Fitzgerald, *Way Out There in the Blue*, p. 198.

[38] Craig R. Eisendrath *et al. The Phantom Defense: America's Pursuit of the Star Wars Illusion* (Westport, CT: Praeger, 2001) p. 13.

the High Frontier panel had virtually nothing to do with the President's
speech ... But, then, explaining the initiative by some technical enthusiasm, however bizarre, was better than confessing that technology had
nothing to do with it at all.'[39] An important point to note, however, is
that the question of whether or not Reagan and his aides were actually
in the throes of any 'technological enthusiasm' is in some ways a
secondary point. What is more striking is that they, and several historians with them, have retrospectively elevated technological optimism to
a key theme within this 'myth of origins'. The theme is expected to
resonate, to fit the character of key participants, to make sense. This
'bizarre' language of technological enthusiasm was to become the common sense rhetoric of SDI.

Reagan: a technological optimist?

Reagan was certainly cast in the role of technological optimist after
announcing his new initiative. The *Washington Post* declared in spring
1985 that 'Reagan was fascinated with the prospect of a technological
breakthrough that would create hardware that could stop incoming
missiles. Reagan often called the idea "my dream", which suggests the
magical nature of its hold on him ...'[40] Likewise Reagan biographer Lou
Cannon asserts that 'Reagan totally believed in the science-fiction solution he had proposed without consultation with his secretary of state or
his secretary of defense ... Reagan was convinced that American ingenuity could find a way to protect the American people from the nightmare of
Armageddon. As he saw it, the Strategic Defense Initiative was a dream
come true.'[41]

   Chapter 6 sets out to show how Reagan's obsession with the 'nightmare
of Armageddon' was actually articulated through an opposed, pessimistic
vision of technology, thereby replicating the structure of the American
common sense of technology as outlined in chapter 3. But the question of
how much Reagan was or was not convinced about the potential of
American ingenuity is again of less interest than the way in which a
sense of technological optimism was adapted seamlessly into Reagan's
everyman persona, an optimism that cut across partisan politics. As
Linenthal notes, 'Reagan's [March 1983] speech held out hope to people

---

[39] Fitzgerald, *Way Out There in the Blue*, p. 146.
[40] Quoted in ibid., p. 255.   [41] Cannon, *President Reagan*, p. 333.

of various ideological persuasions that the same scientists who had bur-
dened humankind with nuclear weapons could now, motivated by patriotic fervor and blessed with seemingly God-like technological genius,
provide the only sure path to salvation – the path of missile defense.'[42]
More than this, in a world of rocket scientists and opaque strategic theory
populated by acronyms and obscure concepts, Reagan's speech had a
refreshingly simplistic logic to it. Strategic defence was portrayed as both
innately moral and, thanks to American ingenuity, achievable. In his
March 1983 exhortation 'Reagan [cut] through the arcane and dangerous
knowledge [of MAD] with pure common sense.'[43]

This sense of technological optimism also tallied well with other key
themes promoted by Reagan, with SDI representing the 'ultimate
expression of the Reagan emphasis on national pride'.[44] On 6
February 1985, in the first State of the Union Address of his second
term, Reagan cited SDI as an example of the creative promise of a
'Second American Revolution', declaring that 'There are no constraints
on the human mind ... no barriers to our progress except those we
ourselves erect,' a theme reiterated in a briefing on the SDI in August
1986, when the President spoke of 'expanding the limits of human
potential. The relationship between freedom and human progress has
never been more apparent ...'; and, in a phrase that could be taken as
the epitome of an instrumentalist justification, Reagan concluded that
'The future is literally in our hands. And it is SDI that is helping us to
regain control over our own destiny.'[45]

In such statements, Reagan rejuvenated hopes for missile defence
technology as a revolutionary instrument for US policy. The reason
that Reagan could so confidently redefine the 'limits of human potential'
was, arguably, due to a lack of objective scientific advice in White House
circles prior to the announcement of SDI. Greb asserts that when Reagan
asked America to 'turn to the very strengths in technology that spawned
out great industrial base and that have given us the quality of life we
enjoy today' in March 1983, it was 'with only the bare minimum of

[42] Linenthal, *Symbolic Defense*, p. 11.
[43] Fitzgerald, *Way Out There in the Blue*, p. 26.
[44] Gerald M. Steinberg, 'The Limits of Faith' in Steinberg, *Lost in Space*, p. 151.
[45] Extracts from President Reagan's remarks at a briefing on the Strategic
Defense Initiative, Washington, DC, 6 August 1986. Department of State,
SDI: Progress and Promise, Current Policy No. 858 (Washington, DC: GPO,
1986), emphasis added.

scientific consultation and input [that] he challenged the scientific com-munity'.[46] The free rein taken by Reagan in appealing to American technological ingenuity as a policy instrument for ending the Cold War had significant consequences. In Reagan's public statements the relation-ship between technological innovation and security, previously asso-ciated with the fear of exacerbating or inciting an arms race, had been reconstituted as one of hope. As a result, 'Psychologically and politically, SDI represented a paradigm shift upward in public expectations con-cerning the role of technology in protecting America.'[47] In order to sustain these expectations, the achievability of missile defence would have to be shown. The Reagan administration's attempt discursively to reconfigure the relationship between technology and nuclear strategy had to struggle with technical realities. As Mitchell notes, 'Reagan's visionary claims about SDI put enormous rhetorical pressure on the American military research establishment to produce scientific evidence showing the feasibility of a "leakproof" missile defense system.'[48]

Invoking America's technological heritage

A major obstacle in this respect was that the fact that the American scientific community remained split on the feasibility of missile defences. While familiar critics such as Hans Bethe, Herbert York and Richard Garwin remained unconvinced – and indeed scathing in their criticism of SDI – others such as Robert Jastrow, a former NASA astrophysicist, vigorously defended the initiative. Jastrow published two articles in *Commentary* magazine directly criticising the stance of Bethe, Garwin and others in the Union of Concerned Scientists (UCS) who had dismissed the possibility of even a more limited form of defence based on their own study of directed-energy weapons.[49] In the first of these, 'Reagan vs. the Scientists: Why the President is Right about Missile Defense', published in January 1984, Jastrow stated that in

---

[46] Greb, 'Short-Circuiting the System', p. 27.
[47] Roger Handberg, *Ballistic Missile Defense and the Future of American Security: Agendas, Perceptions, Technology and Policy* (Westport, CT: Praeger, 2002) p. 19.
[48] Mitchell, *Strategic Deception*, p. 48.
[49] This UCS study was reprinted in John Tirman (ed.) *The Fallacy of Star Wars: Based on Studies Conducted by the Union of Concerned Scientists* (New York: Vintage Books, 1984).

regard to protection of Minuteman missiles (or 'point defence'), 'The basic technologies have been proven, they are inexpensive, and they can be put into use with relative rapidity.' Regarding population defence using lasers, Jastrow drew on the assessments of George Keyworth II, Reagan's scientific adviser and Teller's protégé, to argue that 'Among the experts actually working on laser defense or advising the government on it, the consensus is that no basic scientific obstacles stand in the way of success ... The major fundamental problems in every area of [laser defense] have been removed.' In general, Jastrow did not directly confront the technical criticisms raised by the UCS study (cited above). Instead he merely declared that 'scientists do not have a very good track record when it comes to making predictions about the feasibility of bold new ideas'. Jastrow cited an astronomer who declared in 1903 that the laws of physics prevented flight and another who had called satellites 'utter bilge'. He also recalled the prediction of Vannevar Bush – head of the Office of Scientific Research and Development during World War II and overseer of the Manhattan Project – that efforts to develop ICBMs 'can be left out of our thinking'.[50]

Reagan too was keen to stress that 'bold new ideas' sometimes needed to be fostered even in the face of criticism. 'Our country's security today relies as much on the genius and creativity of scientists as it does on the courage and dedication of those in the military services,' he declared in 1986 with the debate over the technical feasibility of SDI more entrenched than ever; but 'It also relies on those with the wisdom to recognize innovation when they see it and to shepherd change over the obstacles and through the maze ...' If the new idea could be shepherded through the initial maze of scientific criticism, Reagan argued, it would eventually reach the point of general acceptance: 'There are three stages of reaction to any new idea as Arthur C. Clarke, a brilliant writer with a fine scientific mind, once noted. First, "It's crazy; don't waste my time." Second, "It's possible, but it's not worth doing." And finally, "I always said it was a good idea."'[51]

[50] Robert Jastrow, 'Reagan vs. the Scientists: Why the President is Right about Missile Defense', *Commentary*, 77:1 (1984) pp. 23–31.

[51] Extracts from President Reagan's remarks at a briefing on the Strategic Defense Initiative, Washington, DC, 6 August 1986. Department of State, *SDI: Progress and Promise*, Current Policy No. 858 (Washington, DC: GPO, 1986).

As Rebecca Bjork notes, Reagan's pleas for technological optimism were grounded as much in historical as in scientific claims, or rather in claims about the history of scientific development in the American context. Reagan frequently peppered his public comments on SDI with examples of innovation in the face of scepticism, liberally drawing on the progressivist-instrumentalist narrative of technological development, outlined in chapter 2, as a resource. In remarks made in March 1986, he argued that American history is replete with dramatic accounts of technological breakthroughs in industry, agriculture and medicine. Thomas Edison, the Wright brothers and Alexander Graham Bell, he argued, were not daunted by the technological pessimists of their day.[52] Other examples referred more directly to the relation between technological change and military innovation:

Back when Fulton was inventing the steamboat and it came into reality, there was a general effort made to sell it to Napoleon in France. And the great general, with all his wisdom, said: 'Are you trying to tell me that you can have a boat that will sail against the tide and the currents and the wind without any sails?' He said: 'Don't bother me with such foolishness.' Well, we know where the foolishness lay, and let's not make the same mistakes … When the time has come and the research is complete, yes, we're going to deploy.[53]

Chief among the analogies employed by Reagan in this respect was that of space exploration. In defending SDI in his 1986 State of the Union Address, Reagan said, 'America met one historic challenge and went to the moon. Now America must meet another – to make our strategic defense real for all the citizens of the planet earth.' Hence Reagan sought to ground his own apparent technological optimism within a broader frame of technological innovation associated with American history, infusing the general theme of technological progress with a particular patriotic zeal – 'I'll put my money on American technology anytime,' Bjork quotes Reagan as saying. 'By calling upon these examples of American genius', she asserts, 'Reagan called forth a compelling sense of history, and used it to support his calls for faith in SDI research,'

[52] United States, Office of the Federal Register, *Weekly Compilation of Presidential Documents* (Washington, DC: GPO, 17 March 1986) p. 341/9; (June 1986) p. 739.

[53] Extracts from President Reagan's remarks at a briefing on the Strategic Defense Initiative, Washington, DC, 6 August 1986. Department of State, *SDI: Progress and Promise*, Current Policy No. 858 (Washington, DC: GPO, 1986). For more on Fulton as a referent point of American technological progress, see chapter 2.

and Steinberg concurs that 'this historical foundation is invoked repeat-
edly' to this effect.[54]

Thus, Reagan attempted to incorporate America's technological past
into SDI in an attempt to take on the positive connotations of past
achievements. Moreover, Bjork argues, Reagan employed this historical
foundation to reinforce his representation of specific 'breakthroughs' in
SDI research in, for example, sensors and homing devices against a
strong current of scientific scepticism. Effectively, 'Reagan re-enacted
the historical and quintessentially American drama of technological
breakthroughs in the face of seemingly insurmountable odds before
the nation's very eyes.'[55] To Gordon Mitchell, this represents a logical
continuation of the theme of the 1983 speech, the view that 'Absolutely,
our ingenuity can surmount any technical challenge.' In fact he argues
that these themes would 'become bread-and-butter moves in missile
defense advocates' rhetorical repertoires'.[56]

A brief survey of the support for SDI lends added credence to this
assertion. General James A. Abrahamson, director of the Strategic
Defense Initiative Organization (SDIO) reiterated several of the themes
touched upon by Jastrow and Reagan. In the immediate wake of
Reagan's March 1983 speech, Abrahamson strongly endorsed the
President's optimism and even went further, declaring that 'I don't
think anything in this country is technically impossible. We have a
nation which can indeed produce miracles.' Testifying before a House
committee in 1984, Abrahamson spoke of his 'great faith in just what
American technology can do'.[57] In the same hearing Abrahamson also
reinforced the assertion that, based on his experience, technicians, not
scientists, would be the key players in achieving the goals of SDI: 'I guess
my experience as a technologist and as a manager with a long career in
this effort is that we indeed can produce miracles.' Brushing aside
criticisms of the programme, he declared that:

There is very little question that we can build a very highly effective defense
against ballistic missiles someday . . . I am a little dismayed at some of the critics
who keep saying that we can't do something. I don't think that the history of

---

[54] Bjork, *The Strategic Defense Initiative*, pp. 72–3; Steinberg, 'The Limits of Faith',
p. 148.
[55] Bjork, *The Strategic Defense Initiative*, p. 73.
[56] Mitchell, *Strategic Deception*, p. 55.
[57] Steinberg, 'The Limits of Faith', pp. 148–9.

what we have done in this country technically is something that supports a lot of their pessimism.[58]

Such pessimism, Abrahamson believed, was especially unhelpful given the potentially revolutionary effect that SDI technology could have on America's destiny. 'With SDI', he claimed, 'we have explicitly recognized our strength in the development and application of technology, and we have chosen this as the gateway to the third century of our existence as a nation.'[59] Abrahamson, even more explicitly than Reagan, cast himself in the role of visionary working to effect an epochal shift against a tide of technological pessimism.

I like to think of SDI as part of the new space renaissance. The science and technology which developed in the seventeenth century were the tools which Renaissance man needed to complete his emancipation from the Middle Ages. In the twentieth century, another Renaissance was brought about by the space program. Our work in space opened new opportunities for expanding our understanding of the universe and for improving the quality of human life. The space renaissance brought to us much of our microelectronics capability, as well as more accurate forecasting of weather and natural disasters, low-cost global communication and navigation and the surveillance from space which has proven so vital for our national security.[60]

Moreover, while some charged SDI as driven by financial interests, Abrahamson argued that the programme would have a beneficial restorative effect for all by stimulating the US economy, acting as a boon to America's hi-tech industry and opening up new markets.

Clearly, the potential for an economic payoff from investment in the SDI technologies is great. The introduction of new, advanced technologies historically enhances a society's rate of growth ... I am confident that most of the emerging SDI technologies can, over time, readily be adapted for other space activities and for the consumer market ... With a lot of patience and a little creativity and innovation, the SDI program can create technological and economic opportunities that could be among the most important in our history.[61]

[58] Quoted in Fitzgerald, *Way Out There in the Blue*, p. 248.
[59] James A. Abrahamson, 'SDI: a Personal Vision' reprinted in Steven W. Guerrier and Wayne C. Thompson (eds.) *Perspectives on Strategic Defense* (Boulder, CO: Westview Press, 1987) p. 52.
[60] Abrahamson, 'SDI: a Personal Vision', p. 52.   [61] Ibid., p. 53.

As with Reagan, therefore, Abrahamson attempted discursively to link SDI both to specific technologies (microelectronics, space surveillance technologies) and to an overarching narrative of progress spanning from the Middle Ages onwards. Abrahamson also joined Reagan and Jastrow in invoking America's technological legacy as a response to scepticism from some parts of the scientific community.

I am convinced that these opponents will join the legions who said that man would never fly, who said that man would never go to the moon. As one who, in 1969, thrilled at watching man standing on the moon, I am not discouraged by these criticisms. I might add that neither is my friend, Sir Frank Whittle. In 1940 the National Academy of Science concluded that 'the gas turbine could hardly be considered a feasible application to airplanes.' Whittle first became aware of this opinion in 1976, long after his invention was commonplace. Not bad for something that was not feasible!

The SDIO chief also charged these opponents, much as Teller had decades earlier, with misunderstanding the process of technological development and underestimating the potential for novelty and scientific change:

I frankly think that many of our critics fail to appreciate the dynamic character of science. New discoveries are constantly changing technology and adding to its potential for new processes and new products. I remain convinced that there is little that the alliance of American science and technology cannot provide for our armed forces and for our nation! I remain convinced that anything that is theoretically possible will be achieved in practice, especially if we want it.[62]

As a national endeavour, then, SDI held the potential to unite Americans under a banner of technological innovation. Here Abrahamson looked to the techno-romanticism of an earlier time, blending philosophy, economics and moral principles:

In the 1930s, one of my favourite authors and a great aviator, Antoine de St Exupery, decried the so-called moralists who viewed technology as 'the enemy of spiritual civilization.' He stated that technological accomplishments 'have the single aim of bringing men together.' In my vision, so does SDI ... In my vision, SDI holds unlimited opportunities for strengthening our defense; for amassing new scientific knowledge; for inspiring our

---

[62] Ibid., p. 54.

young; for reinvigorating our economy; and for promoting peace and good will. In my vision, SDI will benefit the whole human race.[63]

Notable here is Abrahamson's wilful avoidance of the question of what impact SDI might have on the strategic balance. He jumps from the particular ('my vision', 'our defense') to the universal ('the whole human race') as the beneficiaries. Ultimately then, technological and moral imperatives fused for Abrahamson: 'we must be dedicated to using whatever our advantages are in space, on the ground, at sea, and in the air – everywhere – to find the way to ensure that we endure long enough and safely enough so that human solutions can finally be found'.[64]

Many of these themes and techniques were also echoed by ardent supporters of the concept of missile defence as it was re-imagined in the guise of SDI. On the question of the influence of these enthusiasts Fitzgerald (as was noted earlier) is sceptical, describing their perceived role as 'yet another legend surrounding the origin of Star Wars . . . In reality, Wallop, Graham and Teller did not inspire Reagan with their technical enthusiasms or persuade him to make the 1983 speech, though they tried hard enough.'[65] But even Fitzgerald concedes that:

in other ways they [Wallop, Graham and Teller] played an important role in launching the SDI program . . . besieging the Congress and the Pentagon as well as the White House, and publicizing their concepts through the press. In the process they created a public stir around the idea of missile defenses and kept the issue alive throughout the days of apostasy in Weinberger's Pentagon. Then, too, partly as a result of their efforts, the particular technologies they espoused later became major elements of the SDI program.[66]

These advocates of missile defence infused their arguments with a degree of technological enthusiasm which, though it may or may not have had direct influence on the Reagan administration prior to 1983, bears close resemblance to the types of rhetoric and argumentation employed by administration officials once the programme had been initiated. Senator Wallop, for example, had written in a 1979 letter to Reagan that technology was rendering the balance of terror 'obsolete' and was promising a 'considerable measure of safety from the threat of ballistic missiles'.[67] In a meeting in early November 1983 held in George

---

[63] Ibid.; de St Exupery (1900–44) was an early French airpower enthusiast.
[64] Ibid., p. 56.   [65] Fitzgerald, *Way Out There in the Blue*, p. 121.   [66] Ibid.
[67] Quoted in ibid., p. 121.

Keyworth's office at the White House, Teller assured assembled officials that an entire new generation of weapons was coming along, a 'third generation', to succeed the atomic and hydrogen bombs.[68] Nuclear weapons, he argued, were about to be superseded.[69]

Although Graham's claims for a partial defence (that is, of individual cities rather than the USA as a whole) were in some ways more modest,[70] his optimism was more ostentatious. Aspects of Graham's arguments echo closely those made later by Reagan, Jastrow and Abrahamson:

The United States is faced with an historic, but fleeting, opportunity to take its destiny into its own hands ... confidence in the future of free political and economic systems can be restored ... To accomplish this we need only take maximum advantage of one priceless legacy handed down to us by those free institutions – superiority in space technology ... We can confound the prophets of doom by opening the vast and rich High Frontier of space for industrialization ... The technology is available, the costs are reasonable, and the alternatives are not promising solutions to our security problems.[71]

But Graham was even more insistent about the potential benefits to be accrued from taking the 'High Frontier' of space for US defences. 'Throughout man's history', he argued, 'those nations which moved most effectively from one arena of human activity to the next have reaped enormous strategic advantages. For instance, when man's activities moved from land to the coastal seas, the Vikings established an extraordinary dominance by excelling at sailing those seas.'[72] In a 'Proposed Statement of US Policy' published in his *The Non-Nuclear*

---

[68] Ibid., p. 136.

[69] See Edward Teller, *Better a Shield than a Sword: Perspectives on Defense and Technology* (New York: The Free Press, 1987).

[70] Daniel O. Graham and Gregory A. Fossedal were themselves sceptical about the possibility of rendering nuclear weapons entirely obsolescent writing in 1983 that 'You will never have a perfect defense, not against the bullet, not against the tank, and not against nuclear weapons. What you can do is vastly complicate an attacker's calculations, blunt his force, and save millions of lives' – *Wall Street Journal*, 8 April 1983.

[71] Gen. Daniel O. Graham, *The Non-Nuclear Defense of Cities: the High Frontier Space-Based Defense against ICBM Attack* (Cambridge, MA: Abt Books, 1983) p. 1.

[72] Ibid., p. 3.

Defense of Cities: the High Frontier Space-Based Defense against ICBM Attack in 1983, Graham declared that:

In April of 1981, the Space Shuttle Columbia made its dramatic maiden voyage into space and back safely to Earth. This event was not merely another admirable feat of American space technology. It marked the advent of a new era of human activity on the High Frontier of space. The Space Shuttle is a development even more momentous for the future of mankind than was the completion of the transcontinental railway, the Suez and Panama Canals, or the first flight of the Wright brothers. It can be viewed as a 'railroad in space' over which will move the men and materials necessary to open broad new fields of human endeavour in space and to free us from the brooding menace of nuclear attack.[73]

By continuing this path of technological and engineering excellence, not only could the USA solve the problem of assured destruction, but technology could also become the means to solve many of the modern world's most pressing problems:

We can thus open the doors of opportunity to develop entire new space based industries, promising new products and new jobs for our people on Earth ... This will not only enhance the prosperity of the advanced, industrialized nations of our Free World, but will also provide the means to solve many of the hitherto intractable problems of the developing countries.[74]

Graham argued that the technological capability necessary to achieve these ends was essentially ready to go.[75]

Secretary of Defense Weinberger was not generally seen as an advocate of missile defence prior to 1983 as was seen in his earlier refutation of Graham's representations. But Weinberger himself swiftly adopted the language of technological optimism and the tendency to reference America's technological legacy once the initiative had been declared. Days after Reagan's speech, he argued that the Apollo project showed 'how quickly America can achieve things that have been felt to be impossible when the full strength of our very considerable resources are deployed behind them'.[76] He also replicated the practice of rejecting scientific criticism through the selective use of historical examples: 'The

---

[73] Ibid., p. 13.   [74] Ibid., p. 14.
[75] Edward Reiss, *The Strategic Defense Initiative* (Cambridge: Cambridge University Press, 1992) p. 43.
[76] *Washington Times*, 25 March 1983, p. 6

nay-sayers have already proclaimed that we will never have such technology, or that we should never try to acquire it. Their arguments are
hardly new ... In 1945 President Truman's Chief of Staff, Admiral
William Leahy, said of the atomic bomb: "That's the biggest fool
thing we've ever done. The bomb will never go off, and I speak as an
expert in explosives."'[77] Here, Weinberger can be seen to try and
reconfigure the discursive field in a manner that would elevate (his)
political expertise over its scientific counterpart. He dismissed technical objections in a similar fashion: 'Many scientists said a few years
ago that we couldn't ever reach the moon ... many scientists have said
a great many things that have proven to be wrong once the work has
been done,' he told NBC news. Critics he deemed 'traditional thinkers'
and people 'congenitally opposed to new ideas'.[78] Likewise John
Hughes, an assistant secretary of state during Reagan's first term in
office, asserted that scientists' protests against SDI violated the 'can-do
spirit' of America, constituting a negation of 'confident American
ingenuity that has taken us to the moon and provided other technological breakthroughs'.[79]

This line of argument even extended to strategic analysts. In a chapter
entitled 'Heavier-than-air Flying Machines are Impossible', Keith B.
Payne acknowledged that a significant proportion of the scientific community were sceptical about defence against ballistic missiles, and that
some technical analyses supported such assessments. On this basis he
asserted that 'It is reasonable ... to be cautious in anticipating what
technology can achieve.' In addition, though, he cautioned that 'one
also should be reluctant to accept the judgement, even from experts,
that a particular technological task is "impossible", particularly in
reference to a decades-long project such as building a comprehensive
defense system'.[80] Payne noted that 'Expert opinion in the past concerning "the impossible" can be quite humorous' and proceeded to list
several such arguments:

---

[77] Quoted in Ashton B. Carter, *Directed Energy Missile Defense in Space:
Background Paper* (Washington, DC: Office of Technology Assessment, 1984)
p. 67.
[78] Quoted in Fitzgerald, *Way Out There in the Blue*, p. 248.
[79] Quoted in Linenthal, *Symbolic Defense*, p. 33.
[80] Payne, *Strategic Defense*, p. 63.

'Rail travel at high speed is not possible because passengers, unable to breathe, would die of asphyxia.' (Dr Dionysus Lardner (1793–1859), professor of natural philosophy and astronomy at University College, London)

'Heavier-than-air flying machines are impossible.' (Lord Kelvin, British mathematician, physicist, and president of the British Royal Society, *c.* 1895)

'It is apparent to me that the possibilities of the aeroplane, which two or three years ago were thought to hold the solution to the [flying machine] problem, have been exhausted, and that we must turn elsewhere.' (Thomas Alva Edison, 1895)

'To affirm that the aeroplane is going to "revolutionize" naval warfare of the future is to be guilty of the wildest exaggeration.' (*Scientific American*, 16 July 1910)

'I can accept the theory of relativity as little as I can accept the existence of atoms and other such dogmas.' (Ernst Mach, professor of physics, University of Vienna, 1913)

Payne added to these Leahy's dismissal of the atomic bomb cited previously by Weinberger, and Vannevar Bush's rejection of the notion of ICBMs which was also cited by Jastrow.[81] 'Current scepticism concerning the impossibility of an effective BMD', Payne concluded, 'may, in the twenty-first century, appear as short-sighted as past statements concerning the impossibility of flying machines, rail travel, ICBMs, and the atomic bomb.' To him a consensus concerning the future potential for ballistic missile defence did not therefore constitute 'a conclusive indictment against the SDI'. Payne preferred to remain upbeat about the prospects for defences, approvingly quoting Professor James Fletcher's assertion that 'The technical issues surrounding the development of effective defenses have many possible solutions and should not at this stage be the primary focus of the debate.'[82]

Imagining SDI

Despite these arguments that technological innovation would come good as it had done for America in the past, confusion reigned as to

[81] Payne reproduces these quotes from Christopher Cerf and Victor Navasky, *The Experts Speak* (New York: Pantheon Books, 1984) p. 232.
[82] Payne, *Strategic Defense*, p. 66.

precisely what form SDI was supposed to take. The Fletcher panel and
the Hoffman commission, both charged with assessing the possibilities
for strategic defence, did not make any fixed recommendations on
what shape the programme should take but advocated instead a
'flexible R&D program designed to offer early options for the deployment of intermediate systems'. This had two important practical consequences. The first was that the concept of missile defence was
endorsed as an objective but its exact format was left unspecified,
thus legitimating a diversity of research projects and a massive R&D
budget favourable to several of the defence industry interests represented on both panels.[83] The second, as Reiss notes, was that although
a research programme for future administrations became the effective
rationale for SDI by 1985, 'the Administration never publicly with-
drew the more popular idea of a "space shield"'.[84] Thus the appeals to
America's history of technological innovation made by Reagan,
Abrahamson, Weinberger *et al.* were intended to create a degree of
certainty for a programme with a necessarily uncertain outcome, and
to provide resonant parallels with great innovations begun in (supposedly) similar circumstances.

Key to sustaining the credibility of these appeals, as indicated briefly
earlier, was the presentation of 'breakthroughs' in the development of
SDI technologies. What counted as a breakthrough, though, was itself
a broad category given the largely unspecified nature of the programme's format. The most prominent initial advance was
Lockheed's Homing Overlay Experiment (HOE) of 10 June 1984,
which destroyed a mock ballistic missile in mid-flight with an interceptor missile. Reiss asserts that the 'video sequence, relayed around
the globe, encouraged widespread belief in "Star Wars" systems', even
though it constituted 'a far cry from dealing with the whole arsenal of
an enemy who could use an array of counter-measures'.[85] Moreover,
the HOE was based on the principle of kinetic (that is, missile-to-
missile) intercept and not the laser-based programmes which took up
the bulk of SDI funding as the programme progressed. Gary Guertner
also asserted in 1989 that the validation of 'components rather than

---

[83] See Reiss, *The Strategic Defense Initiative*, pp. 60–71.
[84] Ibid., p. 52.   [85] Ibid., p. 56.

systems reliability', epitomised by the celebration of advances in sensor and tracking technologies, constituted an ambiguous standard of proof of the overall feasibility of SDI but helped to keep the programme going.

> If Congress could clearly see the final price tag, strategic defense would have little chance of surviving the scrutiny of deficit-minded legislators. But incremental funding, technological optimism, ambiguous standards of proof – for example, validation of components rather than systems reliability – and predictably shrill Soviet reactions may combine to propel it through the appropriations process for many years.[86]

Mitchell takes this critique further, arguing that ambiguous standards of proof were reinforced by a consciously directed policy of 'perception management' by the Reagan administration aimed at presenting SDI research in the best possible light. He argues that 'numerous deceptive manoeuvres executed by missile defense officials and scientists during the Star Wars era appear to have been authorized by several legal instruments that codified governmental prerogatives to censor speech, manipulate scientific results, and deceive external audiences'.[87] Much of the evidence for Mitchell's argument only became available after SDI had been wound down. In 1993, for example, the Clinton administration released documents confirming suspicions that the HOE of 10 June 1984 had been rigged in order to allow for a near-miss to look like a success. Other evidence obtained by virtue of post-Cold War freedom of information suggests that the public face of SDI was carefully managed and co-ordinated from the top-down. On 30 May 1985, Reagan issued National Security Decision Directive 172 – 'Presenting the Strategic Defense Initiative' – to 'provide guidance in the manner in which I want the Strategic Defense Initiative and the SDI research program presented'. The directive specified that statements, briefings, reports, speeches, articles and op ed. pieces by administration officials regarding SDI had to be cleared by the Assistant to the President for National Security Affairs. When asked about these disclosures, former Secretary of Defense Caspar Weinberger told the

---

[86] Gary L. Guertner, 'What is Proof?' in Kenneth N. Luongo and W. Thomas Wander (eds.) *The Search for Security in Space* (Ithaca: Cornell University Press, 1989) p. 191.

[87] Mitchell, *Strategic Deception*, p. 72.

New York Times, 'you're always trying to practice deception. You are obviously trying to mislead your opponents and make sure they don't know the actual facts.'[88]

Management of the perception of SDI extended well beyond administration statements though. For the various elements advocating SDI – including the administration, advocacy groups and defence contractors involved – it also required illustrating and illuminating what exactly SDI was and could be. In keeping with the theme of technological optimism propounded in the rhetoric of SDI supporters, proponents of the programme employed diagrams, pictorial representations and illustrations in order to fill in the gap of imagination for what SDI would look like. The badge of the SDIO presented, quite literally, a shield in space. Linenthal points to the example of a drawing accompanying an article on the morality of SDI in *Policy Review* which depicted an American eagle swooping down on incoming missiles, ready to pluck them out of space.[89] *Newsweek*'s April 1983 front cover presented readers with a comic book-style rendering of an X-ray laser battlestation under the headline of 'Reagan's New Nuclear Strategy: Will Space Be the Next Battleground?'.[90] Even Keith Payne accompanies his previously cited cautionary assessment of experts' predictions with an 'Artist's Conception of Space-Based Non-Nuclear Rocket Defense System'.[91] Newspapers and advocacy groups faithfully reproduced diagrams from the SDIO of how, when and where ICBMs would be intercepted in their flight, while television coverage likewise ran computer-generated simulations of the same, and key contractors in SDI produced information booklets and technical reports accompanied with detailed illustrations for the perusal of Pentagon officials and Congressmen.[92] In this sense, the goals of SDI were primarily 'political and ideological rather than military', and 'Its symbolism was perfectly adapted to this end: an impenetrable sheltering dome, American high technology in full control, a shield rather than a nuclear sword.'[93]

---

[88] Ibid., p. 63.
[89] Linenthal, *Symbolic Defense*, p. 43.   [90] Mitchell, *Strategic Deception*, p. 46.
[91] Payne, *Strategic Defense*, p. 83.
[92] Reiss, *The Strategic Defense Initiative*, pp. 165–78.
[93] Edwards, *The Closed World*, p. 293.

Conclusion

These invocations of America's technological heritage in the promotion
of SDI all textually embedded a key unquestioned assumption: that SDI
technology would eliminate America's nuclear security problem.
Sympathisers and critics alike presume that this instrumental understanding of technology undoubtedly resonates with the 'American
ethos', and that is something the promotion of SDI tapped into.
Michael Vlahos argued at the time that:

> To the progressive, technology is the instrument of American destiny: it is
> what made us and preserved us. It created the hope of a free world. SDI is
> embraced by progressives ... [It] is seen as a national deus ex machina, *the
> intervention of an ancestral, almost godlike instrumentality that will return us
> to the romantic landscape of security we once enjoyed* ... It is almost instinc-
> tively understood by Americans. It resonates to our national hymn.[94]

E. P. Thompson at his most caustic warned that such faux cultural
innocence merely masked what SDI *really* signified – an American desire
to return to the strategic superiority of the immediate post-war years. It
was, he opined, attuned to the worst kind of 'eschatological zeal that
has long been found in the traditions of American populism':

> Star Wars is a populist's dream. It is the Rococo Epiphany, the ultimate
> technological fix, the all-singing-all-dancing-all-praying-all-answering
> machine. It has struck a gusher of American rhetoric in whose fountains
> there float and jostle incompatible elements ... It evokes a nostalgic golden
> past Before the Bomb (or before the machine got into the garden) at the same
> time as it appeals to generations brought up on sci-fi, on space invaders, on
> Darth-Vader and Luke Skywalker movies, and on their own home-terminal
> computer games ... It combines the citizen's faith that whatever the US of A
> does must be moral – and that the Bomb is God's gift to protect the 'Free
> World' –with the energetic and innovative American tradition of 'fixing'
> things, and of looking for technological solutions to political, social or even
> psychological problems.[95]

Undoubtedly, as we have seen, the propagation of this instrumentalist,
progressivist view of technology was present in the promotion of SDI.

---

[94] Michael Vlahos, *Strategic Defense and the American Ethos: Can the Nuclear
   World be Changed?* (Boulder, CO: Foreign Policy Institute, 1986) pp. 18–19,
   emphasis added.
[95] Edward P. Thompson, 'Folly's Comet' in Thompson, *Star Wars*, pp. 138–9.

This in turn had a strategic impact in the sense of furthering specific political and economic interests. There are two further points to note here though. The first is that even critiques of this view, such as Thompson's, acknowledge a prior understanding, history and experience of technology presumed as particularly appropriate and common to the advocacy of missile defence. The second, as will be argued in the next chapter, is that the promotion of SDI in instrumentalist terms was in fact itself born out of a prior substantivist vision which, as will be addressed later, casts the use and appeal of the arguments covered here in a very different light and brings the contradictory, disjointed and fragmentary nature of the common sense argument for SDI to the fore.

6 | *'Star Wars' and technological determinism*

Introduction

This chapter revisits the arguments surrounding the Reagan administration's Strategic Defense Initiative (SDI). It makes the case that the instrumentalist justifications for SDI examined in chapter 5 were themselves only made possible by the use and integration of substantivist framings of the nuclear threat. To show this, the chapter examines the context in which the Reagan administration came to power. In particular it focuses on how the intelligence revisions proposed by reports from 'Team B' and the 'Committee on the Present Danger' foreshadowed the Reagan administration's increased defence restructuring by invoking a quasi-substantivist logic. This restructuring, in turn, led to a purer, more thoroughgoing form of substantivist critique by the political left, which seriously threatened the Reagan administration's commitment to defence spending. Reagan's argument for SDI, particularly his March 1983 presidential appeal, sought to co-opt this latter impulse and to build it into the case for strategic defence, and in conclusion the chapter employs Gramsci's notion of *transformismo* as a means of understanding how this co-optation occurred. As a consequence of this co-optation of substantivist arguments, it is argued, the justification of SDI was based not purely on instrumentalism but rather on a familiar common sense of technology in which potentially contradictory elements of instrumental and substantive understandings of technology formed a 'heteroglossic' composite.

Détente and its discontents

In Part Two we saw how proponents of missile defence such as Edward Teller and General Daniel Graham, having been dealt a major blow by the 1972 ABM Treaty, refocused their efforts on persuading subsequent US policy-makers of the viability of a range of 'exotic' defence proposals. To this missile defence constituency, the rationale for defence remained as strong as ever, if not stronger, post-1972. To recap, the very notion of arms control was argued to be based on a misguided conception of technological development and an equally misguided perception of Soviet intentions. A taken-for-granted assumption of missile defence proponents in the 1970s was that the Soviet Union placed a higher premium on defence than did the United States and, by consequence, was willing to invest the time and effort in developing and deploying an effective strategic defence, even under the ABM Treaty's supposed restrictions, that the USA was not.

In these views, missile defence advocacy once again drew intellectual succour from critics of deterrence theory, and tapped into a broader intellectual sense of dissatisfaction with the quality of intelligence on Soviet strategic forces. Here again Albert Wohlstetter proves to be an influential figure. In a series of articles in the mid-1970s, Wohlstetter chastised the US intelligence infrastructure, the CIA in particular, for underestimating Soviet missile deployment.[1] More generally, the conservative right likewise asserted that the CIA's estimates on Soviet military spending and long-term strategic plans – which were in keeping with the practice of estimates emphasised by McNamara (see chapter 4) – produced an artificially low sense of 'real' Soviet spending and hence the true Soviet threat.[2] The accuracy of such criticism has itself long been questioned.[3] It suffices merely to note here that a growing consensus on the need for a revision of intelligence estimates was to have significant implications for missile defence advocacy in the late 1970s. Familiar faces sympathetic to the cause of missile defence were closely allied in this process of revision. The perceived need for a new assessment, for example, was to be met by President Ford's Foreign Intelligence Advisory Board (PFIAB), the membership of which was dominated by political conservatives and included Edward Teller and John Foster. The former stood as the foremost proponent of missile defence, the latter

---

[1] Albert Wohlstetter, 'Is There a Strategic Arms Race?', *Foreign Policy*, 15 (1974) pp. 3–26; 'Rivals but No Race', *Foreign Policy*, 16 (1974) pp. 170–98; 'Optimal Ways to Confuse Ourselves', *Foreign Policy*, 20 (1975) pp. 997–1002.

[2] Paul Nitze, 'Assuring Strategic Stability in an Era of Détente', *Foreign Affairs*, 54:2 (1976) pp. 207–32.

[3] See, for example, John Prados, *The Soviet Estimate: US Intelligence Analysis and Soviet Strategic Forces* (Princeton, NJ: Princeton University Press, 1986).

as a defence-enthusiastic physicist who, as we saw in the last chapter, was keenly aware of the dynamics for promoting new defence initiatives.

The group assigned by the PFIAB to correct intelligence 'deficiencies', the infamous 'Team B' (or B Team), likewise counted several key missile defence enthusiasts among its ranks. Among those who engaged in this 'experiment in competitive threat assessments' (approved by then Director of Central Intelligence George H. W. Bush) were core political proponents of missile defence: Teller, Graham, William Van Cleave, Paul Wolfowitz and Paul Nitze.[4] Under the leadership of the Harvard professor of Russian history Richard E. Pipes, Team B came up with significantly increased projections for Soviet missile accuracy, and therefore of American vulnerability, than those contained in the National Intelligence Estimate of the time (NIE 11–8–76). Whereas the original NIE indicated that détente would continue without major threat to the USA, the B Team's report speculated that the Soviet intentions extended to disrupting ocean transport and fuel supplies to the USA, and creating a nuclear 'war-winning' capability that would assure global dominance.[5] Graham sought to publicise the general emphasis of the report when writing in the September 1976 *Reader's Digest*: 'The Soviets have not built up their forces, as we have, merely to deter a nuclear war. They build their forces to fight a nuclear war and [they] see an enormous persuasive power accruing to a nation with confidence in its survival.'[6] Such an analysis found favour with Ford's Secretary of Defense, Donald Rumsfeld, who had previously argued that defence spending should be increased markedly to reverse 'adverse trends' in the US force posture.[7]

The Team B reports stand as an early example of the 'weapons don't make war' argument that Colin Gray would later develop explicitly. They accuse the CIA of consistently underestimating the 'intensity, scope and implicit threat' posed by the Soviet Union by relying on technical or 'hard' data, but neglecting to 'contemplate Soviet strategic objectives in terms of the Soviet conception of "strategy" as well as in light of Soviet history, the structure of Soviet society, and the

[4] Anne Hessing Cahn, 'Team B: the Trillion Dollar Experiment (Part I)', *The Bulletin of the Atomic Scientists*, April (1993) pp. 22–7, p. 22.
[5] Prados, *The Soviet Estimate*, p. 252.
[6] Quoted in Cahn, 'The Trillion Dollar Experiment', p. 25.
[7] Quoted in Prados, *The Soviet Estimate*, p. 254.

pronouncements of Soviet leaders'.[8] The strategic goals (or ends) of the Soviet Union's leaders, rather than its strategic forces (or means), would dictate the conduct of Soviet policy, hence estimates should take this into consideration. At the same time when Team B looked at 'hard' data, as Cahn notes, it always saw worst-case scenarios. Well-known examples include substantial overestimation of the number of 'Backfire' bombers that would be produced by the Soviets, an undetectable non-acoustic submarine which never existed (but could not be disproved precisely because it had supposedly 'succeeded' in its undetectability), and in the field of ABM systems. 'Mobile ABM system components combined with the deployed SAM (surface-to-air missile) system could produce a significant ABM capability,' Team B speculated. A perceived asymmetry in both support and funding for ABM led Team B to the conclusion that 'Understanding that there are differing evaluations of the potentialities of laser and CPB (charged particle beams) for ABM, *it is still clear that the Soviets have mounted ABM efforts in both areas of a magnitude that it is difficult to overestimate*.'[9] Thus, Team B predicted, the USA had entered a new period of peril in which Soviet advances in – and American lack of – missile defence were a key issue.

The Committee on the Present Danger

Team B's predictions repeated several of the characteristics of the reaction to *Sputnik* explored in chapter 4, primarily in effecting 'an inexorable swing from complacency to alarm'.[10] Paul Nitze, for example, was one of the key architects of the Gaither report and, as a founder member of the 'Committee on the Present Danger' (CPD), was intent on the dissemination of similar warnings to the US public.[11] The CPD's

---

[8] United States Central Intelligence Agency, *Intelligence Community Experiment in Competitive Analysis: Soviet Strategic Objectives, an Alternative View: Report of Team 'B'* (Washington, DC: Government Printing Office, 1976), declassified 16 September 1992, p. 1.
[9] Ibid., quoted in Cahn, 'The Trillion Dollar Experiment', p. 26, emphasis in original.
[10] Prados, *The Soviet Estimate*, p. 257.
[11] As Wolfe notes, the CPD of the late 1970s 'borrowed both name and purpose' from an organisation of the 1950s established to warn of the consequences of Soviet atomic weapons for the USA – Alan Wolfe, *The Rise and Fall of the Soviet Threat* (Boston, MA: Southend Press, 1984) p. 4. Wolfe, like Prados, also equates the Gaither and Team B reports.

membership and stance largely grew out of Team B and its aim was, essentially, to encourage public pressure for an expansion of America's defence infrastructure by warning citizens of the impending Soviet threat.[12] Its manifesto declared that 'our country is in a period of danger, and the danger is increasing. Unless decisive steps are taken to alert the nation, and to change the course of its policy, our economic and military capability will become inadequate.'[13]

Notable in this regard is the fact that the CPD's appraisal of the role of technology in the strategic balance uncritically combines contending understandings of technology in its 'common sense' assessment of the immediate danger to the USA.[14] Here again, initially, we see the nightmare vision of a United States made subordinate to a technologically superior Soviet Union:

> If we continue to drift, we shall become second best to the Soviet Union in overall military strength; our alliances will weaken … Then we could find ourselves isolated in a hostile world, facing the unremitting pressures of Soviet policy backed by an overwhelming preponderance of power. Our national survival would be in peril, and we should face, one after another, bitter choices between war and acquiescence under pressure.[15]

According to the CPD the Soviets' goal was 'not to wage a nuclear war but to win political predominance without having to fight'.[16] Fear of technological domination, through nuclear blackmail, was hence reiterated. As Dalby notes, 'In the long tradition of the "worst-case" analyses of US strategic thinking … Pipes estimates that the USSR is aiming at achieving a nuclear superiority which will effectively paralyse US political actions in the 1980s.'[17]

This vision of technological domination, somewhat paradoxically, was grounded on the construction of the Soviet adversary as an instrumentalist thinker who would actually *use* nuclear weapons as part of a

---

[12] Simon Dalby, *Creating the Second Cold War: the Discourse of Politics* (London: Pinter, 1990).

[13] Committee on the Present Danger, 'Common Sense and the Present Danger' in Charles Tyroler II (ed.) *Alerting America: the Papers of the Committee on the Present Danger* (Washington, DC: Pergamon-Brassy's, 1984), January 1977, p. 1

[14] Dalby, *Creating the Second Cold War*, see especially pp. 47–52.

[15] Committee on the Present Danger, 'Common Sense and the Present Danger', p. 5.

[16] Ibid., p. 41.   [17] Dalby, *Creating the Second Cold War*, p. 128.

'war-fighting' strategy.[18] Nowhere is this more apparent than in the writings of Richard Pipes, the figurehead of both Team B and the CPD. In *US–Soviet Relations in the Era of Détente*, for example, Pipes pre-empts several of the arguments made much later in Colin Gray's 'weapons don't make war' thesis and applies them to Soviet strategic policy:

> Soviet military theorists reject the notion that technology (i.e., weapons) decides strategy. They perceive the relationship to be the reverse: strategic objectives determine the procurement and application of weapons. They agree that the introduction of nuclear weapons has profoundly affected warfare, but deny that nuclear weapons have altered its essential quality.[19]

'In other words', Pipes continues, 'military strategy, rather than a casualty of technology, has, thanks to technology, become more central than ever. By adopting this view, Soviet theorists believe themselves to have adapted modern technological innovations in weaponry to the traditions of military science.'[20] Given this pervasive Soviet instrumentalism the logical, common sense, thing to do was therefore to analyse the traditions of military science adhered to by the Soviets. Here Pipes was convinced of the essentially 'Clausewitzian' nature of Soviet strategic thought. 'It is well known that the essential nature of *war as a continuation of politics does not change with changing technology and armament*,' Pipes enthusiastically quotes a fellow commentator on Soviet strategy.[21] The Soviet Union would hence have no qualms about military build-up, and was likely to reject the suggestion that there was anything destabilising about unhindered technological innovation – both key predicates of deterrence theory. But then, as Pipes speculated, 'In addition (though we have no solid evidence to this effect) it seems likely that Soviet strategists reject the mutual-deterrence theory on several technical grounds of a kind that have been advanced by American critics of this theory such as Albert Wohlstetter, Herman Kahn, and Paul Nitze.'[22]

[18] Nitze, 'Assuring Strategic Stability in an Era of Détente'; Colin S. Gray, 'Nuclear Strategy: the Case for a Theory of Victory', *International Security*, 4:1 (1979) pp. 54–87; Richard Pipes, 'Why the Soviet Union Thinks it Could Fight and Win a Nuclear War', *Commentary*, 64:1 (1977) pp. 21–34.
[19] Richard Pipes, *US–Soviet Relations in the Era of Détente* (Boulder, CO: Westview Press, 1981) pp. 155–6.
[20] Ibid., p. 156.
[21] Quoted in Pipes, *US–Soviet Relations*, p. 99, from V. D. Sokolovskii, *Soviet Military Strategy* (New York: Praeger, 1963), emphasis added by Pipes.
[22] Pipes, *US–Soviet Relations*, p. 157.

A further likelihood for Pipes, based on his assessment of Russian history, was that 'Such a country tends to assess the rewards of defense in much more realistic terms,'[23] and implicit in this assessment of Soviet 'realism' was a critique of the existing American stance on defence. 'Mutual deterrence postulates a certain finality about weapons technology: it does not allow for further scientific breakthroughs that could result in the deterrent's becoming neutralized'; the Soviets, by contrast, had recognised that 'on the defensive [side], satellites which are essential for early warning of an impending attack could be blinded and lasers could be put to use to destroy incoming missiles'.[24] The CPD likewise concluded that:

The Soviets believe in the importance of air defense of their homeland, whereas the United States has abandoned air defense on the premise that it is not useful in the absence of ballistic missile defense. The Soviets also believe in ballistic missile defense. They signed the ABM Treaty in 1972 because the United States had a long technological lead, not because we had converted them to the concept of mutually assured destruction (MAD), the mutual-hostage theory ... While we deactivated and partially dismantled our sole permitted ABM site, and have cut back our ABM research and development program, the Soviets have maintained their Moscow site and are vigorously pursuing ABM research and development ...[25]

Whereas the USA continued voluntarily to restrict itself in the fields of both active and passive defence, the Soviets were assumed to be pursuing 'Clausewitzian' offensive–defensive combinations apace:

The Soviet leadership seems to strive to obtain a marked superiority in all branches of the military, in order to secure powerful forward-moving shields behind which the politicians can do their work. To reach this objective, the Soviet Union must have open to it all options – to be able to fight general and limited conventional wars near its borders and away from them, as well as nuclear wars employing tactical and/or strategic weapons.[26]

The paradox in all this, identified best by Robert Johnson, is that despite the emphasis placed by Pipes on the Soviet 'character', Soviet military capabilities, embodied in military hardware, remain the prime source of danger to the USA in Pipes's thinking. Hence, ultimately, 'No

[23] Ibid., p. 167.   [24] Ibid., p. 157.
[25] Committee on the Present Danger, 'Common Sense and Present Danger', pp. 42–3.
[26] Pipes, *US–Soviet Relations*, p. 94.

knowledge of Soviet history or of the complex structure of Soviet political goals and motivations is required. The relevance of history and politics is, in fact, denied by the claim that Soviet international behaviour is dominated by Soviet perceptions of the strategic balance.'[27] The response formulated by Pipes, Nitze and especially Colin Gray was therefore to meet this Soviet perception, with equal stress on military-technological superiority, and an accompanying theory of victory to make this superiority meaningful. As Dalby notes, 'the possession of enough weapons is not enough on its own, it requires a plausible theory of victory to be completely convincing. Providing this has been Gray's self-appointed task.'[28] Here, the CPD was not merely advocating a military build-up, based on strategic principles which would (re)include pursuing defensive options, but was focused initially on assuring the superiority of America's offensive nuclear weapons.[29]

The 'Window of vulnerability'

The connections between the CPD and the Reagan administration are well documented.[30] Reagan's election campaign drew on themes developed by the CPD, and in January 1979 he became a member of its executive board. In turn, CPD members formed the core of Reagan's defence team when he came into power. 'In effect', Fitzgerald argues, 'the CPD had become the Reagan campaign's brain trust for defense and foreign policy,' and the shape of Reaganite defence policy reflected this in its heavy emphasis on military spending.[31] The prime example of the CPD's influence was of course the 'window of vulnerability', the phrase consistently used by Reagan and his campaigners to denote an interval (or window) between the Soviet deployment of the SS-18, a

---

[27] Robert H. Johnson, 'Periods of Peril: the Window of Vulnerability and Other Myths', *Foreign Affairs*, 61:4 (1983) pp. 950–71.

[28] Dalby, *Creating the Second Cold War*, p. 147.

[29] Colin S. Gray and Keith B. Payne, 'Victory is Possible', *Foreign Policy*, 39 (1980) pp. 14–27.

[30] Frances Fitzgerald, *Way Out There in the Blue: Reagan, Star Wars and the End of the Cold War* (New York: Simon and Schuster, 2000) pp. 98–106; Dalby, *Creating the Second Cold War*; Robert H. Johnson, 'Periods of Peril'.

[31] Fitzgerald, *Way Out There in the Blue*, p. 98. As Fitzgerald notes, Reagan's national security bureaucracy was dominated by right-wing Republican and neoconservative political appointees, approximately fifty of whom – including figures such as Van Cleave, Fred Ikle and Richard Perle – belonged to the CPD – p. 156.

nuclear missile boasting improved guidance systems, and American deployment of an equivalent ICBM capable of surviving an SS-18 attack. More broadly, though, as used in Reagan's 1980 presidential campaign, the phrase 'conveyed the specter of a Soviet diplomatic offensive the like of which had never been seen'.[32] Thus the 'window' idea shares many of the attributes of the Gaither report, connoting a new period of peril once again premised on the general theme of Soviet technological innovation.[33] Fitzgerald argues that Reagan's electioneering rhetoric was based on his own reinterpretation of the CPD 'doomsday scenario': America's bombers and missiles were outdated, its nuclear submarines outdated, and its efforts at civil defence inadequate.[34] 'The Soviet Union has used détente to build the biggest military force the world has ever seen,' Reagan claimed during the 1980 election campaign.[35] His proposed remedy likewise fitted the CPD's recommendations. The case for the MX missile, for example, became subsumed within the window of vulnerability argument even though the MX was technically not a 'survivable' option in the event of a Soviet first strike. On the subject of defence, Reagan indicated that he was prepared to countenance all possibilities during the campaign:

I don't know about the backyard shelters with today's technology or not, but as I say, one of the first things I would do would be to turn to those who are knowledgeable in military affairs, knowledgeable in the weaponry that would be coming at us, and so forth, to find out what we could do. Now it could well be that maybe there is another defense, maybe there is a defense through having superior offensive ability to keep them from doing this.[36]

Thus, Fitzgerald argues, far from being a naive everyman with little sense of America's strategic capabilities when on his 'inspirational' visit to NORAD in the summer of 1979, Reagan was more likely 'thoroughly immersed in the CPD's arguments about strategic nuclear policy'.[37] Indeed, the massive defence build-up endorsed by Reagan seems to reflect the influence of the Republican right and the CPD in particular. Once in office, however, the limitations of the CPD's 'doomsday

---

[32] Cahn, 'The Trillion Dollar Experiment', p. 23.   [33] Johnson, 'Periods of Peril'.
[34] Fitzgerald, *Way Out There in the Blue*, p. 107.
[35] Quoted in Wolfe, *The Rise and Fall*, p. 1.
[36] Robert Scheer, *With Enough Shovels: Reagan, Bush, and Nuclear War* (New York: Random House, 1982) pp. 232–4.
[37] Fitzgerald, *Way Out There in the Blue*, p. 98.

scenario' became evident. Questions soon rose about how it was exactly that investment in offensive weapons was supposed to avert this scenario, and it quickly became apparent that neither the CPD nor the Reagan administration had a monopoly on the evocation of substantivist fears. Their critics were in fact prepared to develop these fears even more vividly.

Substantivism and the anti-nuclear movement

Whereas those advocating a military build-up invoked substantivism to some extent, radical critics of this same campaign took this view much further. Far from seeing nuclear weapons as a new development that simply required a new theory of victory, influential commentators such as Jonathan Schell argued that nuclear weapons rendered the very categories of victory and defeat effectively meaningless. 'These bombs were built as "weapons" for "war",' Schell acknowledged in *The Fate of the Earth*, 'but their significance greatly transcends war and all its causes and outcomes. They grew out of history, yet they threaten to end history. They were made by men, yet they threaten to annihilate men. They are a pit into which the whole world can fall – a nemesis of all human intentions, actions, and hopes.'[38] Furthermore, Schell held out little hope for a technological fix that would prevent a nuclear war: 'To return to safety through technical measures alone, we would have to disarm matter itself, converting it back into its relatively safe, inert, non-explosive nineteenth-century Newtonian state – something that not even the physics of our time can teach us how to do.'[39] Schell's hope for reducing the threat of nuclear war rested not, as in the CPD view, in technological predominance, but on a radical conception of human agency that could only be inspired by a universal desire to prevent nuclear war.[40] Science and technology, as in the typical substantivist view, were inhibitors of this agency. 'Science', Schell argues, 'is a process of submission, in which the mind does not dictate to nature but seeks out and then bows to nature's laws, letting its conclusions be guided by that which *is*, independent of our wills.'[41]

---

[38] Jonathan Schell, *The Fate of the Earth* (London: Picador, 1982) p. 3.
[39] Ibid., p. 100.   [40] Jonathan Schell, *The Abolition* (London: Picador, 1984).
[41] Schell, *The Fate of the Earth*, p. 105, emphasis in original.

Schell's *Fate of the Earth* famously drew on a hypothetical scenario in which New York was destroyed by a nuclear bomb as a means to inspire revulsion at the potential consequences of the ongoing arms race. 'It may only be by descending into this hell in imagination now that we can hope to escape descending into it in reality sometime later,' Schell argued.[42] The work of Helen Caldicott, Jack Geiger and Carl Sagan all followed broadly similar lines of argument, while the ABC channel's made-for-television movie *The Day After* visually depicted the aftermath and after-effects of a nuclear attack on the United States, thereby bringing the nightmare vision home to a prime-time audience. The substantivism of anti-nuclear activists was thus of a qualitatively different nature to that evoked by defence advocates. Those within the CPD and Reagan administration were arguably most worried about the ability of the Soviet Union to 'blackmail' the USA into submission, as opposed to nuclear war itself. Schell, Caldicott *et al.* were convinced that such thinking was itself a contributory factor in heightening the likelihood of nuclear war. Moreover, the CPD's pro-nuclear, pro-weapons technology position assumed that rational calculations and decisions would guide the course of nuclear war, neglecting the possibility that accidents and misperceptions could instigate a nuclear confrontation.

Several commentators invoked a more thoroughgoing substantivist understanding as a way of depicting this seeming nuclear illogic. Such accounts can be seen as engaged in a textually enacted struggle, armed with their own bleak vocabulary and literary allusions, with the pro-nuclear position epitomised by the CPD's viewpoint over the exact implications of a further arms build-up.[43] 'The uncontrollable arms race is proof enough that the nuclear state lacks the internal means to stave off annihilation. Those who seem to control it are, in fact, slaves,' argued Joel Kovel. 'Who of us has not felt utter helplessness in the face of the juggernaut of nuclear weaponry? Our puny individual strength is simply not drawn on the same scale. There is more to it than the power of the weapon itself.'[44] Kovel likened the domination of nuclear technology to Faust's bargain; to Shelley's *Frankenstein*, seeing it as 'the

[42] Ibid., p. 5.
[43] Norman Fairclough, 'Linguistic and Intertextual Analysis within Discourse Analysis' in Adam Jaworski and Nikolas Coupland (eds.) *The Discourse Reader* (London: Routledge, 2004) p. 198.
[44] Joel Kovel, *Against the State of Nuclear Terror* (London: Pan, 1983) pp. 42–3.

realization of this grim verdict against industrialization and technology'; and to William Blake's image of 'dark satanic mills', endorsing Blake's conclusion that 'Thy self-destroying, beast form'd Science shall be thy eternal lot'.[45] Echoing Jacques Ellul's theory of a technological society, Kovel declared that:

In technological society, people are swathed in technology, fascinated by it, yet inevitably estranged from and ignorant about it. This should be no mystery, since the other side of estrangement is the privileged use by the minority of owners and masters. Technology has always been trumpeted as the great bringer of social equality. When used under the aegis of technocracy, it does no such thing, but only perpetrates inequality at a higher overall level of material acquisition ... Nuclear weaponry is not just an aberration but the logical result of an entire attitude toward the world.[46]

Robert Lifton likewise used a substantivist framing to describe what he saw as the psychological effects of nuclearism: 'Technology comes to shape and render belligerent the mind-set, rather than the mind-set controlling and restraining the technology.'[47] E. P. Thompson, also invoking Blake's imagery, saw fit to designate this condition with a new category:

There is an internal dynamic and reciprocal logic here which requires a new category for its analysis. If 'the hand-mill gives you society with the feudal lord; the steam-mill, society with the industrial capitalist', what are we given by those Satanic mills which are now at work, grinding out the means of human extermination? I have reached this point of thought more than once before, but have turned my head away in despair. Now, when I look at it directly, I know that category which we need is that of 'exterminism'.[48]

In his well-known essay of the time 'Notes on Exterminism, the Last Stage of Civilization', Thompson tacitly endorses the Heideggerian view that instinctive instrumentalism in relation to nuclear weapons had precipitated a modern crisis. 'Weapons are things, and strategies are instrumental plans for implementing policies which originate elsewhere. Thus what we must do is examine the ruling elites and their

[45] Ibid., pp. 98–99.   [46] Ibid., pp. 122–3, 131.
[47] Robert Jay Lifton and Richard Falk, *Indefensible Weapons: the Political and Psychological Case against Nuclearism* (New York: Basic Books, 1982) p. 9.
[48] Edward P. Thompson, 'Notes on Exterminism, the Last Stage of Civilization' in Edward P. Thompson (ed.) *Exterminism and Cold War* (London: Verso, 1982) pp. 44–5.

political intentions. All the rest can be taken as given,' Thompson notes in words that would have aptly described the view of weaponry expounded by the CPD. 'This sounds like commonsense,' he continued, 'but it is wrong. It is to foreclose analysis of self-generating independent variables before it has even commenced. Nuclear weapons (all weapons) are things: yet they, and their attendant support-systems, seem to grow of their own accord, as if possessed by an independent will. Here at least we should reach for that talisman, "relative autonomy".'[49] 'Weapons', Thompson concluded, animating the lifeless tools of the instrumentalist view, 'are political agents also ... Weapons, and weapons systems, are never politically neutral.'[50]

The nuclear freeze and the 'vulnerability' of anti-nuclear discourse

Thompson's and Kovel's anti-nuclear rhetoric is imbued with an overt sense of technology-out-of-control that was not endorsed by all. Raymond Williams, Thompson's fellow-traveller on the British left, criticised Thompson's notion of 'exterminism' on the grounds of technological determinism, arguing that nuclear weapons were 'consciously sought and developed ... for known and foreseeable ends'.[51] On similar grounds did Robert W. Tucker seek to unpack the pervasive sense of crisis of the early 1980s:

what has brought the crisis to a point where the "destabilizing" weapons seem almost to "take over" and to undermine deterrence is a political process, a process out of which the conviction increasingly grows that war is inevitable ... if there is a necessity at work here, it is not one imposed by technology but by man's nature and the historical situations in which the statesman must act.[52]

---

[49] Ibid., p. 5.
[50] Ibid., p. 7. See also Freeman Dyson, *Weapons and Hope* (London: Harper and Row, 1984).
[51] Raymond Williams, 'The Politics of Nuclear Disarmament' in Thompson, *Exterminism and Cold War*, pp. 65–86. Williams's sympathetic critique of Thompson argued that 'Technological determinism ... is, when taken seriously, a form of intellectual closure of the complexities of social process' – p. 68.
[52] Robert W. Tucker, *The Nuclear Debate: Deterrence and the Lapse of Faith* (New York: Holmes and Meier, 1985) p. 65.

That said, the arguments of critics such as Thompson formed the more radical articulation of a general sense shared by the anti-nuclear movement in Europe and, increasingly, also in the United States. Moreover, 'when descriptions of these gruesome details [of nuclear war] were combined with appeals to common sense, pro-freeze discourse attempted to convince citizens that, although the nuclear issue is daunting and difficult to think about, ordinary people could contribute to preventing nuclear war'.[53] As Rebecca Bjork notes, in the early 1980s the fatalism and frustration explicit in substantivist critiques of the arms race had already 'erupted into a massive grassroots effort to redefine the role of nuclear weapons in America's defense posture', the 'nuclear freeze' campaign.[54]

The freeze campaign's principal demand was a suspension of the testing, manufacture and deployment of nuclear weapons by both superpowers. This naturally ran counter to the orientation of the Reagan administration as indicated above. By 1982, however, the campaign had reached a level that the administration could no longer afford to ignore. Over a million people in the USA were working to promote the freeze, and the resolution was on the agenda in numerous city, county and state elections.[55] In March of the same year, Senators Edward Kennedy and Mark Hatfield introduced the nuclear freeze resolution into the Senate. The freeze, they argued, and not technical or scientific expertise, offered the only sensible hope of escape from the substantivist nightmare that nuclear weapons represented:

The freeze concept has the inestimable political virtues of simplicity and practicality. Its benefits to humanity are readily apparent to ordinary human beings, rather than to only a select handful of scientists and strategic analysts. There would be no mistaking the moral implications of an agreement to stop the arms race now, and an intense national and international

---

[53] Rebecca S. Bjork, *The Strategic Defense Initiative: Symbolic Containment of the Nuclear Threat* (New York: State University of New York Press, 1992) p. 53.

[54] Ibid., p. 16.

[55] Bjork, *The Strategic Defense Initiative*, p. 16. For a general overview of the contemporaneous debates see The Union of Concerned Scientists, *Beyond the Freeze: the Road to Nuclear Sanity* (Boston: Beacon Press, 1982); Steven E. Miller, *The Nuclear Weapons Freeze and Arms Control* (Cambridge, MA: Ballinger, 1985); Adam M. Garfinkle, *The Politics of the Nuclear Freeze* (Philadelphia: Foreign Policy Research Institute, 1984); from a pro-nuclear perspective Keith B. Payne, *The Nuclear Freeze Controversy* (Lanham, MD: University Press of America, 1984).

campaign for ratification could be effectively mounted. To a world increasingly apprehensive over the awesome dangers and technological complexities
of the arms race, a freeze offers the symbol and the substance of hope.[56]

In August 1982, the House of Representatives narrowly defeated the
resolution by a vote of 204 to 202, but in the intervening period
750,000 freeze protestors had gathered in New York City, and later
the general sense of moral revulsion at the prospect of nuclear war was
also articulated in a much-publicised pastoral letter by America's
Catholic bishops.[57] By the end of the year public support for increased
military spending had plummeted from 80 per cent (in 1980) to 20
per cent, Congress refused to appropriate further funds for the MX
system, and the House awaited a new vote on the freeze resolution in the
spring of 1983. Simultaneously, as economic recession combined with
general anxieties about the superpowers' relations, Reagan's approval
ratings dropped significantly.[58] Scientist George Yonas, who would
come to oversee the SDI programme, later recalled that: 'The opposition
to MX and the freeze movement were very close to succeeding; the
Catholic Bishops' pastoral letter … at one point said nuclear weapons
were immoral. All of us working in the weapons game were aware of
that whole business, including the anti-nuclear movement in Europe.
There was a lot of frustration.'[59]

Bjork identifies five main themes in the discourse of nuclear freeze
advocates: 'faith in common sense'; 'fear of nuclear war'; 'concern
about nuclear overkill'; 'a sense of urgency'; and 'impatience with traditional arms control'.[60] Though these themes were initially highly successful in motivating the freeze campaign, she argues that they were innately
vulnerable when challenged by Reaganite discourse. 'Warfighters' within
the Reagan administration characterised the freeze movement as part of a
pro-MAD constituency. A freeze on weapons production, they argued,

---

[56] Edward M. Kennedy and Mark O. Hatfield, *Freeze! How You Can Help Prevent
Nuclear War* (New York: Bantam Books, 1982) p. 143.
[57] 'The Challenge of Peace: God's Promise and Our Response', 1983, in Philip J.
Murnion (ed.) *Catholics and Nuclear War* (New York: Crossroad, 1983)
pp. 1–103.
[58] Fitzgerald, *Way Out There in The Blue*, p. 156. The freeze resolution did
eventually pass Congress in May 1983, in a much-watered-down form –
Garfinkle, *The Politics of the Nuclear Freeze*, p. 90.
[59] Quoted in Bjork, *The Strategic Defense Initiative*, p. 17.
[60] Bjork, *The Strategic Defense Initiative*, p. 50.

would simply enshrine a disparity in military force between the two superpowers and, with it, the 'delicate balance of terror' itself. Colin Gray, for example, expressed alarm at the widespread popularity of Schell's *Fate of the Earth*, admonishing it as 'conscious spreading of fear and despondency asymmetrically in the West'.[61] As Goldfischer notes in line with the analysis above, 'It is instructive ... that even as US victory theorists were beguiled by dreams of harnessing the West's technological and economic security to achieve a usable nuclear advantage, they were simultaneously beset by fear that disarmament-oriented democracies might simply relinquish parity.'[62]

At the same time, to some extent at least, the 'simplicity and practicality' of the freeze proposal, as lauded above by Kennedy and Hatfield, left it open to caricature as a complete rejection of nuclear deterrence – as was the position of victory theorists. Fitzgerald, for example, argues that Jonathan Schell's rhetoric was 'not unlike that of the Committee on the Present Danger, only the enemy was not the Soviet Union but nuclear war itself'.[63] In Robert Tucker's estimation, 'The peace movement had been marked above all by a sudden lapse of faith in deterrence ... the President's Strategic Defense Initiative (SDI) ... in its own way reflected the same lack of faith in deterrence as did the peace movement ... For both Jonathan Schell and Ronald Reagan ... the goal we must now strive after is the transcendence of mutual deterrence and not its mere enhancement.'[64]

Reagan, SDI and the co-optation of substantivism

'Literalists', Frances Fitzgerald argues with reference to SDI, 'were always inclined to believe that Reagan was a fantasist dreaming of science-fiction weapons.'[65] As recounted in chapter 5, Fitzgerald questions the narrative reconstruction of Reagan as a naive technological optimist subsequent to the announcement of the SDI programme. In her view, the more likely rationale for SDI came from the impasse that had

---

[61] Colin S. Gray, 'Dangerous to Your Health: the Debate over Nuclear Strategy and War', *Orbis*, 26 (1982) pp. 327–49, p. 338.
[62] David Goldfischer, *The Best Defense: Policy Alternatives for US Nuclear Security from the 1950s to the 1990s* (Ithaca: Cornell University Press, 1993) p. 44.
[63] Fitzgerald, *Way Out There in the Blue*, p. 181.
[64] Tucker, *The Nuclear Debate*, pp. 93–4.
[65] Fitzgerald, *Way Out There in the Blue*, p. 108.

been met in Reagan's defence build-up, and the opposition of the nuclear freeze movement. In fact, to her the failure to mention the importance of the latter is akin to having 'the score of a piano concerto with the piano part missing'.[66] Foreign policy adviser Robert McFarlane, she notes, informed Reagan in December 1982 that he was working on a concept that would 'outflank the Freeze'.[67] McFarlane would later recall of the decision-process leading to SDI that 'Reagan's view of the political payoff was sufficient rationale as far as he was concerned ... By that I mean providing the American people with an appealing answer to their fears – the intrinsic value of being able to tell Americans, "For the first time in the nuclear age, I'm doing something to save your lives. I'm telling you that we can get rid of nuclear weapons."'[68] First, though, Reagan would have to articulate those fears in such a way that would satisfy popular anti-nuclear sentiment, yet be commensurate with his administration's investment in the US military infrastructure and continuing emphasis on technology as the key instrument of US power.

As such, when we re-examine the context of Reagan's appeal to common sense instrumentalism in his March 1983 speech on strategic defence, we find it is already grounded in a substantivist vision of technology previously associated primarily with the anti-nuclear movement. It consequently had all the hallmarks of American technological common sense in its combination of a vision of autonomous nuclear technology with an appeal to a supposedly innate American faith in technology to overcome even the greatest of challenges, combining elements of folklore, strategic analysis and appeals to science in the process.[69] The text-structure of Reagan's speech of 23 March 1983 certainly follows this pattern. Although best remembered for its final section, the greater part of Reagan's speech was devoted to justifying the massive increase in US defence expenditures under his tenure, along a

[66] Ibid., p. 199.
[67] Ibid., p. 200. Fitzgerald bases this argument on the account found in Donald R. Baucom, *The Origins of SDI, 1944–1983* (Lawrence, KS: University Press of Kansas, 1992) p. 204.
[68] Quoted in Hedrick Smith, *The Power Game: How Washington Works* (London: Collins, 1988) p. 609.
[69] Cf. Antonio Gramsci, *Selections from the Prison Notebooks*, ed. and trans. by Quintin Hoare and Geoffrey Nowell Smith (London: Lawrence and Wishart, 1973) p. 323.

similar rationale to that provided by the CPD years earlier. As Mitchell puts it, 'for much of the Star Wars address, Reagan painted a gloomy picture of the cold war, where surging Soviet strength combined with increasing American vulnerabilities to cast dark clouds of doubt on the future'.[70] The picture portrayed would have been familiar to those who had followed Reagan's presidential campaign and his period in office up until then: 'the Soviets, for example, have enough accurate and powerful nuclear weapons to destroy virtually all of our missiles on the ground', Reagan declared.[71] He goes on, in substantivist fashion, to suggest that the development of modern weapons technology conditioned US policy in this respect:

There was a time when we depended on coastal forts and artillery batteries, because, with the weaponry of that day, any attack would have to come by sea. Well, this is a different world, and our defenses must be based on recognition and awareness of the weaponry possessed by other nations in the nuclear age.[72]

Reagan also portrayed the Soviet Union as machine-like and relentlessly efficient in its pursuit of technological superiority:

For 20 years the Soviet Union has been accumulating enormous military might. They didn't stop when their forces exceeded all requirements of a legitimate defensive capability. And they haven't stopped now. During the past decade and a half, the Soviets have built up a massive arsenal of new strategic nuclear weapons – weapons that can strike directly at the United States.[73]

Rebecca Bjork argues that up until this point in the speech, Reagan downplays the role of human agency, choice and free will – all classic hallmarks of substantivism:

Humans have lost control over their destiny, are subject to the whim of nature. Free will has been surrendered to materialistic determinism, as human agents are caught in a scene over which they have no control. Reagan, in describing the nuclear arms race and Soviet threat, described

---

[70] Gordon R. Mitchell, *Strategic Deception: Rhetoric, Science and Politics in Missile Defense Advocacy* (East Lansing: Michigan State University Press, 2000) p. 54.

[71] Ronald Reagan, 'Address to the Nation on Defense and National Security', 23 March 1983, http://www.atomicarchive.com/Docs/Missile/Starwars.shtml [last accessed 20 January 2009].

[72] Ibid.   [73] Ibid.

such a scene, and explained how it was dangerous and menacing ... By focusing on the ever-present shadow of the nuclear arms race, Reagan portrayed a dismal and hopeless scene from which there seemed to be no escape; the arms race seems to have a life of its own. Humanity can find no way out of the nuclear dilemma.[74]

Had Reagan's address ended on this note, then little would have changed from his previous arguments. In some ways, though, the section of the speech introducing SDI acts as both a tacit recognition of the limits of the appeal of the CPD argument – that more (offensive) nuclear weapons would ameliorate the arms race – and as a response to the fears raised by the anti-nuclear movement. As Tucker notes of Jonathan Schell's appeal to human agency, 'Schell's scheme ... depended on politics rather than technology and for this reason lacked any attraction for those who have always looked to technology for eventual salvation from the nuclear peril.'[75] The latter part of Reagan's speech sought to satisfy both impulses. Reagan, as Bjork puts it, shifts from 'scene' to 'purpose'.[76] He wasn't simply describing a world conditioned by nuclear weapons (a 'sad commentary on the human condition'); he was proposing to do something about it by rejuvenating agential capacity ('I've become more and more deeply convinced that the human spirit must be capable of rising above dealing with other nations and human beings by threatening their existence').[77] This rejuvenation would occur *through* technology – namely, missile defence technology.

It is against this backdrop that Reagan grounded his appeal to 'turn to the very strengths in technology that have spawned our great industrial base and that have given us the quality of life we enjoy today'.[78] Subsequently Reagan embellished the sense that the idea for SDI had emerged from his own musings over how to transcend a world conditioned by technology, one represented in the seemingly arcane and opaque concepts of nuclear strategy. Bjork argues that Reagan, intentionally or not, portrays himself as being 'as confused as the average American citizen by the esoteric language, jargon, and logic embedded in the doctrine of mutually assured destruction. MAD depends upon

[74] Bjork, *The Strategic Defense Initiative*, p. 67.
[75] Tucker, *The Nuclear Debate*, p. 94.
[76] Bjork, *The Strategic Defense Initiative*, p. 75.
[77] Ronald Reagan, 'Address to the Nation on Defense and National Security'.
[78] Ibid.

paradoxes ... States must *possess* nuclear weapons and, in fact, continue to *build* them, in order to someday *eliminate* them. Citizens must put *faith* in the weapons that they *fear* so much.'[79]

In doing so, Reagan metaphorically swapped the vocabulary of deterrence theory, in which defences were problematic, in favour of an approach that used a story-telling style to make his point – one which is more folkloric and seemingly commonsensical. A recurrent example of this is the metaphor of 'cocked pistols', cited initially by Reagan in the first question and answer session after his speech: 'it's inconceivable to me that we can go on thinking down the future, not only for ourselves and our lifetime but for other generations, that the great nations of the world will sit here, like people facing themselves across a table [*sic*], each with a cocked gun and no one knowing whether someone must tighten their finger on the trigger'.[80] Four days later Reagan reiterated that: 'To look down an endless future with both of us sitting here with these horrible missiles aimed at each other and the only thing preventing a holocaust is just so long as no one pulls the trigger – this is unthinkable.'[81] Again, the story Reagan tells fits the criteria we associate with substantivism, notably in its vision of a seemingly inescapable, technologically determined future. In fact, it's hard to see how there could be any remedy to such a situation other than for both sides to lower their 'pistols'; but, Reagan continues, 'There is another way, and that is if we could, the same scientists who gave us this kind of destructive power, if they could turn their talent to the job of, perhaps, coming up with something that would render these weapons obsolete. And I don't know how long it's going to take, but we're going to start.'[82]

To some extent Reagan effectively replicated the pattern familiar from CPD argumentation, and from chapter 4, in his March 1983 address and subsequent embellishment of it. In keeping with Robert H. Johnson's appraisal of 'period of peril' arguments, Reagan's vision 'simplifies a complex and confusing international environment by focusing upon its bipolar dimension and upon the issues of survival', as exemplified in the pistols metaphor. This in turn 'provides a conceptual basis for heroic rhetoric' which 'promises to simplify the increasingly complex domestic politics of US foreign policymaking by

[79] Bjork, *The Strategic Defense Initiative*, p. 14, emphasis in original.
[80] Quoted in Fitzgerald, *Way Out There in the Blue*, p. 208.   [81] Ibid.
[82] Ibid.

offering a simple, unifying theme' – in this case, the theme of American technological ingenuity invoked by Reagan initially and developed further by other proponents of SDI (see chapter 5).[83] Additionally though, in the process, Reagan arguably sought to co-opt and defuse the contending popular appeal of the nuclear freeze movement. His speech and the subsequent rhetoric of his administration eloquently adopted and then adapted a fear of nuclear war and technological determinism that had already been articulated by the radical critique of the freeze movement. This broadly corresponds to what Gramsci terms *trasformismo* – 'transformism', or co-optation of political opposition. Here 'dissent is channelled into existing structures or marginalized by dismissing it as "radical" or unrealistic'.[84] The term transformism was originally used to describe the formation of loose alliances between factions of the left and right in late nineteenth-century Italian politics.[85] Gramsci extended it to denote a system of transformation in which 'there is no real opposition or alienation in power'.[86] Instead there is a piecemeal absorption of oppositional ideas by the ruling elite, 'even of those which came from antagonistic groups and seemed irreconcilably hostile'.[87] Here Gramsci emphasises 'intellectual, moral and political hegemony' ('one should not count only on the material force which power gives in order to exercise an effective leadership') and the incorporation of opposing common sense arguments in popular appeals as a means of effecting a 'passive revolution'.[88]

Several commentators argue that in his March 1983 appeal, and in his administration's subsequent rhetoric, Reagan effectively co-opted the themes of the anti-nuclear movement, thereby weakening its prior status as a form of radical-utopian critique.[89] 'Using the equation "BMD=disarmament" as a template for public argumentation,' Mitchell argues, 'Star Wars visionaries were able to "steal the language

[83] Johnson, 'Periods of Peril', p. 967.
[84] Dalby, *Creating the Second Cold War*, p. 13.
[85] David Forgacs (ed.) *The Antonio Gramsci Reader: Selected Writings 1916–1935* (New York: New York University Press, 2000) p. 424; see Gramsci, *Selections from the Prison Notebooks*, pp. 59–61.
[86] Forgacs, *The Antonio Gramsci Reader.*
[87] Gramsci, *Selections from the Prison Notebooks*, p. 59.   [88] Ibid.
[89] Bjork, *The Strategic Defense Initiative*, p. 75; Edward T. Linenthal, *Symbolic Defense: the Cultural Significance of the Strategic Defense Initiative* (Urbana: University of Illinois Press, 1989) p. 65.

and cause" of activists calling for nuclear disarmament.'[90] Linenthal argues that:

The Grand Vision speech brought about a striking transformation in conservative rhetoric. Sounding like members of the anti-nuclear movement, for which they previously had voiced nothing but contempt, some SDI enthusiasts began attacking deterrence as an immoral national strategy that might lead to the tragic, needless death of millions of innocent Soviet citizens. Whereas before the utopian visions of a denuclearized world were found mainly among certain segments of the antinuclear movement, after the speech SDI enthusiasts began utilizing these same visions, which they once criticized as hopelessly naïve.[91]

Similarly, Paul N. Edwards argues that 'Whatever its technical merits, the *rhetorical* power of the SDI proved considerable, since it allowed its proponents to claim that they were supporting defensive rather than offensive weapons,'[92] allowing the supporters of SDI to take the moral high ground against proponents of disarmament.

Gramsci's theory of co-optation can be augmented here by reference once again to Herbert Marcuse's concept of 'one-dimensionality', 'the weakening and even the disappearance of all genuinely radical critique, the integration of all opposition in the established system'.[93] Writing in 1964, Marcuse portrays a possibility that could be applied directly to Reagan's vision and the way in which it used fear of technologically determined disaster to legitimate continued reliance on a vast weapons infrastructure:

Does not the threat of an atomic catastrophe which could wipe out the human race also serve to protect the very forces which perpetuate this danger? The efforts to prevent such a catastrophe overshadow the search for its potential

---

[90] Mitchell, *Strategic Deception*, p. 85. See also J. Michael Hogan, *The Nuclear Freeze Campaign: Rhetoric and Foreign Policy in the Telepolitical Age* (East Lansing: Michigan State University, 1994).

[91] Linenthal, *Symbolic Defense*, p. 65.

[92] Paul N. Edwards, *The Closed World: Computers and the Politics of Discourse in Cold War America* (Cambridge, MA: MIT Press, 1996) p. 292, emphasis in original.

[93] Douglas Kellner in introduction to Herbert Marcuse, *One-Dimensional Man: Studies in the Ideology of Advanced Industrial Society*, 2nd edition (London: Routledge, 1991; first published 1964) p. xii. Kellner argues that 'In particular, Reagan and Reaganism exemplified one-dimensional "positive thinking" to an extreme degree' – p. xxxviii.

causes in contemporary industrial society. These causes remain unidentified, unexposed, unattacked by the public because they recede before the all too obvious threat from without – to the West from the East, to the East from the West ... We submit to the peaceful production of the means of destruction, to the perfection of waste, to being educated for a defence which deforms the defenders and that which they defend.[94]

The apparatus of co-optation occurred, in Gramsci's terms, 'In forms, and by means, which may be called "liberal" – in other words through individual, "molecular", "private" enterprise (i.e. not through a party programme worked out and constituted according to a plan, in advance of the practical and organisational action).' In other words, the pre-existing base of missile defence advocates picked up the President's vision and ran with it, complementing the administration's subsequent arguments for SDI and effectively acting as a stratum of 'organic intellectuals'.[95] Post-1983, missile defence enthusiasts such as Teller now cited scenarios akin to those described by Jonathan Schell as further justification for their high-cost proposals. High Frontier, the lobby group established by Daniel Graham to promote missile defence from space, declared 'ABC's *The Day After* Could Be Prevented by High Frontier' on the cover of its November 1983 newsletter.[96] Prominent space-weapons advocates now argued that strategic defence would 'offer the peace marcher one of his most cherished hopes'.[97]

SDI proponents argued that strategic defence addressed the main weakness of the nuclear freeze concept: it offered hope of rendering nuclear weapons 'obsolete', to use Reagan's term, whereas a nuclear freeze would merely lock the superpowers into the existing stalemate. Thus freeze proponents could now be portrayed as seeking to perpetuate, rather than eradicate, MAD. With Reagan's common sense appeal to America's technological strength, and his stated faith in the possibility that 'a shield could protect us from nuclear missiles just as a

---

[94] Marcuse, *One-Dimensional Man*, p. xli.
[95] Gramsci, *Selections from the Prison Notebooks*, p. 60 – 'organic intellectuals' negatively conceived of course, just as Gramsci himself applies the term to liberal Italian 'Moderates' as well as the vanguard socialist party.
[96] Cited in Linenthal, *Symbolic Defense*, p. 13.
[97] Daniel O. Graham and Gregory A. Fossedal, *A Defense that Defends: Blocking Nuclear Attack* (Old Greenwich, CT: Devin-Adair, 1983) p. 11.

roof protects a family from the rain',[98] the freeze movement's seeming rejection of technology and scientific expertise was also made to appear misguided. No one could deny that it was common sense to try and avoid nuclear war, but was it really so commonsensical to reject America's strength in science and technology in the process? SDI, it was argued, required no such rejection, and SDI proponents effectively portrayed nuclear freeze campaigners as neo-Luddites. Simultaneously, as discussed in chapter 5, it was impossible to disprove that a techno-logical fix to prevent the nuclear nightmare could be found. As Bjork notes, 'the Reagan Administration's SDI rhetoric, especially its claim that SDI was only a research project, created a symbolic niche for the program whereby it was insulated from strong criticism, and, simulta-neously, was rhetorically self-perpetuating'; thus, there was also a kind of productive uncertainty about the potential for missile defence tech-nology, constantly reiterated, as was shown in the previous chapter, by reference to America's technological heritage.

Conclusion

The process of *trasformismo* effected by the Reagan administration was complete to the point where both substantivism and utopianism, pre-viously considered the 'exclusive property of the left fringe', had now become incorporated into the pro-missile defence arguments of the Republican right.[99] SDI unlocked a new raft of defence spending, the stated rationale of which was to rid the world (or at least the United States) of the fear of nuclear weapons. In turn, 'The freeze campaign's rejection of technology created an opportunity for Reagan to do what he did best: express optimism and faith in the American way of life. Saying no to the inexorable march of technology, progress, American ingenuity, and optimism is difficult to sustain given America's self-image as a moral and progressive nation with new frontiers to con-quer.'[100] Indeed, supporters of SDI could now invoke this self-image in the first instance, and revert to a substantivist understanding of technol-ogy as justification when necessary. This illustrates the kind of 'common

[98] United States, Office of the Federal Register, *Weekly Compilation of Presidential Documents* (Washington, DC: GPO, June 1986) p. 839.
[99] Linenthal, *Symbolic Defense*, p. 65.
[100] Bjork, *The Strategic Defense Initiative*, p. 63.

sense' formation that in some ways transcends – or perhaps better brackets – the philosophical opposition between instrumentalism and substantivism and transforms it into a source of discursive (and thereafter political and economic) productivity. In Part Four the case will be made that this style of argument has essentially been replicated under the administration of George W. Bush, and that here too substantivist visions are frequently invoked to ground and legitimate current US nuclear posture in general, defence spending and missile defence in particular.

Contemporary missile defence

7 | Ballistic missile defence: 'Technology, working for you now'

Introduction

Under the presidency of George W. Bush, missile defence – as both a programme and a concept – underwent something of a renaissance. Campaigning for the presidency in 1999 Bush made a firm commitment to investment in missile defence and defence spending in general, promising to deploy anti-ballistic missile systems 'at the earliest possible date'.[1] He based this promise on the familiar self-image of American strength in technology which had created 'a revolution in the technology of war ... This revolution perfectly matches the strengths of our country – the skill of our people and the superiority of our technology. The best way to keep the peace is to redefine war on our terms.'[2] To achieve this redefinition of war, however, increased spending would be required: 'The real goal is to move beyond marginal improvements – to replace existing programs with new technologies and strategies. To use this window of opportunity to skip a generation of technology. This will require spending more – and spending more wisely.'[3] In signing the defence appropriations bill in January 2001, Bush was even more succinct in tying together the themes of technological advance and missile defence as a justification for an overhaul of defence funding:

Our nation must also look even farther into the future so that the next generations of weaponry take advantage of our nation's decisive technological edge. That's why I'm pleased to see that this year's defense bill contains almost $50 billion for research and development, including nearly $8 billion for missile defense.[4]

---

[1] George W. Bush, 'A Period of Consequences', speech at the Citadel, South Carolina, 23 September 1999, www.citadel.edu/pao/addresses/pres_bush.html [last accessed 20 January 2009].
[2] Ibid.   [3] Ibid.
[4] President George W. Bush, remarks as delivered by the President at the signing of the defence appropriations bill, January 10, 2001, www.defenselink.mil/speeches/2002/s20020111-secdef.html [last accessed 20 January 2009].

Nor was this the only familiar argument rehabilitated under the new administration. In May 2001 President Bush argued that:

We need new concepts of deterrence that rely on both offensive and defensive forces. Deterrence can no longer be based solely on the threat of nuclear retaliation. Defenses can strengthen deterrence by reducing the incentive for proliferation ... We need a new framework that allows us to build missile defenses to counter the different threats of today's world. To do so, we must move beyond the constraints of the 30 year old ABM Treaty.[5]

Here, Bush not only reiterates broad themes consistent with the instrumentalist conception examined in previous chapters, but makes them appear as particularly applicable to contemporary security: deterrence, in its Cold War, assured destruction form, is inadequate; overemphasis on offensive force is in itself potentially detrimental; and self-limitation in the field of defensive development makes no sense. Regarding the last point, Bush explicitly reinforced the view that the ABM Treaty, or any other treaty, that inhibited America's potential to develop technology for itself and others could not be tolerated.[6] While tacitly acknowledging the depth of difficulty involved in developing even a limited national anti-missile system, Bush assured the American public that the nation was up to the task: 'We recognize the technological difficulties we face and we look forward to the challenge. Our nation will assign the best people to this critical task.'[7] Withdrawing from the ABM Treaty (which the USA proceeded to do in December 2001) would only be a positive step as it would leave America free to direct its creative energies into missile defence technology and, finally, create a usable defensive instrument of policy.

Even in the wake of 11 September 2001 – widely perceived as taking emphasis away from the issue of missile defence – Bush continued to invoke these arguments for a national anti-missile system. Returning to the Citadel in December 2001, Bush again made reference to the technological basis of American power ('Our technological strengths produce great advantages, and we will build on them'), referring specifically to the US military's flagship technologies such as unmanned aerial vehicles like the 'Global Hawk' and the 'Predator', and precision-guided

---

[5] President George W. Bush, remarks by the President to Students and Faculty at National Defense University, Washington, DC, 1 May 2001, www.whitehouse. gov/news/releases/2001/05/20010501–10.html [last accessed 7 March 2007].
[6] Ibid.   [7] Ibid.

munitions. Bush also referenced 9/11 as a further reason to push ahead with missile defence:

The attacks on our nation made it even more clear that we need to build limited and effective defenses against a missile attack ... Last week we conducted another promising test of our missile defense technology. For the good of peace, we're moving forward with an active program to determine what works and what does not work. In order to so, we must move beyond the 1972 Anti-Ballistic Missile Treaty, a treaty that was written in a different era, for a different enemy. America and our allies must not be bound to the past. We must be able to build the defenses we need against the enemies of the 21st century.[8]

The terrorist attacks on the USA appeared to have strengthened rather than shaken the Bush administration's resolution to deploy a national anti-missile system, with financial backing for missile defence remaining constant in spite of the cost of the campaigns in Afghanistan and Iraq.[9]

When neo-conservative ...

Bush's turn towards missile defence came in the context of an administration dominated by missile defence enthusiasts. Among the members of the Bush foreign policy team who had a long history in missile defence promotion were Deputy Secretary of Defense Paul Wolfowitz and chairman of the Defense Policy Board Richard Perle. Donald Rumsfeld, while rejecting the tag of missile defence advocate and describing himself as 'not an expert at all on ... ballistic missile defense', had, before becoming Secretary of Defense, chaired Congressional commissions on the threat of ballistic missile proliferation and on US space capabilities respectively, the latter of which he proposed extending to include greater missile defence capability.[10]

---

[8] President George W. Bush, remarks by the President at the Citadel, South Carolina, 11 December 2001, www.whitehouse.gov/news/releases/2001/12/20011211–6.html [last accessed 7 March 2007]. See also President George W. Bush, 'Presidential Directive to Deploy Missile Defenses', 16 December 2002, www.fas.org/irp/offdocs/nspd/nspd-23.htm [last accessed 20 January 2009].

[9] David E. Mosher, 'The Budget Politics of Missile Defense' in James Clay Moltz (ed.) *New Challenges in Missile Proliferation, Missile Defense and Space Security* (Southampton: Centre for Nonproliferation Studies, 2003) p. 22.

[10] Secretary of Defense Donald H. Rumsfeld, Interview with Group of Reporters, 11 July 2001, www.defenselink.mil/transcripts/2001/t07132001_t0711sd.html [last accessed 20 January 2009].

Wolfowitz, Perle and Condoleezza Rice, among the administration's self-styled 'Vulcans',[11] shared a common antipathy towards arms accords and arms control in general, which they viewed as an outdated legacy of the Cold War that unnecessarily perpetuated US vulnerability, views that quickly became the hallmark of Bush's speeches on strategic policy.[12] Aside from the high-profile missile defence proponents such as Perle and Wolfowitz, as Graham notes, 'In filling key jobs at the under-secretary and assistant secretary levels, Bush drew heavily from a crop of intellectual talent deeply rooted in scepticism toward the existing arms control framework.'[13] Examples included Douglas Feith, Undersecretary for Defense for Policy; Jack (J. D.) Crouch, Assistant Secretary of Defense for International Security Policy; and John Bolton, Undersecretary of State for Arms Control and International Security.[14]

Additionally, key to understanding the Bush administration's attachment to missile defence was its broader strategic doctrine on nuclear weapons and the intellectual origins of this approach.[15] A highly significant influence on administration in this respect was the National Institute for Public Policy (NIPP), a Washington think-tank led by Keith Payne, long-time proponent of missile defence as we saw previously. In 1999, the NIPP initiated a study intended to prescribe the future shape of US nuclear weapons policy.[16] The central themes of the study were

[11] Rice, though not a neo-conservative, has generally been counted among the 'Vulcans'. See Ivo H. Daalder and James M. Lindsay, *America Unbound: the Bush Revolution in Foreign Policy* (Washington, DC: The Brookings Institution, 2003) pp. 17–34.

[12] See George W. Bush, 'New Leadership on National Security', 23 May 2000, www.fas.org/spp/starwars/program/news00/000523-natlsec.htm [last accessed 20 January 2009].

[13] Bradley Graham, *Hit to Kill: the New Battle over Shielding America from Missile Attack* (New York: Public Affairs, 2003) p. 354.

[14] The key tenets of this worldview are paralleled in the Project for the New American Century's *Rebuilding America's Defenses: Strategy, Forces and Resources for a New Century* (2000), www.newamericancentury.org/RebuildingAmericasDefenses.pdf [last accessed 20 January 2009]. On the influence of neo-conservativism, Michael C. Williams, 'What is the National Interest? The Neoconservative Challenge in IR Theory', *European Journal of International Relations*, 11:3 (2005) pp. 307–37.

[15] See Aaron Karp, 'The New Indeterminacy of Deterrence and Missile Defense', *Contemporary Security Policy*, 25:1 (2004) pp. 71–87.

[16] This report was published as [Keith B. Payne *et al.*] *Rationale and Requirements for US Nuclear Forces and Arms Control*, National Institute for Public Policy (January 2001).

that post-Cold War nuclear proliferation had rendered Cold War deterrence untenable and arms control anachronistic. This, the report concluded, necessitated a more flexible framework that would allow for defensive as well as offensive systems. By dint of the fact that several participants in the study assumed senior posts in the Bush administration (Steven Hadley, Deputy National Security Advisor, Steven Cambone, senior aide to Donald Rumsfeld, William Schneider, Defense Science Advisor) the report – entitled *Rationale and Requirements* – became, as Graham puts it, 'a road map for strategic revolution'.[17]

... met 'neo-Clausewitzian'

In effect, with respect to nuclear strategy in the new administration, the NIPP became a locus of what Gramsci would term 'organic intellectuals': a specialised elite of politically active intellectuals with a clear vision to promote.[18] While *Rationale and Requirements* exerted a largely unofficial influence, its key precepts were adapted virtually wholesale into the administration's 2002 *Nuclear Posture Review* (NPR), authorised by Secretary of Defense Rumsfeld. Payne can thus be credited as a key architect of NPR 2002 along with Robert Joseph, Hadley and Schneider, all members of the NIPP and all holders of positions within the administration.

Not originally intended for public viewing, excerpts of the NPR have since been made available on the internet after elements were leaked in the print media.[19] It set out to provide 'the direction for American nuclear forces over the next five to ten years', and the review makes it explicitly clear that missile defences will form a major part of this direction. Indeed defences are to comprise one leg of a 'New Triad' composed of: 'Offensive strike systems (both nuclear and non-nuclear); Defenses (both active and passive)' and 'A revitalized defense infrastructure that will provide new capabilities in a timely fashion to meet

[17] Graham, *Hit to Kill*, p. 354.
[18] Antonio Gramsci, *Selections from the Prison Notebooks*, ed. and trans. by Quintin Hoare and Geoffrey Nowell Smith (London: Lawrence and Wishart, 1973) p. 15.
[19] Department of Defense, 'The Nuclear Posture Review' [excerpts], 8 January 2002, www.globalsecurity.org/wmd/library/policy/dod/npr.htm [last accessed 20 January 2009].

emerging threats.'[20] The NPR goes on to claim that 'The addition of defenses (along with the prospects for timely adjustments to force capabilities and enhanced C2 and intelligence systems) means that the US will no longer be as heavily dependent on offensive strike forces to enhance deterrence as it was during the Cold War.' By 'dissuading' potential adversaries from engaging in nuclear blackmail, missile defence is argued as crucial to the process of providing 'insurance against the failure of traditional deterrence'.[21]

The NPR's allusions to the further development and potential use of small, 'tactical' nuclear weapons quickly attracted the attention of anti-nuclear and arms control activists, particularly given that Keith Payne had first come to prominence during the Cold War as the co-author of a 1980 article entitled 'Victory is Possible', which advocated a more forceful stance towards the Soviet Union.[22] Payne has since gone to great lengths to alleviate concerns about similar 'war-fighting' tendencies in the NPR on the basis that 'We need research on new, low-yield nuclear weapons because that research may contribute to a deterrent that is believable.'[23] Low-yield nuclear weapons and missile defences act as complementary instruments towards the end of dissuading adversaries from developing their own nuclear programmes, so the argument goes.

What is important to note from our perspective is that at the heart of this approach to nuclear strategy beats an avowedly instrumentalist perspective, one in which the concept of missile defences holds a special place. The ideas, concepts and attitudes that informed the Bush administration's nuclear weapons policy have not emerged *de novo*; in fact it can be argued that they are derived from a particular approach to

---

[20] Ibid. For further analysis, see Karp, 'The New Indeterminacy of Deterrence and Missile Defense'.

[21] Ibid.

[22] Colin Gray and Keith Payne, 'Victory is Possible', *Foreign Policy*, 39 (1980) pp. 14–27.

[23] Keith B. Payne, 'Weaponry: the Nuclear Jitters', *The National Review*, 30 June 2003, www.nipp.org/Adobe/the%20nuclear%20jitters.pdf#search=%22Weaponry%3A%20The%20Nuclear%20Jitters%22 [last accessed 20 January 2009]. See also Keith B. Payne, 'The Nuclear Posture Review and Deterrence for a New Age', *Comparative Strategy*, 23 (2004) pp. 411–419; and 'The Nuclear Posture Review: Setting the Record Straight', *The Washington Quarterly*, 28:3 (2005) pp. 135–151.

nuclear weaponry that shares several features with justifications offered for missile defence in previous periods. Not least is the fact that the intellectual powerhouses behind the NIPP and, in turn, the NPR, have long supported the concepts of active and passive defences in general, and the Strategic Defense Initiative in particular. Chief among these are founder members of the NIPP Colin S. Gray and Keith B. Payne.

Gray's work in particular provides an explicit, theoretically grounded rationale for missile defence based on overtly instrumentalist precepts. Indeed Gray's 1993 work *Weapons Don't Make War*, as was noted in Part One, stands as *the* statement of an instrumentalist approach to military security.[24] In the book's introduction, Gray asserts that 'When Clausewitz wrote that "war should never be thought of as *something autonomous* but always as an instrument of policy," he provided the guiding light that can drive away darkness on the complex subject of this book. For "war" substitute weapons, arms races and arms control processes, and the thrust of this book is revealed.'[25] This theme is constantly hammered home throughout the book. Elsewhere Gray writes that: 'Weapons in the hands of a satisfied state or coalition have a strategic meaning different from weapons in the hands of a revolutionary, "super-rogue", or even "crazy" state ... This generalization holds whether the subject is knives or ICBMs. Policy determines whether they serve offensive or defensive functions.'[26] As the text's title indicates, this position is reducible to one guiding principle: 'Weapons have a meaning imposed only by the policy that directs them.'[27] To Gray this maxim should form the 'common sense' basis of all strategic thinking: 'The idea that offensive or defensive strategies can function as autonomous factors that make for war or for peace independent of policy choice is a plausible fallacy. Policy makes war, not types of weapons, character of strategy, or operational style.'[28]

It follows for Gray that those advocating arms control and radical disarmament are prone to 'the inappropriateness of treating weapons as the disease rather than as the symptoms they are' and are unduly obsessed with weapons technology.[29] The former he charges as guilty of the 'technicist fallacy' of 'reducing the rich complexities of arms

[24] Colin S. Gray, *Weapons Don't Make War: Policy, Strategy and Military Technology* (Lawrence, KS: University Press of Kansas, 1993).
[25] Ibid., p. 3, emphasis in original.   [26] Ibid., p. 31.   [27] Ibid., p. 177.
[28] Ibid., p. 28.   [29] Ibid., p. 29.

competition to the simple model of a clockwork universe'; the latter of 'a Luddite approach to the problem of security'.[30] Both are doomed to failure.[31]

Efforts at limiting developments in defensive weaponry – namely the ABM Treaty – represented an elevation of this fallacy to a new level 'since the driving idea behind it was the speculative theory that fear of defenses fuels the offense'.[32] Such limitation, for Gray, resulted in ignorance of a key strategic concept: defence. In 1993 Gray conceded that 'At present, offense is the strongest form of "strategic" nuclear war, at least in the limited sense that defensive means of all kinds cannot reliably prevent large numbers of offensive weapons either from being launched or from completing their flights.' However, drawing on the well-known Clausewitzian dictum, Gray argues that:

> [I]n a truly strategic sense – bearing upon means *and ends* – defense is the stronger form of war, *by way of countervailing offense*, in that offensive weapons cannot disarm an enemy of his like weapons. In principle, though not necessarily in practice, two unstoppable strategic offensive instruments should have the same implications for statecraft as would a standoff between two impenetrable defenses.[33]

This is what Gray designates as 'the vital synergism' between offence and defence, where each 'should work synergistically to reduce the performance required of either to a manageable level'. Gray argues that this synergism can only make good sense in terms of how military effort is expended: 'This point is explained most easily with reference to the tactical synergism between sword and shield/body armor. A swordsman bereft of shield and armor is obliged to take inordinate risks in quest of a quick kill or to devote himself almost totally to defensive swordplay.'[34] This point, though, needed to be noted by those in power in the USA: 'As history marches into the disorderly 1990s, the arguments for and against active missile defences need to be refocused and in many cases wholly rewritten to reflect the changing orientation in US defence policy.'[35] Otherwise, Gray warned (with wanton hyperbole):

---

[30] Ibid., pp. 38, 161.
[31] As also argued at length in Colin S. Gray, *House of Cards: Why Arms Control Must Fail* (Ithaca: Cornell University Press, 1992).
[32] Gray, *Weapons Don't Make War*, p. 38.
[33] Ibid., p. 15, emphasis in original.   [34] Ibid., p. 17.   [35] Ibid., p. 27.

Pyrrhic victory is likely. Neglect of the principle of protection virtually invites the enemy to find a "knight's move" that evades the opponent's offensive strength (witness the U-boat campaigns of both world wars) … A Pyrrhic victory, while preferable to defeat, is a victory achieved at a price seriously disproportionate to the gain. The ghost of Pyrrhus moves as a dire warning through the halls of nuclear-armed governments.[36]

In sum, for Gray, an instrumental view of technology and defensive strategy are complementary Clausewitzian virtues that had both been lost in deterrence theory, with potentially dire consequences for US defence policy.

These views are paralleled in Keith Payne's arguments.[37] There is, Payne argues, an inverse relation between faith in deterrence and interest in missile defence and 'markedly reduced confidence in the reliability of deterrence has led to an increased appreciation of the need for NMD [National Missile Defense] in the post-Cold War period – to provide a hedge of protection for the United States in the event deterrence fails'. In sum, Payne concludes, 'a generally accepted proposition now is that because the deterrence of missile attack can not be considered reliable, the United States must have some defense'.[38] In other words defence is common sense. Payne likewise addresses those concerned about the prospect of a missile-defence-inspired arms race with similar arguments to those made by Gray:

Defensive measures have frequently, and for long stretches of history, dominated the offense. Athens's defensive walls, for example, precluded a bloody invasion by Sparta in the Peloponnesian War. The defensive walls of Constantinople provided security for nearly a thousand years. British air and naval defenses shut down the planned Nazi invasion of the British Isles, Hitler's "Operation Sea Lion". Of course, Karl von Clausewitz considered defense in general to be the strongest form of warfare …

---

[36] Ibid., p. 17.
[37] Keith B. Payne, 'The Case for a National Missile Defense', 27 May 2005, downloaded from the National Institute for Public Policy, www.nipp.org/publications.php [last accessed 7 March 2007], p. 7. Also published in *Orbis* (Spring 2000). For a more detailed discussion of the point see Keith B. Payne, *Deterrence in the Second Nuclear Age* (Lexington, KY: University Press of Kentucky, 1996).
[38] Payne, 'The Case for a National Missile Defense', p. 7. See also Keith B. Payne, *The Fallacies of Cold War Deterrence and a New Direction* (Lexington, KY: University of Kentucky Press, 2001).

Payne concedes that missile defence would need to be highly effective given the destructive capacity of nuclear-armed missiles. However, pursuing missile defence still makes sense in this 'second nuclear age' on the basis that limited, 'rogue' adversaries are the opponent. Hence, 'Complete security ... is not the declared US goal.' Echoing his defence of research into SDI cited in chapter 5, Payne goes on to speculate that 'whether powerful new defensive technologies such as "exotic" beam weapons, will make this type of defense possible in the future is not known; but it can hardly be ruled out as if by some inevitable law of history.'[39] Again, this view is also echoed in Gray's work: 'it is an error simply to argue that "defense does not work in the nuclear era." In this second nuclear age, the challenge is to be able to defeat missile threats far more modest in scale and sophistication than was the case in the 1970s and 1980s in the great Cold War [*sic*].' More than just a policy choice, the increasing likelihood of 'terroristic efforts at blackmail' made missile defence a policy imperative for Gray by the late 1990s: 'Probably the closest to an identifiable requirement for a major shift in US policy and strategy is the need today for the declining reliability of deterrence to be offset by a new emphasis upon military denial by offensive and *especially defensive*, counterforce.'[40]

America's technological heritage (revisited) and contemporary missile defence

Even by speaking of a 'second nuclear age', it will be argued in the next chapter, Gray and Payne invoke an understanding of technology starkly opposed to the instrumentalist version examined here, and their arguments are in this sense the kind of 'episodic', oscillating view of technology characteristic of American technological common sense. This latent contradiction, though, seems to go unnoticed. Indeed their arguments have become highly prominent in political discourse promoting missile defence. As was indicated above, the Nuclear Posture Review takes on key precepts advocated by Gray and Payne, while Bush's early speeches

---

[39] Keith B. Payne, 'Action–Reaction Metaphysics and Negligence', *The Washington Quarterly*, 24: 4 (Autumn 2001) pp. 109–21, p. 113.

[40] Colin S. Gray, *The Second Nuclear Age* (Boulder, CO: Lynne Rienner, 1999) pp. 98, 102, 153, emphasis, tellingly, in the original.

on nuclear strategy reflect similar notions. Questions of where the lines of influence run to and from are in some ways secondary. What is important is the prevalence, acceptance and reiteration of a set of key shared ideas that came to be encapsulated in the NPR. Secretary of Defense Rumsfeld, for example, propounded the NPR's terminology of a 'New Triad', 'dissuasion' and the need for offensive–defensive combination as advocated by the NPR, melding it with the rhetoric of defence transformation carried on from the 1990s.[41] Others, such as Deputy Secretary of Defense Paul Wolfowitz, also informed and endorsed the general orientation of the NPR especially in relation to missile defence and deterrence theory.[42] Not long into his tenure in the Pentagon Wolfowitz asserted that 'work on ballistic missile defense has been hamstrung by an obsolete theory', echoing a generally held truism within missile defence advocacy and likewise lamenting an assumed range of 'promising technologies' that had been ignored as a consequence.[43] Similarly, Wolfowitz took the line that missile defence would provide a valuable service in that 'We would preserve the freedom of action that we have today.' Again the theme of avoiding nuclear blackmail is reiterated: 'Obviously the greatest danger is if [nuclear missiles] are actually used. But even short of their use is the danger that they will give freedom of action to international bullies like Iraq, like Iran, like North Korea.' Ultimately, for Wolfowitz, 'it makes no sense whatsoever – in an era when technology allows us to take away the ability to attack us with a single missile or a few missiles – to leave ourselves vulnerable to that threat. It might have been something we had to live

---

[41] See Donald H. Rumsfeld, '"21st Century" Transformation of the US Armed Forces' (Remarks as Prepared for Delivery), National Defense University, Washington, DC, 31 January 2002, www.defenselink.mil/speeches/2002/s20020131-secdef.html [last accessed 20 January 2009]; and Donald H. Rumsfeld, 'Global Posture' (Testimony as Prepared for Delivery), Senate Armed Services Committee, Washington, DC, 23 September 2004, www.globalsecurity.org/military/library/congress/2004_hr/040923-rumsfeld.pdf#search=%22Rumsfeld%2BGlobal%20Posture%22 [last accessed 20 January 2009].

[42] See as an example Paul Wolfowitz, Prepared Statement on Missile Defense to Combined Procurement and R&D Subcommittees of the House Armed Services Committee, 27 June 2002, www.defenselink.mil/speeches/2002/s20020627-depsecdef1.html [last accessed 20 January 2009].

[43] Paul Wolfowitz, Prepared Testimony on Ballistic Missile Defense to the Senate Armed Services Committee, Thursday, 12 July 2001, www.defenselink.mil/speeches/2001/s20010712-depsecdef.html [last accessed 20 January 2009].

with during an earlier period. We don't have to live with it now, and we shouldn't.'[44]

Here Wolfowitz clearly postulates technology, in keeping with the instrumentalist view, as something simply to be used ('technology allows us') to achieve predetermined ends. In his view this is the common sense approach to the problem of defence against ballistic missiles. However, a significant problem faced by the Bush administration, particularly in the early years of its tenure, was that not everyone was equally convinced of what technology would allow with respect to missile defence. The fact that there was a natural place for a national missile defence in the administration's overall nuclear strategy did not of itself overcome the questions of technical feasibility that continued to plague the programme. The administration's expanded plans for missile defence required Congressional endorsement of funding. In Congressional Committee hearings and in public members of the administration quickly embellished their strategic rationale with references to America's technological heritage. In similar fashion to the SDI advocacy examined in chapter 5, members of the administration employed these references as a means of downplaying concerns over testing procedures and scientific criticism. In short, they sought to embellish an instrumentalist approach to missile defence with optimistic, common sense appeals to America's technological heritage.

Analysing speeches, statements and testimony from the period 2001 to 2005, familiar techniques of argumentation are apparent in this respect. For example, responding in a television interview in August 2001 to the revelation that a beacon on the dummy ICBM had been used in a prior "hit-to-kill test" of a missile defence interceptor, Secretary Rumsfeld replied:

Let's take the worst case. Let's say the test had failed, which it did not fail. It was a very successful test. But let's say it had failed. Indeed, that would have not said anything at all about ballistic missile defense ... The Corona program had 11 straight failures before it succeeded. The Wright brothers tried to fly many, many times. I think there are floating around the country some people who are theologically opposed to missile defense and are determined to try

---

[44] Paul Wolfowitz, Deputy Secretary of Defense, interview for PBS Frontline 'Missile Wars', 12 June 2002, www.pbs.org/wgbh/pages/frontline/shows/missile/interviews/wolfowitz.html [last accessed 20 January 2009].

and drag up any argument they can make to criticize the program. The test, believe me, was very successful.[45]

Here Rumsfeld combines a specific example of trial-and-error in the case of the Corona (the first photo reconnaissance satellite system) with the more general archetype of technological genius represented by the Wright brothers. In testimony before the Senate Armed Services Committee in July 2001, Wolfowitz put forward a similar line of argument, even elevating test failure to the status of a virtue by comparing missile defence with a series of other defence programs:

there will certainly be bumps along the way. We expect there to be test failures. There is not a single major technological development in human history that did not begin with a process of trial and error and many of our most successful weapons developments have been marked by testing failures: the Corona satellite program, which produced the first overhead reconnaissance satellites, suffered 11 straight test failures; the Thor Able and Thor Agena launch programs failed four out of five times; the Atlas Agena launches failed 5 out of 8 times; the Scout launchers failed 4 out of 6 times; the Vanguard program failed 11 of its first 14 tries; the Polaris failed in 66 out of 123 flights. Mr Chairman, from these failures came some of the most effective capabilities ever fielded. Failure is how we learn. If a program never suffers test failures, it means someone is not taking enough risks and pushing the envelope. Intelligent risk taking is critical to any advanced development program – and it will be critical to the development of effective ballistic missile defenses.[46]

Here Wolfowitz, like Rumsfeld in the passage above, attempts to re-contextualise interceptor test failings by drawing on the analogy of (eventually) successful technologies, thus attempting to elevate test failure as a necessary virtue. The purpose of Wolfowitz's argument is to associate contemporary missile defence with a heroic technological narrative specific to the American military by using it as a symbolic resource.

---

[45] Secretary of Defense Donald H. Rumsfeld, Interview with KNBC-TV Los Angeles, Tuesday, 14 August 2001, www.defenselink.mil/transcripts/2001/t08162001_t814nola.html [last accessed 20 January 2009]. Assistant Secretary Victoria Clarke repeated the same examples verbatim in a 17 August 2001 Interview with WKZO-AM, www.defenselink.mil/transcripts/2001/t08172001_t817wkzo.html [last accessed 20 January 2009].

[46] Wolfowitz, Prepared Testimony on Ballistic Missile Defense to the Senate Armed Services Committee, Thursday, 12 July 2001.

   In the same hearing, Wolfowitz condemns the preceding administration for a distinctly un-American approach to a technological challenge
by again invoking America's record of technological achievement:

For the past decade, our government has not taken seriously the challenge of
developing defenses against missiles. We have not adequately funded it, we
have not believed in it, and we have given the ABM Treaty priority over it.
That is not how America behaves when we are serious about a problem. It is
not how we put a man on the moon in just 10 years. It is not how we
developed the Polaris program or intercontinental ballistic missiles in even
less time.[47]

Wolfowitz's selection of analogies is significant as they are based
around time-frames for (allegedly comparable) crash programmes
(that is, rapid programmes of development and production); at this
point the administration had assigned itself a deadline of 2005 at the
latest to deploy some form of missile defence system.
   Such discursive techniques attempt to take the focus off missile
defence's problematic testing record. Ultimately though, nothing succeeds like actual "success", even in missile defence. Wolfowitz put talk
of failure in the cause of progress to one side in the wake of the July
2001 intercept test that employed the beacon on the target (referred to
by Rumsfeld above) to make the case that, properly resourced and
unfettered, missile defence was feasible and could be achieved quickly:

The ability to defend the American people from ballistic missile attack is
clearly within our grasp. But we cannot do so unless the President has
Congress' support to expand and accelerate the testing and development
program. This weekend's test shows the potential for success is there. Let us
not fail because we did not adequately fund the necessary testing, or because
we artificially restricted the exploration of every possible technology.[48]

Similar sentiments were echoed in arguments made by those within
the Ballistic Missile Defense Organization, upgraded to agency status
in January 2002 to reflect the administration's emphasis on missile

[47] Ibid. Wolfowitz repeats the 'man on the moon' and 'Polaris' examples in his
speech to the American Jewish Committee, Washington, DC, 4 May 2001, www.
defenselink.mil/speeches/2001/s20010504-depsecdef.html [last accessed 20
January 2009].
[48] Paul Wolfowitz, Prepared Testimony on Ballistic Missile Defense to the Senate
Armed Services Committee, 17 July 2001, www.defenselink.mil/speeches/2001/
s20010717-depsecdef1.html [last accessed 20 January 2009].

defence. Lt General Ron Kadish, director of the Missile Defense Agency (MDA), responded to queries about the reliability of interceptors with:

Well, when you look at the Wright brothers in the first days of flight, they went on to their second generation of airplanes very quickly, and they improved very rapidly. Within eight years, the whole aviation industry was born, and it certainly didn't look like the first Wright flyer ... Same issue here with the technology. We learn things about the employment of kill vehicles, how they should be built, what kinds of things we ought to be putting in them to solve the problems we find during testing. It's a natural evolution that we ought to get better in our kill vehicle technology.[49]

Kadish used the flight analogy again to speculate on the expected level of progress for missile defence ('there's a time frame here we've just got to be patient about'[50]) and employed an example familiar from chapter 5 to address the issue of scientific scepticism: 'If my memory of history serves me well, it was Lord Calvin [sic], a very eminent scientist at the time, who said that man will never fly. So I respect the opinions of the people who say that because they worked on those types of issues. But over time, we have good ways of solving those types of problems.'[51] Likewise Kadish's overall view of scientific scepticism paralleled that of his precursors in the 1980s: 'I think that's the nature of technological development in history, is that there's always sceptics, but if you only worked on the sceptics' view of the world, we wouldn't make any progress.'[52] Rumsfeld argued that the implementation of GMD (Ground-Based Midcourse Defense) in 2004 'represent[s] the triumph of hope and vision over pessimism and scepticism'.[53]

---

[49] Lt General Ron Kadish, director of the Missile Defense Agency, interview for PBS Frontline 'Missile Wars', 22 May 2002, www.pbs.org/wgbh/pages/frontline/shows/missile/interviews/kadish.html [last accessed 20 January 2009].

[50] Lt General Ron Kadish, Special Briefing on Missile Defense, 25 June 2002. Taken from World Space Flight News, 2005 Complete Guide to Ballistic Missile Defense [DVD-ROM] (compiled and published by Progressive Management, 2005).

[51] Kadish, interview for PBS Frontline 'Missile Wars', 22 May 2002.

[52] Lt General Ron Kadish, Testimony before the House Armed Services Committee on Ballistic Missile Defense, 19 July 2001, www.defenselink.mil/speeches/2001/s20010719-depsecdef2.html [last accessed 20 January 2009].

[53] Secretary of Defense Donald H. Rumsfeld, Remarks at the Seventh Annual Space and Missile Defense Conference, 18 August 2004, www.defenselink.mil/transcripts/2004/tr20040818-secdef1201.html [last accessed 20 January 2009].

The administration's broader ideological support base in the Republican right also tends to reinforce its view of missile defence as a positive instrument of American policy by taking scientific criticism, and very often the scientific community, as its target. 'I think the technological pessimists, by and large, have been wrong over the years,' Richard Perle asserted in 2002. 'The things that were thought to be difficult, impossible, at least daunting, have been done. They've been done in quite amazing ways.'[54] Newt Gingrich wonders where the microwave oven would be if its inventors had to put up with the same level of criticism.[55]

I look at people who doubt our ability to create this [missile defense], and I think, what century are you living in? For the last 250 years, humans have been increasingly good at inventing science and technology that accomplished things. Arthur C. Clarke once said, "If a famous scientist tells you something can be done, he's almost certainly right. If he tells you something can't be done, you don't have a clue," because the record of famous scientists being wrong is so constant ... So I would just say I'd rather gamble on science and technology; my friends would rather gamble on lawyers and diplomats. I think the historical record is pretty decisive. The countries that rely on lawyers and diplomats get killed. Countries that rely on science and engineering tend to win.[56]

Another obvious manifestation of this self-image of a progressive vanguard lies in a frequently cited analogy with the issue of air-defences in 1930s Britain. Congressman Curt Weldon (R–PA) reminded those present at a committee on ballistic missile defence that:

There were those in Britain who wanted to make sure that Britain was properly prepared, and they were working on one specific new, cutting-edge technology that those who wanted to appease Hitler and Germany thought would provoke a conflict ... I think there's a parallel here, and I would hope that those who are adamantly opposed to missile defense

---

[54] Richard Perle, chairman of the Defense Policy Board, interview for PBS Frontline 'Missile Wars', 19 March 2002, www.pbs.org/wgbh/pages/frontline/shows/missile/interviews/perle.html [last accessed 20 January 2009].

[55] Newt Gingrich, speaker of the House of Representatives, 1995–9, speaking as a member of the Defense Policy Board, interview for PBS Frontline 'Missile Wars', 22 May 2002, www.pbs.org/wgbh/pages/frontline/shows/missile/interviews/gingrich.html [last accessed 20 January 2009].

[56] Ibid.

would just remember that, I think, related story that occurred not too long ago.[57]

Gingrich refers more specifically to those who championed radar as exemplars and as a cautionary tale against turning missile defence into a partisan issue.

Without radar, Britain would have lost the Second World War. People like Winston Churchill worked very, very hard to develop radar when lots of people didn't know why they were doing it. They didn't believe it would work. I think today we have a similar situation, I wish this could be dealt with as a national security issue, not a political issue.[58]

Some European commentators on missile defence have also propounded this comparison. Hans and Michael Ruhle argue that the lessons to be learnt from the successful defence of Britain in the 1930s and '40s is that 'As far as military technology is concerned, the history of scientific and technical predictions has been a history of errors. The dictum "the bomber will always get through" is just one of the most fateful examples ... there is no law of nature according to which the offense is permanently superior to the defense.'[59] Margaret Thatcher asserted to a likeminded audience at the NIPP that 'human ingenuity is such that a way will always be found to counter new weapons, however destructive or smart ... With the improved perspective which the end of the Cold War permits we can see that the renunciation of the means to defend our cities against missiles was, in historical terms, an aberration.'[60]

Conservative think-tanks on security policy generally tend to take America's technological legacy for granted as evidence that defence against ballistic missiles is possible. Baker Spring of the Heritage Foundation, for example, characterised that group's position as 'we thought that it was illogical, in so far as the overall military effort of

[57] Representative Curt Weldon, in Testimony before the House Armed Services Committee on Ballistic Missile Defense, 19 July 2001, www.defenselink.mil/speeches/2001/s20010719-depsecdef2.html [last accessed 20 January 2009].
[58] Gingrich, interview for PBS Frontline 'Missile Wars', 22 May 2002.
[59] Hans Ruhle and Michael Ruhle, 'A View from Europe – Missile Defense for the 21st Century: Echoes of the 1930s', *Comparative Strategy*, 20 (2001) pp. 221–5, pp. 224–5.
[60] Margaret Thatcher, 'Deterrence is not Enough: Security Requirements for the 21st Century', *Comparative Strategy*, 18 (1999) pp. 211–20, p. 220.

the United States compared to other countries is concerned, that technology has always been our strong suit and it's in this kind of area, in missile defences which is a technology-heavy area, that the United States should be able to lead, if you will, in terms of addressing this particular kind of threat.'[61] Other groups such as Missile Defense Advocacy Alliance regularly produce polls that suggest most Americans already believe they have a defence against ICBMs in place, the implication being that the average American citizen naturally expects this to be a threat they should be able to defend against.[62] Wolfowitz also claimed that 'most of the American people don't realize that we have no capability whatsoever',[63] providing echoes of Reagan's self-portrayal as the American everyman horrified to discover that the USA, for all its trappings of technological progress, had not yet found a way to deal with this threat.

'It is/it's not rocket science'

A recurring theme in missile defence advocacy, as we have seen, is to juxtapose the efficacy of science and technology with the assumed naivety of arms control on the basis that the former will always trump the latter. Yet, as we have also seen, scientists have been a persistent source of criticism of missile defence efforts. Particularly in relation to the process of discrimination (of ICBM countermeasures from real warheads) the argument has even been made in scientific quarters that the Missile Defense Agency is dealing with an intractable problem of physics in its attempts to develop a functioning missile defence system. Missile defence proponents, as a consequence, have increasingly sought to portray the development of a national anti-missile system as an *engineering* challenge rather than a scientific problem:

There were some famous German physicists, including some Nobel Prize-winners, who said it wasn't possible to build an atom bomb. I'm a little sceptical of people who aren't engineers, trying to solve a problem, saying

[61] Baker Spring, interview with the author, Heritage Foundation, Washington, DC, 26 May 2005.
[62] See www.missiledefenseadvocacy.org/ [last accessed 20 January 2009].
[63] Paul Wolfowitz, Testimony before the House Armed Services Committee on Ballistic Missile Defense, 19 July 2001, www.defenselink.mil/speeches/2001/s20010719-depsecdef2.html [last accessed 20 January 2009].

it's impossible to solve a problem. History is just littered with problems that were supposed to be impossible.[64]

A corollary of this type of assertion is the portrayal of engineering, rather than science in a 'pure' or abstract sense, as a typically American strong suit: 'today ballistic missile defense is no longer a problem of invention, it is a challenge of engineering. It is a challenge this country is up to.'[65] In short, what missile defence requires is application rather than invention: 'at this point for the technologies we're pursuing, there are no inventions required to do it, it's a matter of very difficult engineering activities ... it's an engineering challenge rather than an inventions challenge for the types of systems that we're looking at very early in this process'.[66] As Trey Obering, Kadish's successor as head of the MDA, put it, 'We're no longer simply doing experiments – we're now actually making a mark on history by implementing layered missile defenses. We can all be proud of this achievement.'[67]

In one sense this anti-science/pro-engineering stance may be making a virtue of necessity. While the Federation of American Scientists and the Union of Concerned Scientists and scientific luminaries such as Richard Garwin (Nobel Prize-winning physicist) and Theodore Postol (professor of science and technology at MIT) have consistently continued to be sceptical of missile defence, few scientists have emerged to become the equivalents of Edward Teller, Robert Jastrow and others who backed earlier missile defence initiatives. It might be argued that this is due in part to the drastic decline in American students pursuing scientific careers, especially within government.[68] More speculatively, it could

---

[64] Paul Wolfowitz, interview for PBS Frontline 'Missile Wars', 12 June 2002.

[65] Wolfowitz, Prepared Testimony on Ballistic Missile Defense to the Senate Armed Services Committee, Thursday, 12 July 2001.

[66] Lt General Ron Kadish, Testimony before the Senate Armed Services Committee on Ballistic Missile Defense, 12 July 2001, www.defenselink.mil/speeches/2001/s20010712-depsecdef2.html [last accessed 20 January 2009].

[67] Lt General Trey Obering III, USAF Director, Missile Defense Agency, Remarks to the Multinational BMD Conference, Berlin, 19 July 2004, www.mda.mil/mdalink/pdf/oberng04.pdf#search=%22Obering%2BBerlin%2BJuly%2019%2B2004%22 [last accessed 20 January 2009].

[68] The US military has reportedly looked to Hollywood to portray scientists in a flattering light in a bid to reverse the trend – 'US Military Sends Scientists to Film School', *Guardian*, 5 August 2005.

be argued that the anti-science stance in relation to missile defence fitted with the Bush administration's general attitude to the American scientific community.[69]

Regardless, this bypassing of scientific debate has important consequences. One is that it allowed the Bush administration to collapse prior distinctions made between various types of missile defence. Early in 2001 Secretary of Defense Rumsfeld declared that 'I've concluded that "national" and "theater" are words that aren't useful.'[70] The previous difference between the two had been based on the fact that theatre or tactical missiles have significantly different characteristics (in terms of velocity, range and countermeasures) and operate in different environments than do ICBMs; hence they provide a radically different challenge in terms of defence. This distinction was enshrined in the ABM Treaty, although its finer points were always problematic, especially in the latter years of the Clinton administration, when theatre defence systems became more expansive in their nature. Rumsfeld argued that the distinction imposed an unnecessary limitation on missile defence's technological progress. As a result of eliminating this demarcation, different forms of missile defence were now seen – in principle and at an institutional level under the MDA – as equivalent. Thus, the generally perceived success of the Patriot PAC-3 tactical missile defence in the 2003 invasion of Iraq against Scud missiles could now be argued as proof of the feasibility of a national missile defence operating in miniature.[71]

An even more significant implication of this discursive shift towards emphasising an 'engineering' orientation in missile defence relates to changes in testing and acquisition procedures, which ultimately have massive bearing on the funding of missile defence. The Bush administration adopted what is variously known as an 'evolutionary approach' to development of missile defences, or 'spiral development'. NSPD 23 states that 'The United States will not have a final fixed missile defence architecture ... Rather, we will deploy an initial set of capabilities that

[69] See Chris Mooney, *The Republican War on Science* (New York: Basic Books, 2005).

[70] Secretary Rumsfeld, Joint Media Availability – Secretary Rumsfeld and Secretary General Robertson (News Conference), 8 March 2001, www.defenselink.mil/transcripts/2001/t03082001_t308sd2a.html [last accessed 20 January 2009].

[71] Centre for Defense Information, '24 Patriots Launched So Far against Iraqi Missiles', www.cdi.org/missile-defense/technology.cfm (2003) [last accessed 20 January 2009].

will evolve to meet the changing threat and to take advantage of technological developments.'[72] Indeed in marked contrast to the traditional procedure of setting a requirement and testing against that requirement, the administration carried out this promise to field elements of a system without ever setting exact targets for an overall system and whilst continuing to test the system "in the field".

At its core, this approach makes several key assumptions that use explicit technological optimism as a justification and a reason to keep the faith in the instrumental value of missile defence. On the one hand, it is assumed that missile defence is technically possible and that the necessary technology will emerge over time. On the other, it is assumed that no one can be completely sure what final form that technology will take, or preclude the possibility of a technological breakthrough. Hence missile defence requires a substantially more lenient approach to acquisition than is normally applied. As Kadish defended the approach with respect to the traditional testing and evaluation process:

This approach takes a different tack. It says that technology is so difficult and so uncertain that we think we can accomplish this, we know we have a good shot at it, from an engineering perspective, but we're going to take the approach that we're going to do this incrementally. We're going to have this idea of the military requirement out there, but we're going to provide the military decision-makers and users what we can produce and ask them a very simple question – "We can do this technically; is this good enough for you to use?" – all right? – instead of working very hard, very high risk, trying to meet a requirement that they say they need.[73]

This in itself requires an even stronger faith in technology to come good. The examples of technological achievement cited by Rumsfeld, Wolfowitz, Kadish *et al.* earlier all relied heavily on appeals to empirical trial and error rather than to abstract plans. However, by leaving the shape of missile defence unspecified and through commitment to fielding, testing and deploying simultaneously, trial and error become reduced to such an opaque status that it renders traditional standards of success and failure virtually meaningless. Two (abortive) intercept

[72] National Security Presidential Directive 23, signed 16 December 2002, www.fas.org/irp/offdocs/nspd/nspd-23.htm [last accessed 20 January 2009].
[73] Lt General Ron Kadish, Special DoD Briefing on Missile Defense Program and Testing, 13 July 2001, www.defenselink.mil/news/Jul2001/t07142001_t0713m da.html [last accessed 7 March 2007].

tests in December 2004 and February 2005, for example, were described as 'disappointments, but they were not, by any measure, serious set-backs'.[74] Secretary of Defense Rumsfeld even argued in his budget request of 2003 that 'It makes sense to waive [operational testing] when reasonable people look at the situation and say that it's time to do that.'[75] Information on testing has become increasingly restricted under the Bush administration, and much of the 'progress' claimed for missile defence is frequently made on the basis of computer simulations rather than actual tests. Modelling and simulation activity is, according to Kadish, 'an even more powerful system verification tool'.[76]

Moreover, this largely open-ended process of engineering, it is argued, requires the appropriation of further defence funds by virtue of its very unpredictability and opacity:

Over the past 20 years, the computer systems and the sensor capability and the miniturization capability we have in this country has brought us to the point where those are no longer barriers they once were . . . It, I think, is borne out by history. It's more expensive to do the engineering because you buy hardware and, quite frankly, you buy the talent, the people who can – very smart people who can put these things together. And you need a lot of them, unfortunately, to bring these weapons systems into being.[77]

Here Kadish once more invokes a sense of American technological achievement – with the qualifier that such achievement comes with a price in the case of missile defence. Wolfowitz employed a similar argument before a House Procurement Committee in 2002:

If those inflation savings are not available, it could also force the lay off of hundreds of people – the bulk of them engineers – and thereby adversely affect

[74] Lt General Trey Obering III, USAF Director, Missile Defense Agency, Missile Defense Program and Fiscal Year 2006 Budget, Spring 2005, www.mda.mil/mdalink/pdf/spring06.pdf [last accessed 20 January 2009].
[75] Quoted in Victoria Samson, 'Skipping Missile Defense's Operational Testing is Unwarranted and Could Deliver a Blow to Confidence in US' Arsenal' (6 March 2003), www.cdi.org/friendlyversion/printversion.cfm?documentID=981&from_page=../program/document.cfm [last accessed 20 January 2009].
[76] Lt General Ron Kadish, Missile Defense Program and Fiscal Year 2005 Budget, Spring 2004, www.mda.mil/mdalink/pdf/spring04.pdf [last accessed 20 January 2009].
[77] Kadish, Special DoD Briefing on Missile Defense Program and Testing, 13 July 2001.

our ability to attract and retain the finest minds of our nation to address one of its greatest technological challenges and field an effective system at the earliest possible date.[78]

Once again, then, the funding of missile defence is portrayed as an imperative – in somewhat self-referential terms – of using American technological know-how in a manner that will sustain and foster this culture of engineering excellence.

Industry and contemporary missile defence

These arguments invoking a self-image of American strength in technology are, in sum, a form of symbolic power:[79] they employ a particular rendition of this self-image to imply and legitimate increased investment in missile defence and the particular political, institutional and material forms of power that follow from this. The defence-industrial infrastructure is a prime instance where mutual interests are maintained through discursive rearticulation of the role industry has played in fostering this tradition of engineering excellence. Hence, the political economy of missile defence is embedded in and justified in relation to a broader cultural narrative.

MDA head Lt General Trey Obering, for example, cites the conclusion of an independent report that 'described the rapid development and initial deployment of the system as comparable to other major military efforts, such as the initial deployment of the Minuteman and Polaris ballistic missiles'.[80] His predecessor, Kadish, also likened the programme in this respect to 'such diverse and pioneering efforts as the Manhattan Project; the Mercury, Apollo and ICBM programmes; and the experience with the Space Shuttle'. In each case, he argues, 'The solution lay in forging a much closer relationship between government and industry than normal practice entails.'[81] Unsurprisingly, defence

---

[78] Wolfowitz, Prepared Statement on Missile Defense to Combined Procurement and R&D Subcommittees of the House Armed Services Committee, 27 June 2002.

[79] Cf. Pierre Bourdieu, *Language and Symbolic Power*, ed. and introduced by John B. Thompson (Cambridge: Polity Press, 2005).

[80] Obering, Missile Defense Agency, Missile Defense Program and Fiscal Year 2006 Budget, Spring 2005.

[81] Lt General Ron Kadish, Statement before the Senate Armed Services Committee, Strategic Forces Subcommittee Regarding the Reorganization of the Missile Defense Program, 13 March 2002, www.mda.mil/mdalink/pdf/kadish13mar02,

contractors are eager to endorse this reading. Northrop Grumman, for example, describes missile defence as 'one of the most complex technology challenges the nation has ever faced'. Success is possible, but 'depends on drawing on the greatest scientific and military talents of the nation and collaborative teamwork across industry and government', including its own 'proven leadership and unparalleled technology innovation'. Spiral development is roundly endorsed as the procedure that can best facilitate this success: 'This approach allows the prudent use of new developments and lays the groundwork for intelligent production decisions.'[82]

This general pattern of argument recurs frequently in marketing presentations of key missile defence contractors, supplemented by glitzy brochures, video footage and computer-generated simulations, and artists' impressions of futuristic technologies (such as the failure-prone 'Airborne Laser') in action. The defence industry's marketing of missile defence concepts sought to fill the lacuna of imagination left open by the Bush administration's vaguely specified system architecture. Taken at face value, with pictorial representations of ballistic missiles being intercepted at all stages of flight from land, sea, air and even space, as well as cities and regions protected by Plexiglas bubbles, missile defence appears entirely conceivable. This marketing effort has been led by a number of select interests. The American defence industry has come to be dominated by a handful of large corporations, including Lockheed, Boeing, Raytheon, Northrop Grumman and BAE Systems, which effectively necessitates that the MDA relies on a relatively small group of programme developers. Close institutional ties have developed as a consequence. The chief executive of Lockheed Martin, Robert J. Stephens, even describes his company as operating at 'the intersection of policy and technology ... thinking through the policy dimensions of national security as well as technological dimensions'.[83] Personnel

pdf#search=%22Kadish%2BStatement%20before%20the%20Senate%20Armed%20Services%20Committee%2C%20Strategic%20Forces%20Subcommittee%20Regarding%20the%20Reorganization%20of%20the%20Missile%20Defense%20Program%22 [last accessed 20 January 2009].
[82] Northrop Grumman Space and Mission Systems Corp., 'JRDC: JNIC Research and Development Contract', 'Systems Engineering for Successful Missile Defense Integration' and 'Space Tracking and Surveillance System: Capability Multiplier for Missile Defense' – promotional brochures, 2005. Taken from World Space Flight News, *2005 Complete Guide to Ballistic Missile Defense* [DVD-ROM].
[83] 'Lockheed and the Future of Warfare', *New York Times*, 28 November 2004.

involved in policy aspects frequently have connections with industrial interests and vice versa. The previously mentioned Stephen J. Hadley, for example, is among a number of former Lockheed employees who went on to serve in the Bush administration.[84]

But to view missile defence simply as an instance of the 'military-industrial complex' is, paradoxically, something of an oversimplification. Missile defence is, in many ways, emblematic of the process of defence reorganization under the Bush administration that legitimated these close ties between government and industry in terms of an instrumentalist view of military technology – a *belief* that defensive technology can and should be a key instrument of US power. Exceptional acquisition procedures that seem to favour industrial interests are justified in terms of this perspective. The NPR declares that:

The third leg of the New Triad is a responsive defense infrastructure. Since the end of the Cold War, the US defense infrastructure has contracted and our nuclear infrastructure has atrophied. New approaches to development and procurement of new capabilities are being designed so that it will not take 20 years or more to field new generations of weapon systems.[85]

Likewise Colin S. Gray, writing in 1993, advocated an approach to weapons technology that could well be mistaken as a blueprint for contemporary missile defence:

Traditionally, engineering excellence (broadly understood) has been the military-competitive long suit of the United States, and applied technology has been the cutting edge of the US military effectiveness. But in recent years, "little and late" is a fit characterization of the application by US science-based industry of new, or radically improved, technologies to defense. By far the most important competitive strategy for the US in the technological area would be a revised acquisition process that allowed expedition in the transition from technology to weapon when such expedition is necessary. The United States devalues the currency of technological advantage by acquiring too few systems, and by acquiring them much later than they could have and therefore at a much higher cost.[86]

On this basis Gray defends the cost of "hi-tech" weapons systems as a virtue:

---

[84] Ibid., Hadley became National Security Advisor in 2005.
[85] 'The Nuclear Posture Review', 8 January 2002.
[86] Gray, *Weapons Don't Make War*, p. 82.

Procurement practices and styles that work well for the acquisition of technically undemanding products at the lowest cost are almost wholly inadequate
for the purchase of major weapons, and weapon support systems that are
literally beyond the state of the art at the time of contract award. Toilet seats
can be bought on a competitive, least-cost basis on the open market; ICBMs,
"stealthy" bombers, nuclear powered attack submarines cannot.[87]

Similarly, Rumsfeld's 'defence revolution' dictated that 'We must promote a more entrepreneurial approach to developing military capabilities – one that encourages people to be proactive, not reactive, and to
behave less like bureaucrats and more like venture capitalists.'[88] The
archetype to be imitated here is an ideal-type private sector, market-
oriented approach where technological development progresses with
minimal strictures. Kadish defended this imitation on the basis that:

A capability-based approach provides for significant discipline. It is just
guided by different mileposts. Instead of the traditional process where
users define the requirement in great detail, then, subsequently, developers
translate the requirements into specifications, we intend to do both at the
same time. In doing so, we can accrue the same advantages the commercial
world enjoys.[89]

The market, where technology can "grow" freely, can be as good for
missile defence as missile defence is for the market. Here, Kadish,
Rumsfeld and Gray all attempt to incorporate the vocabulary of
private sector industry and vaunt the vaguely specified 'advantages'
of the commercial world. The implication is that the rigidities of the
past in terms of funding and acquisition inhibit America's ability to
make the best use of its technology, a reiteration of the instrumentalist
view. The development of a 'responsive defence infrastructure' is
therefore argued to be imperative for the achievement of usable missile
defence.

---

[87] Ibid., p. 83.
[88] Rumsfeld, ' "21st Century" Transformation of the US Armed Forces' (Remarks
as Prepared for Delivery), National Defense University, Washington, DC,
31 January 2002.
[89] Kadish, Statement before the Senate Armed Services Committee, Strategic Forces
Subcommittee Regarding the Reorganization of the Missile Defense Program,
13 March 2002.

The marketing of missile defence: 'Technology, working for you now'

This last theme is expressed most obviously in the promotion of missile defence as industrial opportunity. The marketing discourse of ballistic missile defence is underpinned by a simple instrumentalist precept that missile defence, in a very literal sense, is a case of 'technology, working for you now', as one report on the application of missile defence technologies puts it.[90] In other words, missile defence is not just something that can be used to achieve American security in the future; it already has utility value.

A November 2000 factsheet produced by the BMDO (Ballistic Missile Defense Organization, the forerunner of the MDA) argued that 'BMDO, through the US industrial and scientific community, provides research and development capabilities, technical and design expertise, advanced technologies, and manufacturing infrastructure to acquire active missile defense.' Moreover, it recommended that the BMDO should 'Aggressively move defense technology into the private sector' to 'enhance economic security' and as a means of according America's technology 'the competitive edge in what is now an extremely dynamic international marketplace'.[91] This discourse of technology transfer and "spin-offs" is directed primarily towards industrial interests but is couched within a generic argument that investment in hi-tech military industry has knock-on benefits for all society:

The incorporation of advanced technology into competitive industries is a forward-looking approach; it allows businesses to race miles ahead of competition; it allows the United States to maintain economic competitiveness in a global market; and, in many cases, as often felt in the power industry, it improves the quality of life for millions of Americans.[92]

---

[90] Ballistic Missile Defense Organization, Office of the Chief Scientist (BMDO/ST) Technology Applications Program, *The 2000 BMDO Technology Applications Report: Technology, Working for You Now* (2000), www.mda.mil/mdalink/ html/specialreports.htm [last accessed 7 March 2007].

[91] BMDO Factsheet, November 2000. Taken from World Space Flight News, *2005 Complete Guide to Ballistic Missile Defense* [DVD-ROM].

[92] Ballistic Missile Defense Organization, *BMDO Technology and the Electric Utility Industry* (1997), downloaded from www.mda.mil/mdalink/html/ specialreports.htm [last accessed 7 March 2007], from the conclusion.

BMDO has found that a route through commercial applications for this "technology-in-waiting" can be very beneficial for both BMDO and its sponsors – the Nation and its taxpayers.[93]

Though the bulk of investment in missile defence goes to a select group of industrial contractors, this promotional material emphasises the potential trickle-down effect of economic growth for small and new businesses. Not only this, in their "advanced technology applications" literature both the BMDO and the MDA make the argument that missile defence, by being good for the commercial sector, already makes a substantial difference to the quality of American everyday life:

While being developed for very complex missile defense systems, some of BMDO's most sophisticated innovations can be found in products that are working for you now. You will find them in portable computers, cooling the processors; in cars, ensuring the air bags deploy correctly if needed; in industrial equipment, improving the manufacture of electronic devices; and even in ophthalmic laser systems, helping doctors more precisely perform corneal surgeries.[94]

The technologies are advanced, and their technical names are confusing to a non-technical reader; their names do not make clear the technologies' uses in the day-to-day lives of the general public. But, what if the technologies were called a 'precisely focused laser that can kill cancer cells and leave healthy ones intact,' or 'a mobile generator that can run off the engine of a car continuously for days and nights without any maintenance,' or 'an e-mail program controlled by the user that prevents all spam from entering an inbox?' When described this way, the usefulness of MDA-funded technologies to the general public is apparent ...[95]

The marketing of missile defence thus pulls together in a glossy format key themes discussed in chapter 2. The areas in which technology transfer are said to occur with most frequency are those that resonate with the narrative of technological progress: manufacturing,

---

[93] Ballistic Missile Defense Organization, Office of the Chief Scientist (BMDO/ST) Technology Applications Program, *The 2000 BMDO Technology Applications Report: Technology, Working for You Now* (2000), www.mda.mil/mdalink/html/specialreports.htm [last accessed 7 March 2007] p. 5.

[94] Ibid., p. 21.

[95] Missile Defense Agency Advanced Systems (MDA/AS) Technology Applications Program, *2004 Technology Applications Report* (2004), www.mda.mil/mdalink/html/specialreports.htm [last accessed 7 March 2007] p. 6.

communication, computers, transport, medicine, space exploration and so on. In addition, although the MDA has been forced to expend much effort in meeting the requirements of environmental impact assessments for its intercept tests, the BMDO used to play up its contribution to improving the environment. For example, a benefit of tracking satellites – primarily intended to detect incoming missiles – is that 'Without understanding the environmental impact of mankind's activities from a global perspective, it is very difficult for policy makers, scientists, and industry leaders to make sound decisions that will protect our planet's ecosystems.'[96]

Other highlights included 'BMDO R&D May Help Meet Clean Air Standards' and even 'BMDO R&D Controls Mollusks Without Polluting Lakes'.[97]

Here too, heroes of science and engineering are reverentially referenced. One report approvingly quotes Einstein ('The whole of science is nothing more than a refinement of everyday thinking') and Edison ('There ain't no rules around here. We're trying to accomplish something!'). It concludes that:

Significant leaps in technology are needed to make the vision of superior missile defense a reality. These leaps offer the potential to push forward the boundaries of known science and engineering to allow scientists and engineers to create ever-more-sophisticated technology ... Sometimes a large investment must be made to make the very discovery that overcomes a technology barrier.[98]

---

[96] Ballistic Missile Defense Organization, *1998 BMDO Technologies – Improving the Environment* (1998), www.mda.mil/mdalink/html/specialreports.htm [last accessed 7 March 2007] p. 30.

[97] Ibid., pp. 38, 36. Other examples available from the MDA website: *Venturing through the Forbidden Band ... a Glance at MDA's Investment in Wide-Bandgap Technology* ['Defense and commercial uses for wide-bandgap semiconductors and highlights many of the projects funded by the Missile Defense Agency and its predecessors ...']; *Emergency Response Tools – Missile Defense Technology: Applied* [Applications in fire-fighting and search and rescue]; *Missile Defense Agency Sensors: Making the Unknown Known* [Sensor and imaging technology]; *Missile Defense Technologies: Tools to Counter Terrorism 2002* [counter-terrorism applications], www.mda.mil/mdalink/html/specialreports.htm [last accessed 7 March 2007].

[98] Missile Defense Agency Advanced Systems (MDA/AS) Technology Applications Program, *2003 Technology Applications Report* (2003), www.mda.mil/mdalink/html/specialreports.htm [last accessed 7 March 2007] p. 8.

(Re)making space for missile defence?

As with SDI, one of the boundaries that contemporary missile defence advocates seek to 'push' is outer space.[99] In early January 2001, the bipartisan Rumsfeld Space Commission 'unanimously concluded that the security and well-being of the United States, its allies and friends depend on the nation's ability to operate in space' and advocated 'using the nation's potential achievements in space to support its domestic, economic, diplomatic, and national security objectives'.[100] Signals from within the administration also seemed to back this view. President Bush argued that 'In space, we must be able to protect our network of satellites essential to our flow of commerce and defense of our country.'[101] Likewise US Air Force and US Space Command have designated space as within *Joint Vision 2020*'s mandate of 'full spectrum dominance': 'Our nation may find it necessary to disrupt, degrade, deny or destroy enemy space capabilities in future conflicts.'[102]

Missile defence advocates, though, have been quick to point out that space may be naturally better suited to defensive rather than offensive purposes. Gray argues that:

> Overall, it is by no means self-evident that the offense must be the strongest form of war in space. For the technologies of the 1990s, it is plausible to argue that the offense is the strongest form of war in low earth orbit, but that in high earth and geosynchronous orbits the defense enjoys critical advantages – of distance from credible threats and ability to hide in orbits not easily surveilled.[103]

While some, such as O'Hanlon,[104] express concern about the latent dual-use capabilities of such defensive technologies, this, for Gray, is again a question of whether or not technology (as an instrument of

---

[99] See Michael E. O'Hanlon, *Neither Star Wars nor Sanctuary: Constraining the Military Uses of Space* (Washington, DC: Brookings Institution Press, 2004).

[100] Kevin McLaughlin, 'Would Space-Based Defenses Improve Security?' in Alexander T. J. Lennon (ed.) *Contemporary Nuclear Debates: Missile Defense, Arms Control, and Arms Races in the Twenty-First Century* (Cambridge, MA: MIT Press, 2002) p. 75.

[101] Bush, 'A Period of Consequences', speech at the Citadel, South Carolina, 23 September 1999.

[102] Statement by the US Space Command, quoted in O'Hanlon, *Neither Star Wars nor Sanctuary*, p. 1.

[103] Gray, *Weapons Don't Make War*, p. 15.

[104] O'Hanlon, *Neither Star Wars nor Sanctuary*.

policy) is used to serve offensive or defensive ends – not of technology itself.

With more specific reference to contemporary missile defence policy Wolfowitz, for example, advocated outer space as the future strategic 'highground' for missile defence:

While we have demonstrated that hit-to-kill works, as we look ahead we need to think about areas that would provide higher leverage. Nowhere is that more true than in space. Space offers attractive options not only for missile defense but for a broad range of interrelated civil and military missions. It truly is the ultimate highground.[105]

Richard Perle concurs that with respect to intercepting ICBMs earlier in their flight, 'space is a very good place to consider'.[106] The Missile Defense Agency has intimated an interest in pursuing options in space, and announced an intention to solicit contracts for space-based systems in 2008.[107] Concurrently the US Air Force has reportedly been agitating for a more aggressive space policy to ensure 'free access in space'. Head of Space Command, General Lance Lord, has asserted that 'Space is not our birthright, but it is our destiny.'[108] Here again is the assumption that technology – most likely missile defence technology – can be the instrument of US military, political and economic dominance of space.

Some analysts estimate that up to $675 million may be spent on space-based missile defence alone by 2010, although gauging exact figures in this regard is difficult.[109] As a doctrinal debate on the future of American defence policy though, the advocacy of space-based defences exhibits several similarities and continuities with arguments examined previously. Firstly, there are the assumed instrumental benefits mentioned above, which take for granted that attempts at

---

[105] Paul Wolfowitz, 'On Missile Defense', speech to Frontiers of Freedom, 24 October 2002, www.defenselink.mil/speeches/2002/s20021024-depsecdef.html [last accessed 20 January 2009].

[106] Perle, interview for PBS Frontline "Missile Wars", 19 March 2002.

[107] Center for Defense Information, Missile Defense Update #4, 6 May 2005, www.cdi.org/friendlyversion/printversion.cfm?documentID=2958#2 [last accessed 20 January 2009].

[108] Missile Defense Briefing Report No. 178, 28 May 2005, www.afpc.org/mdbr/mdbr178.shtml [last accessed 7 March 2007]. See also 'Air Force Seeks Bush's Approval for Space Weapons Program', New York Times, 18 May 2005.

[109] Center for Defense Information Missile Defense Update #4, 6 May 2005, www.cdi.org/friendlyversion/printversion.cfm?documentID=2958#2 [last accessed 20 January 2009].

controlling the military uses of space are doomed to fail just as attempts at arms control are in general. Additionally, space-based options capture the imagination of hawkish conservative interest groups as much today as they did in the 1970s and '80s. 'First from sea, then from space' is the Heritage Foundation's motto on missile defence, while groups such as High Frontier argue that time and money spent on land-based systems are effectively wasted when space continues to provide obvious benefits.[110] Similarly, publications such as *Aviation and Space Weekly* and *Aerospace Daily* continue to devote copy to proposals for space-based defences complete with cutaway diagrams and artists' impressions, just as they did during the days of SDI.

Other similarities lie in the invocation of America's technological heritage in response to those who doubt the wisdom of investing in space defence technologies. One of the foremost academic proponents of the potential for space defences, Professor Everett C. Dolman of the US Air Force School of Advanced Air and Space Studies, states that:

[The] argument that the technology to deploy a missile defense shield will never be developed, is defeated by analogy. History is replete with scientific advances over the popular howlings that a thing can't be done ('man will never fly', comes to mind). The ingenuity of the scientific community accepts such dares willingly. The real technical question is not can the task be done, but can the task be done for the amount of money available? Thirty-five to three hundred billion dollars, the original cost estimates, are in retrospect far too low. Three to five trillion dollars, however, might just turn the trick.[111]

Dolman echoes these typical missile defence arguments with reference to space:

Technologies will be found that were not or could not be foretold, and the foolish policymaker eschews adapting to it until its utility is beyond a doubt. Indeed, it is concern for the unanticipated arrival of technology X that initially motivates my own preference for a policy advocating immediate deployment of space weapons. So long as America is the state most likely to acquire a

[110] See www.highfrontier.org/, http://users.erols.com/hifront/ [last accessed 20 January 2009].
[111] Everett C. Dolman, 'US Military Transformation and Weapons in Space' (2005), background paper available at www.e-parl.net/pages/space_hearing.htm [last accessed 20 January 2009]; see also Everett C. Dolman, *Astropolitik: Classical Geopolitics in the Space Age* (London: Frank Cass, 2002).

breakthrough technology in this area, my concern is limited to the problem of letting technology take us where it will.[112]

Interestingly, though, this line of argument ('letting technology take us where it will') seems to lead away from the notion of policy dictating the pace of technology to a radically different vision in which technological development leads policy, and hints again at both a potentially broader contradiction within the way technology is understood in missile defence advocacy and its status as a form of common sense in which these contending understandings exist side by side.

Conclusion

As we have seen in chapter 3, 5 and 7 there are strong continuities in the instrumentalist arguments propounded by missile defence advocates. Whether or not these arguments have always been credible or success-ful, they exhibit several recurrent commonalities: technology is an instrument of policy, apparent faith in technological development, assumed to the point where arms control becomes a fallacy, and the history of (American) technological development itself as the final best proof of the potential for missile defence. The longevity of missile defence, and its current resurgence in fortunes, would seem therefore to be testament to what one analyst has described as 'the prevalence of advertising over objectivity in a society where the commercialization of war and the cult of technology have reached historic proportions'.[113] Others take a more nuanced view of why advocates persist in their promotion:

For some, missile defense is a touchstone of the Reagan revolution, that they believe that this issue is necessary to prove their bone fides as a true Reagan Republican. For some, it's tied in with the strategic vision of the United States that should be able to project military force anywhere, anytime, and it can have this capability. For some, it's part faith in American technology. If you can put a man on the moon, why can't we shoot down a ballistic missile? For some, it's more careers, profits. There's a lot of money in missile defense. Eight billion dollars a year, $100 billion spent just since the Star Wars speech. There's a lot of money to be made there.

[112] Dolman, 'Weapons in Space'.
[113] Walter C. Uhler, 'Missile Shield or Holy Grail?', *The Nation*, 28 January 2002, www.thenation.com/doc/20020128/uhler [last accessed 20 January 2009]

Thus there are a multiplicity of interests at play in the promotion of missile defence. However, the same commentator concludes, there is an underlying vision of technology as the key instrument of American security underpinning all of these motivations:

For all of them, I think, is this faith in finding a technological solution to American vulnerabilities; if we just have the right vision, if we just have the right political will, we can do what we want, anywhere we want, and protect the homeland from any attack or counterattack. I think that's an illusion, and a dangerous illusion. But it is the vision that fuels the missile defense fervor and keeps alive the myth of missile defense.[114]

Hence, missile defence would seem to represent the archetype of America's optimistic instrumentalism outlined in chapter 2. But is this the complete picture? Instrumentalism, as we saw in the same chapter, has been consistently complemented by a substantivist undercurrent in which technology figures in a radically different way. Indeed, based on several of the arguments covered in this chapter, the instrumentalist assumption of technology as simply something humans can avail of is arguably already problematic in the case for missile defence. The apparent switch to an 'engineering' approach to missile defence seems to imply that technology is something 'out there' that can be willed into existence with enough political and financial backing and appropriate defence restructuring. Justifications for such restructuring frequently rest on the attribution of technology as a kind of entity in itself with its own characteristics ('difficult', 'uncertain', 'evolving'), opening the way to a reading in which humans are not entirely in control of technology and, with this, the formation of a common sense view of technology in which it is both an instrument to be used and an autonomous dynamic within justifications for missile defence. The aim of the next chapter is to trace further manifestations of this substantivist understanding in the history of missile defence advocacy and the manner in which it has been extended to form a key component of the case for contemporary missile defence.

---

[114] Joseph Cirincione, director of the Non-Proliferation Project at the Carnegie Endowment for International Peace, interview for PBS Frontline "Missile Wars", 13 May 2002, www.pbs.org/wgbh/pages/frontline/shows/missile/interviews/cirincione.html [last accessed 20 January 2009].

8 | *The iron cage of proliferation*

Introduction

This chapter aims to show the ways in which the substantivist trope has come to be incorporated into the contemporary case for ballistic missile defence in the United States. It does so initially by tracing the manner in which a discourse of technological fears, centring on the fear of spreading nuclear weapons and ballistic missile technology, emerged in government circles in the 1990s alongside the rhetoric of technological optimism associated with the 'revolution in military affairs' in the same decade. This framing of the missile threat to the USA accords closely with the category of substantivism outlined in previous chapters, as is further illustrated in relation to both literature on nuclear proliferation in general and to missile defence advocacy in particular. However, rather than obviating arguments for missile defence, this language of substantivism has been incorporated into building a common sense case for missile defence, and it acts as a logical counterpart to the more instrumentalist, progressivist understanding of technology examined in the previous chapter. This is shown through analysis of arguments made by key proponents of missile defence within strategic studies, the rhetoric of the Bush administration, and the use of homologous arguments made in the broader promotion of missile defence by government agencies and non-governmental advocacy groups. In doing so these more substantivist representations of technology help replicate the contradictory, common sense view of technology within contemporary justifications of missile defence.

A growing peril: missile defence and proliferation in the 1990s

The 1990s constituted something of an interregnum for missile defence, with events leading to countervailing implications for strategic defence. On the one hand, the collapse of the Soviet Union terminally diminished the rationale for SDI; on the other, the 'success' of the US Army's Patriot (tactical) anti-missile system in the 1991 Gulf War was not only taken by missile defence advocates as verification of the concept of missile defence in principle[1], but even credited in some quarters with initiating a 'revolution in military affairs' (RMA) characterised by technological sophistication.[2]

Whilst Patriot may have served as a source of inspiration to missile defence advocates and RMA proponents alike, development of a national anti-missile system was not, initially at least, a priority of the Clinton administration. At a general level, the Clinton administration was far from immune from invoking the language of instrumentalism and technological optimism in its promotion of defence 'transformation'. Indeed under its auspices technological superiority gained an arguably unprecedented level of prominence in tandem with the RMA debate, frequently construed as a logical continuation of American mastery of technology. Emblematic of this trend was the Joint Chiefs of Staff's *Joint Vision 2010* and its follow-up *Joint Vision 2020*. Backed by Secretary of Defense William Cohen in 1997, *JV 2010* set out 'the conceptual template for how America's Armed Forces will *channel the vitality and innovation of our people* and *leverage technological opportunities* to achieve new levels of effectiveness in joint warfighting'. *JV 2020* likewise invokes America's technological heritage: 'Throughout the industrial age, the United States has relied upon its capacity for technological innovation to succeed in military operations, and the need to do so will continue.' The key unifying theme of both documents was that 'information-age technological advances', one of 'America's core

---

[1] See Francis Fitzgerald, *Way Out There in the Blue: Reagan, Star Wars and the End of the Cold War* (New York: Simon and Schuster, 2000) p. 486; Rebecca S. Bjork, *The Strategic Defense Initiative: Symbolic Containment of the Nuclear Threat* (Albany, NY: State University of New York Press, 1992) pp. 91–114; and especially Gordon R. Mitchell, *Strategic Deception: Rhetoric, Science and Politics in Missile Defense Advocacy* (East Lansing: Michigan State University Press, 2000) pp. 121–59.

[2] Cf. Lawrence Freedman, *The Revolution in Strategic Affairs*, Adelphi Paper 318 (London: International Institute of Strategic Studies, 1998); Mitchell, *Strategic Deception*, pp. 121–79. The actual performance of the Patriot against Iraqi Scud missiles in 1991 was later estimated to be as low as three to five hits out of fifty-one attempts – see Theodore A. Postol, 'Lessons of the Gulf War Experience with Patriot', *International Security*, 16 (1991/2) pp. 119–71.

strengths', would become the new pillar around which organisational change in the US military would take place.[3]

More often than not, though, the Clinton administration's emphasis on defence transformation through technology did not extend to a national-level missile defence. During the 1992 election campaign Clinton had explicitly renounced aspirations of space-based defence and supported only the development of an option for a 'limited' missile defence system within the existing framework of the ABM Treaty.[4] The raised profile of battlefield (as opposed to national) missile defences such as Patriot assured its place in Clinton's plans, but in May 1993, Secretary of Defense Les Aspin announced sweeping changes to the strategic defence programme inherited from the Reagan and Bush administrations. Renaming the SDIO the Ballistic Missile Defense Organization (BMDO), Aspin declared 'the end of the Star Wars era'.[5] The name change indicated that Aspin shared Clinton's view of the redundancy of SDI, as did Aspin's national defence budget which shifted the majority of financing away from efforts at strategic defence (which was downgraded to the status of a 'technology readiness programme') towards the development of defence against short- and medium-range ballistic missiles, or theatre missile defence (TMD).[6] The lesson that Aspin took from the Gulf War was that theatre defences were 'paramount' and technically, militarily and financially distinguishable from national defences.[7]

---

[3] Both documents are available online at www.dtic.mil/jv2010/jvpub.htm [last accessed 20 January 2009]. Emphasis added.

[4] Jack Mendelsohn, 'Arms Control after the Summit', *Arms Control Today*, 23:4 (1993) pp. 10–14, p. 10.

[5] Defense Secretary Aspin, 'Defense Department Briefing', Federal News Service, 13 May 1993, www.fas.org/spp/starwars/offdocs/d930513.htm [last accessed 20 January 2009].

[6] In March of the same year, Aspin had formally announced the proposed national defence budget for financial year 1994 (FY 94). The Clinton administration requested $3.8 billion for SDI, about the same level as FY93; however, money for national ground-based missile defence was to be cut below the FY93 level, with the budget for Theater Missile Defense (TMD) rising from $1.1 billion to $1.8 billion, an increase of more than 60 per cent. By contrast, the $75 million requested for "Brilliant Pebbles" (a futuristic system of spherical, space-based interceptors plagued by cost overruns and eventually discontinued in 1993) was about one-third of the FY93 level. See Mendelsohn, *Arms Control after the Summit*.

[7] Remarks by Les Aspin and William Dickinson, House Armed Services Committee, US Congress, *Defense for a New Era: Lessons of the Persian Gulf War* (Washington, DC: Brassey's, 1992).

Clinton himself never exhibited any particular attachment to the idea of a national missile defence system, describing the concept on one occasion as 'the wrong way to defend America'.[8] This put the President at loggerheads with a core of Republican proponents of missile defence fronted by the 1996 Republican presidential candidate Bob Dole, and vociferously backed by several Senators in the Republican-dominated Congress as well as by conservative think-tanks such as the Heritage Foundation, High Frontier and the Centre for Security Policy.[9] Problematically, elements within Clinton's own administration also seemed to be sympathetic to the views propounded by Republican proponents of missile defence, and here substantivist visions of technological development became increasingly prevalent as a means to (implicitly) question the President's separation of missile defence from the overall tenor of technological enthusiasm associated with the RMA. Aspin's successor as Secretary of Defense, William J. Perry, for example, questioned the assumption that the end of the Soviet Union could be equated with an end to the threat of ballistic missiles:

My generation spent nearly all of our adult lives with the threat of nuclear holocaust hanging over heads like a dark cloud, threatening the extinction of all mankind.

But while the Cold War is over, the missile threat has not gone away. Indeed, another missile threat is emerging. It is the threat of missile technology in the hands of rogue nations hostile to the United States or our allies. The real danger is that those missiles can be coupled with nuclear, biological or chemical weapons and that they will be used to attack our troops in battle theaters, to attack or terrorize our allies or even in the future to threaten our country.[10]

Likewise, for those within the government's Ballistic Missile Defense Organization the post-Cold War missile threat was construed as growing, amorphous and potentially catastrophic should the administration

---

[8] Remarks by the President at United States Coast Guard Academy Commencement, 22 May 1996, www.pbs.org/newshour/bb/election/may96/clinton_coguard_5-22.html [last accessed 20 January 2009].

[9] For overviews of the political debates see Joseph Cirincione, 'Why the Right lost the Missile Defense Debate', *Foreign Policy*, 106, Spring (1997) pp. 39–55.

[10] Secretary of Defense William J. Perry, 'Protecting the Nation through Ballistic Missile Defense', remarks at George Washington University, Washington, DC, 25 April 1996, www.defenselink.mil/Speeches/Speech.aspx?SpeechID=956 [last accessed 20 January 2009].

fail to meet the threat of missile attack with technological ingenuity. 'We are affirming that the threat is there today. We're affirming that it's growing, and it certainly will be there ... certainly it could be within the next couple of years, and the need for getting this program started is an affirmation of the reality of that particular threat.'[11] A similar logic informed the views of Perry's replacement as Secretary of Defense, William Cohen. Before going on to specify the exact (potential) missile threat posed by North Korea, Iraq and Iran to a European audience, Cohen framed the issues in terms of a broader technological dynamic at play globally:

> This habit of adaptation – the constant reevaluation of the threats of our day and age – is the reason that the United States is moving forward in areas such as ballistic missile defense. We must recognize *the iron law of modernity: as technology spreads and improves, the security threats beyond our borders – and the security expectations within our borders – both increase* ... The solution is clear: America needs both theater missile defense systems and a limited national missile defense system.[12]

Here Cohen seems to be working within a clear substantivist trope in order to make the case for missile defence. Note the pseudo-Weberian overtones of an 'iron cage' to his stipulation that the spread of technology determines security; technology as an aspect of modern life has a constrictive effect (externally) that is concomitant with its more progressive impact (domestically – as, Cohen implies, can be the case with missile defence).

Much of the sustenance for these increasingly pessimistic visions of a growing missile threat in the late 1990s came from the findings of the 'Commission to Assess the Ballistic Missile Threat to the United States'.[13] Established in 1998 amidst the growing dissatisfaction of

---

[11] Lt General Lester L. Lyles, BMDO director, DOD News Briefing, 20 January 1999, www.fas.org/spp/starwars/program/news99/t01201999_tgen.htm [last accessed 20 January 2009].

[12] Secretary of Defense William Cohen, 'European Security and Defense Identity', Speech to the 36th Munich Conference on Security Policy, 5 February 2000, www.acronym.org.uk/dd/dd43/43bmd.htm [last accessed 20 January 2009], emphasis added.

[13] Commission to Assess the Ballistic Missile Threat to the United States, *Report of the Commission to Assess the Ballistic Missile Threat to the United States*, Executive Summary, 15 July 1998, www.fas.org/irp/threat/bm-threat.htm [last accessed 20 January 2009].

Republicans in Congress with intelligence estimates of the ballistic missile threat to the USA, the commission's findings have since come to epitomise the threat perception underlying the case for US ballistic missile defence. Intended to provide a bipartisan perspective on the issue of ballistic missile proliferation to Congress, the commission contained several avowed proponents of missile defence – such as Paul D. Wolfowitz and Dr William R. Graham – and a chair, Donald Rumsfeld, who had reluctantly overseen the dismantling of the Sentinel missile defence initiative of the 1970s. Balance, however, was expected to be provided by the presence of several well-known missile defence sceptics – such as Nobel Prize-winning physicist Richard Garwin – and the fact that the commission was under strict instructions not to make specific recommendations as to responses to the threat they were investigating.

From our perspective, the report of the 'Rumsfeld Commission' (as it was to become colloquially known) is significant in several respects. The central finding of the commission was that 'The threat to the US posed by these emerging capabilities [ballistic missiles and WMD] is broader, more mature and evolving more rapidly than has been reported in estimates and reports by the Intelligence Community.'[14] The reason given as to why the intelligence community had so badly misjudged the evolution of such capabilities was that it had failed to recognise 'a dramatically transformed international security environment' that 'provides an ever-widening access to technology, information and expertise that can be and is used to speed both the development and deployment of ballistic missiles and weapons of mass destruction'.[15]

Technological development is construed here as inherently dangerous. Of course the commission had in mind ballistic missile and WMD technology in particular; its report grounds this fear, though, within a broader narrative that emphasises the Janus-faced nature of technological development more generally. The report notes that the current system of global trade, for example, is of course predicated on a technological infrastructure of transport and communication. Simultaneously, however,

Expanding world trade and the explosion in information technology have accelerated the global diffusion of scientific, technical and industrial

---

[14] Ibid.   [15] Ibid.

information. The channels – both public and private, legal and illegal – through which technology, components and individual technicians can be moved among nations have increased exponentially.[16]

Similarly, the commission considered the extent to which taken-for-granted markers of technological advancement, such as reliance on computers on a global level and military-technological superiority in the USA in particular, constituted an inherent weakness (in the form of susceptibility to the 'Y2K' bug and overemphasis on the RMA).[17] This more general framing allows for the particular specification of missile technology as 'technology-out-of-control', as intimated in the earlier quote from Cohen: 'commerce in ballistic missile and WMD technology and hardware has been growing, which may make proliferation self-sustaining ...'.[18] Indeed the commission lamented the fact that as 'the world's leading developer and user of advanced technology' the USA had unwittingly acted as a proliferator: 'The acquisition and use of transferred technologies in ballistic missile and WMD programs has been facilitated by foreign students training in the US, by wide dissemination of technical information, by the illegal acquisition of US designs and equipment and by the relaxation of US export control policies.'[19] Hence, US promotion of technological development in such areas had become its own Achilles heel.

Extrapolating from such trends, the commission sought to go beyond prior intelligence assessments by posing the question of not just 'What is known about the ballistic missile threat?' but also 'What is not known about the threat ...?' Its conclusion was that rather than assume a 'distant threat', the US intelligence infrastructure should revise its estimates 'to reflect the reality of an environment in which there may be little or no warning' of a ballistic missile attack.[20] The commission thus ended up resembling 'Team B' and its views discussed in chapter 4, not least in its proud admission that 'we took into account not only the hard data available, but also the often significant gaps in that data'.[21] Newt Gingrich, speaker of the House at the time of the report's formulation, later reflected that 'The Rumsfeld commission, in some ways, is modelled on a second-team approach that was used in the late 1970s to review the Central Intelligence Agency under President Jimmy Carter,

---

[16] Ibid.   [17] Ibid., Attachment 1 to report.   [18] Ibid.   [19] Ibid.   [20] Ibid.
[21] Ibid.

which also showed, by the way, a huge gap in the two interpretations of reality.'[22]

On 31 August 1998, a matter of weeks after the Rumsfeld Commission had submitted its findings to Congress, US defence satellites spotted what later transpired was a three-stage rocket launched from North Korean soil, the *Taepodong I*. Though the *Taepodong* had broken up before achieving its expected altitude the launch had a profound effect – not least in lending credence to the pessimistic predictions of the Rumsfeld Commission. Prior missile defence sceptics such as Clinton's Secretary of State Madeline Albright began to reconsider their viewpoints: 'I got a sense that there was a whole new element of danger to the United States,' she recalls of the time. 'It's hard not to see it that way.'[23] The North Koreans had 'essentially leapfrogged several developmental levels' with the launch as it had skipped from its previously known capacity of single-stage missiles to a three-stage variant, a feat that had not been predicted by US intelligence (or, for that matter, by the Rumsfeld Commission).[24] If successful, a three-stage rocket of this type could potentially reach the territory of the United States. The launch, as Bradley Graham puts it, had 'shaken the conventional wisdom about foreign missile development. Suddenly, the skies over the United States looked a lot more threatening.'[25]

In the wake of the Rumsfeld report and the North Korean launch, pressure increased markedly on the administration to deploy a missile defence system. The final text of the Missile Defense Act signed into law by Clinton in 1999 ('It is the policy of the United States to deploy as soon as technologically possible an effective National Missile Defense system against limited ballistic missile attack') reflected an assumption of technological feasibility hitherto dismissed by Clinton himself, and represented a major victory for missile defence advocates.[26] Clinton ultimately deferred any decision on deployment to his successor, but by

---

[22] Newt Gingrich, interview for PBS Frontline 'Missile Wars', 27 March 2002, www.pbs.org/wgbh/pages/frontline/shows/missile/interviews/gingrich.html [last accessed 20 January 2009].

[23] Quoted in Bradley Graham, *Hit to Kill: the New Battle over Shielding America from Missile Attack* (New York: Public Affairs, 2001) p. 91.

[24] Ibid., pp. 59, 62.   [25] Ibid., p. 69.

[26] 'National Missile Defense [NMD] Act of 1999', 22 July 1999, www.cdi.org/friendlyversion/printversion.cfm?documentID=1005 [last accessed 20 January 2009].

then US intelligence estimates reflected a revised level of threat awareness that largely echoed the vision of technologically determined threats
espoused by the Rumsfeld Commission. The unclassified public summary of the 1999 National Intelligence Estimate is indicative of a move
towards framing the threat of ballistic missile proliferation in terms of –
to paraphrase the Rumsfeld Commission – what was not known about
the threat. It did so by employing and emphasising conditional language
to foreground the possibilities allowed for by the advancement and
spread of missile technology in the coming decade:

> North Korea *could convert* its Taepo Dong-I space launch vehicle (SLV) into
> an ICBM ... that could deliver a light payload (sufficient for a biological or
> chemical weapon) to the United States ... North Korea is *more likely to
> weaponize* the larger Taepo Dong-II ICBM that could deliver a several-
> hundred-kilogram payload (sufficient for early generation nuclear weapons)
> to the United States ... Iran *could test* a North Korean-type ICBM ... If Iraq
> could buy a Taepo Dong-II from North Korea it *could have a launch cap-
> ability* within months of the purchase ... Sales of ICBMs or SLVs, which have
> inherent ICBM capabilities and could be converted relatively quickly with
> little or no warning, could increase the number of countries able to threaten
> the United States.[27]

Once again, these specific judgements were grounded within a broader
argument. In the view of George J. Tenet, Director of Central Intelligence:

> as we face a new century, we face a new world. A world where technology
> especially information technology, develops and spreads at lightning speed –
> and becomes obsolete just as fast ... where technology has enabled, driven, or
> magnified the threat to us; where age-old resentments threaten to spill-over
> into open violence; and where a growing perception of our so-called 'hege-
> mony' has become a lightning rod for the disaffected. Moreover, this environ-
> ment of rapid change makes us even more vulnerable to sudden surprise.[28]

---

[27] National Intelligence Officer for Strategic and Nuclear Programs, Foreign Missile
Developments and the Ballistic Missile Threat to the United States through 2015,
September 1999, pp. 4–5, emphasis in original, www.dni.gov/nic/
PDF_GIF_otherprod/missilethreat2001.pdf#search=%22Foreign%20Missile%
20Developments%20and%20the%20Ballistic%20Missile%20Threat%20to%
20the%20United%20States%20through%202015%22 [last accessed 20
January 2009].
[28] George J. Tenet, Director of Central Intelligence, Statement before the Senate
Select Committee on Intelligence on the Worldwide Threat in 2000: Global
Realities of Our National Security, 2 February 2000, www.cia.gov/cia/

The proliferation frame and technological fears

Such claims about the nature of the international environment naturally carry and invoke ontological stipulations about the world and the kind of threats that exist in it. Acknowledging this does not require that we reduce everything merely to competing claims about the nature of reality. As Tan See Seng notes:

> Events that ostensibly fuelled the drive for missile defence were 'real': nuclear tests in South Asia; missile tests by North Korea; 'rogue states' committing sizeable levels of resources to developing their ballistic missile capabilities, and their resort to denial and deception to hide the development and deployment of those capabilities; China's and Russia's gross exportation of enabling technologies (including ballistic missile technology per se) to countries 'hostile' to the US; China's defence budget burgeoning by as much as fifty percent in the last decade, or its bellicose rhetoric concerning Taiwan and so on.[29]

The critical point, however, is that acknowledging the fact that an 'event' has autonomous, extra-discursive qualities does not negate the importance of subsequent discursive construction(s) of that event.[30] As Seng contends:

> The difficulty ... lies with the claim that such events could have constituted themselves or 'emerged' as objects outside of any discursive condition of possibility ... These representational modes are not exactly new since they have also figured in past articulations of danger cardinal to the repetitive writing of political identity.[31]

Examples of such repetition can be seen in Perry's invocation of the Cold War analogy for the emerging missile threat, or Gingrich's comparison of the Rumsfeld Commission with 'Team B' and its articulation of the nuclear danger in the late 1970s.[32] These establish a prior

public_affairs/speeches/2000/dci_speech_032100.html [last accessed 7 March 2007].

[29] Tan See Seng, *What Fear Hath Wrought: Missile Hysteria and the Writing of 'America'*, Institute of Defence and Strategic Studies Working Paper (Singapore: Institute of Defence and Strategic Studies, 2002) p. 14.

[30] Jutta Weldes, 'Constructing National Interests', *European Journal of International Relations*, 2:3 (1996) pp. 275–318, p. 280.

[31] Seng, *What Fear Hath Wrought*, p. 14.

[32] See Gordon R. Mitchell, 'Team B Intelligence Coups', *Quarterly Journal of Speech*, 92:2 (2006) pp. 144–73.

framework of meaning through which unfamiliar contexts can be understood and explained by reference to preceding discourses.

With regard to missile defence, a relevant framework of representation is what David Mutimer has termed the 'proliferation metaphor'.[33] Discourse on proliferation rose to prominence in the 1990s, associated particularly (though not exclusively) with WMD and ballistic missile technology, and remains a prominent issue in contemporary security debates. The 'metaphorical' element of the concept of proliferation, Mutimer argues, lies in 'its base biological meaning' which 'refers to an autonomous process of growth and outward spread, internally driven but externally controlled. Danger arises when the controls fail and the natural proliferation of cells produces excessive reproduction.'[34] In figurative terms, therefore, the Manhattan Project 'represented the source cell or organism from which the technology would spread' and, Mutimer argues convincingly, the metaphor has now been extended to include associated technologies, particularly ballistic missiles.[35]

Of particular interest here is the fact that the core characteristics of this metaphor accord acutely with the category of substantivism oulined in Part One. Firstly, Mutimer contends that the discourse of proliferation 'pointed to the movement of technology as the key to producing the problem [of proliferation] in the first place'.[36] Secondly, 'the object of the "proliferation" image is an autonomous technology that *will* spread if left unchecked, with potentially devastating consequences' and, crucially, 'In turn, this framing enables certain practices that aim to check this autonomous technological diffusion.'[37] Finally, again in keeping with substantivism, 'the proliferation metaphor for the problem of nuclear weapons spread is *an extreme technological determinism* ... the metaphor of proliferation applied to the development of nuclear technology highlights the autonomy in the growth of that technology and its problematic weapons variant'.[38] Hence it can well be argued that the discourse of proliferation incorporates several of the features of

---

[33] David Mutimer, *The Weapons State: Proliferation and the Framing of Security* (Boulder, CO: Lynne Rienner, 2000).

[34] David Mutimer, 'Reimagining Security: the Metaphors of Proliferation' in Keith Krause and Michael C. Williams (eds.) *Critical Security Studies: Concepts and Cases* (London: UCL Press, 1997) p. 201.

[35] Mutimer, *The Weapons State*, see p. 29.   [36] Ibid., p. 2.

[37] Ibid., p. 7, emphasis in original.   [38] Ibid., p. 61, emphasis added.

substantivism: autonomous technology, technology-out-of-control and explicit technological determinism.

Of course it could be objected that the proliferation metaphor, as occurs in arguments for missile defence, rarely remains at this level of generality for too long. Rogue states, their leaders, potential motivations and capabilities are all often specified in detail (for example, North Korea, Kim Jong-Il, long-standing hatred of the US/irrationality, the *Taepodong* II). Such specification, though, is invariably framed in terms of a broader and more amorphous dynamic – the spread of technology. This occurs most frequently through the prior nominalisation of the word 'technology': its transformation into a noun-like entity that seems to have inherent capabilities. Thus 'technology spreads and improves', 'technology develops and spreads at lightning speed', 'technology has enabled, driven or magnified the threat to us' and so on (see the previously cited quotations). The agential capacity that is associated with an instrumental view of technology (individuals use technology towards certain ends) consequently comes to be severely diminished as in the substantivist view (technology *itself* determines particular ends).

This latter tendency results in the stipulation of a highly amorphous and petrifying scenario that establishes an initial 'necessity' (or 'basic' fear), which can then be broken down into more manageable problems ('specific' fears).[39] In the context of contemporary missile defence advocacy it will be argued below that the articulation of a broad sense of threat emanating from the fear of technology itself prepares the ground for the promises made for the saving power of missile defence technology examined in the previous chapter. As Seng puts it, 'If missile defence is … the "foolproof recipe" for exorcising the ghosts or demons of missile hysteria, then Bush's national security advisors are the exorcists and shaman as well as the constructors of national insecurity via missile hysteria.'[40]

Substantivism and proliferation

It should be noted that the tendency to construe proliferation in substantivist terms is not the exclusive purview of proponents of missile

---

[39] Robert H. Johnson, *Improbable Dangers: US Conceptions of Threat in the Cold War and After* (New York: St Martin's Press, 1994) p. 12.

[40] Seng, *What Fear Hath Wrought*, p. 27.

defence. In fact it could well be argued that, in a manner broadly analogous to the co-optation of the rhetoric of nuclear fears by SDI proponents in the 1980s, the arguments of missile defence borrow from, overlap with, and are situated in relation to a broader discourse and literature on proliferation that also encourages the nominalisation of technology. Mutimer notes, for example, the implication of the title of Frank Barnaby's 1993 work *How Nuclear Weapons Spread: Nuclear Weapons Proliferation in the 1990s*, arguing that we should 'Notice that the *weapons themselves* spread; they are not spread by some form of external agent – say, a human being or a political institution.' The metaphor is precisely commonsensical in so far as 'Under most circumstances such a title would be unnoticed, for the implications are so deeply ingrained in our conceptual system that they are not recognized as metaphorical.'[41] More recently Victor A. Utgoff has spoken of 'The Specter of Nuclear, Biological, and Chemical Weapons Proliferation', invoking the kind of ghostly presences alluded to by Seng, whilst the title of Michael E. Brown's *Grave New World: Security Challenges in the 21st Century* plays on Aldous Huxley's vision of a technologically structured dystopia.[42]

Other prominent examples of such pessimistic scene-setting occur in Graham Allison's *Nuclear Terrorism: the Ultimate Preventable Catastrophe*.[43] Allison opens with a quote from Albert Einstein that immediately establishes the theme of technology-out-of-control: 'Since the advent of the Nuclear Age, everything has changed save our modes of thinking and we thus drift toward unparalleled catastrophe.'[44] Allison sets out to raise awareness that nuclear weapons have, in a very literal sense, got out of control – as is captured succinctly by the concept of 'loose nukes': 'newspapers carry almost weekly stories of

---

[41] Mutimer, *The Weapons State*, p. 61, emphasis in original; Frank Barnaby, *How Nuclear Weapons Spread: Nuclear Weapon Proliferation in the 1990s* (London: Routledge, 1993).

[42] Victor A. Utgoff, 'The Specter of Nuclear, Biological, and Chemical Weapons Proliferation' in Victor A. Utgoff (ed.) *The Coming Crisis: Nuclear Proliferation, US Interests, and World Order* (Cambridge, MA: MIT Press, 2000); Michael E. Brown (ed.), *Grave New World: Security Challenges in the 21st Century* (Washington, DC: Georgetown University Press, 2003).

[43] Graham Allison, *Nuclear Terrorism: the Ultimate Preventable Catastrophe* (New York: Times Books, 2004). A similar reading is offered by Robert S. McNamara, 'Apocalypse Soon', *Foreign Policy*, May/June (2005) pp. 29–35.

[44] Allison, *Nuclear Terrorism*, quoted on p. 1.

theft of radioactive material, not only in Russia and the former Soviet Union but here at home as well'.[45] The network of arms sales established by the infamous Dr A. Q. Khan, Allison notes, amounts to 'what the International Atomic Energy Agency (IAEA) has called a "Wal-Mart of private-sector proliferation"'.[46]

Again, these specific threats are embedded within the wider spread of technology. Allison quotes at length from the afterword to Tom Clancy's 1991 bestseller *The Sum of All Fears*, where Clancy paints a scenario in which a nuclear device is planted on US soil after falling into the hands of Middle Eastern terrorists:

All of the material in this novel relating to weapons technology and fabrication is readily available in any one of dozens of books ... What required billions of dollars in the 1940s is much less expensive today. A modern personal computer has far more power and reliability than the first Eniac, and the 'hydrocodes' which enable a computer to test and validate a weapon's design are easily duplicated. The exquisite machine tools used to fabricate parts can be had for the asking. When I asked explicitly for specifications of the machine used at Oak Ridge and elsewhere, they arrived Federal Express the next day. Some highly specialized items designed specifically for bomb manufacture may now be found in stereo speakers. The fact of the matter is that a sufficiently wealthy individual could, over a period of from five to ten years, produce a multistage thermonuclear device. Science is all in the public domain, and allows few secrets.[47]

What is notable here is the way that Clancy inverts the familiar narrative/intertext of technological development and progress: everyday technologies such as the personal computer, machine tools and stereo speakers become sources of threat, and the dispersion of scientific knowledge becomes a potential source of weakness. Allison replicates this view:

Nuclear weapons occupy the top of the pyramid of threats, but as we all learned on 9/11, *even the everyday instruments of modern life* (like airplanes) can be turned into weapons. High on the list of potential dangers are the nation's nuclear power plants. The prospect of a terrorist crashing an airplane

---

[45] Ibid., p. 8; see also pp. 43–5, 61.   [46] Ibid., p. 8.
[47] Tom Clancy, *The Sum of All Fears*, 1992 edition as quoted in Allison, *Nuclear Terrorism*, p. 12. Clancy's novel was later made into a successful (2001) movie of the same name.

into a nuclear plant or detonating a powerful truck bomb next to a vulnerable area is among many people's worst nightmares.[48]

This incorporation of 9/11 into the general theme of technological fears is also made in another recent treatise by Jonathan Schell: 'If terrorists could knock down the World Trade Center with airplanes, what might they have done with a nuclear weapon? And nuclear technology [is] spreading.'[49] Later Schell employs the proliferation metaphor to represent a more general trend:

By convention, the word 'proliferation' refers to the actual acquisition of nuclear weapons. However, there is a sort of proliferation that falls short of this but is still highly significant. This is the proliferation of the basic scientific and technical capabilities on which the construction of nuclear arms is based . . . The secret of the bomb is out; it has been published in magazines. The same holds true for missile technology and chemical and biological weapons technology.[50]

On this reading, increasing scientific and technical knowledge is the harbinger of catastrophe, a fact rendered all the more problematic by the modern world's dependence on those same forms of knowledge.

Substantivism, proliferation and defence in the 'second nuclear age'?

Whilst operating within the parameters of substantivism, the commentators cited above could hardly be considered as sympathetic to missile defence. Allison contends that 'Against the threat of nuclear terrorism, this initiative [missile defense] is virtually irrelevant, since terrorists are not likely to acquire a weapon that is small enough to be delivered by missile, and even less so the missile itself. This allocation of funds suggests that the Bush administration and Congress do not fully grasp the nature of the nuclear terror threat.'[51] Schell has declared that 'In the absence of negotiated agreements that are pushing offensive nuclear weapons in the direction of zero, missile defense is a supreme folly.'[52]

---

[48] Allison, *Nuclear Terrorism*, p. 53, emphasis added.
[49] Jonathan Schell, *The Unfinished Twentieth Century: the Crisis of Weapons of Mass Destruction* (London: Verso, 2001) p. xi.
[50] Ibid., pp. 65–6.   [51] Allison, *Nuclear Terrorism*, p. 201.
[52] Schell, *The Unfinished Twentieth Century*, p. 69.

Mutimer's survey of proliferation discourse in the 1990s concentrated on the ways in which the proliferation metaphor was used to build the case for stronger international regulatory frameworks, such as the Non-Proliferation Treaty and the Missile Technology Control Regime (MTCR). 'Proliferation' thereby enabled a series of control practices, and this reassertion of control would come primarily in the form of international law and treaties. Incumbent upon proponents of missile defence, by contrast, has been a need to articulate proliferation fears in such a way as to render missile defence as *the* common sense solution or panacea for these fears, largely in opposition to arms control measures (exemplified by virulent opposition to the ABM Treaty). To do so has required proponents of missile defence to embed the largely positive and instrumental narrative of technology – which, as shown in the previous chapter, they have frequently employed in order to promote missile defence – *within* a substantivist framing of technological development.

Characteristic of this move in terms of strategic thought is the work of Colin S. Gray. The notion of a 'second nuclear age' that came to be espoused by Gray (amongst others) in the late 1990s establishes a significantly different view of weapons technology than he had espoused in his earlier 'Weapons Don't Make War' thesis.[53] The 'second nuclear age', Gray argues, is conditioned by the continued existence of nuclear weapons, an existence that must be given primacy in strategic analysis in spite of purportedly radical political changes associated with the end of the Cold War. Thus, 'the thesis implies nothing in particular about the character of the age in question other than it is a nuclear one'.[54] As was argued in chapter 1, this seems to assign a substantive impact to the continued existence of nuclear weapons technology that is at odds with Gray's earlier views, although Gray seeks to pre-empt any such potential criticism by arguing that 'There is a danger that some scholarly reviewers of this book may "lose the plot" by indulging in unduly rigorous examination of the hypothesis that this is a second nuclear age.'[55]

---

[53] Colin S. Gray, *The Second Nuclear Age* (Boulder, CO: Lynne Rienner, 1999). See also Keith B. Payne, *Deterrence in the Second Nuclear Age* (Lexington, KY: University Press of Kentucky, 1996); Fred C. Ikle, 'The Second Coming of the Nuclear Age', *Foreign Affairs*, 75:1 (1996) pp. 119–29.
[54] Gray, *The Second Nuclear Age*, p. 23.   [55] Ibid., p. 28.

Attempted pre-emption of faultfinding notwithstanding, the architecture of Gray's argument and its relation to his earlier espoused view of weapons technology is worth noting. Though he does not acknowledge this explicitly himself, it could be argued that the conditioning effect of nuclear weapons follows logically from Gray's early notion that weapons don't make war. He seems to resort to the earlier position when he argues that 'Arms are not the problem; rather it is the political demand for arms.' Yet,

Just as we have to cope with drug addiction because we cannot solve the 'problem' of the demand for drugs, so we have to cope – as an extension of the ways in which we do at present – with a more nuclear, indeed more WMD-proliferant world, because we cannot solve the 'problem' of local and regional political demand for the security that is believed to flow uniquely from possession of such weaponry.[56]

In other words, as is characteristic of substantivism, the instrumental value of (nuclear weapons) technology is so self-evident as a seemingly obvious shortcut to power in the international realm that we will logically end up living in a world saturated by that technology.

Gray's notion of nuclear proliferation as a 'condition' stands as a radical acceptance of the technological determinism Mutimer associates with the concept. Hence Gray dismisses attempts at regulating the spread of ballistic missiles and WMD through international regulation as misguided at best: proliferation is out there, unstoppable, and something to be taken as an accepted fact. He thus ends up at the somewhat paradoxical position of chastising American policy-makers in particular for pursuing an instrumental, problem-solving approach to the issue, drawing directly on Hoffman's critique of 'skill thinking':

the United States is an engineering-minded, problem-solving culture, whose analysts are ever vulnerable to cultural seduction by the challenge of yet another problem in need of solution. In other words, the idea that nuclear proliferation might be a condition rather than a problem, and a diversely manifested condition at that, is not one that sits easily in the word processors of some US experts. After all, if the proliferation of WMD and of cruise and ballistic missiles is researchable as a topic ... then that which is researchable should lend itself to treatment with conclusions that allow confident researchers to manipulate their findings with some controlling solutions.[57]

---

[56] Ibid., pp. 59–60.   [57] Ibid., p. 51.

Yet, he contends, 'we are far from helpless', and here Gray offers a very different response than Allison or Schell, but one that is still clearly in the problem-solving mould: 'there are measures that states can take, especially with respect to the provision of robustly layered offensive and defensive counterforce capabilities, that would help us to cope well enough (if not really well) with the perils posed by WMD. Otherwise we are reduced to a condition wherein our security must reside in faith, hope, and UN weapons inspectors.'[58] The measures which he recommends?

> Although there can never be any absolute guarantees, it is as certain as anything can be in this friction-fraught realm that a multitiered US BMD architecture would defeat militarily any missile menace from regional powers ... Multitiered and mobile forward deployable missile defense (TMD), backstopped critically by a national missile defense (NMD) capability – to minimize the option for terroristic efforts at blackmail – should help enable the superpower to extend protection, even by extended deterrence.[59]

At no point does Gray see a contradiction in upholding the instrumental value of weapons on the one hand and the existence of a nuclear condition on the other. Gray's treatise abounds with such contradictions and lacunae: Isn't the separation between politics and technology part of the reason for the 'nuclear condition'? Could not missile defence in itself be seen as a form of problem-solving response in foreign policy that Gray is so keen to dismiss?

In point of fact, and returning to some of the arguments set out in the initial part of this text, Gray's oscillating representations of technological development, and the extent to which human control over it can be established or re-established, is perfectly in keeping with much of the interpretation of technology both at a broader cultural level and in the justifications offered for missile defence historically. Furthermore the ideas contained in Gray's *Second Nuclear Age* foreshadowed much of the orientation of the current US nuclear posture, in terms of not only missile defence, but also the potential utility of 'deep penetration' (or 'bunker-buster') bombs[60] and the instrumental value of a nuclear capacity for 'limited' wars ('one should not be too hasty in recoiling in politically correct horror from the possibility of US first

---

[58] Ibid., p. xii; see also p. 4.   [59] Ibid., pp. 99, 102.   [60] Ibid., p. 136.

use of nuclear weapons for "niche" war-fighting purposes').[61] Gray's fellow-traveller in the 'second nuclear age' Keith B. Payne replicates several of Gray's contentions and was a co-author of the National Institute for Public Policy's *Rationale and Requirements for US Nuclear Forces and Arms Control*, which recommended several of the above measures as US policy. Payne was among the first to tie the 'spectre' of missile proliferation in the 1990s to the case for missile defence,[62] and has argued more recently that 'the variety of factors driving the political consensus in favor of NMD, most notably the continuing pace of missile and WMD proliferation, are *beyond control*' and that 'Proliferation clearly has become an autonomous factor.'[63] Elsewhere he has declared:

How can we control nuclear physics research and development, nuclear knowledge, and even nuclear scientists? It is not feasible to control knowledge of nuclear physics. The scientific knowledge base is at this point extremely widespread and well documented, easily available to and retrievable by any-one with a will to accumulate it. Similarly, most of the basic technologies involved have proliferated as well. Previous attempts at 'technological denial' as a means of controlling access to a militarily useful technology have not always turned out well. Without political assurances of stable security, science will be exploited for military use. And knowledge of nuclear weapons tech-nology will persist indefinitely.[64]

Rationale and Requirements subsequently reflected the general sense in which the actions and motivations of individual state or non-state actors, though assumed to be harmful towards the USA, were in many ways incidental to the fact of spreading technological capacities:

In the post-Cold War period the various complex technical, political and operational factors that must be taken into account in advance of such

---

[61] Ibid., p. 137.

[62] Keith B. Payne, *Missile Defense in the 21st Century: Protection against Limited Threats, Including Lessons from the Gulf War* (Boulder, CO: Westview Press, 1991).

[63] Keith B. Payne, 'National Missile Defense: Why? And Why Now?', *FPRI Wire* (2000), www.nipp. org/Adobe/fpri.pdf#search=%22National%20Missile% 20Defense%3A%20Why%3F%20And%20Why%20Now%3F%22 [last accessed 20 January 2009] p. 4, emphasis added; Keith Payne and Andrei Kortunov, 'The Character of the Problem', *Comparative Strategy*, 16 (1997) pp. 127–32, p. 129.

[64] Keith B. Payne, 'The Case against Nuclear Abolition and for Nuclear Deterrence', *Comparative Strategy*, 17 (1998) pp. 3–44, p. 34.

defence advocacy remains entirely monolithic between Cold War and post-Cold War eras. A subtle change can be noted, for example, in the shifts from the mechanical nature of the principal threat itself (the Soviet 'war machine') to the machinations of particular states and terrorist groups. But between the two the spread of technology beyond the immediate control of the US state remains consistent as a problem. In testimony before the Senate Armed Services Committee in June 2001, for example, Secretary of Defense Rumsfeld emphasises technology as a continuous, if only continuously surprising, source of threat even as it has developed and changed over time:

Consider the track record of my lifetime ... Airplanes did not exist at the start of the century, but by World War II, bombers, fighters, transports and other aircraft had become common military instruments that critically affected the outcome of the war ... Soon thereafter, the atomic age shocked the world. It was a surprise ... That recent history should make us humble. It certainly tells me that the world of 2015 will almost certainly be little like today and, without doubt, notably different from what today's experts are confidently forecasting ... But while it's difficult to know precisely who will threaten us or where or when in the coming decades, it is less difficult to anticipate how we might be threatened.[74]

As the last line of the above excerpt indicates, identity of adversary is in some ways secondary to the fact that threats are allowed for by technological development. Rumsfeld goes on to list as an example 'Our dependence on computer-based information networks today' which 'makes those networks attractive targets for new forms of cyberattack'.[75] Such examples embellish the grim 'reality' of proliferation:

There are some important facts which are not debatable. The number of countries that are developing nuclear, chemical and biological weapons of mass destruction is growing. The number of ballistic missiles on the face of the Earth and the number of countries possessing them is growing as well.[76]

---

[74] Secretary of Defense Donald H. Rumsfeld and Chairman of the Joint Chiefs of Staff General Hugh Shelton, Testimony before the Senate Armed Services Committee: Defense Strategy Review, 21 June 2001, www.defenselink.mil/speeches/2001/s20010621-secdef2.html [last accessed 20 January 2009].
[75] Ibid.   [76] Ibid.

Here again it is the spread of technology itself which is faulted, a view that is echoed across several instances in which Rumsfeld makes the case for missile defence:

In the 20th Century we faced essentially conventional capabilities ... Regrettably the problem of proliferation and the pervasiveness of these technologies and indeed technicians is such today we will have to be very attentive to see that we are able to continue that record of not having those weapons used.[77]

The new threats are on the horizon, and with the speed of change today, where technology is advancing not in decades but in months and years, we can't afford to wait until they have emerged before we prepare to meet them.[78]

As in Gray's argument, though, such pessimistic accounts of technological development in arms slowly build towards one particular weapons technology, and its technicians, that the USA cannot afford to do without in the coming decades:

we're now in the year 2001, and because of proliferation a number of countries have those weapons [ballistic missiles] and we have no ability to defend against them. So it makes a lot of sense to set that [ABM] treaty aside and develop the capability of being able to defend against ballistic missiles from rogue states.[79]

Indeed, this builds into a more general (and more instrumentalist) justification for the continuation of the USA as a weapons-producing state: 'If harnessed by us ... advanced weapons can help us to extend our current peace and security into the new century. If harnessed by our adversaries, those technologies could lead to unpleasant surprises in the years ahead and could allow hostile powers to undermine our current prosperity and peace.'[80]

This attempt to 'harness' advanced weapons is most obvious in the more 'exotic' missile defence options currently being touted, and similar

---

[77] Secretary of Defense Donald H. Rumsfeld, Remarks to the Metro Atlanta Chamber of Commerce, 27 September 2002, www.defenselink.mil/speeches/2002/s20020927-secdef.html [last accessed 20 January 2009].

[78] Rumsfeld, Testimony before the Senate Armed Services Committee, 21 June 2001.

[79] Defense Secretary Donald H. Rumsfeld, Interview with KNBC-TV Los Angeles, 14 August 2001, www.defenselink.mil/transcripts/2001/t08162001_t814nola.html [last accessed 20 January 2009].

[80] Ibid.

One of the most prominent advocates of missile defence, adept at working within the substantivist/proliferation frame, is former Deputy Secretary of Defense Paul Wolfowitz. Making the case for missile defence to the Senate Armed Services Committee in July 2001 Wolfowitz declared categorically that 'The number of missiles on the face of the earth is growing.'[86] He embellished the impact of his point by asking his audience to imagine a scenario in which the USA had deployed its troops in response to a 'rogue state's' invasion of its neighbour:

Suddenly, almost without warning, missiles rain down on our troops, and pound into the densely populated residential neighborhoods of allied capitals. Panic breaks out. Sirens wail, as rescue crews in protective gear race to search the rubble for bodies and rush the injured to hospitals. Reporters, mumbling through their gas masks, attempt to describe the destruction, as pictures of the carnage are instantaneously broadcast across the world.

Wolfowitz delivers his *coup de grâce* by declaring that 'Mr Chairman, the scene I have described is not science fiction. It is not a future conflict scenario dreamed up by creative Pentagon planners. It is a description of events that took place ten years ago – during the Persian Gulf War.'[87]
    Here the Deputy Secretary neatly invokes several intertexts. The first is the Persian Gulf War as an analogy for a missile attack on the USA itself and, by inference, the 'success' of the Patriot in combating Iraqi Scud missiles. Thus, Wolfowitz infers a common theme between the two circumstances. The second is the negative invocation of science fiction and fictional scenarios. Wolfowitz notes elsewhere that 'Someone once said that history has more imagination than all the scenario writers in the Pentagon, and we have a lot of scenario writers here.'[88] Yet in the same interview Wolfowitz responds positively to the suggestion of *The*

---

[86] Deputy Secretary of Defense Paul Wolfowitz, Prepared Testimony on Ballistic Missile Defense to the Senate Armed Services Committee, 12 July 2001, www.defenselink.mil/speeches/2001/s20010712-depsecdef.html [last accessed 20 January 2009].

[87] Ibid. This 'scenario' was repeated verbatim by Wolfowitz days later in Deputy Secretary of Defense Paul Wolfowitz and Lt General Ronald Kadish, Testimony before the House Armed Services Committee on Ballistic Missile Defense, 19 July 2001, www.defenselink.mil/speeches/2001/s20010719-depsecdef2.html [last accessed 20 January 2009].

[88] Deputy Secretary of Defense Paul Wolfowitz, interview for PBS Frontline 'Missile Wars', June 12 2002, www.pbs.org/wgbh/pages/frontline/shows/missile/interviews/wolfowitz.html [last accessed 20 January 2009].

Sum of All Fears as a plausible future scenario, using it to further his argument for missile defence:

> We saw a fictional version of that in the movie, *The Sum of All Fears*, where the terrorists put a nuclear bomb in Baltimore. There are countries that are working today to be able to put nuclear bombs on the end of long-range missiles to be able to attack American cities, and that's why we want to deny them.[89]

Note the fact that Graham Allison uses the same referent point but arrives at a very different conclusion. In similar fashion 9/11 comes to function as a conceptual resource with which to imagine the future, as it was for Jonathan Schell, but again it has a very different implication. Drawing upon it Wolfowitz indulges in another bit of scenario writing of his own:

> these strikes [9/11] were not just an act of war – they were a window into our future: A future where new enemies visit violence on us in startling ways: a future in which our cities are among the battlefields and our people are among the targets; a future in which more and more adversaries will possess the capability to bring war to the American homeland; a future where the old methods of deterrence are no longer sufficient – and new strategies and capabilities are needed to ensure peace and security.[90]

And what allows for this grim future? Once again the (autonomous) spread of technology is cited as the key enabling factor:

> The information revolution that is fuelling the world economy is also putting dangerous technologies into the hands of multiple adversaries, many of whom despise our nation and wish to harm our people.
>
> Along with the globalization that is creating interdependence among the world's free economies, there is a parallel globalization of terror, in which rogue states and terrorist organizations share information, technology, weapons materials and know-how.
>
> This technology will allow new adversaries to get past our Armed Forces and strike our territory without having to confront and defeat them. As technology proliferates, with each passing year our enemies will possess an increasing capability to bring war to the American homeland.[91]

---

[89] Ibid.
[90] Wolfowitz, Prepared Testimony on Ballistic Missile Defense to the Senate Armed Services Committee, 12 July 2001.
[91] Ibid.

On the basis of such predictions, Wolfowitz declares his plea to pursue missile defence as fully and as soon as possible:

it makes no sense whatsoever – in an era when technology allows us to take away the ability to attack us with a single missile or a few missiles – to leave ourselves vulnerable to that threat. It might have been something we had to live with during an earlier period. We don't have to live with it now, and we shouldn't.[92]

The phrase 'technology allows us' restores a reassuring agential capacity that is absent in the prior discussion of technology's spread. Technology is both agent and instrument on this reading, but its character depends on those in possession of it. 'We', the USA, have the scientific and moral capacity to master technology and make it an instrument of 'our' security; 'they', the external adversaries, are deemed to lack such capacities and operate at the behest of the spread of technology itself. Taken in combination with the assumed faith in missile defence technology examined in chapter 7, the logic is, in the Gramscian understanding, pure common sense.

Substantivism and the marketing of missile defence

Why is the theme of technology-out-of-control so prevalent in arguments for missile defence? It is tempting to speculate that the language of substantivism has instrumental value of its own in the sense of being 'used' in attempts to legitimate the current missile defence effort, particularly in Congressional hearings where the financial lifeblood of the programme is at stake. As one prominent staffer on the Senate Armed Services Committee succinctly puts it:

The bottom line is if you feel there's a threat out there and you believe that we're vulnerable to that threat then you support an approach where you have fieldable prototypes and you continue to test and field a system as you go. If you're less concerned about the threat, or you think that you don't need missile defence because you can deter the threat through counter-retaliation … you say let's slow things down, let's make sure the system really works.[93]

[92] Wolfowitz, interview for PBS Frontline 'Missile Wars'.
[93] Interview (conducted by author), 26 May 2005.

As this quote implies, not everyone is convinced by the notion of a threat 'out there'. Analysts such as Cirincione, Wolfstahl and Rajkumar, for instance, refute the view that attempts to regulate and control such trends are merely facile gestures. Even if efforts at controlling the spread of missile and WMD technology have not been completely successful to date, the moderate success of treaties and monitoring arrangements should, in their view, be used as the basis of a stronger non-proliferation regime.[94] Failure to persuade as to the superiority and necessity of missile defence over such alternatives has potentially crucial consequences for the institutional and industrial ensemble surrounding missile defence and makes its pretensions to popular appeal and resonance – the broader cultural-politico-ethical edifice in Gramsci's terms – all the more important.

As David E. Mosher notes, funding and threat perception are in this case innately related, and spiralling costs have often been the downfall of previous initiatives (such as SDI): 'If the threat to the United States is great enough and a weapons system can help counter that threat, cost becomes a secondary issue. But if the threat is not compelling enough or the strategic rationale is not perceived as clearly benefiting national security, cost can play a central role in changing or even terminating the program.'[95] This becomes pertinent once we recall that 'Missile defense programs have experienced inordinately high rates of cost growth – that is, costs have escalated well above the initial estimates made for virtually every program the United States has started.'[96] The current BMD initiative is no exception in this regard. In addition, multiple defence programmes and initiatives compete for an ultimately finite amount of resources. Missile defence has played a distant second fiddle to the dominant defence issue of the 'War on Terror' though this had a differential impact on missile defence, reducing public focus on the issue but simultaneously empowering the President on national security issues.[97] On several occasions President Bush has also sought to designate missile defence as a component of the broader War on

[94] Joseph Cirincione, Jon B. Wolfstahl and Miriam Rajkumar, *Deadly Arsenals: Nuclear, Biological, and Chemical Threats* (Washington, DC: Carnegie Endowment for International Peace, 2005).
[95] David E. Mosher, 'The Budget Politics of Missile Defense' in James Clay Moltz (ed.) *New Challenges in Missile Proliferation, Missile Defense and Space Security* (Southampton: Mountbatten Centre for International Studies, 2003) p. 18.
[96] Ibid., pp. 18–19.   [97] Ibid., p. 20.

Terror, thus rendering Congressional opposition to the former difficult in political terms.[98]

We should, however, reject the temptation to reduce missile defence advocacy, and the role played by substantivism in it, purely to a functional-instrumental account. It would of course be premature to rule out the possibility that parties who stand to gain from missile defence's increasing budgetary resources can be cognisant of the potential utility of a substantivist framing for the marketing of missile defence. However, overemphasis on this point misses out on the fact that such a framing both assumes and requires a depth of resonance, that the framing of 'threats' in this way will make sense at some broader level by being embedded within (and portrayed as) prevailing common sense.

Substantivism in the broader promotion of missile defence

Important to note in this sense is the fact that endorsement and dissemination of the Bush administration's view of the threat continued to come from a range of government agencies, policy think-tanks and advocacy groups, and the same logic and assumptions could even be said to have informed defence planning. The contemporary structuring of missile defence has been justified in terms of a 'capability-based acquisition' approach to missile defence, itself in turn based on the 'capabilities-based model' espoused in the 2001 Quadrennial Defense Review (QDR). The QDR 2001 recommended that defence planning shift from a 'threat-based' model for defence planning to one based on 'capabilities' that would focus 'more on how an adversary might fight rather than who that adversary might be or where a war might occur'.[99] With regard to missile defence, this was seen to be appropriate justification to 'fast-track' deployment:

In sum, capability-based acquisition is a flexible approach to the question of complex systems, incorporating advanced technologies, that permits the early

---

[98] See for example President George W. Bush, remarks by the President at the Citadel, South Carolina, 11 December 2001, www.whitehouse.gov/news/releases/2001/12/20011211-6.html [last accessed 7 March 2007] and 'Graduation Speech at West Point', 1 June 2002, www.whitehouse.gov/news/releases/2002/06/20020601-3.html [last accessed 7 March 2007].

[99] Department of Defense, *Quadrennial Defense Review Report*, 30 September 2001, www.defenselink.mil/pubs/qdr2001.pdf#search=%22Quadrennial%20Defense%20Review%20Report%22 [last accessed 7 March 2007].

deployment of a limited but effective capability that can be progressively enhanced over time as needed. It provides for continuous warfighter involvement and disciplined development aimed at reducing cycle time. It stays relevant to the threat and remains technologically current. That is our vision for the capability-based approach and how we intend to execute it.[100]

This seems, in essence, to lock the USA into an institutionalised pattern of chasing technological development elsewhere, once again devoting primacy to technological development itself rather than the existence of specified adversaries. In an opposed sense to that examined in chapter 7, technology is once again seen to dictate the development of missile defence. Yet this opposition implies a complementary form of defence economics still in keeping with the prevailing neo-liberal agenda of the Bush administration. A 2002 RAND report captures this melding of threat-based and economic imperatives: 'Capabilities-based planning ... is planning, under uncertainty, to provide capabilities suitable for a wide range of modern-day challenges and circumstances while working within an economic framework that necessitates choice. It contrasts with developing forces based on a specific threat and scenario ... [and] emphasizes flexibility, adaptiveness and robustness of capability.'[101]

Beyond the administration, several advocacy groups shared a unity of purpose in articulating a threat to the USA that only missile defence can prevent. These groups share the general conception of the missile threat expressed by the Bush administration and the resultant pressure for further investment in missile defence. Indeed, they even tended to be more vociferous in this regard. The Claremont Institute, for example, created the imaginatively titled 'MissileThreat.com'[102] to raise

[100] Lt General Ron Kadish, USAF Director, Missile Defense Agency, Statement before the Senate Armed Services Committee regarding the Reorganization of the Missile Defense Program, 13 March 2002, www.mda.mil/mdalink/pdf/kadish13mar02.pdf#search=%22Kadish%2BStatement%20before%20the%20Senate%20Armed%20Services%20Committee%2C%20Strategic%20Forces%20Subcommittee%20Regarding%20the%20Reorganization%20of%20The%20Missile%20Defense%20Program%22 [last accessed 20 January 2009].
[101] Paul K. Davis, *Analytic Architecture for Capabilities-Based Planning, Mission-System Analysis, and Transformation*, RAND 2002, MR-1513-OSD, www.rand.org/pubs/monograph_reports/MR1513/index.html [last accessed 20 January 2009].
[102] See www.missilethreat.com/ [last accessed 20 January 2009].

awareness of 'America's complete vulnerability to ballistic missile attack' which 'increases with the proliferation of ballistic missile threats throughout the world'.[103] On the website's opening page, the dangers of 'missile proliferation' are listed on the left of the screen, including not only data on foreign ballistic missile capabilities ('Missiles of the world') but also 'Scenarios' – computer-animated imaginings of 'Ballistic missile attack on Los Angeles', 'Chinese attack on Russia' and 'Ship-based attack on Hollywood' among others.[104] Reading left to right on the opening page we find detailed descriptions of how missile defence can potentially negate the missile threat, and the scenarios include a number of imagined missile intercepts. Thus the 'problem' of protecting America and its solution is reduced to an assumed common sense conjunction where new weapons systems co-exist as both threat and protector.

Such confident predictions of the saving power of missile defence frequently lead advocacy groups to criticism (albeit sympathetic) of the recent level of US investment in missile defence. Appearing on *ABC News* in the wake of renewed North Korean missile testing in 2006, Claremont Institute President Brian T. Kennedy warned that 'The President [George W. Bush] is very well intentioned when it comes to missile defense. It's just that we're not putting enough resources towards it quickly enough.'[105] Similar lines of argument can be found across the websites and publications of other advocacy groups: 'Missile Defense Advocacy Alliance', or MDAA (famed for its polls claiming to show most Americans want/assumed they already had a missile defence);[106] the Center for Security Policy (sample featured articles: 'Minimal Missile Defense Too Little' and 'Needed: Lasers in the Sky');[107] and the Heritage Foundation ('Congress Must Expand the Nation's "Limited Defensive Capability" against Ballistic Missiles').[108] Here too there is a willingness to incorporate 9/11 into the case for missile

---

[103] Ibid.

[104] See www.missilethreat.com/scenarios/ [last accessed 20 January 2009].

[105] 'Kennedy on ABC News, Calling for Urgency to Missile Defenses', 6 July 2006, www.missilethreat.com/news/200607061049.html [last accessed 7 March 2007].

[106] See www.missiledefenseadvocacy.org/ [last accessed 20 January 2009].

[107] See www.centerforsecuritypolicy.org/index.jsp?topic=missile&section= featured [last accessed 7 March 2007].

[108] See www.heritage.org/Research/NationalSecurity/wm1049.cfm, 26 April 2006 [last accessed 20 January 2009].

defence and missile defence in turn in the broader 'War on Terror' even when the administration does not do so itself explicitly. A December 2005 email circular from the MDAA notes President Bush's declaration that 'We saw the destruction terrorists could cause with jet fuel – and we imagined the destruction they could cause with even more powerful weapons.' The circular immediately notes independently a 'successful' (flight) test of an interceptor missile over the Pacific days earlier, assuming a connection not strictly made by the President himself.[109]

In a somewhat more sanitised form, representatives of industry also place significant store in the ability to represent and simulate not only the imagined potentials of missile defence, but also the assumed consequences of a failure to deploy the systems they claim to be able to build. As well as direct lobbying of those in power through meetings, provision of promotional material and testimony to Congressional committees, corporate-sponsored conferences such as the Royal United Services Annual Conference on missile defence in London are replete with increasingly sophisticated presentations from American corporations (as well as their European counterparts and subsidiaries). These evidence a general tendency to contrast, in computer-simulated form, the effects of a ballistic missile attack and the operation of imagined defence capabilities.[110] This has been paralleled in recent years by the US Department of Defense's increasing reliance on 'modelling and simulation', much more than actual testing, as a primary source of data for missile defence development. The MDA's 'Joint National Integration Center' (JNIC) is specifically directed to develop 'battlefield scenarios' and 'wargame' the role of missile defences in such scenarios, giving full rein to imagination and bringing the technological nightmares implicit in substantivism to life. [111]

---

[109] MDAA email circular, 'If We Wait for Threats to Develop, We Will Have Waited Too Long', author's copy. Reference is to President George W. Bush, 'President Discusses Iraqi Elections, Victory in the War on Terror', 14 December 2005, www.whitehouse.gov/news/releases/2005/12/20051214-1.html [last accessed 7 March 2007].

[110] Witness various contributions to 'The Seventh RUSI Missile Defence Conference: International Missile Defence – Shaping the Future from Policy to Technology', 2–3 November 2005.

[111] See www.mda.mil/jnic/HPCC/default.asp [last accessed 20 January 2009].

Conclusion

This chapter has endeavoured to indicate a variety of ways in which
substantivism informs the contemporary case for missile defence. It has
been argued that a substantivist understanding has been highly prevalent in this regard, and that this pessimistic reading of technological
development has been used to pave the way for the supposed utility of
missile defence. Taken on its own terms this understanding has a fairly
consistent logic, and as we have seen it occurs in an array of arguments
supporting missile defence; but read in light of the previous chapter,
which detailed the simultaneous use of an instrumental understanding
of technology in arguments made by the same strategic, political and
economic interests, we arrive at a seeming paradox. These two understandings of technology should logically contradict each other. Strictly
speaking they have mutually contradictory emphases, and they connote
radically different conceptions of the role between technology, society
and, in turn, security. This, it will be argued in the Conclusion, is where
the exact potency of common sense becomes apparent in the case of
missile defence advocacy.

Conclusion: common sense and the strategic use of 'technology'

Introduction

The aim of this book has been to interrogate the relationship between technology and security as it has been discursively configured and understood within a given context – that of ballistic missile defence advocacy in the United States. A primary move made was to eschew the common tendency to treat technology as a discrete object of analysis in the study (and practice) of security, one that is *either* determinate of *or* determined by security relations. Instead, the analysis given here invited us to consider the question of how such *ways of understanding and representing* technology contribute to the manner in which security, specifically nuclear security, is pursued.

Nowhere is this question more pertinent and appropriate than in the case of American ballistic missile defence. US missile defence, historically, is a perfect instance of investment in technology in pursuit of security. In concrete terms this boils down to issues such as whether we can or should expect defensive technologies to progress to a capacity to intercept ICBMs and what the questionable testing record of missile defence implies for its future prospects and funding. Logically, therefore, the way technology is understood and articulated in the promotion of missile defence is of critical importance. Building on the theoretical outline developed in Part One, Parts Two, Three and Four sought to illustrate empirically the ways in which broad cultural reference points – specifically narratives of technological development within and beyond the narrow field of military security – have been invoked by proponents to substantiate the (claimed) technological capabilities of missile defence and embellish its rationale as a component of US defence policy.

This Conclusion revisits the concerns with which we began, the findings made and the issues these raised in the preceding chapters. Specifically, it reiterates the claim that the understanding(s) of technology employed in American ballistic missile defence advocacy constitute

249

a classic case of 'common sense' in the Gramscian sense of a contradictory, fragmentary and episodic view of the world. Following on from this, the Conclusion examines two further aspects that emphasise the importance of this finding. The first is the ways in which in this form of common sense, contradiction actually constitutes a source of discursive strength in the case made for missile defence – rather than causing it to collapse. Here ideas of the Marxist theorist of language Mikhail Bakhtin are used to flesh out the exact formulation of common sense in this case. The second aspect that the Conclusion reiterates and draws out is the manner in which these common sense understandings of technology are used in a 'strategic' fashion by missile defence advocates. The approach to the strategic use of language developed by Pierre Bourdieu, it is argued, is instructive in this sense in helping get beyond rational-utilitarian approaches to language and discourse, and hence complements Gramsci's definition of common sense. Finally, the Conclusion also returns to the question of technology and argues that a primary aim of Critical Security Studies should be the critical interrogation of the ways in which technology is understood in the theory and practice of contemporary military and nuclear security. Such critique and reflection is imperative because the maintenance of these understandings potentially prohibits and constrains possible alternative conceptions of the relationship between technology and security.

Common sense and contradiction in missile defence advocacy

As noted above, this book was structured to probe for the presence of two recurrent understandings of technology – identified and manifested in philosophical and cultural approaches to technology – within a specific form of security discourse, missile defence advocacy. As well as tracing the presence and influence of an instrumental understanding of technology in key 'texts' associated with the historical promotion of missile defence in the USA, it also identifies an alternate understanding of technology that more closely resembles the philosophical approach to technology labelled as substantivism. Yet how can two understandings that are generally seen to be opposed in philosophical terms not only co-exist within the same argument (that is, for missile defence) but build towards the same end? How and why does the progressivism associated with an instrumental view of technology fit with the dystopian substantivist understanding?

That there is a contradiction between these two views becomes clear once we begin to knit the two understandings back together. As a heuristic device, the analysis separated out the instrumental from the substantive. In reality, though, Parts Two, Three and Four cover a shared timeline running from the early espousal of missile defence as a concept in the immediate post-war years through to the present day. In consequence the two understandings have co-existed in a temporal sense, and continue to do so, and are even frequently espoused by the same speakers within and across their arguments for missile defence. As a discursive whole, therefore, missile defence advocacy moves between and combines elements of these two countervailing understandings of technology. The post-war period covered in Part Two, for example, provides us with a view of technological development as *both* the great hope for establishing freedom of action for the United States in the Cold War *and* the main constraint upon American state power respectively. Early proponents of ballistic missile defence such as Edward Teller and Albert Wohlstetter switched between espousing the capacity for American technological innovation and warning of dangers resultant from non-American advances in technology. Chapter 5 illustrated the extent to which the Reagan administration situated the promotion of SDI in a broader narrative that took technology to be an instrument of progress characteristic of American national identity; yet chapter 6 showed the extent to which this promotion was itself predicated on a view of technology (largely co-opted from the anti-nuclear movement) as an autonomous source of danger. Proponents of strategic defence proved themselves adept not only at recounting the glories of American technological innovation in the past, but also at painting a vision of a world beholden to a technologically determined future.

With reference to more recent arguments for missile defence, chapters 7 and 8 evidenced the continuing presence of these countervailing understandings. Political proponents such as Rumsfeld and Wolfowitz cite everyday technologies and weapons innovations as proof of the potential of technological advance; but this is held at one and the same time to be potentially beneficial and potentially catastrophic for the USA. Similarly, proponents within strategic theory such as Gray and Payne oscillate between seeing technological innovation and diffusion as a source of strength *and* weakness in American security relations; a source of US autonomy *and* a constraint upon its ability to act globally; as something that should be promoted as the basis of American military power yet which frequently gets beyond the control of the US state.

In terms of strategic theory, we saw how these contending visions of technology have been upheld and propounded by Gray in particular – in the form of his 'weapons don't make war' and 'second nuclear age' theses – as sustaining the case for missile defence without any apparent awareness or concern for the fact that these two theses rely on ultimately contradictory understandings. With regard to the political discourse advocating missile defence, the same pattern is replicated across speeches and presentations. The 'surprising' nature of technological development, for example, is used variously to defend the patchy testing record of missile defence by reference to unanticipated leaps in weaponry,[1] but this is itself something that is to be feared.[2] The conflicting inferences at play are apparent within assessments from Paul Wolfowitz, quoted in chapter 8, where it is asserted that:

technology will allow new adversaries to get past our Armed Forces and strike our territory without having to confront and defeat them. As technology proliferates, with each passing year our enemies will possess an increasing capability to bring war to the American homeland.[3]

But, simultaneously:

it makes no sense whatsoever – in an era when technology allows us to take away the ability to attack us with a single missile or a few missiles – to leave ourselves vulnerable to that threat. It might have been something we had to live with during an earlier period. We don't have to live with it now, and we shouldn't.[4]

Technology simultaneously 'allows' two opposed possibilities here: in the first instance it allows for the USA to be held hostage to foreign

---

[1] Paul Wolfowitz, Prepared Testimony on Ballistic Missile Defense to the Senate Armed Services Committee, Thursday, 12 July 2001 (see chapter 7).

[2] Secretary of Defense Donald H. Rumsfeld and Chairman of the Joint Chiefs of Staff General Hugh Shelton, Testimony before the Senate Armed Services Committee: Defense Strategy Review, 21 June 2001 (see chapter 8).

[3] Deputy Secretary of Defense Paul Wolfowitz, Prepared Testimony on Ballistic Missile Defense to the Senate Armed Services Committee, 12 July 2001 (see chapter 8).

[4] Deputy Secretary of Defense Paul Wolfowitz, interview for PBS Frontline 'Missile Wars', 12 June 2002 (see chapter 8).

powers; in the second it enables the USA to overcome its adversaries. At no point do these apparent antagonisms appear to be a cause of concern for proponents of missile defence. Any potential contradiction between these two understandings and the arguments they sustain is never acknowledged; both are stipulated (as in the case above by Paul Wolfowitz) as being particularly appropriate in the current international environment. In part this might be explained via the observation that these apparently contradictory understandings of technology are simultaneously bound up with questions of identity and the identification of external threats.[5] The proliferation of technology is identified with 'them', 'our enemies', whilst this is an external threat that 'we', the USA, shouldn't have to live with when 'technology allows us to take away the ability to attack us'.

Yet, even if we accept these understandings as 'second-order explanations' intended to mediate the dynamics of the international system – wherein practices of identity formation are also readily apparent – there is still a logical paradox that comes into play when they are used simultaneously in the manner indicated above: how can technology be two things at one time, especially when these two things contradict? Superficially at least, it seems problematic to respond to a 'threat' caused by innovation in ballistic missile technology by seeking to develop ballistic missile technology further; to both emphasise and chastise the instrumental value that states place on weapons innovation; to simultaneously laud and denigrate the impact of technology on everyday life, and so on.[6] In this sense, the understanding(s) of technology present in missile defence advocacy constitute a perfect example of Gramsci's concept of 'common sense' which, in chapter 1, was

---

[5] On this general theme see David Campbell, *Writing Security: United States Foreign Policy and the Politics of Identity* (Manchester: Manchester University Press, 1992) and Jutta Weldes, Mark Laffey, Hugh Gusterson and Raymond Duvall (eds.) *Cultures of Insecurity: States, Communities, and the Production of Danger* (Minneapolis, MN: University of Minnesota Press, 1999); with specific reference to the strategic discourse associated with ballistic missile defence see especially Natalie Bormann, *National Missile Defense and the Politics of US Identity* (Manchester: Manchester University Press, 2008), which gives an extended application of this reading.

[6] A good example being Fred C. Ikle's chastening claim that 'our attempts to escape the predicted [nuclear] calamity have helped to bring it about', which stands in contradiction to his own favourable disposition towards missile defence – *Annihilation from Within: the Ultimate Threat to Nations* (New York: Columbia University Press, 2006) p. 57.

defined as a conception of the world that 'is not critical and coherent but disjointed and episodic'. In keeping with the precepts of common sense, we might say that the common sense understandings of technology present in missile defence advocacy stand as the folklore equivalent of the philosophy of technology we find in Habermas, Heidegger or the Frankfurt School: halfway between folklore 'properly speaking' (the quasi-mythological narratives of America's cultural-technological heritage), the rhythms, tropes and language of instrumentalist and substantivist philosophy, yet imitative of them, without ever referring to them directly. This certainly seems to fit the Janus-faced nature of the understandings summarised above and examined in detail previously.

Beyond false consciousness: missile defence in the world upside down

What seems to occur, therefore, in missile defence advocacy is the replication of broader philosophical debate on technology within a particular instantiation of security discourse. Given that this philosophical debate has itself had no clear 'winner', we could perhaps be content to note this as a tension within missile defence advocacy, to register it as an unresolved dualism or dichotomy that may exist at multiple levels of thought and discourse. For if philosophers cannot come to terms on the question of technology, why should we expect political practitioners to resolve it? To do so, however, would be to drop the 'critical' aspect of the discourse analysis undertaken in this analysis, and would neglect the emphasis within Critical Theory on the productive (but not necessarily progressive) role of contradiction both in language and in social reality as discussed in chapter 1. Even as the early Frankfurt School were participants in the philosophical debate on technology, and tended increasingly towards its substantivist pole, they sought at a broader level to point out the productive nature of contradictions: the contradictory *mélange* of capitalism from which class consciousness would seemingly never emerge or National Socialism's convoluted mix of illusory pre-modern ideals with modern industrial techniques. The major revision the Frankfurt School theorists added to Hegelian–Marxism in this regard (and here there is a clear parallel in Gramsci's less pessimistic view) was that there is no guarantee that such contradictions would necessarily produce a new and improved 'synthesis'. Progress, as in Horkheimer's view, is *not* guaranteed by 'History'. What Gramsci's concept of common sense adds to this is an awareness of how the practices of historically acting subjects discursively produce and reproduce such contradictions at an 'everyday' level in a largely unconscious fashion, and how this in turn embeds and legitimates stratified social relations. In this sense the presence of the unconcluded dialectic (*unabgeschlossene Dialektik*) of technology at a phenomenal level in missile defence advocacy is no mere issue of semantics.

But what, exactly, are these contradictory understandings of technology productive of in relation to missile defence advocacy? For some commentators these two understandings of technology are usually viewed in passing (and separately) as forms of false consciousness. Critics such as Walter Uhler and Roger Handberg speak of a 'cult of technology' and 'technological utopianism' that has been absorbed and deployed as part of the ideological worldview of the American right.[7] Likewise, the proliferation discourse that forms a key part of the promotion of contemporary missile defence has been described by others as 'a piece of ideological machinery'. Hugh Gusterson argues that the main purpose of this discourse has been to effect a 'system of nuclear apartheid' where nuclear weapons are presumed to be safe in the hands of Western states, but not in those of the 'Third World'. Thus proliferation discourse 'legitimates the nuclear monopoly of the recognized nuclear powers' by representing non-Western states, leaders and cultures as an inherently immature and unreliable 'Other' when it comes to nuclear weapons technology. Yet, Gusterson argues, there is a blatant double-standard being maintained here: 'critics of US military spending have been told for years that military spending stimulates economic development and produces such beneficial economic spin-offs that it almost pays for itself. If military Keynesianism works for "us", it is hard to see why it should not also work for "them".'[8]

---

[7] Walter C. Uhler, 'Missile Shield or Holy Grail?', *The Nation*, 28 January 2002, www.thenation.com/doc/20020128/uhler [last accessed 20 January 2009]; Roger Handberg, *Ballistic Missile Defense and the Future of American Security: Agendas, Perceptions, Technology and Policy* (Westport, CT: Praeger, 2002).

[8] Hugh Gusterson, 'Nuclear Weapons and the Other in the Western Imagination' in his *People of the Bomb: Portraits of America's Nuclear Complex* (Minneapolis, MN: University of Minnesota Press, 2004) pp. 26, 28.

Doubtless there is some validity to these viewpoints, but we should resist being tempted by such arguments to proceed along the lines of 'ideology critique' in its basic Marxist variant:[9] pointing out the errors and mystifications present in missile defence advocacy, and consequently designating the understandings of technology present within this discourse as the deceptive foils of real motivations of political and techno-strategic elites. This requires a number of prior assumptions: that we know what the 'real' motivations behind the push for missile defence are, and that we can presume proponents of missile defence to be rational and calculating actors who are aware of the instrumental value (in terms of the 'strategic' use of language) of deploying contradictory understandings of technology to achieve their aims. As Raymond Williams argues, however, 'if our social and political and cultural ideas and assumptions and habits were merely the result of specific manipulation, of a kind of overt training which might be simply ended or withdrawn, then ... society would be very much easier to move and change than in practice it ever has been or is'.[10] In this spirit, we bracketed questions of 'why' missile defence is being pursued to instead establish more firmly the discursive resources and techniques deployed by its proponents. Having gone through the process of developing this latter aspect in relation to understandings of technology, we are now in a position to offer a more sophisticated account of how these seemingly contradictory understandings are related to each other by proponents of missile defence, and what the possible effects of this relation are.

The idea that a word or concept such as 'technology' can uphold not only multiple but contradictory understandings of the world therefore needs to be explained further. Here two key ideas of the Russian Formalist theorist of language Mikhail Bakhtin are useful in further illustrating and fleshing out the Gramscian concept of common sense in this regard. The first is Bakhtin's notion of the 'heteroglossia' of words, languages and discourses, introduced and discussed in chapter 1. As we have seen previously, the concept of technology as employed within missile defence advocacy has two

---

[9] Karl Marx and Friedrich Engels, *The German Ideology* (London: Lawrence and Wishart, 1965).

[10] Raymond Williams, *Problems in Materialism and Culture* (London: Verso, 1980) p. 37.

broadly distinguishable senses that further invoke and imply (often opposed) understandings of the role and place of technology in social relations more generally. In his key work *The Dialogic Imagination*, Bakhtin sought to explicate a 'philosophy of discourse' in a 'contradictory and multi-language world'[11] and the ways in which 'at both individual and social levels, productive vitality and creativity derive from a continuous dialogic struggle *within and between discourses*' – what he terms 'heteroglossia'.[12] From this perspective, discourse of technological development, and even the very term technology itself, can possess multiple contending meanings in its usage.

Taking the view that language is heteroglossic also renders any attempt at simple ideology critique more problematic, as a seamless ideological construct is itself an unobtainable goal in this view. Indeed, the (relative) fluidity allowed by heteroglossia even allows for diametric opposition within utterances and discourses. In *The German Ideology*, Marx and Engels use the analogy of a camera obscura to denote the way in which 'in all ideology men and their circumstances appear upside-down'.[13] Such inversion is taken on this view to be characteristic of the (pejorative) conceptualisation of ideology. In Bakhtin, the metaphor of the 'world upside-down' serves a very different function, one that helps illustrate the way in which the tension between instrumental and substantive understandings has a potentially productive, stabilising role within the discursive whole promoting missile defence. Bakhtin's notion of 'carnival' and the 'carnivalesque' is particularly relevant here. This may seem a strange resource to draw upon given that Bakhtin developed these notions in his study of the French medieval humanist François Rabelais and ostensibly they have very little to do with the field of missile defence. There are instructive parallels though. Think firstly of the kind of 'double standards' cited by Gusterson, which can be read as a series of inversions: nuclear weapons are permissible for the West, but not for the 'Third World', 'military Keynesianism' is encouraged for one but not for the other, and so on. Bakhtin argues that in the medieval practice of carnival we find a characteristic logic, 'the

---

[11] Mikhail Bakhtin, *The Dialogic Imagination: Four Essays*, trans. C. Emerson and M. Holquist (ed.) (Austin, TX: University of Texas Press, 1981) p. 275.

[12] Pam Morris (ed.) *The Bakhtin Reader: Selected Writings of Bakhtin, Medvedev and Voloshinov* (London: Edward Arnold, 1994) p. 73, emphasis added.

[13] Marx and Engels, *The German Ideology*, p. 37.

peculiar logic of the "inside out" (*á l'envers*), of the "turnabout", of a
continual shifting from top to bottom, from front to rear, of numerous
parodies and travesties, humiliations, profanations, comic crownings
and uncrownings'.[14] In short, 'carnival celebrated temporary liberation from the prevailing truth and from the established order; it
marked the suspension of all hierarchical rank, privileges, norms,
and prohibitions'.[15] The carnival world was thus populated by fool-
kings, giants, dwarfs, monsters and trained animals (collectively
known as 'the grotesque') and, Bakhtin notes, the historic development of such feast-days was linked to actual moments of social crisis
and revolution.[16]

It could be argued that there is something of the carnivalesque about
the stylistic profile of missile defence advocacy given that the two
understandings of technology employed within it imply two very different worlds, which in turn allows us to view the identity formation
aspect of the discourse associated with missile defence promotion in
even greater depth.[17] One, associated with the instrumental understanding, is populated by heroic individuals – inventors, engineers,
visionary leaders. It prioritises agential capacity, valorises technology
as an instrument of control, and places technologically advanced
states (in this case the USA) at the pinnacle of the world order. Here,
the market is a 'good thing' as it encourages and advances the kind
of entrepreneurial spirit associated with technological invention and
innovation. Reasoning is made by analogy: to actual inventors (such
as the Wright bothers), situations (the defence of Britain during
World War II) and technologies (the Corona satellite, Polaris missile,
the space shuttle).

The other world, derived from the substantivist understanding of
technology, largely inverts these tenets: this world is populated by
individuals only to the extent that they are conduits within broader
networks of technology transfer. The proliferation of nuclear and ballistic technology is portrayed as potentially (literally) inverting the
world order by making the world's most powerful state beholden to
some of the weakest. 'Nuclear blackmail' threatens to elect a pauper
as king – again literally in the case of North Korea – by holding the
USA hostage. Structural uncertainty replaces agential control, and the

---

[14] Morris, *The Bakhtin Reader*, p. 200.   [15] Ibid., p. 199.   [16] Ibid., pp. 197–9.
[17] Cf. Bormann, *National Missile Defense and the Politics of US Identity*.

market is definitely not a good thing in this worldview since it is taken to provide the major source and stimulus of weapons proliferation. Metaphor and prediction (in the form of simulated attacks and imagined scenarios of nuclear devastation) largely replace historical analogy. This is a world, in short, populated by the spectral and monstrous presences of the grotesque. It is a world that emerges at moments of identified crisis, 'revolutionary situations in which common words take on opposite meanings', as one modern interpreter of Bakthin puts it:[18] the launch of *Sputnik*, the 'window of vulnerability', North Korean missile launches and, more recently, nuclear tests.

It could be argued that susbtantivist literature in its most heightened philosophical (Heidegger, Ellul, Adorno and Horkheimer) and literary forms (Shelley, Huxley) extend this carnivalesque trope to an extreme by imagining a dystopian future in which technology uses humanity, not the other way round. This tendency parallels the trend of post-medieval literature, what Bakhtin describes as 'Grotesque Realism', which became fixated solely with terror and fear behind which lies 'a terrible vacuum, a nothingness lurks behind it'.[19] In Bakhtinian terms, this actually truncates the original function of carnival, which was to regenerate and rejuvenate the existing order, to restore things to their natural place. Here it might well be argued that missile defence advocacy is closer in form to the folkloristic origins of carnival, where temporary exposure to that which was feared most (Hell, nightmares, disorder) served ultimately to reinforce the 'rightful' social hierarchies of medieval life. We might note in passing that efforts at a comparable Grotesque Realism – actually portraying the visceral effects of a nuclear attack – generally do not feature within the discourse of missile defence advocacy. Such effects are either 'simulated' in a relatively sanitised fashion, or referred to obliquely, for example by reference to Pearl Harbor and 9/11. Hiroshima, Nagasaki and Chernobyl are all notable by their absence.[20] Framing

---

[18] Pierre Bourdieu, *Language and Symbolic Power*, ed. and introduced by John B. Thompson (Cambridge: Polity Press, 2005) p. 40.

[19] Morris, *The Bakhtin Reader*, p. 195.

[20] Compare the deliberate efforts at restoring the grotesque in Hugh Gusterson, *Nuclear Rites: a Weapons Laboratory at the End of the Cold War* (Berkeley, CA: University of California Press, 1996) and *People of the Bomb*; Lynn Eden, *Whole World on Fire: Organizations, Knowledge and Nuclear Weapons Devastation* (New York: Cornell University Press, 2004).

the grotesque in a manageable way through its managed inclusion in the promotion of missile defence arguably serves to effect the carnivalesque function of regeneration or redemption – in this case the redeeming power of technology. As we have seen, the use of substantivist tropes by missile defence advocates is frequently truncated to allow for the restoration of American security through missile defence. Thus what Bjork terms the 'saving power' of strategic defence or Klein's notion of 'technological salvation' is maintained and rejuvenated; hope for American protection and freedom of action, the assumed rightful order, is symbolically restored.[21]

Technology, common sense and the 'strategic' use of language in missile defence advocacy

As was noted at several points previously, missile defence is a concept which the American scientific community remains highly sceptical of. Strong arguments persist that the physical limitations of such a project cannot be overcome, and the adumbrated and frequently questionable nature of testing and evaluation of the system has exacerbated doubts in this regard. In this context, the symbolic restoration of technology's saving power in missile defence advocacy through the common sense juxtaposition of instrumental and substantive understandings is highly potent: it is, in this sense, an exercise of 'symbolic power'.

Pierre Bourdieu's notion of symbolic power closely parallels the dynamics Gramsci associates with hegemony in so much as it refers to the way in which power is frequently exercised in a symbolic rather than material form. Symbolic power consists in the ability to persuade without, or with minimal, exercise of material force or sanctions. This renders it all the more powerful: the lack of explicit coercive content disguises or obscures the extent to which a form of power is being exercised at all, thus symbolic power is 'a mechanism through which power is exercised and simultaneously disguised'.[22] Here common sense, as a form of shared beliefs, plays a crucial role:

[21] Rebecca S. Bjork, *The Strategic Defense Initiative: Symbolic Containment of the Nuclear Threat* (New York: State University of New York Press, 1992) pp. 82–4; Bradley S. Klein, *Strategic Studies and World Order* (Cambridge: Cambridge University Press, 1994) pp. 109–12.
[22] What Bourdieu terms *meconnaissance* – John B. Thompson, 'Editor's Introduction' to Bourdieu, *Language and Symbolic Power*, p. 23.

the exercise of power through symbolic exchange always rests on a foundation of shared belief. That is, the efficacy of symbolic power presupposes certain forms of cognition or belief, in such a way that even those who benefit least from the exercise of power participate, to some extent, in their own subjection. They recognize or tacitly acknowledge the legitimacy of power in which they are embedded; and hence they fail to see that hierarchy is, after all, an arbitrary social construction which serves the interests of some groups more than others.[23]

What is important to note, though, is that this presupposition of forms of cognition or belief (in this case beliefs regarding technology) simultaneously presumes and portrays these beliefs as common to all: as universal and referring to shared cultural and historical experience even when, as with common sense, this is manifested as the 'diffuse, uncoordinated features of a generic form of thought'.[24]

Even those groups that benefit in an obvious material sense from the use of particular conceptions of technology, therefore, refer to the prior sedimentation(s) of understanding Gramsci associates with common sense. Once again, then, symbolic exchange cannot be dismissed as simply the veiling and advance of interests through an instrumental use of language, even if it sustains a particular historic bloc that benefits the interests of some more than others. Although a stratification of groups may exist in terms of social position, these groups still draw on a common language.[25] The role which instrumental and substantive understandings of technology play in this unconscious pursuit of 'symbolic profit',[26] and its relation to profits in a more prosaic sense, becomes apparent in the context of the scientific-strategic interregnum in which missile defence exists: that is, a condition in which the capabilities claimed for missile defence and the ontological status of the threat it is claimed to be addressing are both hotly contested. The invocation of America's technological heritage in response to doubts over the technical prospects of missile defence, for example, discursively

[23] Ibid.
[24] Antonio Gramsci, *Selections from the Prison Notebooks*, ed. and trans. by Quintin Hoare and Geoffrey Nowell Smith (London: Lawrence and Wishart, 1973) p. 330.
[25] Of course we should note that for Bourdieu discourse and common sense sayings are just one dimension of symbolic power; other factors include the bodily 'hexis', as well as institutions and the (cultural and symbolic) capital they possess.
[26] Bourdieu, 'Price Formation and the Anticipation of Profits' in his *Language and Symbolic Power*, p. 67.

fills the gap created by the failure of missile defence testing to date to
validate definitively the system's feasibility. If we 'buy into' the examples cited by Rumsfeld and Wolfowitz – analogies with the development
of airpower, missile and space technology – then concerns about the
current status of missile defence may well be viewed as teething problems rather than fatal flaws. The use of such examples by proponents
of missile defence presumes a number of further conditions, outlined
in chapter 2, that range from the broad assumption that everyone
agrees on technology as an instrument of progress worth pursuing, to
specific cultural referent points such as the first flight of the Wright
brothers and man landing on the moon. As we saw previously, such
referent points form a key part of the effort to discredit critics of
missile defence as misguided naysayers. There is a move here on the
part of missile defence advocates to delineate who can legitimately
speak on the prospects of the programme, a tendency that was particularly prevalent in the promotion of SDI and continues with the current
programme in relation to the sceptical attitudes of the American scientific community.

Likewise, the substantivist understanding rhetorically fixes the nature of the international security environment that missile defence is
supposed to be facing. By drawing on this understanding, proponents
of missile defence populate this uncertain environment with familiar
features such as rapid technological development, the global spread
of technology and everyday instruments of daily life, and hence
attempt to associate broadly familiar attributes of modern technology
that we would all supposedly recognise from common experience.
Through the nominalisation of technology, also discussed in chapter 2,
this occurs in a manner that designates these developments as
the very source of this uncertainty, as is increasingly a feature of
contemporary missile defence advocacy with the removal of the
Soviet Union as a readily identifiable source of technological threat
to the USA. The discursive construction of the threat in these
terms is tremendously powerful. Rebecca Bjork has identified the
fact that since nuclear war never actually occurred during the Cold
War, the rhetorical construction of the threat addressed by SDI
came to be of prime importance.[27] In regard to contemporary missile
defence, this process is now supplemented by the use of pictorial

---

[27] Bjork, *The Strategic Defense Initiative*.

and computer-generated representations of the impact of a nuclear attack on the USA, all of which help to provide, in Krause and Latham's term, a 'grid of intelligibility' for the post-Cold War world.[28]

The extent to which the calamities predicted by missile defence advocates are happening or will happen is, therefore, in some ways secondary to the extent to which consensus exists as to the validity of such predictions. The interpretation of social reality and the embellishment of that reality in discourse thus become crucial, even if it cannot guarantee consensus or assure fixity of meaning. A case in point is recent testing of the North Korean *Taepodong II* missile. The test – timed to coincide with the 4 July 2006 celebrations and America's own display of prowess in rocketry with the launch of the space shuttle *Discovery* on the same day – fell short (literally) of expectations (the *Taepodong II* 'fell apart about 40 seconds into its flight'), giving rise to radically differing interpretations of its implications for current missile defence.[29] Proponents of missile defence have taken this development as an indicator of the emerging threat, but critics declared that the woeful nature of Kim Jong Il's efforts evidenced the 'hype' surrounding the missile threat and the response to it.[30] In the run-up to the North Korean test, reports claimed that the US missile defence system had been 'activated' (rather confusingly given its 'operational' status since 2005) and speaking at Chicago's Museum of Science and Industry in the wake of its failure, President Bush claimed that the USA possessed a 'reasonable chance' of shooting down the missile had it not disintegrated in flight.[31]

---

[28] Keith Krause and Andrew Latham, 'Constructing Non-Proliferation and Arms Control: the Norms of Western Practice' in Keith Krause (ed.) *Culture and Security: Multilateralism, Arms Control and Security Building* (London: Frank Cass, 1999) p. 39.

[29] Center for Defense Information, 'Press Release: North Korea's Launch of Several Missiles Prompts Concern, Confusion', 5 July 2006, www.cdi.org/program/ document.cfm?DocumentID=3577&from_page=../index.cfm [last accessed 20 January 2009]; 'Defiant North Korea Vows to Test more Missiles', *Guardian*, 7 July 2006.

[30] Joseph Cirincione, quoted in 'North Korean "Fireworks Display" Irritates US but Falls Short of Target', *Guardian*, 5 July 2006; Victoria Samson quoted in 'North Korea's Launch of Several Missiles Prompts Concern, Confusion'.

[31] 'US Claims it is "Ready" for Korean Missile Test', *Guardian*, 20 June 2006; President Bush quoted in 'Bush Wants Clear Lines Set for N. Korea', *Associated Press*, 7 July 2006.

The extent to which arguments of the latter kind are convincing is likely to be crucial to the future political and financial prospects of missile defence. Focus on the construction of narratives around these two understandings of technology, then, needs to be related to the broader context in which these understandings are deployed. The relative strength allowed by the broadly Marxian approach to language and discourse invoked here is that it allows us to tie this generation of 'linguistic exchange' not just to events but to broader social structures and the material distribution of power and resources. Although they approach this issue in subtly different ways and with different emphases, critical theorists of discourse such as Gramsci, Bourdieu and Bakhtin all share a sense in which critical analysis of discourse must be related to aspects of social reality that are not reducible solely to discourse and exist at different levels. In terms of missile defence part of this reality, the part frequently prioritised by critics, is indeed the way that the American defence-industrial base (specifically large corporations such as Boeing, Lockheed and Raytheon) benefit financially from the funding of missile defence. US defence firms, like the US state itself, have adapted to the Cold War and post-Cold War political conditions as well as economic shifts,[32] and Gusterson's invocation of a US model of 'military-Keynesianism' is not so far off the mark in this regard. The pursuit of a national-level missile defence for the USA in its variety of guises has undoubtedly been marked by a particularly close overlap between government and industry, but the aim of the approach taken here was to highlight the manner in which understandings of technology legitimate this relationship in different ways. A prominent example is the way in which both instrumental and substantivist understandings in recent missile defence advocacy intersect with the promotion of a neo-liberal model of defence provision that exists at a broader level in the policies of the Bush administration, which emphasises investment in high-tech weapons programmes, stimulation and protection of private sector industries in order to achieve this, and the maintenance of a flexible partnership with the defence industry in order to meet 'evolving threats'.[33]

---

[32] Bob Jessop, *The Future of the Capitalist State* (Cambridge: Polity Press, 2002) p. 183.

[33] Reiterated in the 2006 Quadrennial Defense Review – www.comw.org/qdr/qdr2006.pdf [last accessed 20 January 2009].

This intersection, though, has been largely ignored up to now, and the role symbolic power has played in achieving post-Cold War defence transformation has been largely under-theorised until very recently. The 'cultural turn' in security studies promises some further development of this aspect by refusing to view the strategic use of language as simply a question of utilitarian strategic choice.[34] Gramsci's concept of 'historic bloc' was introduced as a means of taking a more holistic view of an *ensemble* of social relations, one in which the production and reproduction of common sense understandings of technology play an important role, as illustrated above. Otherwise, we risk missing important dimensions of the interrelation between strategic thinking and defence production. At a general level, as argued by Bradley Klein, intellectual practitioners of strategy, for example, play an important contributing role in defining military technology as 'an exogenous variable which affects strategic thinking' and thus 'The political economy of the armaments industry thereby becomes construed as a realm of private activity which neutrally provides technology for either civil or military purposes.'[35] As was shown previously, intellectual proponents of missile defence tacitly and often explicitly endorse an increased role for corporations and industry in the project. In the reverse direction, those seeking to market missile defence make much of the spin-offs investment in the programme can have. Gramsci argues that 'though hegemony is ethical-political, it must also be economic';[36] but the inverse is also true, or rather the economic and 'ethical-political' should be thought of as two interrelated aspects, as Gramsci's concept of historic bloc suggests.[37]

Revisiting the question of technology

The multiple interests that make up missile defence advocacy, it has been argued, draw upon shared linguistic and cultural resources,

---

[34] Jutta Weldes *et al.*, *Culture of Insecurity*; Krause, *Culture and Security*; Michael C. Williams, *Culture and Security: the Reconstruction of Security in the Post-Cold War Era* (London: Routledge, 2007); Stuart Croft, *Culture, Crisis and America's War on Terror* (Cambridge: Cambridge University Press, 2006).

[35] Klein, *Strategic Studies and World Order*, p. 21.

[36] Gramsci, *Prison Notebooks*, p. 3.

[37] Although beyond the scope of this project, there might well be a case for a fuller Bourdieuian 'field analysis' along similar lines – see Williams, *Culture and Security*.

aspiring to symbolic power by invoking the same common sense understandings of technology. They each therefore contribute to what
Ernesto Laclau and Chantal Mouffe term a 'hegemonic formation', as
was illustrated in the empirical analysis of the ways in which these
understandings are constantly and consistently reiterated in the history
of missile defence advocacy over time and across different fields. In
such formations, Laclau and Mouffe argue, distinct 'moments' can
persist – in this case instrumental and substantive understandings of
technology – but are reduced to the 'interiority of a closed paradigm'.
In other words, these 'moments' act as the given horizon of alternatives
and constitute a form of intellectual closure. This allows not only for
the possibility that contradictory moments do not cancel each other
out, but for the fact that it may be the very lack of cancellation that
gives a discourse its cohesion: 'the diverse surfaces of emergence of
the hegemonic relation do not harmoniously come together to form a
theoretical void that a new concept is required to fill'. Instead, hegemony can be constituted by 'a more complex strategic movement requir-
ing negotiation among mutually contradictory discursive surfaces'.[38]

This has powerful implications for our reading of understandings of
technology in the promotion of missile defence. The antagonisms and
contradictions between the two understandings of technology examined here should, superficially viewed, lead to the dissolution of the
discourse and encourage us to develop a new more holistic understanding of technology and security. Instead, the uneven nature of the two
contradictory discursive surfaces is maintained, allowing for strategic
movement between them. This capacity for strategic movement
between the two understandings is a potentially immense source of
symbolic power for those arguing the case for missile defence; for, as
in the Bakhtinian notion of the world upside-down, missile defence
advocacy already seems to contain, *within* itself, alternate visions of
technology. The strength of the understanding(s) of technology
employed by the discourse of missile defence advocacy is that it captures
at the level of political discourse an antagonism that exists in philosophical debate over the questions of technology, but with a level of
interpretive flexibility that is precluded at the philosophical level –
witness their correlation with utopian and dystopian readings of

---

[38] Ernesto Laclau and Chantal Mouffe, *Hegemony and Socialist Strategy*, 2nd
edition (London: Verso, 2001) p. 93.

technological development. This flexibility, moreover, is politically beneficial in the case of missile defence in that it casts security in technologically determined terms: the view of technology as both an instrument of protection and a constraining factor naturalises the assumption that security and technology are inseparable in this instance. Much of the momentum behind the case for missile defence comes from this sense in which security is predetermined by the assumed existence of technological imperatives – whether in the field of defensive innovations or the spread of offensive technology – that exist seemingly independent of human control. Even though instrumentalist and substantivist arguments for missile defence imply very different visions of technology, the net effect of their pervasive presence is to convey a sense that, in Feenberg's words, 'technology is destiny',[39] that social organization (including security relations) must constantly adapt to technological development.[40]

We can, though, acknowledge that the 'question of technology' needs to be addressed in contemporary security debates as much if not more so than ever without succumbing to such technological determinism. There are two steps that can be made in this regard. The first is to recognise the fact that, following Gramsci, even 'common sense', in spite of its contradictory and fragmentary nature, contains a kernel of 'good sense'. In other words, even the partial and truncated nature of the question of technology in missile defence advocacy does point to a question that modern society is still coming to terms with. Indeed, the fundamental questions if and how the relationship between society and technology can be reconfigured in a more emancipatory vein have been on the table at least since Marx posed the issue in terms of how humans, at the level of 'species being', might gain control of that which they produce. In the *Economic and Political Manuscripts of 1844*, for example, Marx dealt with the tension between the fact that 'humanity's life activity' depended on products from nature – and hence advancements in the technological capacity to produce – and that this same necessity had the unfortunate tendency of encouraging '*loss of the object and bondage to it*; appropriation as *estrangement*,

---

[39] Andrew Feenberg, *Critical Theory of Technology* (Oxford: Oxford University Press, 1991) p. 8.
[40] Ibid., pp. 122–3.

as alienation.[41] Francis Wheen notes that Marx believed the railways would lead to economic and hence ultimately technological revolution. Yet Shelley's *Frankenstein* would remain a favourite inspiration for *Das Kapital*, where capitalism would degrade the worker 'to the level of a machine' and 'drag his wife and child beneath the juggernaut of capital'.[42] Here we have an early encapsulation of the tension between the ability to control our environment through technology on one hand and on the other a seeming loss of control by developing a range of techniques in which human beings seem to play only a minimal part.

Though this framing has a well-established historical-philosophical lineage, this does not mean that it is the only way of understanding technology. Much contemporary ecological thinking suggests that we stop thinking of human beings and our environment as separate entities;[43] similarly, recent approaches to understanding technology in the field of cultural studies have sought to de-emphasise the extent to which humans and technology can be thought of independent of one another and, by consequence, the extent to which we can speak of humans as controlling or being controlled by technology.[44] Constructivist theories of technology emphasise design choices and the social context in which they are embedded, speaking of socio-technical systems rather than society and technology independent of one another,[45] and philosophers such as Bruno Latour argue that such divisions 'render invisible' the political processes by which particular technologies are produced.[46]

---

[41] Karl Marx, *The Economic and Philosophic Manuscripts of 1844* (London: Lawrence and Wishart, 1977) p. 63, emphasis in original.

[42] Francis Wheen, *Marx's Das Kapital: a Biography* (London: Atlantic Books) p. 15; Marx quoted in ibid., p. 23.

[43] William Leiss, *The Domination of Nature* (Montreal: McGill-Queen's University Press, 1994).

[44] See, for example, Donna Haraway, *Simians, Cyborgs and Women: the Reinvention of Nature* (London: Free Association, 1991).

[45] Wiebe E. Bijker, Thomas P. Hughes and Trevor J. Pinch (eds.) *The Social Construction of Technological Systems: New Directions in the Sociology and History of Technology* (Cambridge, MA: MIT University Press, 1989); in the realm of military technology see Donald A. MacKenzie, *Inventing Accuracy: a Historical Sociology of Nuclear Missile Guidance* (Cambridge, MA: MIT Press, 1990).

[46] Bruno Latour, *Pandora's Hope: Essays on the Reality of Science Studies* (Cambridge, MA: Harvard University Press, 1999) p. 304.

However, as William Leiss notes, there has to date been a broad inconsistency between empirical work on technological development and evaluations of its social impact:

On the one, historical side we have abundant empirical knowledge about the history of technical innovations, including the conditions of their development and their diffusion within and among different nations. On the other, speculative side, evaluations of the social consequences of technological change remain trapped in the seemingly arbitrary polarization between subjective feelings of pessimism or optimism, and between warnings of doom and complacent advocacy of a 'technological fix'.[47]

Seeking to regenerate Marxian philosophy in its approach to technology in this light, Andrew Feenberg argues that a renewed 'Critical Theory' of technology must chart 'a difficult course between resignation and utopia' – that is, between the views that we cannot escape the negative impacts of technological development and that we must look to it as a saving power.[48] Drawing on constructivist and historical sociological investigations into the design and production of technology, Feenberg argues that the two elements which are separated out in instrumental and substantive understandings of technology need to be unified into an awareness that 'In choosing our technology we become what we are, which in turn shapes our future choices' and that this act of choice 'is technologically embedded and cannot be understood as a free "use" in the sense intended by instrumental theory'. Yet, the act of choosing itself presupposes an element of agency generally precluded by substantivist theory. This is what Feenberg defines as the 'ambivalence' of technology: 'technology is not a thing in the ordinary sense of the term, but an "ambivalent" process of development suspended between different possibilities'. On this view, 'technology is not a destiny but a scene of struggle. It is a social battlefield, or perhaps a better metaphor would be a *parliament of things* on which civilizational alternatives are debated and decided.'[49]

Thus, Feenberg sees struggle, antagonism and contradiction between the two traditional ways of thinking of technology as an inherent but positive space from which to rethink the potentialities

---

[47] William Leiss, *Under Technology's Thumb* (Montreal: McGill-Queen's University Press, 1990) p. 28.
[48] Feenberg, *Critical Theory of Technology*, p. 13.   [49] Ibid., p. 14.

substantivist orientations of critics of the nuclear arms race and contemporary weapons proliferation leave themselves open to co-optation for those arguing for new developments in defensive technology.

Nor can we resort to the simplistic defence of technology as an instrument of progress for, as we have also seen in relation to missile defence advocacy, this assumption can be taken in several different directions that are not necessarily 'progressive' from a standpoint concerned with human emancipation. Proponents of missile defence might well argue that this initiative is inherently directed at the protection of others in times of terror, including those who will prospectively fall under the jurisdiction of the future extension of missile defence systems within and, prospectively beyond, the USA. This, however, is an arch-example of a problem-solving approach to the critical and fundamental issue of the role of nuclear weapons and humanity's relationship to them. Since the creation of these weapons we've been struggling to come to terms with what they mean, how to deal with them and the dangers they pose to modern life. Current missile defence will not ameliorate this danger, and even if a fully functioning missile defence could be achieved, it would only postpone these questions.

More problematic still is the fact that American post-Cold War 'nuclearism' in terms of offensive weaponry is itself seemingly fuelled by 'technological idealism'.[54] Lieber and Press are not alone in their assertion that in the post-Cold War era 'Washington's continued refusal to eschew a first strike [nuclear capability] and the country's development of a limited missile-defence take on a new, and possibly more menacing, look.' They argue that, worryingly, 'The most logical conclusions to make are that a nuclear-war-fighting capability remains a key component of the United States' military doctrine and that nuclear primacy remains a goal of the United States.'[55] The struggle to come to terms with the full implications of the nuclear revolution thus remains on the security agenda even as the threat of nuclear attack is assumed to have receded in the popular mindset in the post-Cold War era – the phenomenon described by some as 'nuclear

---

[54] Ken Booth, 'Nuclearism, Human Rights and Constructions of Security, (Part 2)', *The International Journal of Human Rights*, 3:3 (1999) pp. 44–61.

[55] Kier A. Lieber and Daryl G. Press, 'The Rise of US Nuclear Primacy', *Foreign Affairs*, March/April (2006) pp. 42–54, p. 54. See also Keir A. Lieber and Daryl G. Press, 'The End of MAD? The Nuclear Dimension of US Primacy', *International Security*, 30:4 (2006) pp. 7–44.

amnesia'.[56] Now more than ever we need to be mindful of the ways security policy embeds and legitimates the role of nuclear weapons technology, and the role conventional understandings of technology play in this.

The virtue of Critical Theory – and here the allegorical value of the Frankfurters' oscillation between positive and negative conceptions of technology is as important as the concepts they provide – is in illustrating ways in which the question of (nuclear) technology continues to be framed. Thus far the emphasis within CSS has been on anchoring the theory and practice of security in a broader concern with human emancipation: 'the freeing of people (as individuals and groups) from those physical and human constraints which stop them carrying out what they would freely choose to do'.[57] The threat of nuclear war is, no doubt, one of those constraints we all wish to be free from. However, emancipation from extant constraints can surely only come through an awareness of prevailing forms of common sense and the conditions they help to perpetuate. This is particularly true of those interpretations of present conditions that would – as is the case with missile defence advocacy – promise a utopian endpoint should we support certain courses of action or, conversely, a dystopian future should we fail to accept a prescribed response. If we are truly to come to terms with the existence of nuclear weapons, we must account for the persistence of such antinomies within strategic debates and take account of the ways in which these set the discursive horizon and delimit the options open to us.

With such concerns in mind this analysis has shown that Critical Theory can offer a valuable base from which to approach debates on issues of 'hard' or traditional security by identifying the grounds upon which such debates take place and the common sense assumptions which they are predicated upon. CSS has, it might be said,

[56] Ken Booth, 'Nuclearism, Human Rights and Constructions of Security (Part 1)', *The International Journal of Human Rights* 3:2 (1999) pp. 1–24, 9–17. See also Jack Mendelsohn, 'Delegitimizing Nuclear Weapons', *Issues in Science and Technology*, Spring (2006), www.issues.org/22.3/mendelsohn.html [last accessed 20 January 2009].

[57] Ken Booth, 'Security and Emancipation', *Review of International Studies*, 17:4 (1991) pp. 313–26, p. 319.

come to be *over*-identified with the contested concept of emancipation.[58] As has been illustrated here, the Frankfurt School and the
Gramscian heritage that CSS draws upon both provide rich seams
of intellectual resource that have much, much more to contribute to
the study of contemporary security, and the preceding analysis has
broken new ground within CSS by showing how these traditions
can provide the frameworks and vocabulary with which to address
actual policy debates. Hence to achieve emancipation, in the realm
of nuclear security as in many others, we may first need to forget it.
The continuing relevance of CSS and its critical heritage will also
lie, most immediately, in its potential to illuminate the constraints
that persist within contemporary strategic discourse. In this sense the
engagement between Critical Theory and Security Studies remains,
happily, an unconcluded dialectic.

[58] Cf. Richard Wyn Jones, 'On Emancipation: Necessity, Capacity, and Concrete
     Utopias' in Ken Booth (ed.) *Critical Security Studies and World Politics* (Boulder,
     CO: Lynne Rienner, 2005) pp. 215–35.

Bibliography

Adams, Gordon, *The Politics of Defense Contracting: the Iron Triangle* (New Brunswick, NJ: Transaction Books, 1982).

Adorno, Theodor, *Negative Dialectics* (London: Routledge and Kegan Paul, 1973).

Adorno, Theodor and Max Horkheimer, *Dialectic of Enlightenment*, trans. J. Cumming (London: Allen Lane, 1973).

Allison, Graham, *Nuclear Terrorism: the Ultimate Preventable Catastrophe* (New York: Times Books, 2004).

Anderson, Martin, *An Insurance Missile Defense* (Stanford, CA: The Hoover Institution, 1986).

Revolution: the Reagan Legacy (New York: Harcourt Brace Jovanovich, 1988).

Anderson, Perry, 'The Antinomies of Antonio Gramsci', *New Left Review*, **100** (November 1976–January 1977) pp. 5–78.

Arato, Andrew and Eike Gebhardt (eds.) *The Essential Frankfurt School Reader* (Oxford: Blackwell, 1978).

Armacost, Michael H., *The Politics of Weapons Innovation: the Thor–Jupiter Controversy* (New York: Columbia University Press, 1969).

Augelli, Enrico and Craig Murphy, *America's Quest for Supremacy and the Third World* (London: Pinter, 1988).

Bacevich, Andrew J., *The New American Militarism: How Americans are Seduced by War* (New York: Oxford University Press, 2005).

Bakhtin, Mikhail, *The Dialogic Imagination: Four Essays*, trans. C. Emerson, and M. Holquist (ed.) (Austin, TX: University of Texas Press, 1981).

Barnaby, Frank, *How Nuclear Weapons Spread: Nuclear Weapon Proliferation in the 1990s* (London: Routledge, 1993).

Baucom, Donald R., *The Origins of SDI, 1944–1983* (Lawrence, KS: University Press of Kansas, 1992).

Baylis, John and John Garnett (eds.) *Makers of Nuclear Strategy* (London: Pinter, 1991).

Benjamin, Walter, *Illuminations* (New York: Shocken Books, 1969).

Bjiker, Wiebe E., Thomas P. Hughes and Trevor J. Pinch, *The Social Construction of Technological Systems: New Directions in the*

Sociology and History of Technology (Cambridge, MA: MIT Press, 1989).

Bjork, Rebecca S., *The Strategic Defense Initiative: Symbolic Containment of the Nuclear Threat* (Albany, NY: State University of New York Press, 1992).

Boese, Wade, 'Missile Defense Aims to Hit Target in '06', *Arms Control Today*, September (2004), www.armscontrol.org/act/2005_09/Missile DefenseAims.asp?print [last accessed 20 January 2009].

Booth, Ken, 'Nuclearism, Human Rights and Constructions of Security (Part 1)', *The International Journal of Human Rights*, 3:2 (1999) pp. 1–24.

'Nuclearism, Human Rights and Constructions of Security (Part 2)', *The International Journal of Human Rights*, 3:3 (1999) pp. 44–61.

'Security and Emancipation', *Review of International Studies*, 17:4 (1991) pp. 313–26.

Strategy and Ethnocentrism (New York: Homes and Meier, 1979).

(ed.) *Critical Security Studies and World Politics* (Boulder, CO: Lynne Rienner, 2005).

Booth, Ken and Moorhead Wright (eds.) *American Thinking about Peace and War* (Sussex: Harvester Press, 1978).

Bormann, Natalie, *National Missile Defense and the Politics of US Identity* (Manchester: Manchester University Press, 2008).

Bottomore, Tom, *The Frankfurt School* (London: Tavistock, 1984).

Bourdieu, Pierre, *Language and Symbolic Power*, ed. and introduced by John B. Thompson (Cambridge: Polity Press, 2005).

Boyer, Paul S., *By the Bomb's Early Light: American Thought and Culture at the Dawn of the Atomic Age* (New York: Pantheon, 1986).

Brandist, Craig, 'Gramsci, Bakhtin and the Semiotics of Hegemony', *New Left Review*, **216** (March–April 1996) pp. 94–109.

'The Official and the Popular in Gramsci and Bakhtin', *Theory, Culture and Society*, 13:2 (1996) pp. 59–74.

Braudel, Fernand, *On History*, trans. Sarah Matthews (London: Weidenfeld and Nicolson, 1980).

Broad, William J., '"Star Wars" Traced to Eisenhower Era', *New York Times*, 28 October 1986, pp. C1, C3.

Teller's War: the Top-Secret Story Behind the Star Wars Deception (New York: Simon and Schuster, 1992).

Brodie, Bernard, *Strategy in the Missile Age* (Princeton, NJ: Princeton University Press, 1965).

Bronner, Stephen Eri and Douglas MacKay Kellner (eds.) *Critical Theory and Society: a Reader* (New York: Routledge, 1989).

Brosnan, Mark, *Technophobia: the Psychological Impact of Information Technology* (London: Routledge, 1998).

Brown, Michael E. (ed.) *Grave New World: Security Challenges in the 21st Century* (Washington, DC: Georgetown University Press, 2003).

Brzezinski, Zbigniew (ed.) *Promise or Peril: the Strategic Defense Initiative* (Washington, DC: Ethics and Public Policy Centre, 1986).

Bulkeley, Rip and Graham Spinardi, *Space Weapons: Deterrence or Delusion?* (Oxford: Polity Press, 1986).

Buzan, Barry, *An Introduction to Strategic Studies: Military Technology and International Relations* (Basingstoke: Macmillan, 1987).

Buzan, Barry and Eric Herring, *The Arms Dynamic in World Politics* (London: Lynne Rienner, 1998).

Cahn, Anne Hessing, 'Team B: the Trillion Dollar Experiment (Part I)', *The Bulletin of the Atomic Scientists*, April (1993) pp. 22–7.

Caldicott, Helen, *The New Nuclear Danger: George W. Bush's Military-Industrial Complex* (New York: The New Press, 2004).

Campbell, David, *Writing Security: United States Foreign Policy and the Politics of Identity* (Manchester: Manchester University Press, 1992).

Cannon, Lou, *President Reagan: the Role of a Lifetime* (New York: Simon and Schuster, 1991).

Causewell, Erin V. (ed.) *National Missile Defense: Issues and Developments* (New York: Novinka Books, 2002).

Cerf, Christopher and Victor Navasky, *The Experts Speak* (New York: Pantheon Books, 1984).

Chant, Colin (ed.) *Science, Technology and Everyday Life 1870–1950* (London: The Open University, 1990).

Chayes, Abram and Jerome B. Wiesner (eds.) *ABM: an Evaluation of the Decision to Deploy an Anti-Ballistic Missile System* (London: MacDonald, 1970).

Cirincione, Joseph, 'Why the Right Lost the Missile Defense Debate', *Foreign Policy*, 106, Spring (1997) pp. 39–55.

Cirincione, Joseph, Jon B. Wolfstahl and Miriam Rajkumar, *Deadly Arsenals: Nuclear, Biological, and Chemical Threats* (Washington, DC: Carnegie Endowment for International Peace, 2005).

Codevilla, Angelo, *While Others Build: the Commonsense Approach to the Strategic Defense Initiative* (New York: Macmillan, 1988).

Coker, Christopher, *Waging War without Warriors? The Changing Culture of Military Conflict* (London: Lynne Rienner, 2002).

Cox, Robert W., 'Social Forces, States and World Orders: Beyond International Relations Theory', *Millennium: Journal of International Studies*, **10**:2 (1982) pp. 126–55.

Crockatt, Richard and Steve Smith (eds.) *The Cold War Past and Present* (London: Allen and Unwin, 1987).

Croft, Stuart, *Culture, Crisis and America's War on Terror* (Cambridge: Cambridge University Press, 2006).

Daalder, Ivo H. and James M. Lindsay, *America Unbound: the Bush Revolution in Foreign Policy* (Washington, DC: Brookings Institution Press, 2003).

Dalby, Simon, *Creating the Second Cold War: the Discourse of Politics* (London: Pinter, 1990).

Danchev, Alex (ed.) *Fin de Siècle: the Meaning of the Twentieth Century* (London: I. B. Tauris, 1995).

Der Derian, James, *Virtuous War: Mapping the Military-Industrial-Media-Entertainment Network* (Boulder, CO: Westview Press, 2001).

Dickson, David, *Alternative Technology and the Politics of Technical Change* (Glasgow: Fontana, 1974).

Disch, Thomas M., *The New Improved Sun: an Anthology of Utopian Science Fiction* (New York: Harper, 1976).

Divine, Robert A., *The Sputnik Challenge* (Oxford: Oxford University Press, 1993).

Dockrill, Saki, *Eisenhower's New-Look National Security Policy, 1953–61* (Basingstoke: Macmillan, 1996).

Dolman, Everett C., *Astropolitik: Classical Geopolitics in the Space Age* (London: Frank Cass, 2002).

'US Military Transformation and Weapons in Space' (2005), www.e-parl.net/pages/space_hearing.htm [last accessed 20 January 2009].

Dyson, Freeman, *Weapons and Hope* (London: Harper and Row, 1984).

Eberhart, Sylvia, 'How American People Feel about the Atomic Bomb', *Bulletin of the Atomic Scientists*, 3: 4–5 (April–May 1947) pp. 146–9, 168.

Eden, Lynn, *Whole World on Fire: Organizations, Knowledge and Nuclear Weapons Devastation* (New York: Cornell University Press, 2004).

Edwards, Paul N., *The Closed World: Computers and the Politics of Discourse in Cold War America* (Cambridge, MA: MIT Press, 1996).

Eisendrath, Craig, Melvin A. Goodman and Gerald E. Marsh, *The Phantom Defense: America's Pursuit of the Star Wars Illusion* (Westport, CT: Praeger, 2001).

Ellul, Jacques, *The Technological Society*, trans. J. Wilkinson (New York: Vintage, 1964).

Erickson, John, *The Military Technical Revolution: Its Impact on Strategy and Foreign Policy* (New York: F. A. Praeger, 1966).

Evangelista, Matthew, *Innovation and the Arms Race: How the United States and the Soviet Union Develop New Military Technologies* (Ithaca: Cornell University Press, 1988).

Fairclough, Norman, *Analyzing Discourse: Textual Analysis for Social Research* (London: Routledge, 2003).

Critical Discourse Analysis: the Critical Study of Language (London: Longman, 1995).

Discourse and Social Change (Cambridge: Polity Press, 1992).

Feenberg, Andrew, *Critical Theory of Technology* (Oxford: Oxford University Press, 1991).

'From Essentialism to Constructivism: Philosophy of Technology at the Crossroads', undated paper available from www-rohan.sdsu.edu/faculty/feenberg/talk4.html [last accessed 20 January 2009].

Questioning Technology (London: Routledge, 2001).

Transforming Technology: a Critical Theory Revisited (New York: Oxford University Press, 2002).

Feld, B. T., G. W. Greenwood, G. W. Rathjens and S. Weinberg (eds.) *The Impact of New Technologies on the Arms Race* (Cambridge, MA: MIT Press, 1971).

Fitzgerald, Frances, *Way Out There in the Blue: Reagan, Star Wars and the End of the Cold War* (New York: Simon and Schuster, 2000).

Forgacs, David (ed.) *The Antonio Gramsci Reader: Selected Writings 1916–1935* (New York: New York University Press, 2000).

Franklin, H. Bruce, *War Stars: the Superweapon and the American Imagination* (New York: Oxford University Press, 1988).

Freedman, Lawrence, *The Evolution of Nuclear Strategy*, 3rd edition (Basingstoke: Palgrave, 2003).

The Revolution in Strategic Affairs, Adelphi Paper 318 (London: International Institute of Strategic Studies, 1998).

Fuller, J. F. C, *Armament and History: a Study of the Influence of Armament on History from the Dawn of Classical Warfare to the Second World War* (London: Eyre and Spottiswoode, 1946).

Galbraith, J. K., *The New Industrial State* (Harmondsworth: Penguin, 1974).

Garfinkle, Adam M., *The Politics of the Nuclear Freeze* (Philadelphia: Foreign Policy Research Institute, 1984).

Gill, Stephen (ed.) *Gramsci, Historical Materialism and International Relations* (Cambridge: Cambridge University Press, 1993).

Gilpin, Robert, *American Scientists and Nuclear Weapons Policy* (Princeton, NJ: Princeton University Press).

Gilpin, Robert and Christopher Wright (eds.) *Scientists and National Policy-Making* (New York: Columbia University Press, 1964).

Goldfischer, David, *The Best Defense: Policy Alternatives for US Nuclear Security from the 1950s to the 1990s* (Ithaca: Cornell University Press, 1993).

Graham, Bradley, *Hit To Kill: the New Battle over Shielding America from Missile Attack* (New York: Public Affairs, 2003).

Graham, Daniel O., *The Non-Nuclear Defense of Cities: the High Frontier Space-Based Defense against ICBM Attack* (Cambridge, MA: Abt Books, 1983).

Graham, Daniel O. and Gregory A. Fossedal, *A Defense that Defends: Blocking Nuclear Attack* (Old Greenwich, CT: Devin-Adair, 1983).

Gramsci, Antonio, *Selections from the Prison Notebooks*, ed. and trans. by Quintin Hoare and Geoffrey Nowell Smith (London: Lawrence and Wishart, 1973).

Gray, Colin S., *Another Bloody Century: Future Warfare* (London: Weidenfield Military, 2005).

'Dangerous to Your Health: the Debate over Nuclear Strategy and War', *Orbis*, 26 (1982) pp. 327–49.

'European Perspectives on US Ballistic Missile Defense', *Comparative Strategy*, 21 (2002) pp. 279–310.

The Geopolitics of the Nuclear Era: Heartland, Rimlands and the Technological Revolution (New York: Crane, Russak 1977).

House of Cards: Why Arms Control Must Fail (Ithaca: Cornell University Press, 1992).

'Nuclear Strategy: the Case for a Theory of Victory', *International Security*, 4:1 (1979), pp. 54–87.

Nuclear Strategy and National Style (London: Hamilton Press, 1986).

The Second Nuclear Age (Boulder, CO: Lynne Rienner, 1999).

Weapons Don't Make War: Policy, Strategy and Military Technology (Lawrence, KS: University Press of Kansas, 1993).

Gray, Colin and Keith Payne, 'Victory is Possible', *Foreign Policy*, 39 (1980) pp. 14–27.

Greenwood, Ted, 'Why Military Technology is Difficult to Restrain', *Science, Technology and Human Values*, 15:4 (1990) pp. 412–29.

Gronlund, Lisbeth, David Wright and Stephen Young, 'An Assessment of the Intercept Test Program of the Ground-based Midcourse National Missile Defense System', *Defense and Security Analysis*, 18:3 (2002) pp. 239–60.

Guerrier, Steven W. and Wayne C. Thompson (eds.) *Perspectives on Strategic Defense* (Boulder, CO: Westview Press, 1987).

Gusterson, Hugh, *Nuclear Rites: a Weapons Laboratory at the End of the Cold War* (Berkeley, CA: University of California Press, 1996).

People of the Bomb: Portraits of America's Nuclear Complex (Minneapolis, MN: University of Minnesota Press, 2004).

Habermas, Jürgen, *The Future of Human Nature* (Cambridge: Polity Press, 2003).

Toward a Rational Society: Student Protest, Science and Politics, trans. J. J. Shapiro (London: Heineman, 1971).

Hall, Stuart, *The Hard Road to Renewal: Thatcherism and the Crisis of the Left* (London: Verso, 1988).

Handberg, Roger, *Ballistic Missile Defense and the Future of American Security: Agendas, Perceptions, Technology and Policy* (Westport, CT: Praeger, 2002).

Hanssen, Beatrice, *Critique of Violence: Between Poststructuralism and Critical Theory* (London: Routledge, 2000).

Haraway, Donna, *Simians, Cyborgs and Women: the Reinvention of Nature* (London: Free Association, 1991).

Hartung, William D. with Frida Berrigan, Michelle Ciarrocca and Jonathan Wingo, 'Tangled Web 2005: a Profile of the Missile Defense and Space Weapons Lobbies', report by the World Policy Institute, www.worldpolicy.org/projects/arms/reports/tangledweb.html [last accessed 20 January 2009].

Heidegger, Martin, *The Question Concerning Technology, and Other Essays*, trans. W. Lovitt (London: Harper and Row, 1977).

Held, David, *Introduction to Critical Theory: Horkheimer to Habermas* (London: Hutchison, 1980).

Hildreth, Steven A. (ed.) *Missile Defense: the Current Debate* (New York: Novinka Books, 2004).

Hitch, Charles and Roland McKean, *The Economics of Defense in the Nuclear Age* (New York: Atheneum, 1960).

Hoffman, Stanley, *Gulliver's Troubles, Or the Setting of American Foreign Policy* (New York: McGraw Hill, 1968).

Hogan, J. Michael, *The Nuclear Freeze Campaign: Rhetoric and Foreign Policy in the Telepolitical Age* (East Lansing: Michigan State University, 1994).

Holst, Johan J., and William Schneider, *Why ABM? Policy Issues in the Missile Defense Controversy* (New York: Pergamon, 1969).

Holub, Renate, *Antonio Gramsci: Beyond Marxism and Postmodernism* (London: Routledge, 1992).

Horkheimer, Max, *Critical Theory: Selected Essays*, trans. Matthew J. O'Connell and others (New York: Seabury Press, 1972).

Eclipse of Reason (New York: Seabury Press, 1974).

Hughes, Thomas P., *American Genesis: a Century of Invention and Technological Enthusiasm, 1870–1970* (Chicago: University of Chicago Press, 2004).

(ed.) *Changing Attitudes Toward American Technology* (New York: Harper and Row, 1975).

Humphrey, Hubert H. and William O. Douglas, *Anti-Ballistic Missile: Yes or No?* (New York: Hill and Wang, 1968).

Ikle, Fred C. *Annihilation from Within: the Ultimate Threat to Nations* (New York: Columbia University Press, 2006).

Every War Must End (New York: Columbia University Press, 1971).

'Nuclear Strategy: Can There be a Happy Ending?', *Foreign Affairs*, **63**:4 (1985) pp. 810–26.

'The Second Coming of the Nuclear Age', *Foreign Affairs*, **75**:1 (1996) pp. 119–29.

Ivanov, Igor, 'The Missile Defense Mistake: Undermining Strategic Stability and the ABM Treaty', *Foreign Policy*, **79**:5 (2000) pp. 15–20.

Ives, Peter, *Gramsci's Politics of Language: Engaging the Bakhtin Circle and the Frankfurt School* (Toronto: University of Toronto Press, 2003).

Jacobsen, Carl G. (ed.) *The Uncertain Course: New Weapons, Strategies and Mind-Sets* (Oxford: Oxford University Press, 1987).

Jastrow, Robert, 'Reagan vs. the Scientists: Why the President is Right about Missile Defense', *Commentary*, **77**:1 (1984) pp.23–31.

Jaworski, Adam and Nikolas Coupland (eds.) *The Discourse Reader* (London: Routledge, 2004).

Jervis, Robert, *Perception and Misperception in International Politics* (Princeton, NJ: Princeton University Press, 1976).

Jessop, Bob, *The Future of the Capitalist State* (Cambridge: Polity Press, 2002).

Johnson, Robert H., *Improbable Dangers: US Conceptions of Threat in the Cold War and After* (New York: St Martin's Press, 1994).

'Periods of Peril: the Window of Vulnerability and Other Myths', *Foreign Affairs*, **61**:4 (1983) pp. 950–71.

Kahn, Herman, *On Escalation: Metaphors and Scenarios* (New York: Frederick A. Praeger, 1965).

Kaplan, Fred, *The Wizards of Armageddon* (Stanford, CA: Stanford University Press, 1983).

Karp, Aaron, 'The New Indeterminancy of Deterrence and Missile Defense', *Contemporary Security Policy*, **25**: 1 (2004) pp. 71–87.

Karp, Aaron and Regina Karp, 'Preface: From Strategy to Domestic Debate', *Contemporary Security Policy*, **26**:3 (2005) pp. v–vi.

Katzenstein, Peter J. (ed.) *The Culture of National Security: Norms and Identity in World Politics* (New York: Columbia University Press, 1996).

Kennan, George, *Russia, the Atom and the West* (New York: Harper, 1958).

Kennedy, Edward M. and Mark O. Hatfield, *Freeze! How You Can Help Prevent Nuclear War* (New York: Bantam Books, 1982).

Kennedy, Robert F., *Thirteen Days: a Memoir of the Cuban Missile Crisis* (New York: W. W. Norton, 1971).

Killian, James R., *Sputnik, Scientists and Eisenhower* (Cambridge, MA: MIT Press, 1977).

Klein, Bradley S., *Strategic Studies and World Order* (Cambridge: Cambridge University Press, 1994).

Kovel, Joel, *Against the State of Nuclear Terror* (London: Pan, 1983).

Krause, Keith (ed.) *Culture and Security: Multilateralism, Arms Control and Security Building* (London: Frank Cass, 1999).

Krause, Keith and Michael C. Williams (eds.) *Critical Security Studies: Concepts and Cases* (London: UCL Press, 1997).

Krepon, Michael, 'Weapons in the Heavens: a Radical and Reckless Option', *Arms Control Today*, **34**:9 (2004) pp. 11–18.

Laclau, Ernesto, *Politics and Ideology in Marxist Theory* (London: New Left Books, 1977).

Laclau, Ernesto and Chantal Mouffe, *Hegemony and Socialist Strategy: Towards a Radical Democratic Politics*, 2nd edition (London: Verso, 2001).

LaFeber, Walter, *The American Age: United States Foreign Policy at Home and Abroad, 1750 to the Present* (New York: Norton, 1994).

Landy, Marcia, *Film, Politics and Gramsci* (Minneapolis, MN: University of Minnesota Press, 1994).

Lapp, Ralph E., *Arms Beyond Doubt: the Tyranny of Weapons Technology* (New York: Cowles, 1970).

Lasch, Christopher, *The True and Only Heaven: Progress and its Critics* (New York: W.W. Norton, 1991).

Latour, Bruno, *Pandora's Hope: Essays on the Reality of Science Studies* (Cambridge, MA: Harvard University Press, 1999).

Lebow, Richard N., *Nuclear Crisis Management: a Dangerous Illusion* (Ithaca: Cornell University Press, 1983).

Leiss, William, *The Domination of Nature* (Montreal: McGill-Queen's University Press, 1994).

Under Technology's Thumb (Montreal: McGill-Queen's University Press, 1990).

Lennon, Alexander T. J. (ed.) *Contemporary Nuclear Debates: Missile Defense, Arms Control, and Arms Races in the Twenty-First Century* (Cambridge, MA: MIT Press, 2002).

Lieber, Keir A. and Daryl G. Press, 'The End of MAD? The Nuclear Dimension of US Primacy', *International Security*, **30**:4 (2006) pp. 7–44.

'The Rise of US Nuclear Primacy', *Foreign Affairs*, March/April (2006) pp. 42–54.

Lifton, Robert Jay and Richard Falk, *Indefensible Weapons: the Political and Psychological Case against Nuclearism* (New York: Basic Books, 1982).

Lifton, Robert Jay and Eric Markusen, *The Genocidal Mentality: the Nazi Holocaust and Nuclear Threat* (London: Macmillan, 1991).

Linenthal, Edward T., *Symbolic Defense: the Cultural Significance of the Strategic Defense Initiative* (Urbana: University of Illinois Press, 1989).

Lowy, Michael, *Redemption and Utopia: Jewish Libertarian Thought in Central Europe* (London: Athlone, 1992).

Lukács, Georg, 'Technology and Social Relations', *New Left Review*, **39** (1966) pp. 27–34.

Luongo, Kenneth N. and W. Thomas Wander (eds.) *The Search for Security in Space* (Ithaca: Cornell University Press, 1989).

McCarthy, Thomas, *The Critical Theory of Jurgen Habermas* (Cambridge, MA: MIT Press, 1981).

McClean, Douglas (ed.) *The Security Gamble: Deterrence Dilemmas in the Nuclear Age* (Totowa, NJ: Rowman and Allenheld, 1984).

MacKenzie, Donald A., *Inventing Accuracy: a Historical Sociology of Nuclear Missile Guidance* (Cambridge, MA: MIT Press, 1990).

McLuhan, Marshall, *Understanding Media: the Extensions of Man* (London: Sphere, 1967).

McNamara, Robert, 'Apocalypse Soon', *Foreign Policy*, May/June (2005) pp. 29–35.

   The Essence of Security: Reflections in Office (London: Hodder and Stoughton, 1968).

Maley, Terry, 'Max Weber and the Iron Cage of Technology', *Bulletin of Science, Technology & Society*, **24**:1 (2004) pp. 69–86.

Mao Tse-Tung, 'The Chinese People Cannot Be Cowed by the Atom Bomb', *Selected Works of Mao Tse-Tung*, Vol. V (Peking: Foreign Languages Press, 1977).

Marcuse, Herbert, *Negations: Essays in Critical Theory* (London: Allen Lane, 1968).

   One-Dimensional Man: Studies in the Ideology of Advanced Industrial Society, 2nd edition (London: Routledge, 1991).

   Reason and Revolution (Boston: Beacon Press, 1960).

   Technology, War and Fascism: Collected Papers of Herbert Marcuse, ed. Douglas Kellner (London: Routledge, 1998).

Marx, Karl, *The Economic and Philosophical Manuscripts of 1844* (London: Lawrence and Wishart, 1977).

Marx, Karl and Friedrich Engels, *The German Ideology* (London: Lawrence and Wishart, 1965).

Marx, Leo, *The Machine in the Garden: Technology and the Pastoral Ideal in America* (New York: Oxford University Press, 1964).

Mathers, Jennifer, *The Russian Nuclear Shield from Stalin to Yeltsin* (Basingstoke: MacMillan, 2000).

Mearsheimer, John, 'Why We Will Soon Miss the Cold War', *The Atlantic Monthly*, **266**:2 (1990) pp. 35–50.

Medhurst, Martin J. and H. W. Brands (eds.) *Critical Reflections on the Cold War: Linking Rhetoric and History* (College Station, TX: Texas A&M Press, 2000).

Mehan, Hugh, Charles E. Nathanson and James M. Skelly, 'Nuclear Discourse in the 1980s: the Unravelling Conventions of the Cold War', *Discourse and Society*, 1:2 (1990) pp. 134–65.

Meier, Hugo A., 'The Technological Concept in American Social History: 1750–1860', PhD dissertation, University of Wisconsin, 1956.

Mendelsohn, Jack, 'Arms Control after the Summit', *Arms Control Today*, 23:4 (1993) pp. 10–14.

'Delegitimizing Nuclear Weapons', *Issues in Science and Technology*, Spring (2006), www.issues.org/22.3/mendelsohn.html [last accessed 20 January 2009].

Miller, Steven E., *The Nuclear Weapons Freeze and Arms Control* (Cambridge, MA: Ballinger, 1985).

Milliken, Jennifer, 'The Study of Discourse in International Relations: a Critique of Research and Methods', *European Journal of International Relations*, 5:2 (1999) pp. 225–54.

Mitchell, Gordon R., *Strategic Deception: Rhetoric, Science and Politics in Missile Defense Advocacy* (East Lansing: Michigan State University Press, 2000).

'Team B Intelligence Coups', *Quarterly Journal of Speech*, 92:2 (2006) pp. 144–73.

Moltz, James Clay (ed.) *New Challenges in Missile Proliferation, Missile Defense and Space Security* (Southampton: Mountbatten Centre for International Studies, 2003).

Mooney, Chris, *The Republican War on Science* (New York: Basic Books, 2005).

Morera, Esteve, *Gramsci's Historicism: a Realist Interpretation* (London: Routledge, 1990).

Morgenthau, Hans J., *Scientific Man versus Power Politics* (London: Latimer House, 1947).

Morris, Pam (ed.) *The Bakhtin Reader: Selected Writings of Bakhtin, Medvedev and Voloshinov* (London: Edward Arnold, 1994).

Mouffe, Chantal (ed.) *Gramsci and Marxist Theory* (London: Routledge, 1979).

Mumford, Lewis, *The Pentagon of Power: the Myth of the Machine, Volume II* (New York: Harvest, 1970).

Technics and Civilization (New York: Harcourt, Brace, 1934).

Murnion, Philip J. (ed.) *Catholics and Nuclear War* (New York: Crossroad, 1983).

Mutimer, David, *The Weapons State: Proliferation and the Framing of Security* (Boulder, CO: Lynne Rienner, 2000).

Nelson, Cary and Lawrence Grossberg (eds.) *Marxism and the Interpretation of Culture* (Urbana: University of Illinois Press, 1988).

Neustadt, Richard E. and Ernest R. May, *Thinking in Time: the Uses of History for Decision Makers* (New York: The Free Press, 1988).

Nitze, Paul, 'Assuring Strategic Stability in an Era of Détente', *Foreign Affairs*, 54:2 (1976) pp. 207–32.

Noble, David F., *Forces of Production* (Oxford: Oxford University Press, 1986).

O'Hanlon, Michael E., *Neither Star Wars nor Sanctuary: Constraining the Military Uses of Space* (Washington, DC: Brookings Institution Press, 2004).

Oppenheimer, J. Robert 'Atomic Weapons and American Policy', *Bulletin of the Atomic Scientists*, 9:6 (July 1953) pp. 202–5.

Paret, Peter (ed.) *Makers of Modern Strategy: From Machiavelli to the Nuclear Age* (Oxford: Clarendon Press, 1986).

Payne, Keith B., 'Action–Reaction Metaphysics and Negligence', *The Washington Quarterly*, 24:4 (Autumn 2001) pp. 109–21.

'The Case against Nuclear Abolition and for Nuclear Deterrence', *Comparative Strategy*, 17 (1998) pp. 3–44.

'The Case for a National Missile Defense', 27 May 2005, www.nipp.org/ publications.php [last accessed 7 March 2007].

Deterrence in the Second Nuclear Age (Lexington, KY: University Press of Kentucky, 1996).

The Fallacies of Cold War Deterrence and a New Direction (Lexington, KY: University of Kentucky Press, 2001).

Missile Defense in the 21st Century: Protection against Limited Threats, Including Lessons from the Gulf War (Boulder, CO: Westview Press, 1991).

'National Missile Defense: Why? And Why Now?', *FPRI Wire* (2000), www. nipp.org/Adobe/fpri.pdf#search=%22National%20Missile%20Defense% 3A%20Why%3F%20And%20Why%20Now%3F%22 [last accessed 20 January 2009].

The Nuclear Freeze Controversy (Lanham, MD: University Press of America, 1984).

'The Nuclear Posture Review and Deterrence for a New Age', *Comparative Strategy*, 23 (2004) pp. 411–19.

'The Nuclear Posture Review: Setting the Record Straight', *The Washington Quarterly*, 28:3 (2005) pp. 135–51.

'Weaponry: the Nuclear Jitters', *The National Review*, 30 June 2003, www.nipp.org/Adobe/the%20nuclear%20jitters.pdf#search=%22 Weaponry%3A%20The%20Nuclear%20Jitters%22 [last accessed 20 January 2009].

Strategic Defense: 'Star Wars' in Perspective (London: Hamilton Press, 1986).

Payne, Keith and Andrei Kortunov, 'The Character of the Problem', *Comparative Strategy*, **16** (1997) pp. 127–32.

Peoples, Columba, 'Technology and Politics in the Missile Defence Debate: Traditional, Radical and Critical Approaches', *Global Change, Peace and Security*, **19**:3 (2007) pp. 265–80.

Pipes, Richard, *US–Soviet Relations in the Era of Détente* (Boulder, CO: Westview Press, 1981).

'Why the Soviet Union Thinks it Could Fight and Win a Nuclear War', *Commentary*, **64**:1 (1977) pp. 21–34.

Postol, Theodore A., 'Lessons of the Gulf War Experience with Patriot', *International Security*, **16** (1991/2) pp. 119–71.

Prados, John, *The Soviet Estimate: US Intelligence Analysis and Soviet Strategic Forces* (Princeton, NJ: Princeton University Press, 1986).

'Team B: the Trillion Dollar Experiment (Part II)', *The Bulletin of the Atomic Scientists*, April (1993), pp. 22/27–31.

Pratt, Erik K., *Selling Strategic Defense: Interests, Ideologies and the Arms Race* (Boulder, CO: Lynne Rienner, 1990).

Pursell, Carroll W., Jr., *Readings in Technology and American Life* (New York: Oxford University Press, 1969).

Purvis, Trevor and Alan Hunt, 'Discourse, Ideology, Discourse, Ideology, Discourse, Ideology . . .', *British Journal of Sociology*, **44**:3 (1999) pp. 473–99.

Reiss, Edward, *The Strategic Defense Initiative* (Cambridge: Cambridge University Press, 1992).

Reppy, Judith 'The Technological Imperative in Strategic Thought', *Journal of Peace Research'* **27**:1 (1990) pp. 101–6.

Rhodes, Richard (ed.) *Visions of Technology: a Century of Vital Debate about Machines, Systems and the Human World* (New York: Simon and Schuster, 1999).

Roman, Peter J., *Eisenhower and the Missile Gap* (Ithaca: Cornell University Press, 1995).

Rosen, Steven (ed.) *Testing the Theory of the Military-Industrial Complex* (Lexington, MA: Lexington Books, 1973).

Ruhle, Hans and Michael Ruhle, 'A View from Europe – Missile Defense for the 21st Century: Echoes of the 1930s', *Comparative Strategy*, **20** (2001) pp. 221–5.

Rupert, Mark, 'Globalising Common Sense: A Marxian–Gramscian (re-) Vision of the Politics of Governance/Resistance', *Review of International Studies*, **29** (2003) pp. 181–98.

Producing Hegemony: the Politics of Mass Production and American Global Power (Cambridge: Cambridge University Press, 1995).

Sagan, Scott D. and Kenneth N. Waltz, *The Spread of Nuclear Weapons: a Debate* (New York: W.W. Norton, 1995).

Sarkesian, Sam C. (ed.) *The Military-Industrial Complex: a Reassessment* (Beverley Hills, CA: Sage, 1972).

Scheer, Robert, *With Enough Shovels: Reagan, Bush, and Nuclear War* (New York: Random House, 1982).

Schell, Jonathan, *The Abolition* (London: Picador, 1984).

The Fate of the Earth (London: Picador, 1982).

The Unfinished Twentieth Century: the Crisis of Weapons of Mass Destruction (London: Verso, 2001).

Schelling, Thomas, *Arms and Influence* (New Haven: Yale University Press, 1966).

The Strategy of Conflict (Cambridge, MA; Harvard University Press, 1960).

Segal, Howard P., *Future Imperfect: the Mixed Blessings of Technology in America* (Amherst: University of Massachusetts Press, 1994).

Technological Utopianism in American Culture (Chicago: University of Chicago Press, 1985).

Seng, Tan See, *What Fear Hath Wrought: Missile Hysteria and the Writing of 'America'*, Institute of Defence and Strategic Studies Working Paper (Singapore: Institute of Defence and Strategic Studies, 2002).

Shaw, Martin, *The New Western Way of War: Risk-Transfer War and its Crisis in Iraq* (Cambridge: Polity Press, 2005).

Sheehan, Michael, *The Arms Race* (Oxford: Martin Robertson, 1983).

Silverstein, Ken, *Private Warriors* (London: Verso, 2000).

Slater, Phil (ed.) *Outlines of a Critique of Technology* (London: Ink Links, 1980).

Smith, Hedrick, *The Power Game: How Washington Works* (London: Collins, 1988).

Smith, Steve, Ken Booth and Marysia Zalewski (eds.) *International Theory: Positivism and Beyond* (Cambridge: Cambridge University Press, 1996).

Sokolovskii, V. D., *Soviet Military Strategy* (New York: Praeger, 1963).

Stares, Paul B., *Space Weapons and US Strategy: Origins and Development* (London: Croom Helm, 1985).

Stein, Jonathan B., *From H-Bomb to Star Wars: the Politics of Strategic Decision Making* (Lexington, MA: Lexington Books, 1986).

Steinberg, Gerald M. (ed.) *Lost in Space: the Domestic Politics of the Strategic Defense Initiative* (Lexington, MA: Lexington Books, 1988).

Stern, Thomas A., *The USAF Scientific Advisory Board: Its First Twenty Years, 1944–1964* (Washington, DC: Government Printing Office, 1986).

Talbott, Strobe, *Master of the Game: Paul Nitze and the Nuclear Peace* (New York: Knopf, 1988).

Teller, Edward, *Better a Shield than a Sword: Perspectives on Defense and Technology* (New York: The Free Press, 1987).

Freedom in an Age of Technology: an Address (New York: International and Academic Technical Publications, 1972).

The Legacy of Hiroshima (Garden City, NY: Doubleday, 1962).

Thatcher, Margaret, 'Deterrence is Not Enough: Security Requirements for the 21st Century', *Comparative Strategy*, **18** (1999) pp. 211–20.

Thompson, Edward P. (ed.) *Exterminism and Cold War* (London: Verso, 1982).

(ed.) *Star Wars* (Harmondsworth: Penguin, 1985).

Thompson, John B., 'Rationality and Social Rationalization: an Assessment of Habermas' Theory of Communicative Action', *Sociology*, **17**:2 (1983) pp. 278–94.

Studies in the Theory of Ideology (Cambridge: Polity Press, 1984).

Tirman, John (ed.) *The Fallacy of Star Wars: Based on Studies Conducted by the Union of Concerned Scientists* (New York: Vintage Books, 1984).

Tucker, Robert W., *The Nuclear Debate: Deterrence and the Lapse of Faith* (New York: Holmes and Meier, 1985).

Tyroler, Charles, II (ed.) *Alerting America: the Papers of the Committee on the Present Danger* (Washington, DC: Pergamon-Brassy's, 1984).

Uhler, Walter C., 'Missile Shield or Holy Grail?', *The Nation*, 28 January 2002, www.thenation.com/doc/20020128/uhler [last accessed 20 January 2009].

Union of Concerned Scientists, *Beyond the Freeze: the Road to Nuclear Sanity* (Boston: Beacon Press, 1982).

Utgoff, Victor A. (ed.) *The Coming Crisis: Nuclear Proliferation, US Interests, and World Order* (Cambridge, MA: MIT Press, 2000).

Van Cleave, William, *Fortress USSR: the Soviet Strategic Defense Initiative and the US Strategic Defense Response* (Stanford, CA: Hoover Institution Press, 1986).

Van Creveld, Martin, *Technology and War: From 2000 BC to the Present* (New York: The Free Press, 1989).

Vlahos, Michael, *Strategic Defense and the American Ethos: Can the Nuclear World be Changed?* (Boulder, CO: Foreign Policy Institute, 1986).

Walt, Stephen M., 'Rush to Failure: the Flawed Politics and Policies of Missile Defense', *Harvard Magazine*, **102**, May–June (2000) pp. 31–5.

Waltz, Kenneth, *The Spread of Nuclear Weapons: More May be Better*, Adelphi Paper 171 (London: International Institute of Strategic Studies, 1981).

Theory of International Politics (New York: McGraw Hill, 1979).

Weigley, Russell F., *The American Way of War: a History of the United States Military Strategy and Policy* (New York: Macmillan, 1973).

Weinberger, Caspar W., 'US Defense Strategy', *Foreign Affairs*, **64** (1986) pp. 695–6.

Weldes, Jutta, 'Constructing National Interests', *European Journal of International Relations*, **2**:3 (1996) pp. 275–318.

Weldes, Jutta, Mark Laffey, Hugh Gusterson and Raymond Duvall (eds.) *Cultures of Insecurity: States, Communities, and the Production of Danger* (Minneapolis, MN: University of Minnesota Press, 1999).

Wenger, Andreas, *Living with Peril: Eisenhower, Kennedy and Nuclear Weapons* (Oxford: Rowan and Littlefield, 1997).

Wheen, Francis, *Marx's Das Kapital: a Biography* (London: Atlantic Books).

Williams, Michael C., *Culture and Security: the Reconstruction of Security in the Post-Cold War Era* (London: Routledge, 2007).

Williams, Michael C., 'Rethinking the "Logic" of Deterrence', *Alternatives*, **17** (1992) pp. 67–93.

'What is the National Interest? The Neoconservative Challenge in IR Theory', *European Journal of International Relations*, **11**:3 (2005) pp. 307–37.

Williams, Raymond, *Keywords: a Vocabulary of Culture and Society* (London: Fontana, 1983).

Problems in Materialism and Culture (London: Verso, 1980).

Wilson, H. T., *The American Ideology: Science, Technology, and Organization as Modes of Rationality in Advanced Industrial Societies* (London: Routledge and Kegan Paul, 1977).

Winkler, Allan M., *Life under a Cloud: American Anxiety about the Bomb* (Chicago: University of Illinois Press, 1999).

Winner, Langdon, *Autonomous Technology: Technics-out-of-Control as a Theme in Political Thought* (Cambridge, MA: MIT Press, 1978).

Wirtz, James J. (ed.) *Rocket's Red Glare: Missile Defenses and the Future of World Politics* (Boulder, CO: Westview Press, 2001).

Wohlstetter, Albert, 'The Delicate Balance of Terror', *Foreign Affairs*, **37**:2 (1959) pp. 211–234.

'Is There a Strategic Arms Race?', *Foreign Policy*, **15** (1974) pp. 3–26.

'Optimal Ways to Confuse Ourselves', *Foreign Policy*, **20** (1975) pp. 997–1002.

'Rivals but No Race', *Foreign Policy*, **16** (1974) pp. 170–98.

Wolfe, Alan, *The Rise and Fall of the Soviet Threat* (Boston, MA: Southend Press, 1984).

Wolfe, Tom, *The Right Stuff* (New York: Bantam, 1980).

Wright Mills, C., *The Power Elite* (London: Oxford University Press, 1956).

Wyn Jones, Richard, *Security, Strategy and Critical Theory* (London: Lynne Rienner, 1999).

(ed.) *Critical Theory and World Politics* (Boulder, CO: Lynne Rienner, 2001).

Yanarella, Ernest J., *The Missile Defense Controversy: Technology in Search of a Mission* (Lexington, KY: University Press of Kentucky, 2002).

York, Herbert F., *Race to Oblivion: a Participant's View of the Arms Race* (New York: Simon and Schuster, 1970).

Yost, David S., *Soviet Ballistic Missile Defense and the Western Alliance* (Cambridge, MA: Harvard University Press, 1988).

Zagacki, Kenneth and Andrew King 'Reagan, Romance and Technology: a Critique of "Star Wars"', *Communication Studies*, **40** (1989) pp. 1–12.

Reports

Ballistic Missile Defense Organization, *1998 BMDO Technologies – Improving the Environment* (1998), www.mda.mil/mdalink/html/special-reports.htm [last accessed 7 March 2007].

BMDO Technology and the Electric Utility Industry (1997), www.mda.mil/mdalink/html/specialreports.htm [last accessed 7 March 2007].

Ballistic Missile Defense Organization Office of the Chief Scientist (BMDO/ST) Technology Applications Program, *The 2000 BMDO Technology Applications Report: Technology, Working for You Now* (2000), www.mda.mil/mdalink/html/specialreports.htm [last accessed 7 March 2007].

Barton, David K., Roger Falcone, Daniel Kleppner *et al.*, 'Report of the American Physical Society Group on Boost-Phase Intercept Systems for National Missile Defense: Scientific and Technical Issues, pp. xxi–xxii, www.aps.org/public_affairs/popa/reports/nmd03.cfm [last accessed 7 March 2007].

Carter, Ashton B., *Directed Energy Missile Defense in Space: Background Paper* (Washington, DC: Office of Technology Assessment, 1984).

Commission to Assess the Ballistic Missile Threat to the United States, *Report of the Commission to Assess the Ballistic Missile Threat to the United States*, Executive Summary, 15 July 1998, www.fas.org/irp/threat/bm-threat.htm [last accessed 7 March 2007].

Commission to Assess United States National Security Space Management and Organization, *Report of the Commission to Assess United States National Security Space Management and Organization*, Executive Summary, 11 January 2001, www.defenselink.mil/pubs/space20010111.html [last accessed 7 March 2007].

Congressional Budget Office, *The Long-Term Implications of Current Defense Plans and Alternatives: Detailed Update for Fiscal Year 2006* (2006), http://www.cbo.gov/showdoc.cfm?index=7004&sequence=0&from=7 [last accessed 7 March 2007].

Davis, Paul K., *Analytic Architecture for Capabilities-Based Planning, Mission-System Analysis, and Transformation*, RAND 2002, MR-1513-OSD, www.rand.org/pubs/monograph_reports/MR1513/index.html [last accessed 20 January 2009].

Department of Defense, *Quadrennial Defense Review Report*, 30 September 2001, www.defenselink.mil/pubs/qdr2001.pdf#search=%22Quadrennial%20Defense%20Review%20Report%22 [last accessed 20 January 2009].

Quadrennial Defense Review Report, 6 February 2006, www.comw.org/qdr/qdr2006.pdf [last accessed 7 March 2007].

Hitchens, Theresa, Michael Katz-Hyman, Jeffrey Lewis and Victoria Samson, *Space Weapons Spending in the Fiscal Year 2006 President's Request: a Preliminary Assessment*, 10 February 2005, www.cdi.org/PDFs/FY06–1.pdf [accessed 07 September].

Joint Chiefs of Staff, 'Joint Vision 2010' and 'Joint Vision 2020', www.dtic.mil/jv2010/jvpub.htm [last accessed 7 March 2007].

Missile Defense Agency Advanced Systems (MDA/AS) Technology Applications Program, *2003 Technology Applications Report* (2003), www.mda.mil/mdalink/html/specialreports.htm [last accessed 7 March 2007].

Technology Applications Program, *2004 Technology Applications Report* (2004), www.mda.mil/mdalink/html/specialreports.htm [last accessed 7 March 2007].

National Institute for Public Policy, *Rationale and Requirements for US Nuclear Forces and Arms Control* (National Institute for Public Policy, 2001).

National Intelligence Officer for Strategic and Nuclear Programs, *Foreign Missile Developments and the Ballistic Missile Threat to the United States through 2015*, September 1999, www.dni.gov/nic/PDF_GIF_other prod/missilethreat2001.pdf#search=%22Foreign%20Missile%20Developments%20and%20the%20Ballistic%20Missile%20Threat%20to%20the%20United%20States%20through%202015%22 [last accessed 7 March 2007].

Union of Concerned Scientists, 'Countermeasures', www.armscontrol.org/subject/md/?print [last accessed 7 March 2007].

'Technical Realities: an Analysis of the 2004 Deployment of a US National Missile Defense System', www.ucsusa.org/global_security/missile_defense/

technical-realities-national-missile-defense-deployment-in-2004.html [last accessed 7 March 2007].

United States Central Intelligence Agency, *Intelligence Community Experiment in Competitive Analysis: Soviet Strategic Objectives, an Alternative View: Report of Team 'B'* (Washington, DC: Government Printing Office, 1976); declassified 16 September 1992.

Index

Cambridge Studies in International Relations